Samuel J. P. (Samuel James Pope) Thearle

Theoretical naval architecture : a treatise on the calculations involved in naval design

Samuel J. P. (Samuel James Pope) Thearle

**Theoretical naval architecture : a treatise on the calculations involved in naval design**

ISBN/EAN: 9783742887689

Manufactured in Europe, USA, Canada, Australia, Japa

Cover: Foto ©ninafisch / pixelio.de

Manufactured and distributed by brebook publishing software
(www.brebook.com)

Samuel J. P. (Samuel James Pope) Thearle

**Theoretical naval architecture : a treatise on the calculations involved in naval design**

# PREFACE.

THE favourable reception accorded to the Treatise on *Practical Shipbuilding* and *Laying Off*, which I had the honour of contributing to this Series three years ago, has encouraged me to venture upon the present work. The literature of Naval Architecture in the English language is not at all commensurate with the importance and magnitude of the shipbuilding industries of Great Britain, and that literature which exists is practically beyond the reach of most of those who desire and need acquaintance with it. Without particularising the special defects in this respect of existing books on the *Theory of Naval Architecture*, it may be said that either they are too large and costly, or written too obscurely to place them within the pecuniary or mental grasp of the majority of students, draughtsmen, and workmen.

In preparing the present work, it has been my object to adapt it for the student who possesses simply a knowledge of elementary mathematics, and at the same time to provide for the requirements of those whose studies have been much more advanced. The former will find all the information necessary to enable him to perform the usual calculations of the drawing office, expressed in formulæ, or by rules easily applied; while the latter will be enabled, by following out the investigations by which these formulæ and rules have been obtained, to gather a tolerably clear idea of the principles upon which they are based.

In offering this work to Naval Architects, it is hardly necessary for me to say that I have been indebted to those who have written before me for a large proportion of the ideas which it contains. It would, indeed, be impossible to write usefully upon a science which has been brought to its present state by the contributions of so many minds without being under such obligations.

An effort has been made to simplify the problems involved in calculating the stability of ships by separating the calculations relating to the form of the vessel from those relating to her weight, and the position of her centre of gravity. A few alterations have been made in the usual nomenclature of the subject with a view to greater exactitude of expression. Some of these alterations were suggested by a recent writer in *Naval Science*. To what extent success, or the contrary, has attended my attempts to secure those very desirable objects—simplicity and accuracy, it will be for the reader to decide. At all events, it is hoped that a work based upon such a plan as the author himself would have desired when a student will be of service to the young naval architect by simplifying his studies, and to the draughtsman and shipbuilder by helping them in their daily duties.

S. J. P. THEARLE.

LONDON, *February 1877.*

# CONTENTS.

INTRODUCTION, . . . . . . . . . . . PAGE 9

## PART I.—CALCULATIONS RELATING TO THE FORMS AND DIMENSIONS OF SHIPS.

### CHAPTER I.

#### CALCULATION OF AREAS AND VOLUMES.

Buoyancy—Stability—Hydrostatical Principles—Displacement—Areas of Plane Surfaces—Trapezoidal Rule—Simpson's 1st Rule: Proofs—Fractional Intervals—Simpson's 2nd Rule—One-twelfth Rule—Worked Examples—Centre of Gravity of a Plane Area—Centres of Gravity of various Figures—Principle of Moments—Centre of Gravity of a Plane Area bounded by a Curve—Volumes of Solids—Volume of a Solid bounded by a Plane and a Curved Surface—Calculation of Displacement—Centres of Gravity of Solids—Centre of Gravity of a Volume bounded by a Curved Surface and a Plane—Curve of Areas of Midship Section—Of Sectional Areas—Of Tons per inch of Immersion—Of Displacement—Explanation of a Displacement Sheet—Geometrical Method—Woolley's Rule—Proof—Centre of Buoyancy by Woolley's Rule—Geometrical Application of Wolley's Rule—Angular Measurement of Areas—Volumes and Moments of Wedge-shaped Solids—Moments of Inertia—Examples—Co-efficients of Fineness—Table of Co-efficients of Fineness, 12

## CONTENTS.

### CHAPTER II.

#### THE METACENTRE AND SURFACE STABILITY.

PAGE

The Metacentre—Transverse Metacentre—Surface Stability—Fixed Metacentre—To obtain Position of Transverse Metacentre—Metacentric Surface Stability—Calculation for Transverse Metacentre Explained—More Exact Calculations of Surface Stability—Intersections of Water Planes—Method of Measurement—Specimen Calculation—Dynamical Stability—Dynamical Surface Stability—Specimen Calculation—Surface of Flotation—Centre of Flotation—Axis of Level Motion—Curve of Buoyancy—Surface of Buoyancy—Metacentric—Longitudinal Metacentre—Calculation for Longitudinal Metacentre Explained—Longitudinal Metacentric Surface Stability—Comparative Surface Stabilities of Different Vessels, . . . . . . . . . 86

---

## PART II.—CALCULATIONS RELATING TO THE WEIGHTS AND CENTRES OF GRAVITY OF SHIPS.

### CHAPTER III.

#### STABILITY AND TRIM.

Centre of Gravity—Metacentric Statical Stability—Exact Calculations of Statical and Dynamical Stability—To find the Centre of Gravity by Experiment—Specimen Calculation—Alteration of Trim by Shifting Weights—Moment to alter Trim one inch—Alteration of Trim by adding a Weight—When Weight is inconsiderable—When considerable—Effect on Trim by admission of Water in different ways—Effect on Stability by moving a Weight—By adding or removing a Weight—By admitting Water in different ways, . . 112

### CHAPTER IV.

#### CALCULATIONS OF THE WEIGHTS AND CENTRES OF GRAVITY OF SHIPS.

*Preliminary Calculations:* Approximation to Weight of Hull—To Centre of Gravity—To Centre of Buoyancy—To Value of GM. *Detailed Calculations:* Armour—Backing—Deck Plating—Bottom Plating—Expansion of Bottom—Bottom Planking—Deck Beams—Plating—Flats—Bulkheads—Transverse Framing—Method with Curves—Longitudinal Frames—Fittings, . . . . . . . . . , 151

## CHAPTER V.

### CURVES OF STABILITY.

Metacentric Curves— Curves of Statical and Dynamical Stability —Specimen Calculations—The Body Plan—Measuring the Ordinates — Preliminary Tables— Combination Tables — Volumes and Moments of Assumed Wedges for Statical Stability—Area and Centre of Gravity of Inclined Water Plane—Statical Correction for Layer— For Appendages— Values of BN and GZ—Check Spot—Curve of Dynamical Stability—Dynamical Correction for Layer— For Appendages—Geometrical Method of Calculating Dynamical Stability—Curve of Statical Stability at Light Draught, . . 180

## CHAPTER VI.

### WAVES AND ROLLING.

Still Water Rolling—The Revolving Pendulum—Isochronous and Free Oscillations—The Equivalent Pendulum—Radius of Gyration—Period of Still Water Rolling—Winging out the Weights—Pitching—Still Water Resistances to Rolling —Dipping—Period of Dipping—Waves: their Forms— Motion—Form of Surface—Motion of Wave Surfaces and Sub-surfaces—Sub-surfaces of Uniform Pressure—Resultant Pressure—Effective Wave Surface—Internal Structure of a Wave—Period of a Wave—Rules and Formulæ for Waves— Passive Rolling—Rolling in a Sea-way—Stiffness—Steadiness—Periods of Oscillations of certain Ships, . . . 204

## PART III.—CALCULATIONS RELATING TO THE STRENGTH OF SHIPS.

### CHAPTER VII.

#### LOCAL STRENGTH.

Definitions—Properties of Bodies under Stress—Intensity of Stress—Classes of Stress—Local Stresses—Diameters and Spacing of Rivets — Butt Straps — Edge Connections— Strengths of Butt Straps—Strength of a Shift of Plates— Strength of Pillars—Beams—Shearing Stress—Bending Moment—Bending Moments and Shearing Stresses for Various kinds of Loading and Modes of Support—Resistance to Bending—Specimen Calculations—The Deflections of Beams Examples—Strength of Bent Pillars—Twisting Moments, . 238

## CHAPTER VIII
### Structural Strength.

PAGE

STILL WATER STRESSES—Curve of Buoyancy—Of Weight of Hull—Of Lading—Of Weights—Of Loads—Of Shearing Stresses—Of Bending Moments—STRESSES AMONG WAVES—Curve of Buoyancy—Of Shearing Stresses and Bending Moments—Table of certain Maximum Bending Moments and Shearing Stresses—Application of preceding Results—Neutral Axis of a Ship—Equivalent Girder—Moment of Inertia of a Section—Specimen Calculation—Mr. John's Investigations, . 304

---

# PART IV.—CALCULATIONS RELATING TO PROPULSION OF SHIPS BY SAILS.

## CHAPTER IX.

Masts—Yards—Sails—Rigs—Sailing—Real and Apparent Motion of the Wind—Effective Impulse of the Wind—Trim of Sails—Effect of the Position of Centre of Gravity (Longitudinally) on a Ship's Sailing qualities—Centre of Effort—Speed under Sail—Stability under Sail—Steady Impulse and Small Inclination—Steady Impulse and any Inclination—Effect of a Gust of Wind, . . . . . . . 321

---

# PART V.—CALCULATIONS RELATING TO PROPULSION OF SHIPS BY STEAM ENGINES.

## CHAPTER X.

Reaction of the Water—Slip, etc.—Experiments on H.M. Ship *Greyhound*—Law of Resistance—Comparative Performances of Steam Ships—Constants of Performance—The Measured Mile—Mean Speed—Trials at varied Speeds—Negative Slip, 345

---

# PART VI.—CALCULATIONS RELATING TO THE STEERING OF SHIPS.

## CHAPTER XI.

Steering—The Rudder—Principle of the Rudder—Angle of Maximum Efficiency—Angle of Maximum Efficiency with regard to Power applied—Usual Angle of Rudder—Areas of Rudders—Ratio of Pressure and Velocity—The Balanced Rudder, . 361

# THEORETICAL NAVAL ARCHITECTURE.

## INTRODUCTION.

The work of the Naval Architect is to design a floating structure, stable, seaworthy, and strong; capable of being propelled with facility either by the wind, by steam, or some other motive power, and adapted for the particular service in which it is to be employed, whether as a fighting ship or for carrying merchandise or passengers. In every case certain qualities, viz., stability, sea-worthiness, strength, speed, stowage, and accommodation, have to be fulfilled in a varying ratio according to the purpose for which the ship is intended. In a ship of war certain other qualities have to be obtained, such as power of carrying and fighting guns, and sometimes invulnerability; these too being provided in different ratios of importance according to the duties the ship has specially to perform. It is the art of securing these qualities, and apportioning them in the several degrees necessary to secure the maximum efficiency of the ship in her peculiar vocation, that constitutes the functions of the Naval Architect, and renders his duties among the most difficult and onerous that fall into the hands of man to perform; requiring, as they do, a knowledge of some of the most complex and abstruse physical laws, and a wise discrimination in applying experimental data.

The development of the science of Naval Construction has been very slow until within the last century, notwithstanding that Naval Architecture has a history dating back almost as far as that of land architecture. Indeed, until the application of iron to shipbuilding, no considerable improvement could be observed in the mode of constructing ships during several centuries. The advances that have been made during the past twenty years, especially in regard to war ships, are far greater than can be traced during at least one hundred and fifty years previously. But, while the growth in the mechanical or building branches of the art have been most important, resulting, as they have, from the rapid development of new resources, and the bringing of powerful forces of nature more under our control, it is to the enlargement of our knowledge in the scientific—or, as it is termed, the theoretical department—that we should attribute a large share of the credit for the unparalleled rapidity of our advances; as by it we have been guided safely, in the wide departures from the old lines of experience and routine, into modes of construction which have been rendered necessary by the altered circumstances of the present day.

It is to the French that we are indebted for the first definite and consistent application of scientific truths to Naval Construction; and, until within recent years, the principal text-books on naval science were written by Frenchmen. The superiority over our own ships in point of sailing and sea-going qualities displayed by ships of war which we had captured from the French, during the wars of the last century, caused our own naval architects to frequently build upon the French models; and this continued until, in the year 1811, we began, in earnest, the scientific study of Naval Architecture. From that time, until the present day, England has not been without highly trained men, into whose hands she could confide the responsible task of providing her with trustworthy and suitable ships for the several departments of her warlike and mercantile navies.

It has already been stated that a ship should fulfil a number of conditions, some of these being more prominent than others; in each case prominence being given to those qualities which are essential for the service the ship is especially intended to perform. We purpose in the following pages to discuss these several qualities, and show how the possession of each is to be obtained. This discussion will necessarily involve statements and explanations of scientific truths and mathematical formulæ, also illustrations of *calculations which have to be made in the application of those truths and formulæ.*

In considering the *Theoretical Principles of Naval Architecture*, we propose to treat the several branches of the inquiry in the following order:—

1. Calculations relating to the forms and dimensions of ships.
2. Calculations relating to the weights and centres of gravity of ships.
3. Calculations relating to the strengths of ships.
4. Calculations relating to the propulsion of ships by sails.
5. Calculations relating to the propulsion of ships by steam engines.
6. Calculations relating to the steering of ships.

# PART I.

## CALCULATIONS RELATING TO THE FORMS AND DIMENSIONS OF SHIPS.

---

### CHAPTER I.

#### CALCULATION OF AREAS AND VOLUMES.

Buoyancy — Stability — Hydrostatical Principles — Displacement — Areas of Plane Surfaces — Trapezoidal Rule — Simpson's 1st Rule: Proofs — Fractional Intervals — Simpson's 2nd Rule — One-twelfth Rule — Worked Examples — Centre of Gravity of a Plane Area — Centres of Gravity of various Figures — Principle of Moments — Centre of Gravity of a Plane Area bounded by a Curve — Volumes of Solids — Volume of a Solid bounded by a Plane and a Curved Surface — Calculation of Displacement — Centres of Gravity of Solids — Centre of Gravity of a Volume bounded by a Curved Surface and a Plane — Curve of Areas of Midship Section — Of Sectional Areas — Of Tons per inch of Immersion — Of Displacement — Explanation of a Displacement Sheet — Geometrical Method — Woolley's Rule — Proof — Centre of Buoyancy by Woolley's Rule — Geometrical Application of Woolley's Rule — Angular Measurement of Areas — Volumes and Moments of Wedge-shaped Solids — Moments of Inertia — Examples — Co-efficients of Fineness — Table of Co-efficients of Fineness.

1. The essential qualities sought for in a ship are that she shall be able to float and carry a cargo of some kind with safety; and that, too, at a certain speed when under the influence of a propelling force. In order to do this, it is requisite that she shall possess *buoyancy*, *stability*, and *strength*; also that she shall be of such a form as to move through the water without an undue expenditure of force. We purpose, considering in this and the next division of the subject, the two first of these qualities; and leave the discussion of *strength* and *speed* for succeeding chapters.

2. **Buoyancy** is that quality whereby a ship, or any other floating body, is enabled to support a certain weight: in the case of a ship, it is necessary that that weight should be carried without her sinking too deeply in the water, or floating too lightly on it.

3. **Stability** is that quality, governed both by the form of the ship, and the positions of the weights carried, whereby, when she is inclined out of the upright position, she immediately seeks to recover herself; and, in passing, it may be remarked that this amount of stability should be sufficient to prevent her from heeling, whether under the influence of the wind or waves, to such an extent as to endanger her safety, or produce inconvenience; and, at the same time, should not be so great as to produce abruptness in her movements sufficient to strain or damage the structure or its contents. The influence of the positions of the weights carried upon the stability of a ship will be considered in Part II.; for the present, we propose to confine ourselves to a discussion of the influence of a ship's *form* upon her buoyancy and stability.

4. **Hydrostatical Principles.**—A body floating in a fluid, in a state of equilibrium, *i.e.*, with no disposition to sink deeper, or rise higher with regard to the surface of the fluid, displaces a volume of that fluid exactly equal to its own weight. For instance, suppose a cubical block of wood, each of whose edges is one foot long, when placed in fresh water to sink to a depth of six inches, so that exactly one half of its volume is immersed, and then to float in a state of repose; we at once conclude that, bulk for bulk, the wood weighs just half as much as the water. In other words, taking the weight of a cubic foot of water at 1000 ounces, the cubic foot of wood weighs 500 ounces; for that is the weight of the half of a cubic foot of water that would fill the space occupied by the portion of the block of wood that is immersed.* Should the block of wood sink until the surface

---

* As a fact, it should be here observed that a cubical block of wood, which weighs a half that of an equal volume of water, will not float in equilibrium in the manner here supposed, with one of its sides horizontal, but with one of its angular points upwards. This can be verified by experiment.

of its uppermost face is level with that of the water, we conclude that, bulk for bulk, the wood and water weigh the same.

This may be proved experimentally in the following manner: Fill a bowl with water, and place it in a dish capable of containing water. Then gently place any body, that will float, upon the surface of the water. In sinking to its proper depth of immersion, it will displace a certain quantity of the fluid, which will flow over the edge of the bowl into the dish. When the body is in equilibrium, remove it; and by weighing the body, and then the whole of the water that flowed over the edge into the dish, their weights will be found to be the same. Replace the body, and load it until it sinks deeper into the fluid; weigh the water that again flows over the edge of the bowl, and its weight will be found to be the same as that of the material with which the body was loaded.

Before passing on, it should be remarked that in the case of the cubical block that sank to half it depth in the fluid, the wood of which it was composed was bulk for bulk half as heavy as water; assuming that the water was distilled, then it is said of the wood that its *specific gravity* is $\frac{1}{2}$ or ·5; the term *specific gravity* meaning the ratio of the weight of any body to that of an equal volume of distilled water. In the second case, when the wood weighed the same as an equal volume of water, its *specific gravity* was unity. Should the body sink to the bottom of the fluid, its *specific gravity* is determined by placing it in a bowl full of water, and comparing its weight with the weight of the fluid that flows over; the volumes being evidently identical. By this it will be seen that the specific gravity of a floating body is less than unity, while that of a body that sinks is greater than unity. The accompanying table of specific gravities of materials used in the construction of ships is given, not because of its immediate use at this part of our subject, but because of its bearing upon the principles under consideration. The figures are given upon the authority of Professor Rankine.

## TABLE OF SPECIFIC GRAVITIES OF MATERIALS USED IN THE CONSTRUCTION OF SHIPS.

| Materials. | Specific Gravity. Pure Water = 1. | Materials. | Specific Gravity. Pure Water = 1. |
|---|---|---|---|
| **Timber.** | | **Metals.** | |
| Cedar, | ·486 | Brass, cast, | 7·8 to 8·4 |
| Cowdie, | ·579 | Copper, cast, | 8·6 |
| Elm, | ·544 | ,, sheet, | 8·8 |
| Fir, Red Pine, | ·48 to ·7 | ,, hammered, | 8·9 |
| ,, Spruce, | ·48 to ·7 | Iron, cast, average, | 7·11 |
| ,, American Yellow Pine, | ·46 | ,, wrought, average | 7·69 |
| | | Lead, | 11·4 |
| ,, Larch, | ·5 to ·56 | Steel, | 7·8 to 7·9 |
| Greenheart, | 1·001 | Zinc, | 6·8 to 7·2 |
| Lignum Vitæ, | ·65 to 1·33 | | |
| Mahogany, Honduras, | ·56 | | |
| ,, Cuba, | ·85 | | |
| Mora, | ·92 | | |
| Oak, European, | ·69 to ·99 | | |
| ,, American Red, | ·87 | | |
| Teak, Indian, | ·66 | | |
| ,, African, | ·98 | | |

It must, however, be clearly understood that it is not essential to the buoyancy of a vessel that she should be constructed, even in part, of materials having a specific gravity less than unity. All that is necessary is that *the volume of water displaced*, when floating at the required depth, should be of the same weight as that of the vessel and her contents. As an illustration, we may cite the common phenomena of a porcelain tea-cup or a glass bottle—the materials of each of which have a higher specific gravity than water—floating so long as no more than a certain weight of water, or any other substance is contained in them. The buoyancy depends upon the form as well as the specific gravity of the floating body, and it is to the former quality that we now wish to direct attention.

5. **Displacement.**—The weight of any body floating at rest in a fluid being equal to that of a quantity of the fluid, equal in volume to the portion of the body that is immersed, it consequently follows that if we want to know the weight

of the body, we can determine it by first calculating that volume in terms of some unit of measurement—say a cubic foot—and then multiplying the volume by the weight of a cubic foot of the fluid. Now it happens that in the case of fresh-water, at its ordinary temperature, a cubic foot of it weighs 1000 ounces, or $62\frac{1}{2}$ pounds avoirdupois; in other words, 35·84 cubic feet weigh 1 ton. Salt-water being somewhat denser, 35 cubic feet are found to weigh 1 ton.

It will thus be seen that when the immersed portion of a floating body is of some regular form, admitting of the application of a simple rule or formula in the determination of its volume, the problem of calculating the weight of the body, by the knowledge of this law, is of a very easy character. This was exemplified in the case of the floating cube of wood already referred to. But the bottom of an ordinary ship is not of this regular and well-known form, and, consequently, the problem of determing the *volume of displacement*, or the "*displacement*," as it is usually termed, requires the application of one or other of several rules, which have been investigated by the aid of principles, founded upon the integral calculus, and which are given in such forms as to admit of ready use, without requiring, on the part of the calculator, a knowledge of those principles upon which they are founded. The two principal of these rules are known as "Simpson's* 1st and 2nd Rules," while another is known as "Woolley's Rule." In each case the name is that of the inventor of the formula. These rules we shall presently state.

It must first, however, be understood that displacement calculations are made for two purposes:—*First*, In order to insure, when designing a vessel, that there is a sufficient volume in the portion of the ship when immersed up to a certain height, chosen for the level of the water surface, that the weight of an equivalent volume of water may be as great as that of the total weight which the ship and the cargo she has to carry is expected to have.

*Second*, In order that when a ship is afloat, we may determine, accurately, the total weight of herself and the cargo on board; it being obviously quite impracticable, if not impossible, to determine that weight in any other way, with certainty.

* These are sometimes known as Stirling's Rules.

The elementary principles of buoyancy being thus established, and the reasons given for obtaining the volume, and thence the weight of displacement, we will proceed to explain how that volume is determined in the case of a ship. It is, however, necessary to first consider the areas of plane surfaces, such as those obtained by cutting transverse slices off a ship, and then advance to the discussion of the modes of obtaining the volume of the whole body immersed.

**6. Areas of Plane Surfaces Bounded by Straight Lines.** —The simplest form of plane area that we have to measure is that of a *square* (fig. 1), or *rectangle* (fig. 2), which, it is

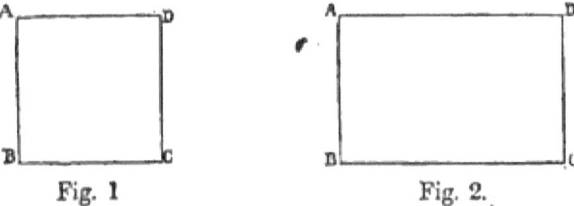

Fig. 1.  Fig. 2.

hardly necessary to say, is obtained by multiplying together two of its adjacent sides, as AB and AD; these being equal in the case of the square. The next form is that of the *triangle* (fig. 3); and since, in the cases we have to consider, it can always be measured in any way thought desirable, its area is simply found by multiplying one side, as BC, by the perpendicular AD, drawn to it from the opposite angle, and then dividing the product

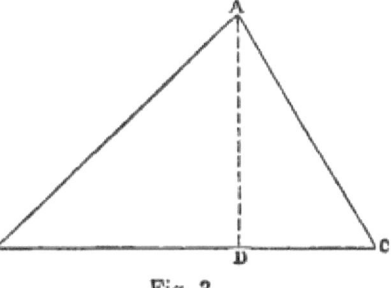

Fig. 3.

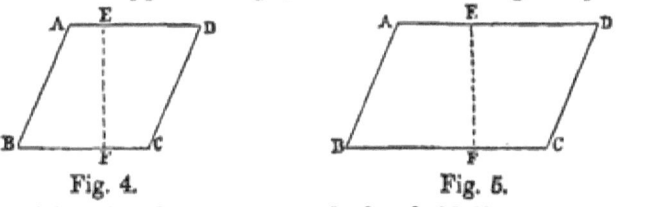

Fig. 4.  Fig. 5.

by 2. The *rhombus* (fig. 4) and *rhomboid* (fig. 5), can each be divided into two equal triangles, and so calculated; or, which is the same thing, the area in each case is found by multiplying either of its sides, say BC, by the perpendicular distance EF, between that side and the side parallel to it. The *trapezoid* (fig. 6), is a four-sided rectilineal, or straight

Fig. 6.

lined, plane figure, only two of whose sides are parallel. Its area is obtained by adding together the lengths of the two parallel sides, AD and BC, and dividing the sum by 2, then multiply this result by the perpendicular distance EF between these sides, and the product is the area. This process is equivalent to obtaining the mean breadth of the figure, and multiplying it by the length; or, in other words, obtaining the area of the equivalent rectangle. The area of the *trapezium* (fig. 7), and that of any other irregular rectilineal plane figure (as in fig. 8), is obtained by dividing

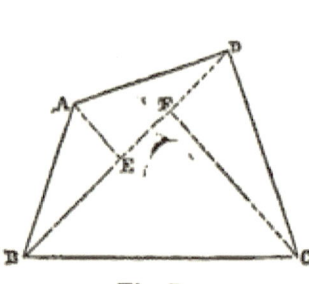 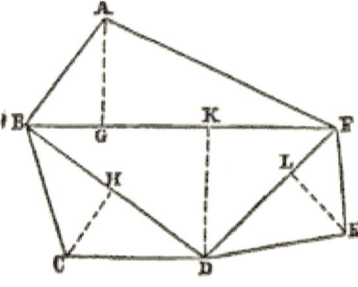

Fig. 7. Fig. 8.

the area into triangles, each of which can be calculated in the manner already described, and then summing the results.

7. **Areas of Plane Surfaces wholly or partially bounded by Curved Lines.**—There is a great number of plane figures, wholly or partially bounded by curved lines, the areas of which can be determined by simple rules; for instance, the circle, segments and sectors of circles, ellipses, parabolas, etc. For our purpose, however, in calculating the areas of such plane figures as are given by the sections of a ship, we do

not concern ourselves with these simple figures, each of which is measured by a separate rule; but attend rather to a rule, or rules, applicable to all plane surfaces bounded by curved lines, and giving results which, while more or less approximate, can always be depended upon for a close degree of accuracy, if sufficient pains are taken in their application. As we shall see presently, these rules are *true* only for certain figures; nevertheless the assumption of their universal accuracy for all curves in a ship's form is not productive of a greater degree of error than is admitted in measuring with a scale from an ordinary drawing.

It is hardly necessary to state that the two "dimensions," or directions for measurement of plane areas, are termed "*length*" and "*breadth*." We will now dispense with these terms, and use in their stead two others which are necessarily employed in the measurement of curved areas. These are "*ordinate*" and "*abscissa*." In figs. 1, 2, 4, and 5, BC and AB are usually termed the length and breadth; in the nomenclature now to be used, AB will be an "ordinate," and BC an "*abscissa*." In Algebraical language, BC is generally known as $x$, and AB as $y$.

In fig. 9, adjoining, ABCD is a trapezoid, the sides AB and CD being parallel. According to the rule already given, the area of this figure is obtained by adding AB and CD together, and then multiplying half of their sum by BC. In Algebraical language, AB would be termed "the ordinate $y_1$," and CD—"the ordinate $y_2$"; also BC would be styled "an abscissa $x$." Consequently, this rule expressed in a formula would appear thus :—

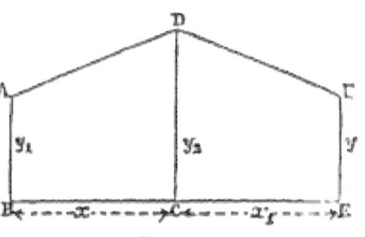

Fig. 9.

$$\text{Area} = \frac{y_1 + y_2}{2} x.$$

Similarly, if another trapezoid be constructed, such as DCEF, having CE in a straight line with BC, and the side DC common to the two figures; then styling EF as $y_3$, and

CE as $x_1$, the area of DCEF is equal to $\frac{y_2+y_3}{2}x_1$. Hence the area of the whole figure ABEF is equal to

$$\frac{y_1+y_2}{2}x + \frac{y_2+y_3}{2}x_1 \quad \ldots\ldots\ldots\ldots\ldots (A)$$

Let BC = CE, or $x = x_1$, and the area becomes

$$\frac{y_1+2y_2+y_3}{2}x \quad \ldots\ldots\ldots\ldots\ldots\ldots\ldots (B)$$

This simple case will serve to familiarise the student with the meaning of the terms *abscissa* and *ordinate;* also of the symbols used to express them, and the manner in which they are employed in expressing the value of an area.

In preparing a plane area for calculation in this manner, the ordinates are always drawn perpendicular to the abscissa, and they are spaced either all equidistant, or else some of the ordinates are a multiple, such as one-half of the distance apart from each other; so that the abscissæ are either all equal, or perhaps a few are some multiple of the other abscissæ.

**8. Trapezoidal Rule for Plane Areas.**—It will, no doubt, have already suggested itself to the student, that the area of a plane surface, bounded by a straight line and a curve, can be easily approximated to by dividing it into a sufficient number of trapezoids, as in fig. 1, Plate I. Suppose the area be required of the plane surface ABECD, bounded by the straight line AD and the curve BEC; also, for simplicity sake, by two end ordinates AB and CD. Divide the base AD into a certain number of equal parts at $a, b, c, F, d$, etc., and draw the ordinates $af, bg, ch, FE, dk$, etc., to the curve; these we shall hereafter term *dividing ordinates*. Then by considering each of the figures BAaf, fabg, gbch, etc., as a trapezoid, and summing their areas, we obtain a result which is less than the true area of ABECD, by the collective areas of the small spaces enclosed between the ticked straight lines Bf, fg, gh, etc., and the curve BEC. It is evident that by taking a sufficient number of ordinates we may obtain, in this way, an area which will differ from the true one by as small an amount as we please. Also, that in the case of a very flat or nearly straight curve, fewer ordinates are required than if the curve is very convex or concave. Again, when a portion of the curve is more concave or convex than the remainder, in order the better to approximate to the area, the ordinates should be closer at that part than elsewhere. Let the lengths of the ordinates $AB$, $af$, $bg$, etc., in fig. 1, Plate I., be expressed by the symbols $y_1$, $y_2$, $y_3$, etc., and the abscissa or common interval between the ordinates, viz., $Aa$ or $ab$, etc., be expressed by $x$. Then by formula (B), in Art. 7, the total area of the trapezoids becomes

$$\frac{y_1 + 2y_2 + y_3}{2}x + \frac{y_3 + 2y_4 + y_5}{2}x + \frac{y_5 + 2y_6 + y_7}{2}x + \frac{y_7 + y_8}{2}x \; \ldots \text{(A)}$$

adding, we get

$$\left( y_1 + 2y_2 + 2y_3 + 2y_4 + 2y_5 + 2y_6 + 2y_7 + y_8 \right)\frac{x}{2} \; \ldots \ldots \text{(B)}$$

or

$$\left( \frac{y_1 + y_8}{2} + y_2 + y_3 + y_4 + y_5 + y_6 + y_7 \right)x \; \ldots \ldots \text{(C)}$$

and by choosing a sufficient number of ordinates, and thereby reducing the size of each trapezoid, we may make this expression represent, as nearly as we please, the area of the figure $ABECD$.

Written out, formula (C) may be stated in the following rule, termed the *trapezoidal rule*:—

*Divide the base into a sufficient number of equal parts, and draw and measure ordinates at the points of division. Add together all the dividing ordinates, and one-half of the end-most ordinates; multiply the sum by the common interval: the product will be the required area, nearly.*

Should it be considered desirable, owing to the greater convexity or concavity of the curve at some parts, to introduce intermediate ordinates at such places, then the areas of these lesser trapezoids, also of the portion made up of the others, must be calculated separately. For further particulars on the mode of dealing with subdivided areas, the student is referred to Art 12, where the mode of expressing the total area in such a case, by one formula, is explained.

9. **Simpson's First Rule.**—The basis of Simpson's rules for the calculation of plane areas is founded upon an assump-

tion, which is practically true for the curves met with in a ship's hull, viz., that they are members of the group known as *parabolic*. The term *parabolic*, as here used, has a wider meaning than that of the ordinary parabola of the conic sections. In the sense the term is here employed, it refers to all curves, any ordinate of which can be expressed by means of one or more terms, each of which is proportional to some power of the abscissa corresponding to that ordinate. The parabolic curve is said to be of the *second order*, the *third order*, etc., according to the exponent of the highest power of the abscissa.

*Simpson's First Rule*, however, is founded upon the assumption that the parabola is of the second order,[*] and therefore that of the conic sections. The result obtained by its application to the curves of ships is found sufficiently correct for all practical purposes. We will now proceed to investigate it by a simple method, based upon a fundamental property of the parabola of the second order, which property it is not necessary to demonstrate in a work of this kind.

10. **Simpson's First Rule—Proof First.**—A parabola of the second order is a curve, such that *the area of any one of its segments is two-thirds of the product of the base and deflection of that segment*. Another property of the common parabola is, that *the deflection of any arc is proportional to the square of its base*.

In fig. 2, Plate I., let $CKD$ be a portion of the arc of a parabola $PKQ$ upon the base $PQ$. Join $CD$, and through the points $C$ and $D$ draw $CA$ and $DB$, ordinates perpendicular to the base $PQ$. Bisect $AB$ at $E$; also bisect $AE$ and $EB$ at $F$ and $G$, respectively. Through the points $F$ and $G$ draw the ordinates $FH$ and $GL$ perpendicular to $PQ$. Join $CK$ and $KD$. Then $KO$, the length of the ordinate $EK$ intercepted between the chord $CD$ and the curve, is termed the *deflection* of the arc $CKD$, also $MH$ and $NL$ are the *deflections* of the arcs $CHK$ and $KLD$, respectively. The property just stated, viz., *that the deflection of any arc is*

---

[*] Mr. C. W. Merrifield has shown that Simpson's First Rule is also true for a cubic parabola, or parabola of the third order. See *Transactions of the Institution of Naval Architects*, Vol. VI.

*proportional to the square of its base*, will be perhaps better understood when we put it thus:

$$OK : HM :: AB^2 : AE^2$$
$$\text{and since } AB : AE :: 2 : 1$$
$$\therefore AB^2 : AE^2 :: 4 : 1$$
$$\therefore OK : HM :: 4 : 1$$
$$\text{and thus } HM = \frac{OK}{4}$$
$$\text{Similarly, } NL = \frac{OK}{4} = HM.$$

Suppose it be required to find the area of the figure $ACKDB$, bounded by the base $AB$, the two end ordinates $AC$ and $BD$, and the parabolic curve $CKD$. Employing the trapezoidal rule, stated at Art. 8, and using only one dividing ordinate, viz., $EK$; the area we obtain is that of the two trapezoids forming the right-lined figure $ACMKNDB$, which is less than the true area by the sum of the areas of the parabolic segments $CHK$ and $KLD$. Again, if we use three dividing ordinates, we obtain the area of the figure $ACHKLDB$, composed of four trapezoids, which is less than the true area by the sum of the four parabolic segments $CH$, $HK$, $KL$, and $LD$. This latter result is more nearly true than the former, inasmuch as it includes the areas of the two triangles $CHK$ and $KLD$, which were neglected in the former. It will readily be seen that by bisecting the portions $AF$, $FE$, $EG$, etc., of the base, and so erecting four intermediate ordinates, we approach the true area by the sum of the four triangles in the segments $CH$, $HK$, $KL$, and $LD$; and by increasing the number of the ordinates indefinitely, we shall approach the truth as nearly as we please. Hence the area of the whole figure $ACKDB$ is made up of the following:—

Trapezoid ACDB + triangle CKD + triangle CHK + triangle KLD + triangles in segments CH, HK, KL, LD + etc., etc.

Neglecting the trapezoid $ACDB$ for the present, we will find the sum of the areas of all the triangles, such as are drawn in the figure, which, *in the limit*, compose the parabolic segment $CKD$.

The area of the triangle $CKD$ is equal to

$$\frac{AB \times KO}{2}$$

Also the areas of the triangles $CHK$ and $KLD$ are each equal to

$$\frac{AB}{2} \times \frac{HM}{2} \text{ or } \frac{AB}{2} \times \frac{NL}{2}.$$
$$\text{but } HM = NL = \frac{OK}{4}.$$

Therefore the areas of the triangles are each equal to

$$\frac{AB}{2} \times \frac{OK}{8} = \frac{AB \times OK}{16},$$

and the sum of the two $= \dfrac{AB \times OK}{8}$,

whence it follows that their sum $= \dfrac{\text{area } CKD}{4}$.

Similarly, it may be shown that the sum of the areas of the triangles in the segments $CH$, $HK$, $KL$, and $LD$, is equal to one-fourth the sum of the areas of the triangles $CHK$ and $KLD$, or one-sixteenth the area of the triangle $CKD$, and so on.

Hence we have for the area of the parabolic segment

$$\frac{AB \times KO}{2} (1 + \tfrac{1}{4} + \tfrac{1}{16} + \tfrac{1}{64} + \tfrac{1}{256} + \text{etc}).$$

By adding together a sufficient number of terms of this endless series, we can approach the true area of the parabolic segment as nearly as we please.

The limit of the series can be found exactly as follows:—
If we take the fraction $\tfrac{3}{4}$ of any unit, and add to it $\tfrac{3}{4}$ of the remaining quarter, or $\tfrac{3}{16}$; then $\tfrac{3}{4}$ of the remaining sixteenth or $\tfrac{3}{64}$, and so on, we obtain successively the sums:

$$\tfrac{3}{4},\ 1\tfrac{3}{16},\ 1\tfrac{3}{64},\ 2\tfrac{3}{256},\ \text{etc.,}$$

which obviously approach nearer and nearer to unity, and may be made to approach as near to unity as we please by carrying on the series far enough. Therefore the *limit* of the sum of the endless series,

$$\tfrac{3}{4} + \tfrac{3}{16} + \tfrac{3}{64} + \tfrac{3}{256} + \text{etc., is 1;}$$

and dividing by 3, we find that the limit of the sum of the endless series,

$$\tfrac{1}{4} + \tfrac{1}{16} + \tfrac{1}{64} + \tfrac{1}{256} + \text{etc.,}$$

is one-third. Consequently, the exact area of the parabolic segment is

$$\frac{AB \times KO}{2}(1 + \tfrac{1}{3}) = \frac{2 \times AB \times KO}{3},$$

as already stated.

Hence the area of the whole figure $ACKDB$ is equal to

$$AB \times \frac{AC + BD}{2} = \text{area of trapezoid,}$$

added to $\tfrac{2}{3}(AB \times KO) = \ldots\ldots$ parabolic segment.
But $\tfrac{2}{3}(AB \times KO) = \tfrac{2}{3}AB(EK - EO)$
$$= \tfrac{2}{3}AB\left(EK - \frac{AC + BD}{2}\right).$$

Hence whole area

$$= AB \times \frac{AC + BD}{2} + \tfrac{2}{3}AB\left(EK - \frac{AC + BD}{2}\right)$$
$$= AB\left(\tfrac{2}{3}EK + \frac{AC + BD}{6}\right)$$
$$= \frac{AB}{6}(AC + 4EK + BD).$$

The same result may be demonstrated when the parabolic arc is concave, by taking $A_1 E_1 B_1$, parallel to $AEB$, as the base, finding the area $A_1 CKDB_1$; and then subtracting the parabolic segment $CKD$ from the trapezoid, $A_1 CDB_1$.

This is the basis of Simpson's First Rule. In the proof we have given, there is only one dividing ordinate; in order to obtain the rule in its general form, we have to place, side by side on a common base, a number of such elementary parabolic areas, as shown by fig. 2, Plate I., and then determine an expression which will represent the area of the whole parabolic figure. In fig. 1, Plate II., let $PRSTQ$ be a parabolic figure on base $PQ$, and divided by the equidistant ordinates $b, c, d$, etc.; $a$ and $g$ being the two end ordinates, and the common interval $h$. Then the area of the space included between the ordinates:

$a$ and $c = \tfrac{1}{3}h(a + 4b + c)$
between $c$ and $e = \tfrac{1}{3}h(c + 4d + e)$
between $e$ and $g = \tfrac{1}{3}h(e + 4f + g)$.

Adding these areas together we obtain

Total area $PRSTQ = \tfrac{1}{3}h(a + 4b + 2c + 4d + 2e + 4f + g)$,

which is the rule for seven ordinates; and, similarly, the

value of the area, in terms of any other odd number of equidistant ordinates and their common intervals, may be expressed by a similar formulæ.

*Simpson's First Rule* may therefore be thus stated:—

Divide the base into any even number of equal lengths, and through these points draw ordinates to the curve, which ordinates will consequently be odd in number. *Multiply the length of each of the even ordinates by* 4, *and that of each of the odd ordinates by* 2, *except the first and last, or bounding ordinates, which multiply by unity. The sum of these products, multiplied by one-third of the common interval between the ordinates, will give the area required.*

The proof we have given depends upon the integral calculus, although the notation of that branch of mathematics is not employed. This will be seen by the assumption made regarding the limit of the sum of the series $\frac{3}{4}+\frac{3}{16}+\frac{3}{64}$, etc., which we have, for very good reasons, taken as unity, without rigidly demonstrating such to be the case.

The nature of the problem is such as to necessitate the employment of the calculus in an exact demonstration. This we now proceed to give. (See fig. 2, Plate II.)

**11. Simpson's First Rule—Second Proof.**—To find the area of the plane figure $BCEGH$, bounded by the base $BH$, the parabolic curve $CEG$, and the end ordinates $BC$ and $GH$. Draw the three dividing ordinates $OD$, $AE$, and $KF$, so that there are five equidistant ordinates, which we will term $a$, $\beta$, $\gamma$, $\delta$, and $\varepsilon$.

Consider the curve $CEG$ as a portion of the parabola, whose equation is
$$y = a + bx + cx^2.$$
Let $O$ be the origin of co-ordinates, and let
$$BO = OA = AK = KH = h.$$
Then the area $CBA = \int y\,dx$, or
$$\text{area} = \int_{-h}^{h}(a+bx+cx^2)dx = 2\left(ah+\frac{ch^3}{3}\right)$$
$$= \tfrac{2}{3}h(3a+ch^2). \quad\ldots\ldots\ldots\ldots\ldots(1)$$
Now when $x = 0 \quad y = a = \beta$ (as seen by the figure)
$\qquad\quad x = h \quad y = a+bh+ch^2 = \gamma$
$\qquad\quad x = -h \quad y = a-bh+ch^2 = \varepsilon$
$\therefore \varepsilon + \gamma = 2(a+ch^2)$
$\text{and } 4\beta = 4a.$

Hence, adding
$$\alpha + 4\beta + \gamma = 2(3a + ch^2), \ldots\ldots\ldots\ldots(2)$$
and the area CBAE by (1) and (2)
$$= \frac{h}{3}(\alpha + 4\beta + \gamma).$$

Similarly, the area $EAHG = \frac{h}{3}(\gamma + 4\delta + \epsilon)$,

∴ the whole area $CBHG = \frac{h}{3}(\alpha + 4\beta + 2\gamma + 4\delta + \epsilon)$,

which proves the Rule.

A very ingenious demonstration, due to Mr. F. K. Barnes, will be found at page 9 of *Shipbuilding, Theoretical and Practical*, which is too lengthy for insertion here.

**12. Fractional Intervals.**—As already mentioned (Art. 8), when a portion of the bounding curve has very great or sudden convexity or concavity, it is desirable, with a view to greater accuracy, to draw ordinates at one-half, or even one-fourth the common interval apart. In such a case, in order to express the total area in terms of the common interval, and the lengths of the ordinates, the multipliers must be altered in the following manner. In fig. 3, Plate II., the curve $RST$ is very concave between $S$ and $T$, with regard to the base $PQ$. Let $a, b, c, d, e$, be an odd number of equidistant ordinates, $h$ being the common interval. Draw the ordinate $f$ midway between $c$ and $d$, the ordinate $g$ midway between $d$ and $e$, the ordinate $k$ midway between $d$ and $g$, and the ordinate $l$ midway between $g$ and $e$, so that we have nine ordinates. Then the area of the space enclosed between

$$a \text{ and } c = \frac{h}{3}(a + 4b + c)$$

$$c \text{ and } d = \frac{h}{6}(c + 4f + d)$$

$$d \text{ and } g = \frac{h}{12}(d + 4k + g)$$

$$g \text{ and } e = \frac{h}{12}(g + 4l + e).$$

Summing these results, we have

$$\text{Total area PRSTQ} = \frac{h}{3}\left(a + 4b + c + \frac{c}{2} + 2f + \frac{d}{2} + \frac{d}{4} + k + \frac{g}{4} + \frac{g}{4} + l + \frac{e}{4}\right)$$
$$= \frac{h}{3}\left(a + 4b + \frac{3c}{2} + 2f + \frac{3d}{4} + k + \frac{g}{2} + l + \frac{e}{4}\right).$$

If a quadrant of a circle (see fig. 4, Plate II.) of a certain radius, say 12 feet, be divided by 9 ordinates in this manner, and the lengths of these ordinates be carefully measured and substituted in this formula, the area so obtained will be 112·93 square feet; whereas the area obtained by taking $\pi = 3\cdot 1416$ will be 113·1. Thus an error of $113\cdot 1 - 112\cdot 93 = \cdot 17$ or ·16 per cent. is made by applying Simpson's First Rule in such an extreme case, using the number of intermediate ordinates shown in the figure.

**13. Simpson's Second Rule for Plane Areas.**—This rule is founded upon the assumption that the bounding curve is a parabola of the third order, *i.e.*, one whose equation may be expressed thus,

$$y = a + bx + cx^2 + dx^3.$$

Let $ABCD$ (fig. 1, Plate III.), be a plane area, bounded by a base $AD$, two end ordinates $AB$ and $CD$, and a parabolic curve of the third order, $BHC$. Divide $AD$ into three equal parts, each equal to $h$, at the points $E$ and $F$, and draw through these points the ordinates $EG$ and $FH$. Let the lengths of the four ordinates be represented by $a$, $b$, $c$, and $d$.

Then area $ABCD = \tfrac{3}{8}h(a + 3b + 3c + d)$.

This may be proved by a somewhat similar demonstration to that given of the First Rule at Art. 11. It is not necessary to state the proof here, the more so as the rule does not generally give quite so close an approximation to the true area as the First Rule.

It will be readily seen that, by dividing the base up into six equal lengths, and drawing ordinates through the divisions, we have two elementary figures as above; and if $a$, $b$, $c$, $d$, $e$, $f$, and $g$ be the ordinates, and $h$ the common interval,

Then area $= \tfrac{3}{8}h\,(a + 3b + 3c + d) + \tfrac{3}{8}h\,(d + 3e + 3f + g)$
$= \tfrac{3}{8}h\,(a + 3b + 3c + 2d + 3e + 3f + g),$

from which the Second Rule may be thus stated:—

Divide the base into equal lengths so that their number may be a multiple of 3, and draw ordinates through the dividing points and the extremities of the base, so that their total number, when divided by 3, gives a remainder of 1. Call the 4th, 7th, 10th, etc., ordinates, *dividing ordinates;* and the others, except the endmost, *intermediate ordinates.*

Add together the endmost ordinates, twice the dividing ordinates, and three times the intermediate ordinates; multiply the sum by three-eighths of the common interval: the product will be the required area, nearly.

14. **Area of Subdivision of a Parabolic Figure.**—It is sometimes required to calculate separately the area of one of the two subdivisions (see fig. 2, Plate I.) into which an elementary parabolic figure $ACKDB$ is divided by the middle ordinate $EK$. For example, supposing it is required to calculate separately the area of the subdivision $ACKE$; let $AC$ be called the *near end ordinate*, and $BD$ the *far end ordinate*, then the rule will be as follows:—*To eight times the middle ordinate, add five times the near end ordinate, and subtract the far end ordinate; multiply the remainder by one-twelfth of the common interval: the product will be the area required.*

The truth of this will be readily seen by considering that the area is made up of the trapezoid $ACOE$, and the half segment $CKO$. For the area of the half segment $CKO$ is equal to

$$\frac{AB}{3}\left(EK - \frac{AC+BD}{2}\right) \text{ (See Art. 10)},$$

and the area of the trapezoid $ACOE$ is equal to

$$\frac{AB}{2}\left(\frac{AC+OE}{2}\right)$$
$$= \frac{AB}{8}\left(3\,AC+BD\right).$$

Hence area of figure $ACKE$

$$= \frac{AB}{3}\left(EK - \frac{AC+BD}{2}\right) + \frac{AB}{8}\left(3\,AC+BD\right)$$
$$= \frac{AB}{24}\left(5\,AC+8\,EK-BD\right)$$
$$= \frac{AE}{12}\left(5\,AC+8\,EK-BD\right)$$

This is sometimes known as the *five-eight rule*.

15. **Example of the Application of Simpson's First Rule.**—The following example will illustrate the application of Simpson's First Rule for measuring a plane area bounded by a curve.

Let the area of the figure $ACB$ (fig. 2, Plate III.) be required, of which the base AB is 40 feet long. Divide AB into a certain even number of, say 8, equal lengths, each of which will therefore measure 5 feet. Erect ordinates through these points; these will necessarily be 9 in number, including the end ordinates; and therefore fitted for the application of Simpson's First Rule. Measure the lengths of these ordinates, which lengths we will suppose to be represented by the dimensions marked against them in the diagram.

| Numbers of Ordinates. | Simpson's Multipliers. | Lengths of Ordinates. | Functions of Ordinates. |
|---|---|---|---|
| 1 | 1 | ·2 | ·2 |
| 2 | 4 | 3·5 | 14·0 |
| 3 | 2 | 5·2 | 10·4 |
| 4 | 4 | 6·6 | 26·4 |
| 5 | 2 | 6·8 | 13·6 |
| 6 | 4 | 6·7 | 26·8 |
| 7 | 2 | 5·8 | 11·6 |
| 8 | 4 | 4·7 | 18·8 |
| 9 | 1 | 1·6 | 1·6 |

$$\phantom{xxxxxxxxxxxxx}123\cdot4$$
$$5 = \text{Common Interval}$$
$$\text{Divisor by Rule} = 3\overline{)617\cdot0}$$
$$\phantom{xxxxxxxxxx}205\cdot66 = \text{Area, nearly.}$$

In proceeding to apply the Rule as in the above table, four *columns* are ruled, and as many *rows* as there are ordinates. The first column shows the distinguishing numbers of the ordinates; the second column contains Simpson's Multipliers, arranged in their proper order, and opposite to their respective ordinates; the third column contains the lengths of the respective ordinates, numbered in the first column; and the fourth column contains what is termed "*the functions of the ordinates*," *i.e.*, the products of the ordinates and their respective multipliers.

The sum of the figures in the fourth column is 123·4, and this has to be multiplied by one-third the common interval, which, in this case, is 5 feet. Hence, 123·4 is multiplied by 5 ft. and divided by 3; thus giving 205·6 sq. ft., which is the area required, nearly.

APPLICATION OF THE TRAPEZOIDAL RULE. 31

Some calculators, in order to reduce the figures in the fourth column, use as multipliers the figures ½, 2, 1, 2, . . . 2, ½, instead of 1, 4, 2, 4, . . 4, 1, and consequently the sum so obtained has to be multiplied by 2 after being multiplied by one-third of the common interval.

**16. Example of the Application of Simpson's Second Rule.**—In this case the number of divisions of the base must be a multiple of 3, and there will, of course, be one more ordinate than division.

Divide the base AB (fig. 3, Plate III.) into, say 6, equal lengths, each being 5 ft., also draw the ordinates and measure them as before.

| Numbers of Ordinates. | Simpson's Multipliers. | Lengths of Ordinates. | Functions of Ordinates. |
|---|---|---|---|
| 1 | 1 | 2·1 | 2·1 |
| 2 | 3 | 3·6 | 10·8 |
| 3 | 3 | 5·3 | 15·9 |
| 4 | 2 | 5·6 | 11·2 |
| 5 | 3 | 5·4 | 16·2 |
| 6 | 3 | 5·0 | 15·0 |
| 7 | 1 | 2·5 | 2·5 |

$$\begin{array}{r} 73\cdot7 \\ 5 = \text{Common Interval} \\ \hline 368\cdot5 \\ 3 \\ \hline 8)\overline{1105\cdot5} \\ \hline 138\cdot19 = \text{Area, nearly.} \end{array}$$

The arrangement of the columns is the same as in the preceding example; the number of ordinates and the multipliers being different according to the Rule. The sum of the figures in the fourth column is 73·7, which is multiplied by three-eighths of the common interval, or $\frac{3}{8} \times 5$ ft., and gives 138·19 ft. which is the area, nearly.

**17. Example of the Application of the Trapezoidal Rule.**—We will use the same diagram and dimensions as in Art. 16,

32   THEORETICAL NAVAL ARCHITECTURE.

| Numbers of Ordinates. | Multipliers. | Ordinates. | Functions of Ordinates. |
|---|---|---|---|
| 1 | ½ | 2·1 | 1·05 |
| 2 | 1 | 3·6 | 3·60 |
| 3 | 1 | 5·3 | 5·30 |
| 4 | 1 | 5·6 | 5·60 |
| 5 | 1 | 5·4 | 5·40 |
| 6 | 1 | 5·0 | 5·00 |
| 7 | ½ | 2·5 | 1·25 |

$\phantom{xxxxxxxxxxxxxxxxxxxxxx}$ 27·2
$\phantom{xxxxxxxxxxxxxxxxxxxxxx}$ 5 = Common Interval
$\phantom{xxxxxxxxxxxxxxxxxxxx}$ 136·0 = Area, approximately.

The area found by this rule is thus 136 sq. ft., whereas by Simpson's Second Rule it was found to be 138·19 sq. ft. If the area be determined by the First Rule, the result will be 138 sq. ft. Simpson's Rules thus practically agree, and as the First Rule can be depended upon to, at least, the same degree of accuracy as the Second, we may take 138 as the area. Thus it will be seen that in this case the use of the Trapezoidal Rule involves an error of 138 − 136 = 2 sq. ft., or about 1·5 per cent. With a curve of greater convexity or concavity the error would, of course, be still more.

**18. Example of the Application of the Rule for Subdivision of a Parabolic Figure.**—(See Art. 14.)  In fig. 2, Plate I., let AC = 5·3, EK = 7·2, BD = 3·1, and AE = 8.

Then area ACKE = $\dfrac{AE}{12}\left(8\ EK + 5\ AC - BD\right)$

$= \dfrac{8}{12}\left(57·6 + 26·5 - 3·1\right) = \dfrac{2}{3} \times 87 = 58$ sq. ft.

By treating the figure as a trapezoid—

$\phantom{xxxxxxx}$ Area $= \dfrac{8}{2}\left(7·2 + 5·3\right) = 50$ sq. ft.

The Trapezoidal Rule thus being relatively in error, 58 − 50 = 8 sq. ft., or 14 per cent. in this particular case.

**19. Centres of Gravity of Plane Areas.**—The centre of gravity of a plane area, termed its *geometrical centre of gravity*, is that point at which, if the surface is uniformly weighted, it can be poised in equilibrium. To illustrate our meaning, we may consider the plane as the surface of a sheet of metal having a uniform thickness, then the centre of gravity of a plate of any form is that point where the plate, if supported thereat, will balance or remain poised in a state of equilibrium. In all our considerations regarding the centre of gravity of a plane area the surface is supposed to be heavy, and the weight of every unit of the area to be the same.

20. **Centres of Regular Figures.**—It will at once be seen that the geometrical centre of gravity* of a circular plane area is its centre. Also, that the geometrical centre of gravity of a square or rectangular area is the point where the two diagonals intersect; for as each diagonal cuts the figure into two similar and equal parts, the centre of gravity must be in each diagonal; and, therefore, at the point common to the two, or where they intersect. The same is true of a rhombus or rhomboid. The centre of gravity of a regular polygon is the centre of the circumscribed circle; for since every diameter of the circle passing through the angular points of the polygon cuts the latter into two similar and equal parts, therefore the centre of gravity of the figure must lie in each diameter, and consequently at the point common to them all, or the centre of the circumscribed circle. The circumscribed and inscribed circles being concentric, the centre of gravity of the latter circle is also that of the regular polygon.

**The Centre of Gravity of a Triangle** is found in the following manner:—*Bisect two sides and join the points of bisection with the opposite angles, then the point of intersection of the two lines so drawn is the centre of gravity of the triangle.*

Let $ABC$ (fig. 1, Plate IV.) be the surface of a triangular plate of uniform weight; bisect $BC$ in $E$, and join $AE$; draw $ceb$ parallel to $CEB$, cutting $AE$ at any point $e$. Then, by similar triangles—

$$ce : CE :: Ae : AE$$
$$\text{and } \quad be : BE :: Ae : AE$$
$$\therefore \quad ce : CE :: be : BE$$
$$\text{but } CE = BE, \therefore ce = be.$$

Hence $AE$ bisects every line in the triangle drawn parallel to $BC$. Therefore each of the strips similar to $ceb$, into which we may suppose the triangle to be divided, will balance on

---

* Hereafter the geometrical centre of gravity will be understood to be meant when referring to forms without weight.

$AE$, and consequently the centre of gravity must be in the line $AE$.

Bisect $AC$ in $F$, and join $BF$; let this cut $AE$ in $G$. Then, as before, the centre of gravity must be in $BF$; but it has been shown to be in $AE$, therefore $G$, the intersection of $AE$ and $BF$, is the centre of gravity.

This point $G$ is situated at one-third the length of $AE$ from the point $E$. To prove this, join $EF$. Then, because $CE = BE$ and $CF = AF$, therefore $EF$ is parallel to $AB$ and $AB = 2FE$; also by similar triangles—

$$AB : EF :: AG : EG;$$
$$EG = \tfrac{1}{2} AG, \text{ or } EG = \tfrac{1}{3} AE.$$

Hence, to find the centre of gravity of a triangle, *bisect any side, join the point of bisection with the opposite angle, and the centre of gravity lies a third of the way up this line.*

It will be useful to observe that the centre of gravity of a triangle coincides with the centre of gravity of three equal weights placed at the angular points of the triangle. For, to find the centre of gravity of three equal weights placed at the points $A$, $B$, $C$, respectively (see fig. 1, Plate IV.), we join $CB$ and bisect it in $E$; then $E$ is the centre of gravity of the weights at $C$ and $B$. Suppose these weights collected at $E$, then join $AE$, and divide $AE$ in $G$, so that $EG$ may be to $AG$ as the weight at $A$ is to that of the two at $E$, that is as 1 : 2; then $G$ is the centre of gravity of the three equal weights. From the construction, $G$ is also the centre of gravity of the triangle $ABC$, as already shown.

**21. Centre of Gravity of a Trapezium.**—From this we may proceed to determine the centre of gravity of a trapezium by drawing a diagonal, and thus dividing it into two triangles. The centre of gravity of these are found, and the points joined by a straight line. Next, the other diagonal is drawn, and the centres of gravity of the two resulting triangles are joined by a straight line. As the centre of gravity of the trapezium is in each of these straight lines, it is evidently the point of their intersection.

The ordinary mode of constructing the figure is, however, as follows:—Let $ABCD$ (fig. 2, Plate IV.) be a trapezium; draw the diagonals $AC$, $BD$ intersecting at $E$. Let $AE$ be greater than $EC$, and $BE$ greater than $ED$. Take $AF = EC$, and $BG = ED$. Set off $ES = \frac{1}{3} EF$, and $ET = \frac{1}{3} EG$; draw $SO$ parallel to $BD$, and $TO$ parallel to $AC$; their intersection $O$ is the centre of gravity of the trapezium. It is evident if we join $GF$, then $O$ is also the centre of gravity of the triangle $EGF$.

The following is the proof of the accuracy of this construction. It will be observed that it is required to demonstrate that the lines $LM$ and $NP$ joining the centres of gravity of the two sets of triangles, into which the diagonals successively divide the trapezium, are parallel to $AC$ and $BD$ respectively; also that $SO = \frac{1}{3} EG$, and $TO = \frac{1}{3} EF$.

Since $HL = \frac{1}{3} AH$, and $HM = \frac{1}{3} HC$, therefore $LM$ is parallel to $AC$. Similarly, $NP$ is parallel to $BD$. This gives the first requirement.

Again, since $BG = ED$, and $BH = HD$, $\therefore GH = HE$. Similarly, $FK = KE$. Also, because $LM$ is parallel to $AC$, and $HM = \frac{1}{3} HC$, $\therefore HT = \frac{1}{3} HE$, and $TE = \frac{2}{3} HE = \frac{1}{3} GE$. Similarly, $SE = \frac{1}{3} EF$, whence the construction.

The centre of gravity of the trapezium being coincident with that of the triangle $EFG$, a very simple mode of determining the point by construction is to bisect $EF$ and $EG$ at $K$ then $H$ respectively; then joining $FH$ and $GK$, their point of intersection is $O$, the centre of gravity of the triangle, and therefore of the trapezium.

22. **The Centre of Gravity of a Trapezoid** is easily found in the following manner: Let $ABCD$ (fig. 3, Plate IV.) be a trapezoid, $AD$ and $BC$ being the parallel sides. Bisect $AD$ in $E$, and $BC$ in $F$, and join $EF$. Then divide $EF$ at the point $G$, so that

$$BC : AD :: EG : GF.$$

$G$ is the centre of gravity of the trapezoid. The truth of this is too obvious to need a proof here.

23. **The Centre of Gravity of an Ellipsoid** is evidently at its centre, or at the intersection of the major and minor axes.

24. **Principle of Moments.**—In obtaining the centres of gravities of the plane areas already examined, we have depended merely upon the symmetry of the figures, whereby we were enabled to draw two lines, each of which contained the centre of gravity, the latter being therefore situated at

the intersection of these lines. We shall presently show how to determine the centre of gravity when there are no symmetrical conditions to assist us. Consequently, we must have recourse to the elements of statical equilibrium as enunciated in the *principles of moments*. The forces we have to consider being those due to gravity, they are therefore parallel, and act in the same direction; a condition which materially simplifies our investigations.

The *moment* of a weight about any point is the product of the weight into the perpendicular distance of its line of action from that point (see fig. 4, Plate IV.). Let the weight $W$ act at the point $A$, perpendicular to the straight line $AB$, then the moment of the weight about the point $B$ is $W \times AB$.

If there is more than one weight acting at different points on the straight line, perpendicular to it, then the sum of the products of the weights into the distances of their points of application from $B$ is the total moment acting about that point. For instance, $W_1$, $W_2$, and $W_3$ (fig. 5, Plate IV.) acting at the points $A$, $C$, $D$, respectively, have a total moment about $B = W_1.AB + W_2.CB + W_3.DB$. It will be readily seen that the three weights $W_1$, $W_2$, and $W_3$ may be applied at some point in the line, so that their moment may be equal to the sum of the three moments as they are at present situated. Let $x$ be the distance of that point from B; then

$$x(W_1 + W_2 + W_3) = W_1.AB + W_2.CB + W_3.DB$$
$$x = \frac{W_1.AB + W_2.CB + W_3.DB}{W_1 + W_2 + W_3}$$

from which $x$ may be readily found by substituting the values of $W_1, W_2, W_3$, and $AB$, $CD$, and $DB$. If $P$ be the position of the point so found, then $P$ is the centre of gravity of the weights; being the point where all the weights collected have the same statical effect as when they were situated as shown in the figure.

In the figure, $AB$, $CB$, and $DB$ are the leverages of the several weights; $B$ is the point about which, it is said, *moments are taken*, and $x(W_1 + W_2 + W_3)$ is the *resultant moment*. Moments may be taken about any other point as well as $B$. For instance, suppose we happen to fix upon $P$ as the point about which moments are taken, then in that case $x =$ zero; also

$$W_1.AP = W_2.CP + W_3.DP.$$

When the point, about which moments are taken, is situated between any of the points of application of the weights, then the distances measured on one side of that point are considered positive, and on the other side negative. If the sum of the moments on one side of the point is equal to that of those on the other, then the weights are in equilibrium about that point, and it is therefore their common centre of gravity, as in the above case, when the moments are taken about $P$. But if the sum of one set of moments is in excess of the other, then the centre of gravity is on that side upon which the greater moments are. For instance, in fig. 6, Plate IV., in which the weights $W_1$, $W_2$, $W_3$, $W_4$, act at the points $A$, $B$, $C$, and $D$, respectively, on the straight line $AD$; then, taking moments about any point $P$,

$$(W_1.AP + W_2.BP) - (W_3.CP + W_4.DP)$$

is the resultant moment. Let $G$ be the centre of gravity of the weights; then

$$PG(W_1 + W_2 + W_3 + W_4) = (W_1.AP + W_2.BP) - (W_3.CP + W_4.DP)$$

$$PG = \frac{(W_1.AP + W_2.BP) - (W_3.CP + W_4.DP)}{W_1 + W_2 + W_3 + W_4}$$

If $W_1.AP + W_2.BP$ is greater than $W_3.CP + W_4.DP$, the point $G$ will be between $P$ and $A$; but if less, then the point $G$ will be between $P$ and $D$. In the figure, we have assumed the latter case.

The value of $PG$ is usually expressed as the *Algebraical sum of the moments* about $P$, divided by the sum of the weights; the *Algebraical sum* being the collective value of the moments when affected by their proper signs, *i.e.*, *plus* or *minus*.

**25. Centre of Gravity of Plane Figure bounded by a Curve.**—To apply the preceding results in obtaining the centre of gravity of a plane figure, such as is commonly met with in Naval Architecture, and to which we have been applying Simpson's Rules for finding its area, we proceed as follows:—

First observe that the figures are in almost every case

symmetrical about a middle line, so that knowing the centre of gravity is somewhere in that line, we have to determine where it is.

Let $ACBD$ in fig. 1, Plate V., be a plane figure, symmetrical about a middle line $AB$, then we know the centre of gravity of the area is in $AB$, also that the centre of gravity of the half area $ACB$, is in the ordinate passing through that point. In accordance with our previous definition, the area is assumed to be uniformly weighted, such as a sheet of metal of uniform thickness. Divide the straight line $AB$ into an even number of equal parts, and draw the ordinates $aa_1$, $bb_1$, $cc_1$, etc., through the points of division. There is thus (including the end ones), an odd number of ordinates, the value of the end ordinates being in this case zero. Assume each of the ordinates to be a narrow strip, so that they each have a weight, the latter being therefore in proportion to the length of the ordinate. Now, if we merely wished to find the centre of gravity of these strips, it would be the same as finding the centre of gravity of nine weights, acting at the points $A$, $a$, $b$, $c$, $d$, etc., the values of the weights being zero, $aa_1$, $bb_1$, $cc_1$, $dd_1$, etc., respectively. It is evident that if the ordinates be very close together, the sum of their moments, about any point on $AB$, would approximate very closely to the total moment of the area $ACB$ about the same point; and by increasing the divisions of the line $AB$, thereby increasing the number of ordinates and reducing the breadths of the strips they represent, we may make the approximation as close as we please. It is here that Simpson's Rules come to our aid, as by assuming the curve $ACB$ to be parabolic, the Rules give us the sum of the areas of all the *very* narrow strips represented by the ordinates when the latter are *very* close together. Hence, if we multiply every ordinate by its distance from the point about which the moments are taken, and consider the results so obtained as the ordinates of a new curve, then the area enclosed by that curve, and the straight line $AB$, will represent the moment of the area $ACB$ about the point.

It will be observed that as the ordinates are equidistant, the distance of every ordinate from any of the points A, $a$, $b$, etc., is a multiple of the common interval; hence, to simplify the work, the multiple only is used in applying the Rule, the result being afterwards multiplied by the common interval.

Let the lengths of the ordinates in feet be those given in the figure, the common interval being 4 ft. Taking moments about $B$, the following is the mode of obtaining the centre of gravity of the area:—

| Number of Ordinate. | Simpson's Multiplier. | Length of Ordinate. | Function of Ordinate. | Multiplier for Leverage. | Function of Moment. |
|---|---|---|---|---|---|
| 1 | 1 | 0 | 0 | 0 | 0 |
| 2 | 4 | 2·5 | 10·0 | 1 | 10·0 |
| 3 | 2 | 4·3 | 8·6 | 2 | 17·2 |
| 4 | 4 | 5·1 | 20·4 | 3 | 61·2 |
| 5 | 2 | 5·5 | 11·0 | 4 | 44·0 |
| 6 | 4 | 5·4 | 21·6 | 5 | 108·0 |
| 7 | 2 | 4·8 | 9·6 | 6 | 57·6 |
| 8 | 4 | 4·0 | 16·0 | 7 | 112·0 |
| 9 | 1 | 0 | 0 | 8 | 0 |

$$97\cdot2 \qquad 410\cdot0$$
$$4 \qquad\qquad 4$$
$$3)388\cdot8 \qquad 3)1640\cdot0$$
$$\text{sq. ft.} \quad 129\cdot6 = \text{Area} \qquad 546\cdot66$$
$$4$$
$$2186\cdot64$$
$$129\cdot6)2186\cdot64 \qquad = \text{moment}$$
$$16\cdot87 \text{ ft.}$$

Hence the centre of gravity of the area is 16·87 ft. from $B$, or ·87 from $d$, on the side of the latter nearest $A$.

It will be seen that the multipliers for leverage, 0, 1, 2, 3, etc., represent the number of times the common interval of 4 ft. that the ordinates $B$, $gg_1$, $ff_1$, $ee_1$, etc., are respectively from $B$, the point about which moments are taken. If the actual leverages were inserted in the fifth column instead of 0, 1, 2, 3, 4, etc., the figures would be 0, 8, 12, 16, etc., and the figures in the fifth column would be 0, 40, 68·8, 244·8, 176, etc.; instead of using these large numbers we afterwards multiply by 4, and so obtain the total moment 2186·64. It may be further remarked that 546·66 represents the area of a plane surface, whose ordinates are multiples of the moments of the ordinates 0, 2·5, 4·3, etc., about the point $B$, that is, whose ordinates are 0, 2·5, 8·6, 15·3, etc.

It is usual to avoid multiplying the sums of columns Nos. 4 and 6 by ⅓ the common interval, as it is a needless process, one product having afterwards to be divided by the other. In the above case the work would be:—

$$
\begin{array}{r}
410{\cdot}0 \\
4 \\
\hline
97{\cdot}2)\overline{1640{\cdot}0} \\
\hline
16{\cdot}87 \text{ ft.}
\end{array}
$$

Again, in practice, it is customary to still further reduce the figures employed in the calculation by taking moments about an ordinate near the middle of the length of $AB$. As, for instance, taking moments about $dd_1$, or No. 5 ordinate.

| Number of Ordinate. | Simpson's Multiplier. | Length of Ordinate. | Function of Ordinate. | Multiplier for Leverage. | Function of Moments. |
|---|---|---|---|---|---|
| 1 | 1 | 0   | 0    | 4 | 0    |
| 2 | 4 | 2·5 | 10·0 | 3 | 30·0 |
| 3 | 2 | 4·3 | 8·6  | 2 | 17·2 |
| 4 | 4 | 5·1 | 20·4 | 1 | 20·4 |
| 5 | 2 | 5·5 | 11·0 | 0 | 67·6 |
| 6 | 4 | 5·4 | 21·6 | 1 | 21·6 |
| 7 | 2 | 4·8 | 9·6  | 2 | 19·2 |
| 8 | 4 | 4·0 | 16·0 | 3 | 48·0 |
| 9 | 1 | 0   | 0    | 4 | 0    |
|   |   |     | 97·2 |   | 88·8 |

$$
\begin{array}{r}
88{\cdot}8 \\
67{\cdot}6 \\
\hline
21{\cdot}2 \\
4 \\
\hline
97{\cdot}2)\overline{84{\cdot}8} \\
\hline
{\cdot}87 \text{ ft.}
\end{array}
$$

Here we have two sets of moments, one positive and the other negative; their difference, or Algebraical sum, is 21·2, which, multiplied by 4 and divided by 97·2, gives ·87 ft., the distance of the centre of gravity of the area from ordinate No. 5 or $dd_1$, and on the side of it nearest to $A$; which is the same result as was obtained before. In this case, the largest multiplier for leverage being 4, the figures in the sixth column are not so large as when the multipliers continually increased to 8. The saving of labour is more apparent in such large areas as are met with in actual practice.

In the preceding examples, Simpson's First Rule has been applied; the same method is adopted with the Second Rule, the number of the ordinates being, of course, different.

In the case of intermediate ordinates being used, the multipliers are, of course, fractional; as for instance, 0, $\frac{1}{2}$, 1, $1\frac{1}{2}$, 2, 3, 4, etc., where two sets of half intervals occur next to the ordinate about which moments are taken. Examples of this kind will be given hereafter.

**26. Volumes of Solids.**—The rules for finding the volumes of regular solids are to be found in any work on Mensuration, so that we shall simply state a few of those most usually required, before proceeding to examine the method of finding the volume of such a solid figure as that of the immersed body of a ship.

**27. Volume of a Sphere.**—Multiply the cube of the diameter by $\cdot 5236 = \frac{\pi}{6}$; or the cube of the radius by $4 \cdot 1888 = \frac{4\pi}{3}$

**28. Volume of Ellipsoid.**—Multiply the product of the three axes by $\cdot 5236$, or the product of the three semi-axes by $4 \cdot 1888$.

**29. Volume of Pyramid or Cone.**—Multiply the area of the base by one-third of the height—the height being measured perpendicular to the base.

**30. Volume of a Solid Figure bounded by a Plane and a Curved Surface.**—Such a figure is to be found in the case of the immersed body of a ship, the bounding plane being that of the water surface.

The body has first to be divided into a number of segments by equidistant parallel planes, which are perpendicular to the bounding plane. *The area of each plane section is found by either of Simpson's Rules, and the results are treated as the ordinates of a new curve, the common interval being the perpendicular distance between the planes; the area of this curve is the volume of the figure.* It is evident that the ordinates of the new curve being in square measure, the area of the curve will therefore be in cubic measure.

In calculating the volume of the immersed body of a ship by this method, the figure being symmetrical about the longitudinal vertical middle line plane of the ship, only one-half of the body is calculated. It is unimportant whether the dividing planes are drawn parallel to the water plane or perpendicular to both the water and middle line planes. In the former case, the bounding curves of the areas are "water lines," and in the latter "square stations" (see *Shipbuilding and Laying Off*, p. 17).* It is usual to calculate the volume by using both sets of dividing planes, in order that one result may check the other, and so prevent inaccuracy. The vertical dividing planes in a large ship are generally spaced from about five to seven times the distance apart that is considered requisite for the horizontal dividing planes.

**31. Example of Calculation of Volume of a Ship's Displacement.**—As a first example of the method of calculating the volume of a ship's displacement, we will assume that the areas of the sections at the dividing planes are already found; those of the endmost sections are evidently zero.

In (fig. 2, Plate V.) showing the immersed body of a small vessel, $ADBC$ is the water plane, and $AB$ its middle line. This latter is divided into 8 equal lengths, each equal to 4 ft., and sections of the body are made by planes passing through these divisions, perpendicular to $AB$ and the plane $ADBC$. The half areas of these planes in square feet are marked upon the figure; those at the extremities $A$ and $B$ being zero.

| Number of Section. | Half Area of Section. | Simpson's Multipliers. | Function of Half Area. |
|---|---|---|---|
| 1 | 0  | 1 | 0   |
| 2 | 15 | 4 | 60  |
| 3 | 25 | 2 | 50  |
| 4 | 30 | 4 | 120 |
| 5 | 32 | 2 | 64  |
| 6 | 28 | 4 | 112 |
| 7 | 23 | 2 | 46  |
| 8 | 13 | 4 | 52  |
| 9 | 0  | 1 | 0   |

$$\begin{array}{r} 504 \\ 4 \\ \hline 3)\overline{2016} \\ \hline 672 \\ 2 \\ \hline 1344 \end{array}$$

$672$ = Half Volume

$1344$ = Total Volume in cubic feet.

---

* Wm. Collins, Sons & Co.'s *Advanced Science Series*; also *Elementary Laying Off*, p. 18.

When the vessel floats to this water plane, she therefore displaces 1344 cubic feet of water (see Art. 4), and as 35 of these weigh 1 ton, hence $\frac{1344}{35} = 38\cdot 4$ tons is the weight of the vessel and its contents at that time. The same result would be obtained by cutting the body into segments by equidistant planes, parallel to the water plane, and using their areas and common interval in the rule instead of those of the vertical sections.

It will be observed that Simpson's First Rule is that which we employed in the example just given, as it is the one commonly used in practice; the other may, however, be adopted, by dividing the figure into the requisite number of divisions.

The volume of displacement is generally obtained direct in one calculation; the data given being the lengths of equidistant ordinates of the several sectional areas, their common interval, and the common interval between the sectional areas.

**32. Centres of Gravity of Solids.**—In speaking of the centre of gravity of a solid, we suppose the latter to be a homogeneous body, *i.e.*, of uniform density; then its centre of gravity is that point at which, if the body were suspended, it would balance or be in equilibrium. In other words, it is that point where, if all the matter composing the body be concentrated, it has the same statical effect as when the body is in its ordinary condition. In the next division of this work, we shall refer also to the centre of gravity of a body composed of a number of other bodies, each of a certain weight (as, for instance, the hull of a ship), in which case the centre of gravity is that point where, if all the bodies could be collected, they would have the same statical effect as when distributed in their respective positions.

**33. Centres of Gravity of Special Solids.**—The centre of gravity of a sphere is evidently at its centre; for, as all planes passing through that point cut the sphere into two equal parts, the centre of gravity of the sphere must be in each of such planes, and therefore at their common intersection, viz., the centre of the sphere.

The centres of gravity of all regular solids, bounded by planes, such as the *tetrahedron, hexahedron, octahedron*, etc., are evidently at the centres of their circumscribing spheres.

The centres of gravity of all cylinders are at half their heights, measured from the centre of gravity of the base of the cylinder.

The centre of gravity of a pyramid or cone is at one-fourth its height, measured from the centre of gravity of its base. That of a hemisphere is at a distance from the centre of its base equal to three-eighths the radius of the sphere.

**34. Centre of Gravity of a Symmetrical Solid, bounded by a Curved Surface and a Plane.**—We will now show how to obtain the position of the centre of gravity of such a homogeneous body as that represented by the volume of a ship's displacement. The figure is first divided by two sets of equidistant parallel planes, each set perpendicular to the other, such as we have just employed in determining its volume. In that case it was stated that the two sets of planes might be used, in order that the result obtained by using one set could act as a check upon the result obtained by using the other; but, in the present calculation, it is necessary to use the two sets, in order that the position of the centre of gravity may be fixed, by having its distances from two planes at right angles to each other; knowing, at the same time, it is in the longitudinal vertical middle line plane of the body or ship.

Referring to fig. 2, Plate V., consider the body (or immersed portion of the ship) to be divided by a series of equidistant parallel planes as there shown, whose areas are as marked in the several sections. Then, by the same reasoning as was employed at Art. 25, it will be seen that the centre of gravity of the whole volume coincides with that of all the infinitely thin slices into which it can be cut by an infinite number of such planes as are shown. So that by taking the planes sufficiently numerous, and therefore close together, we may, by obtaining the position of the centre of gravity of these planes, approach as closely to the true centre of gravity of the whole volume as we please. Simpson's Rules again come to our aid, as by their use we, in fact, interpolate the values of the moments of those thin slices which can be cut between the sections drawn in the figure, in the same way as when calculating the volume we, in reality by the rule, interpolated the volumes of these thin slices.

Hence, to obtain the longitudinal position of the centre of gravity (*i.e.*, the position on the line $AB$ at which a section would pass through the centre of gravity), we multiply the areas of the sections by their perpendicular distances from the parallel plane, about which moments are taken (termed the *axis*), and then, having affected these by Simpson's multipliers, we obtain the total moment of the volume about that axis. If the moment so found be divided by the volume, the result gives the perpendicular distance of the centre of gravity of the volume from the plane about which moments were taken. As in the case of finding the centre of gravity of a plane area, it is not necessary to multiply the areas by their perpendicular distances from the axis, but by the common multiple of that distance, which is the numerical number of the plane area, reckoning from the axis. The result is afterwards multiplied by the common interval between the planes, and this gives the actual distance of the centre of gravity.

35. **Example of Method of Calculating Position of Centre of Gravity in one Direction.**—Using the areas given on fig. 2, Plate V., and taking moments about No. 5 section.

| Numbers of Sections. | Areas of Sections. | Simpson's Multipliers. | Functions of Areas. | Multipliers for Leverage. | Functions of Moments. |
|---|---|---|---|---|---|
| 1 | 0 | 1 | 0 | 4 | 0 |
| 2 | 15 | 4 | 60 | 3 | 180 |
| 3 | 25 | 2 | 50 | 2 | 100 |
| 4 | 30 | 4 | 120 | 1 | 120 |
| 5 | 32 | 2 | 64 | 0 | 400 |
| 6 | 28 | 4 | 112 | 1 | 112 |
| 7 | 23 | 2 | 46 | 2 | 92 |
| 8 | 13 | 4 | 52 | 3 | 156 |
| 9 | 0 | 1 | 0 | 4 | 0 |
| | | | 504 | | 360 |

$$\begin{array}{r} 360 \\ 400 \\ \hline 40 \\ 4 \text{ Common Interval} \\ \hline 504)\overline{160} \\ \cdot 3 \text{ feet.} \end{array}$$

The figures in the above table will be readily understood by the student, if attention has been given to the preceding pages. The result shows that the centre of gravity of the volume is in a plane parallel to the planes of section in the figure, and at a distance of ·3 feet from section 5, on the side of it nearest $A$, or, in other words, the plane will cut the line $AB$ at a point distant 15·7 feet from $A$.

**36. To Fully Determine the Position of the Centre of Gravity,** we must discover at what perpendicular distance from the line $AB$ the point is in that plane. To do this we divide the figure by a series of equidistant planes parallel to the water plane, the number of dividing planes being in accordance with the rule. Then, finding the areas of these planes, and taking moments about the water plane $ADB$, we find at what distance from the line $AB$ the horizontal plane is that contains the centre of gravity, the calculation being performed in a similar manner to that first shown.* By this means the position of the centre of gravity is fixed, as we know that it is in the longitudinal vertical middle line plane of the ship.

The two processes we have just described are performed simultaneously in actual practice, one tabular form serving for the calculation of the areas of all the vertical and longitudinal sectional areas, the volume of the figure and the two distances (longitudinal and vertical) necessary to fix the position of the centre of gravity. Other properties, which will be referred to hereafter, are also calculated on the same sheet of paper, commonly termed the "Displacement Sheet," a specimen of which is given at Table No. 1 in the accompanying volume.

It is well, perhaps, to observe that in the case of the volume of the immersed portion of a ship (which, as we have previously stated, is termed the *displacement*), its centre of gravity is termed "the centre of gravity of displacement," or "centre of buoyancy," the reason for the latter name will be given in the next chapter.

**37. Curves of Areas of Midship Section.**—It is often

---

* The Algebraical expression for the moment in this case is $\int\int z^2 dx dy$, while $\int\int x^2 dy dz$ represents that in Art. 34.

necessary to know the area of the immersed midship section at any mean draught of water. It is at once seen that it would be quite impracticable to do this by expressing in figures the several areas to water lines very close together, as the results would be very numerous; and, besides, if the area to any line, between two consecutive water lines at which areas are known, were required, it would have to be interpolated by the draughtsmen, and might be incorrect. It is therefore usual to draw upon the back of the "displacement sheet" what is termed "*a curve of areas of midship section*," and this is done in the following manner.

The areas of the midship section to the several horizontal ordinates or water lines are calculated by one or other of Simpson's Rules, or the rule given at Art. 14; the particular rule employed being such as is required by the number of ordinates in each case. A base line is then drawn to scale to represent the total draught of water that may reasonably occur. The scale may be any, suited to the dimensions of the "displacement sheet;" that of the *sheer draught* being usually adopted. Points are taken in this line to represent the positions of the water lines, and ordinates are drawn from the points. Distances are then measured to scale upon these ordinates equal to the areas of the midship section up to the respective water lines; the scale being so many square feet, say 50 or 100 to a quarter or half inch. The curve drawn through these points is termed the "*curve of areas of midship section.*" It is at once seen by reference to the specimen curve shown by fig. 1, Plate VI., that the area of midship section to any draught of water can be readily determined by the simple use of a scale.

In consequence of these areas being calculated from the midship section of a ship at a certain "*trim*," *i.e.*, draught of water at bow and stern, it is not strictly accurate when we use the mean draught at any other trim; and in cases where the ship is considerably deeper at the bow or stern than when the calculation was made, a correction has to be made in accordance with the circumstances of the case.

38. **Curve of Sectional Areas.**—The late Mr. Peake introduced the use of curves for calculating the displacement from the areas of the vertical sections, or square stations, by

drawing to scale a base representing the length of the ship, drawing ordinates therefrom at the points corresponding to the positions of the square stations, and measuring to scale upon these ordinates the areas of the respective sections. The curve drawn through these points was termed the "*curve of sectional areas*," and the area of it represented to scale the volume of the displacement. (See fig. 2, Plate VI.)

**39. Tons per Inch of Immersion.**—When a ship is floating at a certain draught of water, the load required to sink her to a deeper draught is, of course, the weight of the additional water displaced. If the increase of draught be small, especially in the neighbourhood of the load water line, the additional volume of displacement is equal to the area of the load water plane multiplied by the increase of draught. It is therefore customary to state upon the "displacement sheet" the number of tons required to sink the ship to a parallel depth of one inch when floating at any draught of water parallel to a certain line. This is called the "*tons per inch of immersion;*" and it is sometimes expressed graphically as a "*curve of tons per inch of immersion.*"

Let $A$ be the area in square feet of a certain water plane, then $\dfrac{A}{12 \times 35}$ = the number of tons to sink the ship 1 inch when floating at that water plane.

Either the figures obtained from the values of $A$ at certain equidistant parallel draughts are stated in a table, or else a curve is drawn in the following manner (see fig. 1, Plate VII.)—Draw a base line representing to scale the total mean draught; draw ordinates through the points on this line representing the positions for which the values of $A$ have been obtained (usuallly the water lines); and set off to scale the values of $A$ on the respective ordinates, the curve drawn through the points so obtained is termed the "curve of tons per inch of immersion."

**40. Curve of Displacement.**—The displacement paper shows the total displacement to the load water line; it is, however, customary to supplement this information with calculations, made upon the same sheet, of the displacement of the ship when floating to each of the water lines which are employed in calculating the total displacement. By referring to the specimen Displacement Sheet, given in Table No. 1, these calculations will be seen. In determining the several volumes of displacement, the various rules already given are required. For instance, the displacement as high as No. 2 water line (the next below the load water line) is usually obtained by deducting the volume included between these two water lines from the total volume of displacement, the former being calculated by means of the five-eight rule, stated at Art. 14.

The displacement as high as the next water line (No. 3) is found by treating the areas of the load and two succeeding water planes by Simpson's First, or one-third, rule, and the result deducted from the total volume gives the displacement in cubic feet to No. 3 water line. For the volume as high as the next water line (No. 4), the three-eight rule is required, for the next the one-third, and so on.

It is usual to give these several calculations on the Displacement Sheet, and then tabulate them as shown.

As is evident, such calculations merely furnish the displacement of the ship when floating at the several water lines used in the calculation. It is, however, very necessary that we should know the displacement at every intermediate parallel draught of water, and for this purpose it is customary to construct from the preceding data a curve termed the "*Curve of Displacement.*" A base line is drawn representing to any convenient scale the whole draught of water, and ordinates representing the water lines are set up at their proper positions. Distances are measured upon the ordinates representing to scale the displacement in tons to the several water lines, and a curve is drawn through the points so obtained.

It will be seen that besides its primary purpose this curve serves as a check upon the accuracy of the several calculations of displacement to the water lines, as in ordinary cases the curve should be fair or continuous.

When this curve is drawn, we are enabled to determine, by measurement, the displacement at any draught of water from the keel to the load line, and by following the curve of the batten we are also able to tell, very nearly, the displacement, to some distance above the load line. (See fig. 2, Plate VII.)

This curve of displacement being calculated and drawn to parallel draughts of water, it is not strictly accurate for an alteration of trim; but, by experience, it is found sufficiently trustworthy for all the ordinary variations which occur in the trim of an equipped ship, especially near the load water line. The minimum alteration of trim which will necessitate a separate calculation being made by means of a new set of water lines, varies with the form of the vessel; it being clear that when the fore and after bodies are made unlike in form, the necessity becomes more imperative than when there is a similarity between these bodies. In the case, too, of an overhanging stern becoming immersed by the change of trim, the calculation from parallel draughts would be misleading. These points must be left to the discretion of the calculator.

It will be remarked that the curve of displacement is the geometrical integration of the curve of sectional areas referred to in Art. 38. Farther on, at Art. 42, will be found a method of obtaining these curves by a geometrical process, recommended by Mr. Scott Russell.

Plate VIII. shows the general manner of arranging the curves already referred to on the back of the ordinary displacement sheet, so as to keep all the particulars of this kind together.

**41. General Explanation of Displacement Sheet.**—Before proceeding further, we will explain the details of an ordinary "displacement sheet," a specimen of which is given on Table I. It is necessary, however, to state that this sheet usually includes other calculations, such as that of the transverse and longitudinal metacentres, etc., as will be seen by referring to the Table; these will be considered in their proper places.

The specimen calculation shown is that of a vessel whose displacement is 620 tons. The draught of water in this case is 10 ft. forward and 12 ft. aft, and the lowest water line is drawn at 8 ft. below the L.W.L., thus leaving a portion of the body (termed an "appendage") to be calculated separately. This "appendage" is, therefore, 2 ft. deep forward, and 4 ft. deep aft. In order to calculate the volume of the main portion of the body, *i.e.*, between the load and fifth water lines by Simpson's First Rule, the depth of 8 feet is divided into four equal parts, thus giving five water planes. Again, since the after perpendicular is situated at the after side of the rudder post, and this being a single screw ship, the length of the immersed body, measured from the fore ordinate (or ·5 feet abaft the fore perpendicular) to the after ordinate (which is at the after side of the body post) is 141 ft. This length is divided into ten equal divisions by eleven dividing planes (including the endmost). Hence the number of ordinates of both the vertical and horizonal sections is odd, being five in the former and eleven in the latter case, the common intervals being 2 ft. and 14·1 ft. respectively.

We will suppose the body, half-breadth, and sheer plans to be drawn with the lines contained in these sections; we have next to measure off the lengths of the ordinates and insert them in a tabular form, as shown by Table I. Referring to the example before us, it will be seen that the ordinates of the water lines are arranged successively in vertical columns, these ordinates being usually and preferably measured in the half-breadth plan. When the ordinates of the water lines are thus set down, the ordinates of the vertical sections will be found arranged successively in horizontal rows. It need hardly be mentioned, in explanation to the student of "Laying Off," that this is owing to the same ordinates appearing in both the body and half-breadth plans. For instance, 12 feet is the breadth of the fourth W.L., at No. 5 vertical section; and in the same way, 12 feet is the breadth of No. 5 vertical section at the fourth W.L.

In the specimen calculations, the lengths of the ordinates are shown in ordinary type, while the dark figures in the tabular form are the products obtained in the calculation.

At the head of the calculation are stated the principal dimensions of the ship, including the draught of water, also the spacing of the water lines and the vertical sections; the intersection of the latter with the former being the ordinates which are measured. We have, also, a record of the positions of the extreme ordinates with regard to the perpendiculars, and of the middle ordinate with regard to a square station on the drawings, *i.e.*, the joint or side of a frame. This record will enable a future calculator to reproduce the lines used in this case, or accurately apply the results obtained therefrom in any other kind of calculation made upon the ship.

As already stated, the foremost ordinate in this particular calculation is situated at ·5 feet abaft the fore perpendicular; this is done in order that, by neglecting the portion of the body on the fore side of that ordinate, a proper allowance may be made for having assumed the whole of the fore foot of the ship to extend forward to the same ordinate instead of being rounded away. The first ordinate of No. 5 water line is considered nil for the same reason. This is a point which is decided by the experience of the calculator. In any special case, as that of a ram-shaped bow, an actual calculation should be made of the volume before the ordinate, and also of that which is to be deducted, owing to the curvature given to the lower part of stem. The same remark applies to the other portions either not included in the main piece of displacement when they belong to the body, or included when they should not be, such as shaft tubes, propeller brackets, screw aperture, etc.

The first column on the left hand side of the specimen sheet contains the numerical names of the ordinates stated in succession; it being observed that in this case, in order to determine with reasonable accuracy the volumes at the highly curved parts of the bow and stern, a half ordinate is added at each extremity, viz., Nos. $1\frac{1}{2}$ and $10\frac{1}{2}$. (See Art. 12.)

The second column contains Simpson's Multipliers for the First Rule, the number of ordinates being odd. It will be seen that the half ordinates cause a modification in the multipliers such as has already been explained.

Passing over for the present the portion of the calculation referring to the "appendage," we find five columns, each headed with the number of the respective water line, followed by its proper Simpson's Multiplier. The ordinates, as measured from the half-breadth plan, are then placed in their proper order.

It has been already stated at Art. 36 that, in practice, the volume of displacement is calculated simultaneously from the areas of both the water planes and vertical sections, and that the results thus obtained serve to check each other. This will be seen in the specimen calculation. Considering the numbers now in the tabular form as consisting of *columns* only, each ordinate in a column is multiplied by the Simpson's

Multiplier for that column, and the product is written immediately below the ordinates, as shown in dark figures. This being done for all the *columns*, the products in the *rows* thus produced are added together, and the sums written in the same row and in the column headed "*Functions of Areas.*" Similarly, considering the numbers in the tabular form as consisting of *rows* only, each ordinate in a row is multiplied by Simpson's Multiplier for that row, and the product is written down on the right hand side of the ordinate, as shown in dark type. This being done for all the *rows*, the products in the *columns* thus produced are added together and the sums written in the same column, and in the row at the left of which is written "*Functions of Areas.*" We thus have two sets of functions of areas, the former being those for obtaining the areas of the vertical sections, and the latter for obtaining the areas of the water planes. In the former case, the area of the water plane is obtained by multiplying its function by $\frac{2}{3}$* × 2 ft.; and in the latter, the area of the vertical section is obtained by multiplying the function of the area by $\frac{2}{3}$* × 14·1 ft. The displacement, however, is found without any such intermediate calculation. The column and row of "*Multiples of Areas*" are the products of the functions in the adjacent columns and rows when multiplied by their respective Simpson's Multipliers, as the sums of these two sets of multipliers are such that we have to multiply each of them by $\frac{2}{3}$ × 2 ft. × $\frac{1}{3}$ × 14·1 ft., in order to obtain the volume of displacement in cubic feet; it is therefore evident that if the preceding work is done correctly, they will agree. In the example given, this is found to be the case; therefore the sum of each set of Multiples of Areas being 3178, as shown, the volume of the main portion of the displacement is thus equal to 19915·46 cubic feet, which, when divided by 35 (35 cubic feet of sea water weighing 1 ton), gives 569·013 tons, which is the weight of a quantity of sea water equal in volume to the portion of the ship inclosed between the foremost and aftermost vertical sections from the load to the fifth water lines.

Before showing how the volume and weight of the remainder

---

* The 2 here is for both sides of the ship, the ordinates being merely those of half the immersed body.

of the displacement is obtained, we will proceed with the calculation for the position of the centre of gravity of the portion of the displacement already found. This point is generally styled the "centre of buoyancy" (or C.B.) of the main portion of the displacement.

In the specimen calculation, the position of this centre of buoyancy is determined with regard to the middle ordinate (No. 6), and moments are taken about that vertical section. In the column headed "multipliers for leverage," it will be seen that opposite each ordinate is written the numerical order of its position with regard to No. 6, or, in other words, the number of times 14·1 feet that the ordinate is distant from the section about which moments are taken. Thus, the multipliers opposite ordinates Nos. $1\frac{1}{2}$ and $10\frac{1}{2}$ are in both cases $4\frac{1}{2}$; each of these vertical sections being $4\frac{1}{2} \times 14\cdot1$ ft. = 63·45 ft. from No. 6.

The reason for using the multipliers in preference to the actual distances, and the manner in which the actual distances are afterwards included in the work, have been explained in Art. 25. The column headed "Moments" contains the products of the "Multiples of Areas" and their respective "Multipliers for Leverage." The moments before and those abaft No. 6 ordinate are totalled separately, and the difference between the totals, viz., 82·5 is a function of the preponderance of the forward over the after moments. The actual resultant forward moment is

$$82\cdot5 \times \frac{14\cdot1}{3} \times \frac{2}{3} \times 14\cdot1 \times 2 = 7289\cdot7 \text{ cubic feet}$$

acting at a leverage of 1 foot, or $\frac{7289\cdot7}{35} = 208\cdot2$ foot tons.

In the above expression, $\frac{14\cdot1}{3} \times \frac{2}{3}$ is the product of one-third of each of the common intervals, as required by Simpson's Rule for a volume; 14·1 is the factor (previously neglected) of the "multipliers for leverage," and 2 is for both sides of the ship. There is, however, no advantage, but rather the contrary, in calculating the exact moment, for since the total 3178 of the "multiples of areas" is in the same terms as $82\cdot5 \times 14\cdot1$; the former being the same function of the volume that the latter is of the resultant moment; therefore $\frac{82\cdot5 \times 14\cdot1}{3178} = \cdot366$ feet, is the horizontal distance of the centre of buoyancy of the 569 tons of displacement before No. 6 ordinate. This is proved by mutiplying 569 tons by ·366 feet, which gives 208·2 foot tons—the same result as before.

Similarly, the vertical position of the same centre of buoyancy with regard to the load water line is found as shown at the foot of the tabular form. The sum of the functions of moments (or "moments" as they are generally styled) is, in this case, 5606·3; hence $\frac{5606\cdot3 \times 2}{3178} = 3\cdot528$ feet, the distance of the C.B. of 569 tons of displacement below the load water line.

There now remains to be calculated the volumes of displacement and positions of the centres of buoyancy of the portions of the immersed body not included in the calculation already made. The principal of these is the volume below the fifth water line, not including the keel. On the left hand side of the sheet this calculation will be seen. In the column headed "half areas," are stated the half areas of the portions of the vertical sections, at the several ordinates, between the fifth water line and upper side of keel. These are calculated by the simple rules of Mensuration, the figures being usually trapezoidal or approximately so. After the preceding description of the calculation for the main portion, the figures in the other columns do not require explanation. It must, however, be remarked that as the figures refer to areas and not linear dimensions as in the previous case, the total 159·55 has merely to be multiplied by $\frac{14\cdot1}{3}$, and afterwards by 2, in order to obtain the volume for both sides of the ship in cubic feet. In regard to the moments, the figures 322·185 and 159·55 are in the same terms, and, therefore, $\frac{322\cdot185}{159\cdot55} = 2\cdot019$ feet is the horizontal position of the centre of buoyancy of the appendage from No. 6 ordinate; it being in this case on the aft side.

Immediately below the calculation just alluded to will be found those for the volume and weight of the displacement of the few minor portions of the immersed body not yet estimated. These, in this case, consist of the rudder and rudder post, bilge keels, wood keel, a continuation of the keel under the aperture, and the body post. These are calculated by the elementary principles of Mensuration, and the weights in tons are found by dividing the volumes by 35. Their centres of buoyancy, including the vertical position of that of the principal appendage, can easily be obtained by simple measurement.

We have now to collect the results already found, and from them determine the total displacement; also the longitudinal and vertical positions of its centre of buoyancy. Immediately beneath the calculation regarding the main portion of the displacement, the total result is given. The total displacement being merely the sum of the several components, it is found to be 620·158 tons of sea water, or 21705·53 cubic ft. The positions of the centres of buoyancy with regard to No. 6 ordinate are stated in the column headed "leverage," and the moments of the components are given in the next two columns —one being for the forward, and the other for the after moments. The resultant after moment is found to be 35·2 foot-tons, and this being divided by the total displacement, 620·158 tons, gives ·056 feet, the distance abaft No. 6 ordinate at which the centre of buoyancy of the total displacement is situated. The two remaining columns show the distances of the centres of buoyancy of the several components below the L.W.L., and their moment about that line respectively. All these moments being on the same side of the axis about which moments are taken, their sum (2449 foot tons) is the total moment of the displacement about the L.W.L. Hence, $\frac{2449}{620·158} = 3·95$ feet, the distance below the L.W.L. at which the C.B. of the total displacement is situated. Thus having the vertical and horizontal positions of the point, it is fully determined, and we are now able to use this knowledge in our future calculations.

An explanation of the curve of areas of midship section was given at Art. 37; at the lower left hand corner of the specimen calculation will be found the work required in determining the ordinates for constructing the curve in this case. The area of the whole midship section to the L.W.L. is found calculated on the extreme right of the calculation for the centre of buoyancy of the whole displacement; the value 158·45 there employed being obtained from the column headed "functions of areas," and in the row belonging to No. 6 ordinate, which is situated at the fullest part of the ship. This function of the midship sectional area is multiplied by one-third the common interval between the water lines, viz., 2 feet, which gives 105·63, to this is added the half sectional area of the "appendage" at ordinate 6 (see column of "half areas,") also those of the keel and bilge keels; the total, 117·78 sq. ft., when multiplied by 2 for both sides, giving 235·56 sq. ft., the total area of the midship section. In obtaining the areas as high as the several water lines below the load line, the areas of the portions included between the latter and the respective water lines are calculated, and the results are deducted from the whole area. The five-eighth rule is employed for the area as high as the second W.L., the one-third for the area to the next, and the three-eighth rule for that to the fourth W.L.; the areas of the keel and appendage added together being the area to the fifth W.L. The mode of constructing the curve with the ordinates thus found has already been explained in Art. 37, and the curve itself is shown by fig. 1, Plate VI.

A "curve of sectional areas" may be constructed by determining the areas of the vertical sections at the other ordinates, in the same manner as already done for that at No. 6—the midship section. See fig. 2, Plate VI.

At the middle of the right hand side of the Table is shown the mode of obtaining the "tons per inch of immersion" at the several water lines. The "functions of areas" of the several water lines, as found in the row at the foot of the tabular form, are multiplied by one-third of 14·1 (the common horizontal interval), which gives one-half the areas of the respective water planes in square feet, or, if considered as cubic feet, it represents a slice having a surface of that area, and one foot thick. Hence, upon dividing by 12 and 35, we obtain the weight of such a volume of sea water having that area, but only an inch thick; and multiplying by

2 we obtain the weight of both sides. The "tons per inch" at the several water lines in this case are shown on the sheet; the mode of constructing the "curve of tons per inch" was explained at Art. 39.

We have now to explain the portion of the specimen calculation referring to the "curve of displacement." As stated at Art. 40, the displacement when the ship is floating at each of the several water lines has first to be calculated, and ordinates are then drawn to a certain scale representing the several displacements. The displacement to the L.W.L., viz., 620·158 tons, has already been obtained. At the foot of the right hand side of the specimen sheet will be seen the calculations for the remaining water lines. As in the case of the areas of midship section, the displacements between the L.W.L. and the other water lines are first calculated; and the results deducted from the total displacement give the displacement below the several lines. The five-eighth rule is employed for the second water line, the one-third rule for the third, and the three-eighth rule for the fourth water line; while the displacement to the fifth water line consists of the sum of the displacements of the appendage, wood keel, rudder, posts, etc. If there were seven instead of five water lines, the one-third rule would be used for the displacement to the fifth, and the three-eighth rule for that to the sixth water line, while the displacement to the seventh W.L. would be found similarly to the fifth in the present example. When the several displacements are calculated, the curve of displacement is constructed in the manner explained at Art. 40. (See fig. 2, Plate VII., also Plate VIII.) The remainder of the calculations shown on the specimen sheet will be explained hereafter.

**42. Geometrical Method.**—We will now show how the displacement, centre of buoyancy, etc., are determined by a purely geometrical process, based upon the principles already discussed. The curves of the water lines and vertical sections are assumed to be parabolas of the second order, as in Simpson's First Rule. It will be remembered that at Art. 10, this parabola was defined as "a curve such that the area of any one of its segments is two-thirds of the product of the base, and deflection of that segment." Referring to fig. 2,

Plate I., the area of $ACHKE$ is made up of the trapezoid $ACKE$, together with the parabolic segment $CHK$.

Hence area $ACHKE = \dfrac{AC+KE}{2} \times AE + \tfrac{2}{3}HM \times AE$

$= AE(MF + \tfrac{2}{3}HM)$

Similarly, area $EKLDB = EB(GN + \tfrac{2}{3}LN) = AE(GN + \tfrac{2}{3}LN)$.

Hence, whole area $ACKDB = AE\left\{\left(MF + \dfrac{2}{3}HM\right) + \left(GN + \dfrac{2}{3}LN\right)\right\}$

If then a point O, fig. 1, Plate IX., be taken so that $OM = \tfrac{2}{3}HM$* and a point $P$, such that $PN = \tfrac{2}{3}LN$.

Then area $ACKDB = AE(FO + GP)$.

From this it is seen that $FO + GP$ is a multiple of the area $ACKDB$, so that a line $EQ = FO + PQ$ will represent the area to a certain scale. For instance, if $AE = 4$ ft., and $EQ$ is found to measure 9 ft., then we know that the area is $4 \times 9 = 36$ sq. ft., or that 9 ft. is the area of the curved space on the scale of 3 in. = 1 sq. ft.† This is the principle upon which the geometrical calculations we are about to consider are based. The distance $EQ$ is set off upon the middle ordinate, or that ordinate produced, for the sake of convenience in further calculations, as will be seen hereafter. In order to keep the geometrical construction within the limits of an ordinary sheet of paper, the scale of length of the new ordinates, such as $EQ$, is reduced; for instance, $ER$ may represent the area, where $ER = \tfrac{1}{2}EQ$; only in that case the scale would be $1\tfrac{1}{2}$ in. = 1 sq. ft., or upon the supposition contained in the foot note the scale would be $\tfrac{1}{32}$ in. = 1 sq. ft., in other words, 1 in. = 32 sq. ft.

The preceding illustration is for an elementary case of three ordinates; referring to Plate X., a more general example will be seen, in which certain other curves are constructed by a continuation of the principle.

* If the curve is convex, with regard to the base line, as in fig. 2, Plate IX., then the chord and the point O will be on the other side of the curve, and the length $OM$ must be deducted from $FM$, or in other words, $OH$ must be added to $FH$ instead of being deducted from it as in fig. 1.

† This is upon the supposition that the ordinates $AC$, $EK$, $BD$, and the abscissæ $AE$ and $EB$ are drawn to full size, if they are already upon a reduced scale, say $\tfrac{1}{4}$ in. to a ft., then the scale of $EQ$ will be $\tfrac{1}{16}$ in. = 1 sq. ft.

Fig. 2, on Plate X., is the half-breadth plan of a ship, and, for simplicity sake, it is constructed with five water lines, the lowest being at the keel; and five ordinates, the endmost being at the extremities of the bow and stern. In this way the whole of the immersed body is represented in the plan; the common distance between the water lines being given. It is perhaps unnecessary to state that to secure these conditions the ship is assumed to be floating at "an even keel," and that her extremities are perpendicular to the L.W.L.; by this assumption, we are not bothered with appendages of any kind. In actual practice, allowances can easily be made for these, and represented in the curves. Fig. 1 in the Plate shows only one of the water lines, viz., the L.W.L.; the mode of working with the others is exactly similar, but they are not repeated in this figure, in order to avoid confusion of lines.*

The first curve to be determined is that termed the "curve of areas of water lines," this being constructed from ordinates equal, to scale, to these areas. Beginning with the L.W.L., drawn in fig. 1; chords are drawn joining the upper extremities of adjacent ordinates (this process has already been explained; the chords are omitted in Plate X.), the abscissæ are bisected and intermediate ordinates drawn through the bisections to points situated at two-thirds the deflections of the arcs cut by the chords, measuring from the latter. The sum of the lengths of these intermediate ordinates is obtained by means of a strip of paper applied to each ordinate in succession, the measurements upon the strip being adjacent to each other. This length is set off upon No. 1 original ordinate produced, so that it now serves for L.W.L. as well. In the figure it is drawn to half size to suit the dimensions of the drawing; and it is such, that if measured with the scale to which the drawing is made, and then multiplied by 2, and by the common interval between the original ordinates, the result is the half area of the water plane. The functions of the areas of the other water planes are found by measure-

* It will be observed by reference to the figure that the same lines serve for the ordinates of the half-breadth plan and for water lines; this is done for convenience' sake, it being remembered that the common interval used for the ordinates is 40 ft., while that for the water lines is 3 ft.

ment with a strip of paper in a similar manner, and half the lengths so found are set off upon Nos. 2, 3, 4, and 5* original ordinates (produced if required), which now serve for Nos. 2, 3, 4, and 5 water lines. A line passed fairly through the points thus found is the *curve of areas of water planes.* To determine from it the half area of any other water plane than those used, an ordinate must be drawn through a point on the base line representing the position of the water plane with regard to the others, and the length of this ordinate to the curve must be multiplied by 2, and by the common interval between the vertical section ordinates. For instance, if these ordinates (Nos. 1, 2, etc.) are 40 ft. apart, and if the length of an original ordinate of the curve of areas at No. 2 W.L. (which is a draught of, say, 9 ft., the total draught being 12 ft. in this case) is, measured with the scale, 23 ft.; then:

$23 \times 2 \times 40 = 1840$ sq. ft. for one side only,
or 3680 sq. ft., the total area of No. 2 water plane.

A *curve of areas of vertical sections* can be obtained in a similar manner, by using the body instead of the half-breadth plan; observing that the nature of the curvature in the body plan is such as to render less accuracy probable.

We next proceed to construct a *curve of displacement* by means of the curve of areas of water planes just drawn. Retaining the original and intermediate ordinates already in the figure, but produced, if necessary; draw the chords of the curve of areas as before, and discover the points at two-thirds the deflections of the arcs from the chords. Next consider that the total displacement is the sum of the areas of all the water lines that can be conceived at an infinitely small distance apart, or, in other words, that the total displacement is the area of the space inclosed by the curve of areas of water lines, the base line, and No. 1 ordinate. Hence, with a strip of paper, measure the sum of the lengths of the intermediate ordinates to the points already determined, and this total length will be a function of the whole displacement. In fact, if we call the length so found $l$, the vertical interval

* The area at No. 5 is nothing, as the ship is assumed to have no projecting keel.

between water lines $= h$, and the horizontal interval between ordinates $= k$, then

$$l \times 2 \times h \times k = \tfrac{1}{2} \text{ displacement.}$$

Thus if

$l = 73$ ft. when measured with the scale,
$h = 3$ ft. and $k = 40$ ft.
$73 \times 2 \times 40 \times 3 = 17{,}520$ cubic ft.
or $35040$ cubic ft. $= 1001$ tons $=$ total displacement.

In the curve of displacement drawn, the distances set off upon the ordinates are half the results of the measurements; this being done in order to keep the figure within bounds. A similar reduction in scale is also found desirable in practice. This half length is then set off upon No. 1 ordinate (produced, if necessary), and, as shown, represents the total displacement to scale.

For the displacement as high as No. 2 water line, the area of the curve enclosed by No. 2 ordinate is similarly measured, and half the length is set off upon that ordinate, and so on with the others. The area to the fifth water line is, of course, nothing. A line drawn fairly through the points thus obtained, as shown, is the curve of displacement; being (if drawn upon the same scale) identical with the curve constructed from the results of the displacement sheet.

A curve of displacement can also be constructed from the curve of vertical areas, and the total displacement shown thereby will be the same as that given by the curve just drawn. The remainder of such a curve is, however, practically useless for the purpose of determining displacements, as the length of an ordinate gives the displacement included between an extremity of the vessel and a vertical section at that ordinate.

We have next to show how to obtain the position of the centre of buoyancy from these results. By the aid of the curves already determined, we are enabled to construct another curve from which we can determine the position, vertically, of the centre of buoyancy, when the ship is floating at any line, parallel to the load line, between the latter and the keel. This is done by constructing a curve, the ordinates of which represent to scale the leverage, about either the keel or the L.W.L., of each of the water planes used in the sheer draught.

## GEOMETRICAL METHOD OF DETERMINING DISPLACEMENT. 63

Supposing we take moments about the L.W.L., and construct such a curve (known as the "curve *for* vertical moment"), then the area of the space enclosed by the curve, the base, and any ordinate, is a known multiple of the moment of displacement to the corresponding water line about the L.W.L. Hence, dividing the moment by the volume of displacement, up to the line in question, the quotient is the distance of the centre of buoyancy of that displacement below the L.W.L.

To construct the "curve for vertical moments" (we will first take moments about the L.W.L.): multiply the first ordinate of the curve of areas of water lines by 0; the second by 1; third by 2, and so on; and pass a curve through the points so found: such a line will be the "curve for vertical moments." It is such that any ordinate of it is a known multiple of the moment of the area of a water plane at that ordinate, about the L.W.L. In this case, when we take moments about the L.W.L., the curve cuts the base line at the first and fifth ordinates, the latter being each $= 0$. As will be seen by the figure, when moments are taken about the keel, the curve cuts the base line at the keel, or fifth water line, only.

Next, to construct the "curve of vertical moments," draw the chords of the curve just obtained, joining the extremities of the ordinates; also, draw the intermediate or half ordinates as used in constructing curves of areas and displacement, and stop them at two-thirds the deflections of the arcs, measured from the chords. Then, by the aid of a strip of paper, obtain the sum of the lengths of these intermediate ordinates, and set off the total upon ordinate No. 5 produced; also the sums of the lengths of the half ordinates between Nos. 1 and 4 ordinate, and set off the result upon No. 4, and so on. In fig. 1, where the curves are shown, only half the lengths are set off in order to keep the figure within reasonable proportions. A curve passed through the points thus found is the "curve of vertical moments." We will now give an instance of the mode of using this curve, in obtaining the vertical position of the centre of buoyancy to any water line, say at 3 ft. below the L.W.L., or at No. 2 W.L. The length of this ordinate when measured with a scale is found to be, say, 70 feet.

$$\therefore 70 \times 2 \times 2 \times 40 \times 3 \times 3 \times 2 = 201{,}600 \text{ foot cubic feet,}$$

= moment of displacement to second W.L., about L.W.L. But displacement to second W.L. is 850 tons = 29,750 cubic feet; therefore

$$\frac{201,600}{29,750} = 6\cdot 8 \text{ feet,}$$

which is the depth below the L.W.L of the centre buoyancy of the displacement when the ship floats at No. 2 water line.

In the above expression the figure 2 is used twice in order to allow for the two reductions in scale which have been made in order to keep the diagram small; 40 is the horizontal common interval; 3 is the vertical common interval, which is used twice, viz., once for volume and once for leverage; and the last 2 is for both sides of the ship.

Sometimes, for the sake of convenience, separate curves are constructed for the fore and after bodies; in which case, the sums of the moments and displacements for the water line in question, as found from the two sets of curves, must be used. Plate XI. shows the curves of the fore and after bodies of a vessel constructed in this way. It will be observed that the curves are drawn upon a prepared sheet, ruled, so as to enable a calculator to work without a scale. Being divided into a number of large squares, the side of each of which is equal to 5 ft. on a $\frac{1}{4}$ inch scale,* and each of these squares being again subdivided into squares, each of whose sides is 1 foot, a very close degree of accuracy can be obtained in setting off distances and dividing or multiplying ordinates without the aid of either compasses or scale.

The curves shown on Plates X. and XI. are those obtained from water lines, and while they give all the information we need regarding the displacement, the only information which they contain regarding the position of the centre of buoyancy is its distance from the L.W. plane. In order to obtain its longitudinal position, it is necessary to construct the curve of areas of vertical sections as already explained, and from this determine, by an analagous process to that just gone through, the longitudinal position of the centre of buoyancy

* Plate X. is drawn upon $\frac{1}{10}$ of the usual scale, to get the diagram within the limits of the page. Usually there are 400 squares instead of 100, and the side of each square is $1\frac{1}{4}$ in. instead of $\frac{3}{8}$ in. as shown. This ruled sheet was devised by Mr. C. W. Merrifield, F.R.S.

with regard to any vertical section about which it may be thought convenient to take moments.

The geometrical method of obtaining the displacement and centre of buoyancy, while furnishing in a compact form a quantity of information, readily extracted if required, yet occupies longer time in construction than is taken about an ordinary displacement sheet for the same ship, and although more labour is required in extracting from the latter particulars regarding various draughts of water than in the case of the geometrical method, yet for general use in the drawing office the displacement sheet is the preferable of the two, as it contains all that is usually required, and in such a form that it can be used at once. Nevertheless, the geometrical sheet, such as is partly shown by Plate XI., is a valuable adjunct which might with great advantage be more generally used than it is at present.

**43. Dr. Woolley's Rule.**—A Rule has been devised by Dr. Woolley, late Director of Education to the Admiralty, for the purpose of obtaining the displacement direct from the ordinates without going through the intermediate process of determining the functions of the areas of the water planes or vertical sections.

Fig. 1, Plate XII., shows a solid bounded by a curved surface, and five planes which intersect at right angles. The immersed body of a ship is made up of a number of such solids. This elementary solid is divided into four parts by two planes at right angles to each other, and dividing the rectangular base into four equal parts. The intersections of these planes with the sides, base and curved surface give nine vertical ordinates, marked $a_1$, $a_2$, $a_3$, $b_1$, $b_2$, etc., in the figure. Let $p$ and $q$ be the sides of one of the rectangles of the base; or if the base be a portion of the vertical middle line plane of a ship, then $p$ and $q$ will be the vertical and horizontal common intervals. The volume of this solid is found thus:—

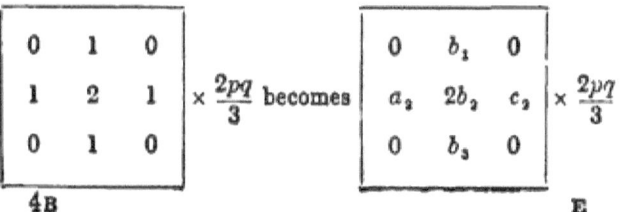

The nine numbers enclosed in the square on the left are the multipliers by the Rule, arranged in order; these are multiplied by the ordinates in order, as shown by fig. 1, Plate XII.

Thus,
$$\begin{array}{lll} a_1 \times 0 = 0 & b_1 \times 1 = b_1 & c_1 \times 0 = 0 \\ a_2 \times 1 = a_2 & b_2 \times 2 = 2b_2 & c_2 \times 1 = c_2 \\ a_3 \times 0 = 0 & b_3 \times 1 = b_3 & c_3 \times 0 = 0. \end{array}$$

The sum of the products multiplied by $\frac{2pq}{3}$ is the volume required. For instance, let

$$\begin{array}{lll} a_1 = 3 & b_1 = 6 & c_1 = 6 \\ a_2 = 4 & b_2 = 6 & c_2 = 5 \\ a_3 = 5 & b_3 = 6 & c_3 = 4 \\ & p = 3, \text{ and } q = 4. \end{array}$$

Then the products enclosed in the preceding square are

$$\begin{array}{|ccc|} \hline 0 & 6 & 0 \\ 4 & 12 & 5 \\ 0 & 6 & 0 \\ \hline \end{array} \times \frac{2 \times 3 \times 4}{3} = (4 + 24 + 5)\,8 = 264.$$

The multipliers of Simpson's First Rule, if expressed in a similar manner, would be

$$\begin{array}{|ccc|} \hline 1 & 4 & 1 \\ 4 & 16 & 4 \\ 1 & 4 & 1 \\ \hline \end{array} \times \frac{pq}{9}$$

and the products, by using the same ordinates, would be

$$\begin{array}{|ccc|} \hline 3 & 24 & 6 \\ 16 & 96 & 20 \\ 5 & 24 & 4 \\ \hline \end{array} \times \frac{3 \times 4}{9} = (24 + 144 + 30)\,\tfrac{4}{3} = 264,$$

which is the same result as above; only, as will be observed, after a greater expenditure of labour, by reason of the magnitude of the multipliers in Simpson's as compared with Woolley's Rule.

So far, we have only been considering the application of Woolley's Rule to an elementary solid, divided by two planes, at right angles to each other. From the preceding, however, an expression is readily found by which a volume of displacement can be calculated with any odd number of vertical sections and water lines. For instance, let us take a case of 5 water lines and 9 vertical sections; we have then eight elementary solids arranged as below:—

|        | No.1 | No.2 | No.3 | No.3 | No.4 | No.5 | No.5 | No.6 | No.7 | No.7 | No.8 | No.9 |   |
|--------|------|------|------|------|------|------|------|------|------|------|------|------|---|
| L.W.L. | 0 | 1 | 0 | 0 | 1 | 0 | 0 | 1 | 0 | 0 | 1 | 0 |   |
| 2 W.L. | 1 | 2 | 1 | 1 | 2 | 1 | 1 | 2 | 1 | 1 | 2 | 1 |   |
| 3 W.L. | 0 | 1 | 0 | 0 | 1 | 0 | 0 | 1 | 0 | 0 | 1 | 0 |   |
| 3 W.L. | 0 | 1 | 0 | 0 | 1 | 0 | 0 | 1 | 0 | 0 | 1 | 0 | $\times \dfrac{2pq}{3}$ |
| 4 W.L. | 1 | 2 | 1 | 1 | 2 | 1 | 1 | 2 | 1 | 1 | 2 | 1 |   |
| 5 W.L. | 0 | 1 | 0 | 0 | 1 | 0 | 0 | 1 | 0 | 0 | 1 | 0 |   |

which, when combined, appears thus—

|        | No.1 | No.2 | No.3 | No.4 | No.5 | No.6 | No.7 | No.8 | No.9 |   |
|--------|------|------|------|------|------|------|------|------|------|---|
| L.W.L. | 0 | 1 | 0 | 1 | 0 | 1 | 0 | 1 | 0 |   |
| 2 W.L. | 1 | 2 | 2 | 2 | 2 | 2 | 2 | 2 | 1 |   |
| 3 W.L. | 0 | 2 | 0 | 2 | 0 | 2 | 0 | 2 | 0 | $\times \dfrac{2pq}{3}$ |
| 4 W.L. | 1 | 2 | 2 | 2 | 2 | 2 | 2 | 2 | 1 |   |
| 5 W.L. | 0 | 1 | 0 | 1 | 0 | 1 | 0 | 1 | 0 |   |

From this example it will be seen how to express the multipliers for any odd numbers of vertical stations and water lines.

**44. Proof of Woolley's Rule.**—For the benefit of the advanced student, we now propose giving a proof of the rule just stated. Referring to fig. 1, Plate XII., let $O$ be the origin and $OX$, $OY$ and $OZ$ the axes of co-ordinates.

The general expression for the volume of the solid is

$$\iiint dx\,dy\,dz.$$

It is assumed that the curved surface is that of a cubic paraboloid, the general equation for which is

$$z = a + bx + cx^2 + dy + ey^2 + fxy + gx^2y + hxy^2 + kx^3 + ly^3.$$

Let $p$ be the common interval along the axis $OX$, and $q$ that along the axis $OY$.

Then we have—when

$x = 0$, $y = q$, $z = a_3 = a + dq + eq^2 + lq^3$
$x = 0$, $y = -q$, $z = a_1 = a - dq + eq^2 - lq^3$
$x = 0$, $y = 0$, $z = a_2 = a$
$x = p$, $y = 0$, $z = b_2 = a + bp + cp^2 + kp^3$
$x = p$, $y = q$, $z = b_3 = a + bp + cp^2 + dq + eq^2 + fpq + gp^2q + hpq^2 + kp^3 + lq^3$
$x = p$, $y = -q$, $z = b_1 = a + bp + cp^2 - dq + eq^2 - fpq - gp^2q + hpq^2 + kp^3 - lq^3$
$x = 2p$, $y = 0$, $z = c_2 = a + 2bp + 4cp^2$
$x = 2p$, $y = q$, $z = c_3 = a + 2bp + 4cp^2 + dq + eq^2 + 2fpq + 4gp^2q + 2hpq^2 + 8kp^3 + lq^3$
$x = 2p$, $y = -q$, $z = c_1 = a + 2bp + 4cp^2 - dq + eq^2 - 2fpq - 4gp^2q + 2hpq^2 + 8kp^3 - lq^3$

But the volume of a solid

$$= \iiint dx\,dy\,dz$$
$$= \iint z\,dx\,dy$$

and this particular volume

$$= \int_0^{2p} \int_{-q}^{q} z\,dx\,dy$$

$$= \int_0^{2p} \int_{-q}^{q} (a + bx + cx^2 + dy + ey^2 + fxy + gx^2y + hxy^2 + kx^3 + ly^3)\,dx\,dy.$$

$$= \int_0^{2p} \left(2aq + 2bxq + 2cx^2q + \frac{2}{3}eq^3 + \frac{2}{3}hxq^3 + 2kx^3q\right)dx$$

$$= 4apq + 4bp^2q + \frac{16}{3}cp^3q + \frac{4}{3}epq^3 + \frac{4}{3}hp^2q^3 + 8kp^4q$$

$$= \frac{pq}{3}\left(12a + 12bp + 16cp^2 + 4eq^2 + 4hpq^2 + 24kp^3\right)$$

but $a_2 + b_1 + 2b_2 + b_3 + c_2 = \frac{1}{2}$ (the above expression in brackets.)

as may be deduced from the values of $a_2$, $b_1$, $b_2$, etc., which have been already found.

Hence we have—

$$\text{Volume} = \frac{2pq}{3}(a_2 + b_1 + 2b_2 + b_3 + c_2)$$

Or, arranging the ordinates as they stand upon the base of the solid—

$$\frac{2pq}{3} \times \begin{vmatrix} 0 & b_1 & 0 \\ a_2 & 2b_2 & c_2 \\ 0 & b_3 & 0 \end{vmatrix}$$

from whence, by using only the multipliers, we get the general expression—

$$\frac{2pq}{3} \times \begin{vmatrix} 0 & . & 1 & . & 0 \\ 1 & . & 2 & . & 1 \\ 0 & . & 1 & . & 0 \end{vmatrix}$$

**45. Centre of Buoyancy by Woolley's Rule.**—The preceding result has been obtained upon the general assumption that the curved surface is a cubic paraboloid; as may be seen by looking into the investigation, the same result would have been obtained if the equation to the ordinary paraboloid had been used, that equation being

$$z = a + bx + cx^2 + dy + ey^2 + fxy.$$

We will now show how to obtain the co-ordinates of the centre of buoyancy by Woolley's Rule, using the above equation to the surface.

First, to find the longitudinal position of the centre of buoyancy. Referring to fig 2, Plate XII. (which represents the base of the solid shown by fig. 1), we will take moments about the plane of $YZ$, which is represented by the line $a_1 a_3$, $a_2$ being the origin.

Let $T$ be the distance of the centre of gravity from that plane,

$$\text{Then Volume} \times T = \int_0^{2p} \int_{-q}^{q} xz\,dx\,dy$$
$$= \int_0^{2p} \int_{-q}^{q} x(a + bx + cx^2 + dy + ey^2 + fxy)\,dx\,dy.$$

Integrating between the limits we have

$$\text{Volume} \times T = \frac{4}{3} p^2 q (3a + 4bp + 6cp^2 + eq^2)$$

But if the equation

$$z = a + bx + cx^2 + dy + ey^2 + fxy$$

represent the surface, we find by equating the co-efficients, as in the last Art., that

$$(b_1 + 2b_2 + b_3) + 2 \times c_2 = 6a + 8bp + 12cp^2 + 2eq^2.$$

Hence Volume $\times T = \frac{2}{3} p^2 q \{(b_1 + 2b_2 + b_3) + 2c_2\}$

$$\therefore T = \frac{\frac{2}{3} p^2 q \{(b_1 + 2b_2 + b_3) + 2c_2\}}{\frac{2}{3} pq \{a_2 + (b_1 + 2b_2 + b_3) + 2c_2\}}$$

Or $T = p \dfrac{a_2 \times o + (b_1 + 2b_2 + b_3) \times 1 + c_2 \times 2}{a_2 + (b_1 + 2b_2 + b_3) + c_2}$

a form which the reader will probably recognise, being that which we have previously employed, only with Simpson's instead of Woolley's Multipliers.*

The value of T, expressed in a form fit for the immediate substitution of the lengths of the ordinates, is—

$$T = p \times \begin{array}{|ccc|} 0 & b_1 & 0 \\ 0 & 2b_2 & 2c_2 \\ 0 & b_3 & 0 \\ \hline 0 & b_1 & 0 \\ a_2 & 2b_2 & c_2 \\ 0 & b_3 & 0 \end{array}$$

* Should the similarity not be obvious, it may be desirable to point out that the functions of the first set of ordinates are multiplied by zero, those of the second by unity, and of the third by 2, the same as when taking moments in the centre of buoyancy calculation upon the ordinary displacement sheet. This is what we might have expected, but we have here proved it independently. If there were a greater number of sections, the multipliers would continue thus:—3, 4, 5, etc.

the sum of the upper products being divided by that of the lower.

As an example, we will substitute the values of the ordinates, and the common intervals given in the preceding Art.

$$T = 3 \times \dfrac{\begin{array}{ccc} 0 & 6 & 0 \\ 0 & 12 & 10 \\ 0 & 6 & 0 \end{array}}{\begin{array}{ccc} 0 \;.\; 6 \;.\; 0 \\ 4 \;.\; 12 \;.\; 5 \\ 0 \;.\; 6 \;.\; 0 \end{array}} = 3 \times \dfrac{34}{33} = 3\tfrac{1}{T} \text{ from the plane YZ}.$$

Using Simpson's Multipliers we shall get

$$T = 3 \times \dfrac{\begin{array}{ccc} 0 & 24 & 12 \\ 0 & 96 & 40 \\ 0 & 24 & 8 \end{array}}{\begin{array}{ccc} 3 & 24 & 6 \\ 16 & 96 & 20 \\ 5 & 24 & 4 \end{array}} = 3 \times \dfrac{204}{198} = 3\tfrac{1}{TT} \text{ from the plane YZ}$$

which is the same result as before.

The other co-ordinate of the centre of buoyancy, *i.e.*, its distance, measured from the plane $ZX$, may be found in a similar manner, only that it is preferable in this case to shift the origin to $a_3$ in fig. 2, or, which is the same thing, to $O_1$, fig. 1, and thus find the distance of the centre of buoyancy from the plane $Z_1 X_1$. The result will be similar to that given above. Let $T_1$ be the distance, then

$$T = q \times \dfrac{\begin{array}{ccc} 0 & a_2 & 0 \\ 0 & 2b_2 & 2b_1 \\ 0 & c_2 & 0 \end{array}}{\begin{array}{ccc} 0 & b_1 & 0 \\ a_2 & 2b_2 & c_2 \\ 0 & b_3 & 0 \end{array}}$$

which, in the example already employed, gives

$$T_1 = 4 \times \cfrac{\begin{array}{ccc} 0 & 4 & 0 \\ 0 & 12 & 12 \\ 0 & 5 & 0 \end{array}}{\begin{array}{ccc} 0 & 6 & 0 \\ 4 & 12 & 5 \\ 0 & 6 & 0 \end{array}} = 4 \times \frac{33}{33} = 4 \text{ from the plane } Z_1 X_1,$$

which happens in this case to be in the plane containing the ordinates $a_2$, $b_2$, and $c_2$, or the plane $ZX$.

The application of Simpson's Rule gives

$$T_1 = 4 \times \cfrac{\begin{array}{ccc} 0 & 16 & 6 \\ 0 & 96 & 48 \\ 0 & 20 & 12 \end{array}}{\begin{array}{ccc} 3 & 24 & 6 \\ 16 & 96 & 20 \\ 5 & 24 & 4 \end{array}} = 4 \times \frac{198}{198} = 4 \text{ from the plane } Z_1 X_1,$$

which again confirms the result by Woolley's Rule.

From the results obtained by the use of the elementary solid, we may readily write down the multipliers by which the centre of buoyancy is found in a case where any odd number of ordinates is given in either direction. In the example with which we conclude Art. 43, the distance of the centre of buoyancy, from vertical section No. 5, is found by first multiplying the ordinates by the following multipliers given in order, and then multiplying the difference between the moments on the two sides of No. 5 by the common interval, and dividing the result by the sum of the products given for the displacement at the end of that Article. It will be observed that in the upper parts of the following tabular

# CENTRE OF BUOYANCY BY WOOLLEY'S RULE.

forms, the multipliers by Woolley's Rule are affected by the multipliers for leverage similarly to the method when Simpson's Rule is employed.

$$T = p \times \begin{vmatrix} \begin{array}{|ccccc|ccccc|} 0 & 3 & 0 & 1 & 0 & 0 & 1 & 0 & 3 & 0 \\ 4 & 6 & 4 & 2 & 0 & 0 & 2 & 4 & 6 & 4 \\ 0 & 6 & 0 & 2 & 0 & 0 & 2 & 0 & 6 & 0 \\ 4 & 6 & 4 & 2 & 0 & 0 & 2 & 4 & 6 & 4 \\ 0 & 3 & 0 & 1 & 0 & 0 & 1 & 0 & 3 & 0 \end{array} \\ \begin{array}{ccccccccc} 0 & 1 & 0 & 1 & 0 & 1 & 0 & 1 & 0 \\ 1 & 2 & 2 & 2 & 2 & 2 & 2 & 2 & 1 \\ 0 & 2 & 0 & 2 & 0 & 2 & 0 & 2 & 0 \\ 1 & 2 & 2 & 2 & 2 & 2 & 2 & 2 & 1 \\ 0 & 1 & 0 & 1 & 0 & 1 & 0 & 1 & 0 \end{array} \end{vmatrix}$$

$$\text{also } T_1 = q \times \begin{vmatrix} \begin{array}{ccccccccc} 0 & 0 & 0 & 0 & 0 & 0 & 0 & 0 & 0 \\ 1 & 2 & 2 & 2 & 2 & 2 & 2 & 2 & 1 \\ 0 & 4 & 0 & 4 & 0 & 4 & 0 & 4 & 0 \\ 3 & 6 & 6 & 6 & 6 & 6 & 6 & 6 & 3 \\ 0 & 4 & 0 & 4 & 0 & 4 & 0 & 4 & 0 \end{array} \\ \begin{array}{ccccccccc} 0 & 1 & 0 & 1 & 0 & 1 & 0 & 1 & 0 \\ 1 & 2 & 2 & 2 & 2 & 2 & 2 & 2 & 1 \\ 0 & 2 & 0 & 2 & 0 & 2 & 0 & 2 & 0 \\ 1 & 2 & 2 & 2 & 2 & 2 & 2 & 2 & 1 \\ 0 & 1 & 0 & 1 & 0 & 1 & 0 & 1 & 0 \end{array} \end{vmatrix}$$

The distance in this latter case being measured from the L.W.L. In both the above, the order of the water lines and vertical sections is the same as in Art. 43.

**46. Geometrical Application of Woolley's Rule.**—Mr. C. W. Merrifield has suggested a convenient and practicable mode of applying Woolley's Rule for the volume of displacement. Fig. 3 of Plate XII. represents the half-breadth plan of a ship, from the L.W.L. to the keel; there are five water lines and seven ordinates, including the two endmost, which in this case are each zero. The lowest water line is placed at the keel, for the sake of simplicity. At the intersections of the water lines and ordinates, the respective Woolley's multipliers are written down. Then take a long strip of paper, having a clean straight edge, and with a sharp pencil measure off upon it the length of every ordinate which has a number at the head of it on the plan, taking twice those marked 2, and neglecting those marked zero. Each ordinate is to begin on the strip where the previous one ends, so that the whole length on the strip will represent the sum of the ordinates when affected by their proper multipliers. The measurements are obtained by actually applying the strips to the ordinates, in the same way as we have already constructed the displacement and moment curves (see Art. 42). It only remains to multiply the total length of the strip (when measured by the scale) by two-thirds of the product of the length and depth intervals, and the displacement is obtained in cubic feet.

As it is not possible to obtain the areas of the water planes and vertical sections with Woolley's Rule, the latter is not often used in ship calculations. It is, however, peculiarly adapted for rapidly obtaining the volume of displacement and position of the centre of buoyancy in the preliminary stages of a design; but for obtaining all the particulars calculated upon a displacement sheet, Simpson's Rules are better suited, and invariably employed.

**47. Angular Measurement of Areas.**—The area of a figure bounded by a curve and two intersecting straight lines, such as $WSW_1$, fig. 3, Plate V., may be found in the following manner:—Divide the angle $WSW_1$ into an even number of equal intervals by radiating lines $Sw_1$, $Sw_2$, and $Sw_3$. *Measure the lengths of the radiating ordinates, $SW$, $Sw_1$, $Sw_2$, $Sw_3$,* and

$SW_1$, and treat their half squares as the ordinates of a new curve. Multiply these half squares by their respective Simpson's Multipliers, as in the one-third rule, and then multiply the sum of the products by one-third the circular measure * of the angular interval between the radiating ordinates; the result will be the area required.

For instance, let the values of $SW$, $Sw_1$, $Sw_2$, $Sw_3$, and $SW_1$, be 5, 5·2, 5·7, 6·4, and 7·3, respectively; also let the common angular interval be 5 degrees: the area will be calculated thus:—

| Numbers of Ordinates. | Ordinates. | Half Squares of Ordinates. | Simpson's Multipliers. | Functions of Half Squares. |
|---|---|---|---|---|
| 1 | 5·0 | 12·500 | 1 | 12·500 |
| 2 | 5·2 | 13·520 | 4 | 54·080 |
| 3 | 5·7 | 16·245 | 2 | 32·490 |
| 4 | 6·4 | 20·480 | 4 | 81·920 |
| 5 | 7·3 | 26·645 | 1 | 26·645 |

$$\frac{\text{circular measure of }5°}{3} = ·02908$$

$$\text{Area of WSW}_1 = 6·038$$

**48. Explanation of the preceding.**—Let $WS = r$ and $WSW_1 = \theta$. Consider an indefinitely small angle $WSw_1$ which will thus be $d\theta$. Then $Ww_1 = rd\theta$, and therefore the area of

$$WSw_1 = \frac{r}{2} \times rd\theta = \frac{r^2 d\theta}{2}.$$

Hence the whole area $WSW_1$, made up of an infinite number of these elementary areas, is equal to $\int \frac{r^2}{2} d\theta$. Now the area of a plane figure bounded by a curve and rectangular ordinates and abscissa is $\int y dx$, and this expressed by Simpson's First Rule is $\frac{h}{3}(a_1 + 4b_1 + c_1)$; whence we see by analogy that $\int \frac{r^2}{2} d\theta$ expressed by that rule is

$$\frac{\theta}{3}\left(\frac{a_1^2}{2} + \frac{4b_1^2}{2} + \frac{c_1^2}{2}\right)$$

* The *circular measure* of any angle is found by multiplying the number of degrees in it by ·01745.

This may be rigidly demonstrated by using the polar equation to the parabola.

**49. Volumes of Wedge-shaped Solids.**—The volumes of solids of a wedge form, such as $PW_1T$ (fig. 3, Plate V.), bounded by a curved surface $PWW_1P_1$ and two planes $PWST$ and $P_1W_1ST$ meeting at a straight edge $ST$; and having cross sections such as $WSW_1$, may be found in the following manner:—Divide the angle $WSW_1$ between the bounding planes into an even number of equal intervals by an odd number of radiating planes which meet at the line $ST$, as shown by $p_1w_1ST$, $p_2w_2ST$, etc. Divide the line $ST$ into an even number of equal divisions, and through these points of division draw planes, such as $RR_1U$, perpendicular to the bounding planes, and to the line $ST$. The intersections of these perpendicular planes with the radiating planes will give ordinates which are to be treated as follows:— *Find the half squares of the ordinates for each plane $PWST$, $p_1w_1ST$, etc., and treat them as the ordinates of a new curve, the area of which find by Simpson's Rule in the ordinary way.* (As will be seen, the ordinates for the plane $P_1W_1ST$ are $W_1S$, $R_1U$, $P_1T$; their half squares being $\dfrac{\overline{W_1S}^2}{2}$, $\dfrac{\overline{R_1U}^2}{2}$, and $\dfrac{\overline{P_1T}^2}{2}$.) *Next treat the areas\* thus found in the same manner as the half squares were treated in Art. 47, and the result will be the volume of the wedge.* Thus if $A_1$, $A_2$, $A_3$, $A_4$, and $A_5$, are the areas found for the planes by using the half squares of their ordinates, then

$$(A_1 + 4A_2 + 2A_3 + 4A_4 + A_5)\frac{i}{3}$$

is the volume of the wedge.

As an illustration of the practical application of the rule: suppose 50, 55, 62, 71, and 82, to be the areas found by using ordinates equal to the half squares of the actual ordinates of the planes $PWST$, $p_1w_1ST$, $p_2w_2ST$, etc., respectively, then to find the volume.

---

\* It may be noticed in passing that these areas are equivalent to the moments of the respective radiating planes about the axis $ST$.

| Number of Plane. | Area by using $\dfrac{ord^2}{2}$ | Simpson's Multipliers. | Functions. |
|---|---|---|---|
| 1 | 50 | 1 | 50 |
| 2 | 55 | 4 | 220 |
| 3 | 62 | 2 | 124 |
| 4 | 71 | 4 | 284 |
| 5 | 82 | 1 | 82 |

$$\frac{\text{circular measure of } 5°}{3} = \frac{\cdot 02908}{22 \cdot 1}\ 760$$

$$= \text{volume of wedge.}$$

**50 Moments of Wedge-shaped Solids.**—The moment of a wedge-shaped solid, such as is shown by fig. 3, Plate V., may be found with regard—

1. To a transverse sectional plane, such as $WSW_1$.
2. To a longitudinal plane $AC$, through its edge, and perpendicular to one of the radiating planes $P_1W_1ST$.
3. To a longitudinal radiating plane $P_1W_1ST$.

In the first case, the areas of the transverse sections, such as $WW_1S$, $RR_1U$, $PP_1T$, have to be calculated by the rule given in Art. 47, and these areas and the whole volume of the wedge treated in the manner described in Art. 34.

In the second case: Divide the solid in the manner described in Art. 49 when determining its volume. Treat each of the longitudinal sections $PWST$, $p_1w_1ST$, $p_2w_2ST$, as follows:—Measure its ordinates (as $W_1S$, $R_1U$, $P_1T$), and *compute the third parts of their cubes; treat those quantities as the ordinates of a new curve, and find its area. Then multiply each area by the cosine\* of the angle made by the plane to which the area corresponds with the plane that is perpendicular to the one about which moments are taken; and by the multiplier corresponding to its position, according to Simpson's Rule. Add together these products, and multiply their sum by one-third of the common angular interval in circular measure; the result will be the moment required.* In fig. 3, Plate V., $P_1W_1ST$ is "the plane perpendicular to the one about which moments are taken;" $AC$ being the latter. The cosines used

\* Chambers' *Tables of Logarithms*, etc., contains a table of the values of the sines, cosines, and tangents of angles.

in this case are those of the angles $WSW_1$, $w_1SW_1$, $w_2SW_1$, $w_3SW_1$, and zero.

In the third case, proceed as in the second case, *multiplying by the sines of the angles instead of the cosines.*

**51. Explanation of the Preceding.**—The proof of the first case has already been gone into in an analagous question. (See Art 34.)

With regard to the second case, consider an elementary wedge $Pw_1ST$ containing an indefinitely small angle $d\theta$, and of an indefinitely small thickness $dx$. Let the whole angle $WSW_1$ be $\theta$; also, let $WS = r$, then, as stated in Art. 47, the area $WSw_1 = \dfrac{r^2 d\theta}{2}$. Now, its centre of gravity is distant $\dfrac{2}{3}r$ from $S$, therefore the moment of this elementary area about $W_1S$ is

$$\tfrac{2}{3}r \cos\theta \times \tfrac{r^2}{2} d\theta = \tfrac{r^3}{3} \cos\theta\, d\theta.$$

Hence the moment of the elementary wedge $Pw_1ST$ about $W_1S$ is

$$\int \tfrac{r^3}{3} \cos\theta\, dx d\theta,$$

and thus the moments of the whole wedge is

$$\int\int \tfrac{r^3}{3} \cos\theta\, dx d\theta$$

The Algebraical expression for the moment of a solid measured rectangularly, about the plane $AC$, is

$$\int\int xy\, dy dz.$$

If we compare this expression with the rule given in Art. 34 for the moment of a solid about a plane, the reason for the rule given for the second case in the preceding article will be apparent.

The expression for the third case is

$$\int\int \tfrac{r^3}{3} \sin\theta\, dx d\theta.$$

We do not purpose giving an example of the practical

application of these rules at present, as in the next chapter we shall have occasion to make frequent reference to them in consequence of their great importance in calculating the stability of a ship.

**52. Moments of Inertia.**—As the *moments of inertia* of plane figures and solid bodies are frequently required in solving the problems of stability and strength of ships, we purpose devoting a small space to the consideration of the modes of obtaining their value for some of the elementary forms which occur in our investigation.

As in the case of simple moments, when considering the moment of inertia of a plane, it is supposed to be a uniformly weighted surface, or a thin sheet of some heavy material; also, solids are supposed to be homogeneous. In other words, the geometrical moments of inertia are referred to.

1. If the mass of every particle of a material system be multiplied by the square of its distance from a straight line, the sum of the products so formed is called the *moment of inertia* of the system about that line.

2. If $M$ be the mass of a system, and $K$ be such a quantity that $MK^2$ is its moment of inertia about a given straight line, then $K$ is called the *radius of gyration* of the system about that line.

3. If two straight lines $Ox$, $Oy$, be taken as axes, and if the mass of every particle of the system be multiplied by its two co-ordinates $x$, $y$, the sum of the products is called the *product of inertia* of the system about these two axes.

4. The moment of inertia of a body or system of bodies about any axis is equal to the moment of inertia about a parallel axis, through the centre of gravity, plus the moment of inertia of the whole mass collected at the centre of gravity about the original axis.

5. The product of inertia about any two axes is equal to the product of inertia about two parallel axes through the centre of gravity, plus the product of inertia of the whole mass collected at the centre of gravity about the original axis.*

* These five statements which are here given as definitions (although only the first three are strictly such) are taken from *Routh's Rigid Dynamics*.

**53. Moments of Inertia of Certain Figures.**—The following are values of the geometrical moments of inertia for several figures about the axis mentioned:—

1.) *A Rectangle* about an axis in its plane, through its centre of gravity and parallel to the shorter side—
   Length of longer side $= h$
   Length of shorter side $= b$
   Area of rectangle $= A = bh$.
   $$= \frac{bh^3}{12} = \frac{Ah^2}{12}$$

(2.) *A Rectangle* about an axis in its plane, through its centre of gravity, and parallel to the longer side—
   Dimensions as before.
   $$= \frac{b^3h}{12} = \frac{Ah^2}{12}$$

(3.) *A Square* about an axis in its plane, through its centre of gravity and parallel to either side—
   Side of square $= h$
   Area $= A = h^2$.
   $$= \frac{h^4}{12} = \frac{Ah^2}{12}$$

(4.) *A Circle* about a diameter—
   Diameter $= h$
   Area $= A = \frac{\pi h^2}{4}$.
   $$= \frac{\pi h^4}{64} = \frac{Ah^2}{16}$$

(5.) *An Ellipse* about its longer axis—
   Longer axis $= h$
   Shorter axis $= b$
   Area $= A = \frac{\pi bh}{4}$.
   $$= \frac{\pi h^3 b}{64} = \frac{Ah^2}{16}$$

(6.) *An Ellipse* about its shorter axis—
   Dimensions as before.
   $$= \frac{\pi h b^3}{64} = \frac{Ah^2}{16}$$

(7.) *A Sphere* about a diameter—
   Diameter $= h$
   Volume $= V = \frac{1}{6}\pi h^3$.
   $$= \frac{\pi h^5}{60} = \frac{Vh^2}{10}$$

(8.) *An Ellipsoid* about an axis—
   The axes being $b$, $h$, and $l$.
   Volume $= V = \frac{1}{6}\pi bhl$.
   The result is given about the axis $b$.
   $$= \frac{\pi bhl}{120}(h^2 + l^2)$$
   The others may be obtained by observing the symmetry of the expression.
   $$= \frac{V}{20}(h^2 + l^2)$$

(9.) *A Cube* about any axis through its centre of gravity—
   Side of cube $= h$
   Volume $= V = h^3$.
   $$= \frac{h^5}{6} = \frac{Vh^2}{6}$$

## 54. Specimen Investigations.

The determination of these moments of inertia involves a knowledge of the integral calculus, and, as the subject is an extensive one, we have omitted the solutions of the problems and merely given the results.

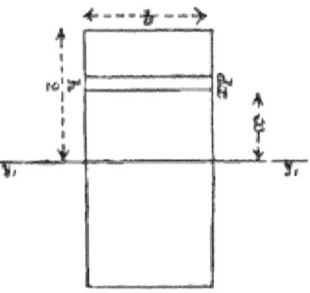

Fig. 10.

(1.) As a specimen investigation, we will, however, show how the moment of inertia of a rectangle is obtained, about an axis in its plane passing through its centre of gravity, and parallel to either of its sides. (See fig. 10.)

Let $h =$ the longer side.
 ,, $b =$ the shorter side.
 ,, $w =$ the weight of a unit of area.

$y_1 y_1$ is the axis about which the moment of inertia is found.

Consider a small strip of the rectangle parallel to $y_1 y_1$ whose breadth is infinitely small, or $dx$, and let $x =$ the distance of this strip from the axis.

Then the area of the strip is $b\,dx$,
and its weight $= wb\,dx$.
Its moment of inertia $= wbx^2 dx$,

and the moment of inertia of the half of the rectangle on one side of $y_1 y_1$

$$= wb \int_0^{\frac{h}{2}} x^2 dx.$$

and integrated between the limits this becomes

$$= \frac{wbh^3}{24}$$

Hence the moment of inertia of both sides of the rectangle about the axis is

$$\frac{wbh^3}{12}.$$

Neglecting $w$, as we merely require the geometrical moment of inertia, we have

$$\text{M. of I. of rectangle} = \frac{bh^3}{12},$$

which is the result already given.

(2.) Hereafter we shall have frequent occasion to use the moment of inertia of a plane figure, bounded by a curve and straight line, about that straight line. The following method is employed in determining it:—

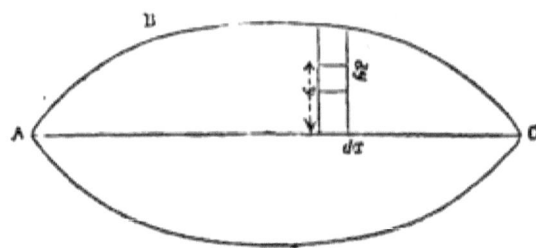

Fig. 11.

Let ABC (fig. 11) be such a figure, represented in practice by a half-load water plane, AC being the middle line. Required, the geometrical moment of inertia of the area ABC about the axis AC.

Consider an infinitesimal element of the area, whose length is $dy$, and breadth $dx$, the element being distant $y$ from AC.

The area of this element is $dxdy$.
Its moment of inertia is $y^2 dxdy$.

and the moment of inertia of the whole area $ABC =$

$$\iint y^2 dx dy = \frac{1}{3} \int y^3 dx.$$

The second integration is performed by the aid of Simpson's Rule, by taking the cubes of the ordinates of the curve and treating them as the ordinates of a new curve; one-third the area of this curve is the geometrical moment of inertia of the area ABC, about the axis AC; or, multiplying by two for both sides, two-thirds the area is the moment of inertia of the whole water plane about AC.

**55. Co-efficients of Fineness.**—If there are two vessels of similar form, but of different dimensions, so that every ordinate of every water plane or transverse section in one of them bears a uniform proportion to the corresponding ordinate in the corresponding water plane or transverse section of the other, then it is evident that the displacements of these vessels are to each other in the ratio of the products of their lengths, breadths, and draughts of water; that is, of the rectangular solids or parallelopipedons circumscribing their immersed bodies. Hence if the displacement of a vessel is found to be some fraction of that of the circumscribing parallelopipedon, the displacement of any other vessel of similar form, but of different dimensions, may be found by multiplying the product of her length, breadth, and draught of water by that fraction. The fraction referred to is termed the *co-efficient of fineness of displacement.*

Similarly, the ratio between the area of a water plane or transverse section to that of the circumscribing rectangle is termed the co-efficient of fineness of the water plane or transverse section in question. Hence, having found the value of this co-efficient, for any water plane or transverse section in one vessel, the area of the corresponding water plane or transverse section in another vessel of similar form is found by multiplying the product of the principal dimensions of the plane or section by the co-efficient.

The co-efficients of area usually employed are those of the midship section and load water plane.

**Co-efficient of Fineness of Displacement.**—The value of this co-efficient is a very good criterion of the fineness of the immersed body, even in comparing vessels having slightly different ratios of length, breadth, and draught of water. Also, in the preliminary stages of a design when it is decided what degree of fineness shall be given to the vessel with a view of obtaining a certain speed; by knowing the co-efficients of fineness of other vessels of about the same size, which have attained the required speed with about the same propelling power as it is contemplated employing, we are enabled to determine at once, with a tolerable degree of accuracy, what displacement is available with the proposed length, breadth, and draught of water. It should be remarked that the mean draught of water is always employed, also the length and breadth at the load water line.*

---

* Strictly speaking, when the ship is not floating at an even keel, it is incorrect to say "circumscribing parallelopipedon;" we should rather say "a solid of the same length, breadth, and mean depth as the displaced body."

The value of this co-efficient generally ranges from ·5 to ·7, a common value being about ·6.

**56. Co-efficient of Fineness of Water Lines.**—The co-efficient for the load water line is most commonly required, being the ratio of the area of the load water plane to that of its circumscribing rectangle. Its value commonly ranges from ·7 to ·8.

The co-efficient of fineness of any other water line is also the ratio of its area to that of its circumscribing rectangle, the value of the co-efficient diminishing as the water lines are farther from the load water line.

**57. Co-efficient of Fineness of Midship Section.**—This affords a more valuable criterion of the speed which will probably be obtained with a certain propelling power than does that of the load water line. More will be said on this subject in Part IV. Its value usually varies between ·6 and ·9; a common value being ·8.

**58. Mean Co-efficient of Fineness of Water Lines.**—The mean co-efficient of fineness of all the water lines of a ship is obtained as follows:—Multiply the greatest immersed area of midship section by the length of the load water line, and divide the displacement by the product.

The co-efficient of fineness of the displacement is equal to the product of the co-efficient of fineness of the midship section, multiplied by the mean co-efficient of fineness of the water lines.

By consulting the following table it will be seen that the co-efficient of fineness of displacement is generally greatest in vessels having the greatest ratio of length to breadth, even although the latter have bodies better adapted for high speed, this being due to the greater length of midship body in such vessels. In the same way, the co-efficients of fineness of the water lines of long vessels having very fine bows and sterns sometimes exceeds those of much bluffer but shorter vessels. The small co-efficient for the midship sections of the wooden vessels is due to the very rising floor which they have—the midship sections of modern war and merchant steam-ships being usually much flatter and fuller in this respect, in order to carry the engines low, and obtain greater displacement.

## 59. TABLE OF CO-EFFICIENTS OF FINENESS.

| Class of Ship. | Length. | Breadth. | Mean Draught. | Co-efficient of Displacement. | Co-efficient of Water Line. | Co-efficient of Mid. Section. |
|---|---|---|---|---|---|---|
| | ft. | ft. | ft. | | | |
| Pacific S. N. Co. | 390·0 | 42·5 | 21·0 | ·609 | ·77 | ·86 |
| Royal Mail Co. | 344·0 | 40·5 | 21·0 | ·590 | ·76 | ·84 |
| National Line Co. | 385·0 | 42·0 | 22·0 | ·659 | ·80 | ·88 |
| Anchor Line. | 350·0 | 35·0 | 21·0 | ·687 | ·84 | ·85 |
| Armour-clad Frigate. | 325·0 | 59·0 | 25·2 | ·637 | ·82 | ·90 |
| Turret Ship. | 320·0 | 75·0 | 24·0 | ·674 | ·79 | ·92 |
| Line of Battle Ships (3 decks) | 260·0 | 61·0 | 25·5 | ·537 | ·82 | ·76 |
| Line of Battle Ships (2 decks) | 238·0 | 55·8 | 23·8 | ·530 | ·84 | ·66 |
| Wood Frigate. | 251·0 | 52·0 | 21·3 | ·453 | ·79 | ·64 |
| Iron Unarmoured Frigate | 337·3 | 50·3 | 23·0 | ·490 | ·73 | ·79 |
| Composite Sloop. | 160·0 | 31·3 | 13·0 | ·495 | ·76 | ·79 |

# CHAPTER II.

## THE METACENTRE AND SURFACE STABILITY.

*The Metacentre—Transverse Metacentre—Surface Stability—Fixed Metacentre—To obtain Position of Transverse Metacentre—Metacentric Surface Stability—Calculation for Transverse Metacentre Explained—More Exact Calculations of Surface Stability—Intersections of Water Planes—Method of Measurement—Specimen Calculation—Dynamical Stability—Dynamical Surface Stability—Specimen Calculation—Surface of Flotation—Centre of Flotation—Axis of Level Motion—Curve of Buoyancy—Surface of Buoyancy—Metacentric—Longitudinal Metacentre—Calculation for Longitudinal Metacentre Explained—Longitudinal Metacentric Surface Stability—Comparative Surface Stabilities of Different Vessels.*

**60. The Metacentre.**—If a vessel, floating upright in still water, be inclined, the centre of buoyancy will evidently move in the same direction as that in which the ship is heeled. Supposing the angle of inclination to be indefinitely small, then the point where the vertical, drawn through the centre of buoyancy in the inclined position, intersects that drawn through the centre of buoyancy when the ship is upright, is termed the *metacentre*. When the ship is inclined transversely the point is termed the "*transverse metacentre,*" and when inclined longitudinally, it is styled the "*longitudinal metacentre.*" The term *metacentre* is usually employed when referring to the transverse metacentre; but when the longitudinal metacentre is referred to, the latter name is invariably used.

**61. Transverse Metacentre.**—The name metacentre was first given to the point by Boguer, a French mathematician and writer on Naval Architecture. Although, strictly speaking, the term is only applicable when the angle of inclination is indefinitely small, yet it has now obtained a wider meaning, being often used to denote the point of intersection at any finite angle of heel. As we shall presently show, it is only in the case of bodies of a certain special form that the position of the intersection remains fixed for all inclinations. In ordinary ships the point is practically fixed up to about 15 degrees, and for some ranges beyond that angle the intersections in well-formed ships are always higher. In the following pages, the term "*metacentre*" will refer to the intersection at an indefinitely small angle of heel, being the limiting position to which the intersection continually comes closer and closer as the angle of heel is indefinitely diminished. By the term "*fixed metacentre*" will be meant the point of intersection when it is fixed, or assumed to be fixed, for different angles of heel. When the point is not supposed to be fixed, but is considered (as it usually does), to vary in position for different inclinations, then the point will be termed the "*shifting metacentre.*"

We will now consider the influence of the position of the metacentre upon the stability of the ship. Fig. 1, Plate XIII., represents a transverse section of a ship at amidships, $WL$ being the load water line, and $B$ the centre of buoyancy when the ship is upright; $W_1L_1$ is the load water line when the ship is inclined through a certain angle. For the present, we will consider the angle as being of appreciable magnitude. It will be observed that the intersection $S$ of these two lines is not at the middle line of the ship, but at the side of it, towards which the ship is inclined;* the mode of obtaining the position of this point $S$ will be a subject for future consideration. When the ship is inclined, a portion of the section, viz., $LSL_1$, becomes immersed, while another portion of the section, viz., $WSW_1$, emerges from the water. These areas $LSL_1$ and $WSW_1$ are transverse sections of two wedge-shaped portions of the ship's body, which are named respectively the "*wedges of immersion and emersion,*" and sometimes the "*in and out.*" Since the displacement of the ship remains the same however she may be inclined, the volumes of these wedges are consequently equal.

As the alteration in the form of the immersed portion of

* This is the usual position of the point $S$ in ordinary ships when inclined at moderate angles.

the body is due to the transference of the volume contained by the wedge $WSW_1$ to the other side of the ship in the form of the wedge $LSL_1$, it consequently follows that the alteration in the position of the centre of buoyancy will also be due to the shifting of these volumes. Let $E$ and $I$ be the centres of buoyancy of the wedges of emersion and immersion, respectively; and join $EI$. Through $B$ draw $BB_1$ parallel to $EI_1$, then the new position of the centre of buoyancy will be somewhere in the line $BB_1$.

Let $V$ = the known volume of either wedge,
and $D$ = the volume of the whole displacement.

Then by a simple rule of statics,

$$V \times \text{EI} = D \times x,$$

where $x$ is the distance of the new centre of buoyancy from $B$ along $BB_1$,

$$\text{Wherefore } x = \frac{V \times \text{EI}}{D}.$$

Hence if a distance $BB_1$ be set off equal to $x$, then $B_1$ is the centre of buoyancy in the inclined position.

Through $B_1$ draw $B_1M$ perpendicular to $W_1L_1$, intersecting $BM$ at the point $M$, then if the angle $BMB_1$ be indefinitely small, $M$ is the metacentre; if the angle is less than about 15 degrees, the point $M$ is a good approximation to the metacentre, but in every case when the inclination is some finite angle the point $M$ will have a different position for each angle, and be termed a shifting metacentre.

Through $B$ draw $BN$ perpendicular to $B_1M$, and through $E$ and $I$ draw $EH$ and $IK$ perpendiculars to the new water line $W_1L_1$. Now suppose the centre of gravity of the weight of the ship and her contents to be at the point $B$, this weight, now that the ship is inclined, will act downwards in the direction $BO$, perpendicular to $W_1L_1$; hence there are in this case two forces, constituting *a couple*, acting upon the ship, viz., her weight (which is equal to the displacement), downward through $B$, and the upward pressure of the water (also equal to the displacement), through $B_1$. This couple—which evidently tends to "right" the ship, or restore her to the upright position—is equal to

$$D \times BN.$$

If the centre of gravity of the ship is below the point $B$, the "righting moment" will evidently be greater than $D \times BN$, and if the centre of gravity is above the point $B$, the righting moment is less. The latter becomes continually less until the centre of gravity coincides with $M$, when it is zero; while, if above $M$, the couple is a negative or upsetting one. These statements are made at this stage in order to show the importance of the point $M$.

**62. Surface Stability.**—By surface stability is meant that tendency of a vessel, when inclined, to return to the upright position, which is due to her form, irrespective of the influence due to her centre of gravity not coinciding with the centre of buoyancy. For instance, referring to fig. 1, Plate XIII., the moment of surface stability at the inclination shown is equal to

$$D \times BN, \text{ or } D \times BM \sin BMB_1 \dots\dots\dots\dots(1)$$

When the centre of gravity coincides with $B$, this is the whole moment of stability at that inclination; but if the centre of gravity is below $B$, then the whole moment of stability is in excess of the surface stability, and if above, then it is less.

$$\text{Since } D \times BB_1 = V \times EI$$
$$\therefore D \times BN = V \times HK, \dots\dots\dots\dots (2)$$

whence $V \times HK$ is another expression for the moment of surface stability at that inclination.

**63. Fixed Metacentre.**—It was stated at Art. 61, that it is only in the case of bodies of a certain form that the intersections, given by different angles of heel, coincide with the metacentre itself, the point $M$ being in that case termed the fixed metacentre. It will be readily seen that the case referred to is that of a body with circular cross sections having their centres in one longitudinal axis. We will now show how to obtain the value of $BM$ in such a case.

Fig. 2, Plate XIII., represents any cross section of a vessel, such that in the vicinity of the water line, and throughout the whole of the angle of heel considered, the curvature is that of a circle described about the point $O$. We will first show how to obtain the moment of surface stability for a foot in length of such a ship, from which we will deduce the value of $BM$. In this figure, $WL$ and $W_1L_1$ are the upright and inclined load water lines, as before. In the act of heeling the wedge $WSW_1$ is taken from, and the equal wedge $LSL_1$ is added to the displacement. Now as only that portion of the cross section which is circular emerges from or is immersed in the water up to the extent of heel contemplated by us, we may neglect for the present all that portion of the displacement in the foot of length which is not contained within the cylindrical surface $WW_1PQLL_1$, and consider the operation of heeling as equivalent to that of substituting the segment $W_1QL_1$ for the equal segment $WPL$. Hence the required moment of surface stability is equal to the difference between the moments of the equal segments $WPL$ and $W_1QL_1$, relatively to the longitudinal plane passing through $OQ$, the latter being perpendicular to the inclined water line. But the moment of the segment $W_1QL_1$ about that plane is zero, and the moment of the segment $WPL$ is

$$\frac{2}{3}(AW)^3 \times \sin POQ, \quad\quad\quad\quad (3)$$

which result is expressed thus:—

I. *The moment of surface stability per foot of length is equal to two-thirds the cube of the half-breadth multiplied by the sine of the angle of heel.*

From this we proceed to determine the surface stability of the whole vessel by remembering that it is composed of the surface stabilities of all the vertical layers, such as we have been considering. By the application of Simpson's Rule we have the following:—

II. *Divide the length of the load water line into a convenient number of intervals, and measure the half-breadths; treat the cubes of those half-breadths as if they were the ordinates of a new curve, two-thirds the area of that curve multiplied by the sine of the angle of heel will give the surface stability.*

Let $A$ = area of curve so obtained,
,, $\theta$ = angle of heel,
then $\frac{2}{3} A \sin \theta$ = moment of surface stability.
But $D \times BM \sin \theta$ = moment of surface stability,
$\therefore \frac{2}{3} A \sin \theta = D \times BM \sin \theta$,
and $BM = \frac{\frac{2}{3}A}{D}$,

which result is expressed thus:—

III. *Two-thirds of the area of the above curve, divided by* the volume of displacement, is equal to the height of the fixed transverse metacentre above the centre of buoyancy.

In Algebraical language,

$$BM = \frac{\frac{2}{3} \int y^3 dx}{D}.$$

The moments computed by I. and II. are expressed in cubic feet of sea water, at a leverage of one foot; divided by 35 they are reduced to foot-tons.

Now, it happens that two-thirds of the area, whose ordinates are the cubes of the ordinates of the half water plane, is the *geometrical moment of inertia*\* of that water plane about its middle line; hence Rule III. may be expressed thus:—

IV. *Divide the moment of inertia of the load water plane by the volume of the displacement, the quotient will be the height of the fixed tranverse metacentre above the centre of buoyancy.*

**64. To obtain the Position of Transverse Metacentre.**—In the preceding investigation the ship has been assumed to have circular transverse sections throughout the extent of the inclination, and from this an expression has been found for the height of the fixed transverse metacentre.

We now purpose showing that the same expressions and rules are also true for the height of the actual transverse metacentre above the centre of buoyancy, the conditions in this case being, of course, an ordinary form of vessel and an indefinitely small angle of heel.

In this case, the line denoted by the point $S$ (fig. 1, Plate XIII.) continually approaches the longitudinal axis $A$ of the upright water plane. The transverse sections $WSW_1$ and $LSL_1$ of the wedges of emersion and immersion continually approach closer and closer to an equality with a triangle whose base is $AW$; whose height is $AW$, multiplied by the sine of the angle of inclination, and consequently whose area is equal to $\frac{AW^2}{2}$, multiplied by that sine. The sum of the moments of these sections approximate closer and closer to double the moment of the said triangle, relatively to the

\* See Art. 54.

vertical plane through $MO_1$; which double moment is equal to the area of the triangle, multiplied by $\frac{2}{3} AW$, or equal to $\frac{2}{3} AW^3$, multiplied by the sine of the angle of heel, which is the expression (3) on page 90. From this we obtain Rules II. and III. (Art. 63), in the manner already stated, only that in Rule III. the word "fixed" may be omitted, as the expression is now seen to be true for the height of the true metacentre above the centre of buoyancy.

The result just obtained being true for a vessel of any form at an indefinitely small angle of heel, we will now consider in which direction error occurs when the height of metacentre so found is used as the height of the shifting metacentre for any finite inclination of inconsiderable amplitude. If the convexity of the curvature of the cross sections in the vicinity of the load water line is greater than that giving a fixed metacentre, as shown by $ab$, fig. 2, Plate XIII., the actual wedges of immersion and emersion will be smaller than the assumed wedges, and therefore the moment of surface stability as expressed by Rule II., Art. 63, is less than the assumed moment; consequently, the actual position of the shifting metacentre is below the approximate position. This error is on the unsafe side, and will not occur in a skilfully designed vessel.

On the contrary, if the convexity is flatter (as shown by $a_1 b_1$, fig. 2, Plate XIII.) the actual wedges are larger than the assumed wedges, and therefore the actual moment of surface stability is greater than the assumed moment, thus causing the true position of the shifting metacentre to be above the approximate position. This error is on the safe side, and usually occurs in a well designed vessel.

**65. Metacentric Surface Stability.**—When the surface stability is calculated by means of the height of metacentre above centre of buoyancy, it is useful merely as affording a comparison of the surface stability of the ship with others of the same type whose qualities are known. For being true only for an infinitely small inclination, or at the furthest to the extent of 10 or 15 degrees, it furnishes us with no idea of the surface stability of the ship beyond that range, which stability, by reason of singularity in the vessel's form, may soon attain a maximum, and rapidly disappear. The result obtained by its use is termed the *initial surface stability*, and the mode of obtaining it is termed the *metacentric method*.

**66. Transverse Metacentre Calculation Explained.**—We will now show how the result of the preceding investigation is applied in actual practice to obtain the height of metacentre above centre of buoyancy. Referring to the specimen calculation shown in Table I.: upon the right hand side of the sheet will be seen a number of columns of figures headed "**Metacentres.**" The first three columns merely repeat the *numbers of ordinates, Simpson's multipliers,* and *the ordinates of the load water line,* which are found in the adjacent calculation of displacement. The next two columns have the word "**Transverse**," at their head, and it is to these we now wish to call attention. The first of these contains the cubes of the ordinates of the water line, and it may here be remarked that these cubes can be readily found by reference to Barlow's Tables, which, together with Chambers' Logarithms, should be in the possession of every naval architect. The next column, headed "**Functions of Cubes,**" are the products of the cubes of the ordinates and their respective Simpson's multipliers, these being obtained in order that we may determine the area of the curve whose ordinates are the cubes of the ordinates of the load water line. The sum of these functions multiplied by $\frac{14\cdot1}{3} = 4\cdot7$, or one-third the common interval between the ordinates, gives $257954\cdot8$, which is the area of the curve just referred to. This area being again multiplied by $\frac{2}{3}$ gives the moment of inertia of the load water plane, which, being divided by the total displacement, expressed in cubic feet, results in $7\cdot92$ feet, the height of the transverse metacentre above the centre of buoyancy.

The centre of buoyancy having been already found to be $3\cdot95$ feet below the load water line, therefore the transverse metacentre is $7\cdot92$ ft. $- 3\cdot95$ ft. $= 3\cdot97$ ft. above the load water line. This quantity, if multiplied by 620 tons—the displacement—and again by the sine of the angle of heel, will give the *metacentric surface stability* at that angle of inclination. In a vessel of ordinary form, this will practically agree with the true surface stability, as calculated in the manner to be explained hereafter, if the angle is within about 15 degrees.

**67. More Exact Calculations of Surface Stability.**—The method of calculating the surface stability by means of the height of metacentre above centre of buoyancy is due to Boguer, and was considered for some considerable time to be sufficient for the purpose of the Naval Architect. Attwood, however, showed that the method was incorrect for large inclinations, and gave a formula for determining the surface stability at all angles, which formula has been put into a convenient form for calculation by Mr. F. K. Barnes, and still remains in use.

By the method we are now about to explain, the value $V \times HK$ (i.e., the moment of the wedges of immersion and emersion about the plane represented by the line $MB_1$) is calculated, and then, if required, the length of $BM$ at that angle may be readily found by dividing the result by the product of the displacement and the sine of the angle of heel. The rule may be stated thus:—*Divide the moment of the wedges of immersion and emersion by the displacement and the sine of the angle of heel, the quotient will be the height of the shifting metacentre above the centre of buoyancy.*

It will thus be seen that $D \times BN$ represents the surface statical stability in both the metacentric and Attwood's methods, the difference between them being that whereas in the former $M$ is considered a fixed point, by the latter method the point $M$ varies with every different inclination, its position being governed by the moment of the wedges.

$$\text{Since } D \times BN = V \times HK$$
$$\therefore BN = \frac{V \times HK}{D}.$$

$BN$ is styled the *lever of surface statical stability;* being the arm of the righting couple at the inclination in question, the position of the centre of gravity being assumed to coincide with $B$ (see Art. 62).

**68. Intersections of Water Planes.**—In fig. 1, Plate XIII. the intersection $S$ of the inclined with the upright load water planes is shown on the right of the middle line plane represented by the line $BM$, or towards the immersed side of the vessel. That is the direction in which it is found in ordinary well-formed ships at moderate angles of heel. The determination of the exact position of the axis, represented by $S$, is evidently a work of some difficulty, as it must be so situated on the line $WL$ that the volume of the wedge $WSW_1$ shall be equal to that of the wedge $LSL_1$; this being so in order that the displacement may remain unaltered.

In practice, especially when calculating the stability at a great many different angles of heel, it is not found desirable to obtain any trial position, such as $s$ in fig. 1, Plate XIV., but to draw all the lines representing the inclined water planes through the point $A$, the necessary corrections being made in the calculation. Should it, however, be desired to determine the position of $s$, an approximate position for the intersection is first chosen (see fig. 1, Plate XIV.), the general practice being to take $As = \cdot 02$ foot × degrees in angle of heel. A line $w_1 s l_1$ is then drawn through that point, at the required inclination; this will cut off a pair of trial wedges $Wsw_1$ and $l_1 s L$, whose contents, it may be remarked, have to be calculated as a necessary part of the process in determining the statical surface stability. (See preceding Art.) If the volumes of these wedges prove to be unequal, then a correction must be made as follows:—

If the trial wedge of immersion is the greater, then the assumed position of $w_1 s l_1$ is too high.

If the trial wedge of emersion is the greater, then the assumed position is too low.

The perpendicular distance $st$ of the corrected position from the assumed position is

$$st = \frac{\text{Difference of volumes of wedges}}{\text{Area of inclined water section}}.$$

The denominator of this fraction is easily found when calculating the moment of the wedges, as will be seen presently.

If $S$ is the true position of the intersection,

$$Ss = \frac{st}{\sin \text{angle of heel}}.$$

**69. Method of Measurement.**—Fig. 2, Plate XIV., shows the body plan of a vessel, $WL$ being the load water line in the upright position; it is required to find the moment of surface stability when the vessel is inclined through an angle $LS_1L_1$, so that $W_1L_1$ is then the load water line. We will suppose the trial distance of the point of intersection of the water line to be already set off from $A$, on each side, at $S_1$ and $S_2$, then the intersections of $S_1L$ and $S_1L_1$ with the vertical sections give the ordinates of the bounding planes of the fore body portion of the wedge of immersion (measuring from $S_1$), and the intersections of $S_2W$ and $S_2W_1$ with the vertical sections give the ordinates of the after body portion of the same wedge (measuring from $S_2$). Similarly, the intersections of $S_2L$ and $S_2L_1$ give the ordinates of the fore body portion of the wedge of emersion (measuring from $S_2$), and those of $S_1W$ and $S_1W_1$ those of the after body portion of that wedge (measuring from $S_1$). The trace $w_1l_1$ of an intermediate sectional plane, bisecting the angle $LS_1L_1$ is shown; angles not exceeding 20 degrees will not usually require more than one such intermediate section. In the next chapter we shall consider a case where a considerable number of intermediate sectional planes are required.

We have thus six sets of ordinates to be measured, viz., three to each wedge. Upon each of these six sets the following operations are performed. (See Arts. 47 to 51.)

1. Treat their half squares as the ordinates of a new curve, and find its area by Simpson's First Rule. Let the results of this operation be termed, $A_1$, $A_2$, $A_3$, for the wedge of immersion, and $A_4$, $A_5$, $A_6$, for the wedge of emersion. Then,

Volume of wedge of immersion $= (A_1 + 4A_2 + A_3) \times \dfrac{\text{angular interval}}{3}$

Volume of wedge of emersion $= (A_4 + 4A_5 + A_6) \times \dfrac{\text{angular interval}}{3}$

If these volumes are unequal, their difference, divided by the area of the inclined water plane, gives the thickness $st$ (fig. 1, Plate XIV.) of the layer between the assumed and the true positions of the inclined water plane. The area of the inclined water plane is found by the method stated in Arts. 15 and 41; observing, however, that the plane consists in general of two unequal portions, one on each side of the longitudinal axis.

2. Multiply each of the before-mentioned half squares by the longitudinal distance of the ordinate from the foremost

cross section; treat the products as the ordinates of a new curve, and find its area. Let the results of this operation be termed $B_1$, $B_2$, $B_3$ for the wedge of immersion, and $B_4$, $B_5$, $B_6$ for the wedge of emersion. Then the moments relatively to the foremost cross section—

Of the wedge of immersion $= (B_1 + 4B_2 + B_3) \times \dfrac{\text{angular interval}}{3}$

Of the wedge of emersion $= (B_4 + 4B_5 + B_6) \times \dfrac{\text{angular interval}}{3}$.

The work will be much simplified if moments are taken about the midship cross section, treating the area on one side (say forward) as positive, and the other as negative; in this case $B_1$, $B_2$, etc., will each be the difference between two areas, taking care to retain the proper Algebraical sign. (See Art. 25).

With regard to the use of these results, when obtained, it is only necessary at present to state that if the moments of these wedges about any chosen section are unlike, it shows that their centres of gravity are not in the same cross section, and therefore that the centre of buoyancy of the ship is moved forward or aft, as the case may be, when the ship is inclined. Hence in this case transverse heeling is necessarily accompanied with longitudinal heeling also, or, in other words, with an alteration of trim.

3. Treat the third part of the cubes of the ordinates as the ordinates of a new curve, and find its area. Let the results of this operation be termed $C_1$, $C_2$, $C_3$, for the wedge of immersion, and $C_4$, $C_5$, $C_6$ for the wedge of emersion. Then the moment of surface statical stability

$$= \{C_3 + C_6 + 4(C_2 + C_5) \cos \tfrac{1}{2} \text{ angle of heel}$$
$$+ (C_1 + C_4) \cos \text{ angle of heel}\} \times \dfrac{\text{angular interval}}{3}.$$

**70. Specimen Calculation.**—Table II. contains a calculation of the moment of surface stability of a ship when inclined at an angle of 16 degrees; also of the pitching moment due to that inclination. Plate XV. shows the body plan of the same ship, the vertical sections of which are 29·5 feet apart, and the whole displacement 5976 tons. It will be seen that half intervals are taken right forward and aft, for which the proper multipliers are shown, both according to Simpson's Rule and as required for leverage. In this example no trial position of the inclined water plane has been found, but it is drawn so as to intersect the upright water plane at the middle line of the latter; this being the practice usually adopted as it is simpler, besides which equally correct results can be obtained when the "correction for the layer" is made. This "layer," it will be remembered, is the volume included between the inclined water plane, as drawn in the figure, and the plane in its correct position.

The angle of inclination being small, only one intermediate plane is drawn, so that the angles of the wedges are bisected. We have thus the *upright, intermediate,* and *inclined* water planes. The calculations referring to each of these is given under its respective heading, each calculation being termed a "*preliminary table;*" the fourth set of calculations, which combines the results obtained in the *preliminary tables,* and, by the application of the several rules, determines the moment of surface stability, etc., is termed a "*combination table.*"

Referring to the preliminary table for the "upright water plane," it will be seen that the several values $A_1, B_1, C_1, A_4, B_4, C_4$, mentioned in the preceding Article, may be at once determined by multiplying the sums of the "functions of squares," and of the "longitudinal moments" by $\frac{1}{2}$ and then by $\frac{1}{3}$ the common longitudinal interval, also the sums of the "functions of cubes" by $\frac{1}{3}$, and then by $\frac{1}{3}$ the longitudinal interval. Similarly, the values of $A_2, B_2, C_2, A_5, B_5, C_5$, may be found from the preliminary table for the "intermediate water plane," and those of $A_3, B_3, C_3, A_6, B_6, C_6$, from the preliminary table for the "inclined water plane." In practice, these multiplications are, however, performed afterwards on the "combination table." In consequence of the intersections of the planes being taken at the middle line of the upright water plane, the values of $A_1$ and $A_4$, $B_1$ and $B_4$, $C_1$ and $C_4$ are severally equal.

It is unnecessary to explain the several columns of figures in the preliminary tables, as they at once follow from the directions given in the preceding Article. Proceeding then to the combination table, we will notice first the calculation for the volumes of the wedges, which, if found unequal, will render a corresponding correction necessary in the calculation for the moment of surface stability. The calculation shown for the difference of these volumes is evidently equivalent to the expression

$$\frac{\text{Angular interval}}{3} \left\{ (A_1 + 4A_2 + A_3) - (A_4 + 4A_5 + A_6) \right\}$$

The result is found in this case to be 1736 cubic feet.

At the bottom of the combination table will be found a calculation for the true volume of a wedge, *i.e.*, approximately, half the sum of the two unequal wedges, or

$$\frac{\text{Angular interval}}{6} (A_1 + 4A_2 + A_3 + A_4 + 4A_5 + A_6).$$

This is found to be 22,358 cubic feet, or 639 tons.

In order to determine the correction which must be made in computing the moment of surface stability, in consequence of the inclined water plane being drawn above its true position (thus producing unequal wedges, as just shown), it is necessary that we should know the distance of the centre of gravity of the "layer" from the axis. It will be readily seen that the distance of the centre of gravity of the inclined water plane, as drawn from the point $A$, is also, approximately, the distance of the centre of gravity of the layer from that point; we will therefore now call attention to the calculation on the combination table for the centre of gravity of the inclined water plane. We have, first, the functions of the ordinates of that plane copied from the preliminary table, added together and multiplied by one-third the longitudinal interval, thus giving the area of the inclined plane. Next, the difference of the sums of the functions of squares of the ordinates on the two sides, divided by two, gives the function of the resultant moment of the inclined plane about the axis through $A$, and this, when multiplied by one-third the common interval, gives the total resultant moment. Consequently, we have this moment divided by the area, giving ·887 ft., which is a close approximation to the distance of the centre of gravity of the layer from the axis. The volume of the layer, being the excess of one wedge over the other, is 1736 cubic feet; hence the correction for surface statical stability, rendered necessary by drawing the inclined water plane through $A$, as shown in Plate XV., is $1736 \times \cdot 887 = 1540$ cubic feet, at a leverage of one foot. The use made of this result will be seen presently.

We will now consider the main calculation, viz., that for the surface statical stability at 16 degrees. Referring to that part of the combination table, it will be at once seen that the operations performed are such as are indicated by the expression

$$\left\{ C_3 + C_6 + 4\,(C_2 + C_5) \cos 8° + (C_1 + C_4) \cos 16° \right\} \frac{16°}{3}.$$

It will be observed that the correction for the layer is deducted from the result obtained by using the above expression. The rule for making this correction is as follows:—If the centre of gravity of the layer lies towards that side for which the assumed wedge is the greater, then deduct the correction; if it lies towards the opposite side, add the correction.

The displacement of the vessel in this case is equal to 209,156 cubic feet; hence, after making the correction, the remainder is divided by that number, which gives 3·247 feet, the value of $BN$ (fig. 1, Plate XIII.) when $BMB_1$ is 16 degrees. This results from the formula stated at Art. 62:

$$D \times BN = V \times HK$$
$$BN = \frac{V \times HK}{D}$$

$V \times HK$ being equal to 679,284 cubic feet, at a leverage of one foot, and $D$ being equal to 209,156 cubic feet.

$$\text{Since } BM \sin BMB_1 = BN$$
$$\therefore BM = \frac{BN}{\sin BMB_1} = \frac{3\cdot 247}{\sin 16°} = \frac{3\cdot 247}{\cdot 2756}$$
$$BM = 11\cdot 78,$$

a value which is very nearly the same as would be obtained by the method given in Rule II., Art. 63, the angle, viz., 16 degrees, being not very large.

The actual moment of surface stability at this angle is

$$D \times BN \text{ or } 5976 \text{ tons} \times 3\cdot 247 \text{ feet} = 19{,}404 \text{ foot-tons.}$$

We will now examine the last result found in the combination table, viz., the longitudinal positions of the centres of gravity of the wedges. Here again the headings of the several columns will be readily seen to be in accordance with the expression given in the last Article for the moments of the wedges about the foremost vertical section, viz., for the wedge of immersion—

$$(B_1 + 4B_2 + B_3) \times \frac{16°}{3}$$

and for the wedge of emersion—

$$(B_4 + 4B_5 + B_6) \times \frac{16°}{3}.$$

It will be observed, however, that the factor $\frac{16°}{3}$ is not employed; as it is, together with $\frac{\text{longitudinal interval}}{3}$, required in determining the volumes of the wedges; and, since the moment must be divided by the volume, to determine the centre of gravity, the labour of multiplying would be superfluous. (See calculation for centre of buoyancy, Table I.) Hence the sum of the products of longitudinal moments, divided by the sum of the products of the functions of squares, gives a quantity which, when multiplied by the common longitudinal interval, results in the distance of the centre of gravity of the wedge from the foremost cross section. This operation being performed for each of the wedges, gives a result showing that the centre of gravity of the wedge of immersion is 4·7 feet abaft that of emersion.

From this it is seen that heeling the ship to 16 degrees causes the centre of buoyancy of a volume of the displacement equal to that of one of the wedges to travel aft 4·7 feet, thus depressing the bow and raising the stern. The actual moment producing this effect is evidently the displacement of a wedge multiplied by 4·7 feet. We have calculated the volumes of the two assumed wedges at the bottom of the combination table, and divided their sum by two, thus obtaining a close approximation to that of one of the actual equal wedges—the result is 639 tons.

Hence, $639 \times 4·7 = 3003$ foot-tons, the pitching moment produced by heeling the ship traversely through 16 degrees.

**71. Dynamical Stability.**—An important advantage resulting from the exact method of calculating stability, *i.e.*, by determining the actual volume of the transferred wedge at any given angle, is seen in the fact that we are thereby enabled to calculate the *dynamical stability* at that angle. By *dynamical stability* is meant the mechanical work which is performed in forcing a vessel to heel over to a given angle. That work is performed partly in raising the vessel's centre of gravity and partly in depressing her centre of buoyancy. The latter of these effects is evidently due to the vessel's form, and is, therefore, styled *dynamical surface stability;* it is this portion of the mechanical work that we have to consider in the present chapter.

72. **Dynamical Surface Stability.**—The depression of the centre of buoyancy can be conveniently measured from the surface of the water, which evidently remains in a constant position however the vessel may be inclined. Referring to fig. 1, Plate XVI., it will be seen that the depression of the centre of buoyancy is $A_1B_1 - AB$. Suppose the inclined water plane to pass through the point $A$, as in Plate XV., in that case the depression is $A_2B_1 - AB$, and therefore the true depression $A_1B_1 - AB$ is equal to

$$A_2B_1 - AB - A_2A_1$$
$$= A_2N + NB_1 - AB - A_2A_1$$
$$= NB_1 - AB(1 - \cos BMB_1) - A_2A_1$$
$$= NB_1 - AB \text{ versin } BMB_1 - A_2A_1.$$

But the dynamical surface stability is $D(A_1B_1 - AB)$, which is thus equal to $D(NB_1 - AB \text{ versin } BMB_1 - A_2A_1)$, in which expression the value of $D(NB_1 - A_2A_1)$ remains to be determined.

Now $D \times NB_1$ is equal to the difference in the moments, relative to the inclined water plane, of the displacement in its original shape $WPL$, and in its new shape $W_1PL_1$; which difference is equal to the arithmetical sum of the moments of the wedges of immersion and emersion relatively to the inclined water plane $W_1L_1$. If $E$ and $I$ are the centres of buoyancy of the wedges, and $V$ the volume of one of them, then

$$D \times NB_1 = V(EH + IK).$$

We will now proceed to show how the value of the right hand side of this equation is calculated for any specific case, so that by dividing the result by $D$ the value of $NB_1$ can be obtained.

DYNAMICAL SURFACE STABILITY.

In the third case considered in Arts. 50 and 51, it was shown how the moment of a wedge about one of its longitudinal radiating planes may be determined; the Algebraical expression for the same being

$$\int\int \frac{r^3}{3} \sin\theta \, dx \, d\theta.$$

By referring to Art. 69, and fig. 2, Plate XIV., it will be seen that this expression, when put into the necessary form for the application of Simpson's Rule—using the nomenclature there explained—is equal to

$$\left\{ 4(C_2 + C_5) \sin \tfrac{1}{2} \text{ angle of heel} + (C_1 + C_4) \sin \text{ angle of heel} \right\} \times \frac{\text{angular interval}}{3}$$

**73. Specimen Calculation.**—On Table II. will be found a specimen calculation of the dynamical surface stability at an inclination of 16° of the ship whose statical surface stability at that angle has already been calculated. As will be seen, the immediate purpose of this calculation is to find the values of $NB_1$ and $A_1A_2$ (fig. 1, Plate XVI). The only difference between this calculation and that for statical surface stability is in substituting the sines for the cosines of the inclination in the fifth column, and in obtaining the value of $A_1A_2$, which is also required in order to make the correction for the layer. With regard to this correction, it will be seen that we have to find the moment of the layer about the inclined water plane; to do which, we must know its volume and the distance of its centre of gravity from the aforesaid plane. The volume (1827·8 cubic feet) has already been found, and the distance of its centre of gravity may be safely taken at one-half its thickness, or $\frac{A_1A_2}{2}$. The thickness $A_1A_2$ is obtained by dividing the volume of the wedge by the area of the inclined water plane (14,590·7 square feet), the result giving ·12 feet. Hence, $A_1A_2$ is equal to ·12 feet, and the correction is ·06 × 1827·8 = 109·7 cubic feet, lifted one foot. This correction is deducted in every case. Having made the deduction, and divided by the displacement in cubic feet, we obtain the value of $NB_1$ = ·45. The value of $AB$ is obtained from the ordinary displacement sheet; in the present case it is 8·2 feet. $A_1 A_2$ has been found to be ·12 feet, and versin 16 degrees is ·0387.

Hence, $D(NB_1 - AB \text{ versin } 16° - A_1 A_2)$
$= 5976 (·45 - ·317 - ·12)$
$= 5976 \times ·02 = 119·5$ foot-tons of mechanical work,

which is the dynamical surface stability or the work performed, due to the vessel's form, in forcing her over to an inclination of 16 degrees.

As will be seen hereafter, the centre of gravity is raised ·1 foot, thus making the whole mechanical work $5976 \times ·12 = 717$ foot-tons, which is the *dynamical stability*. We may here remark that when the *dynamical stability* is calculated, and not the *dynamical surface stability*, the depression of $B$ and the elevation of the centre of gravity are not measured from the surface of the water, but the increase in the distance of the centre of gravity from $B_1$ over that from $B$ is calculated in one operation. This will be explained more fully in the next chapter.

**74. Surface of Flotation.**—Suppose a vessel to be continually inclined in every possible direction between a direct transverse and a direct longitudinal inclination, so that successive load water planes or *planes of flotation* make indefinitely small angles with each other when drawn upon the vessel's body and sheer plans, and suppose a curved surface to touch all these planes of flotation, so as to be an *envelope* of the planes, then such a surface is called the *surface of flotation*.

Fig. 2, Plate XVI., represents the midship section of a vessel which, when upright, floats at the water line $WL$. Let $wl$, $w_1 l_1$, $W_1 L_1$, be successive water lines, the angles between them being indefinitely small, then the curve $AF$ which touches them will be a transverse vertical section of part of the surface of flotation. Similarly, if the consecutive water lines be drawn upon the sheer plan, a curve touching them will be the longitudinal middle line vertical section of the surface of flotation. Between these two extreme sections, any number of other sections of the same surface may be conceived.

**75. Centre of Flotation.**—*The point of contact of the surface of flotation with any water plane or plane of flotation is the centre of gravity of that plane.*

Let $w_1 l_1$ and $W_1 L_1$ (fig. 2, Plate XVI.) be a pair of planes of flotation indefinitely close to each other, *i.e.*, inclined to each other at an indefinitely small angle, so that their points of contact with the surface of flotation may be considered to coincide with each other at $F$. Hence the straight line of their intersection will be at such an indefinitely small distance from $F$ that it may be considered to traverse that point. Now, this pair of water planes will contain between them a pair of indefinitely thin wedges, viz., a wedge of emersion $w_1 F W_1$ and a wedge of immersion $l_1 F L_1$, and the volumes of these must necessarily be equal to each other. But the volume of either of these wedges is proportional to the moment of the bounding plane of flotation relatively to the line of intersection at $F$. (See Art. 49, foot-note.) Therefore these moments are equal to each other, and hence the line of intersection at $F$ passes through the centre of gravity of the water planes $W_1 L_1$. And since there may be an infinite number of planes of flotation between a direct longitudinal and a transverse heel, all of which planes make the same indefinitely small angle with the plane $w_1 l_1$; therefore there are an infinite number of lines of intersection, all of which contain the centre of gravity of the plane $W_1 L_1$. The point common to all these intersecting lines must be on the surface of flotation, and it is likewise the centre of gravity of the plane of flotation; which proves the proposition. This centre of gravity is termed the *centre of flotation*.

**76. Axis of Level Motion.**—When the vertical transverse section of the surface of flotation is a circle, the centre of that circle is in a line termed the *axis of level motion*. The axis itself is a horizontal line in the middle line longitudinal vertical plane, when the ship is upright, and is so situated that it is at the same height above the water surface when the ship has heeled to a certain angle as when she is upright.

**77. Curve of Buoyancy.**—This name is given to the curve containing all the positions of the centre of buoyancy which occur when a ship is continuously heeled in a transverse direction (see $BB_1$, fig. 2, Plate XVI). This does not take into consideration the effect produced by the change of trim which ships of ordinary form undergo when so inclined. It has, however, been found that in such cases the modifications in the positions of the centre of buoyancy, tending to remove it from a transverse plane, are not of sufficient practical importance to deserve consideration. The curve is evidently symmetrical with regard to the middle line $AP$ of the body, as shown by $B_1BB_2$, and is of an elliptical character. It is often termed the "*locus of centres of buoyancy*," and sometimes the "*metacentric involute*," for a reason which will be seen presently.

**78. Surface of Buoyancy.**—Supposing the ship inclined continually in every direction between a direct longitudinal and a transverse heel, then the surface containing all the different positions of the centre of buoyancy is termed the "*surface of buoyancy*," and sometimes the "*metacentric surface*." The curve of buoyancy $B_1BB_2$ (fig. 2, Plate XVI.) is a transverse vertical section of a portion of this surface.

**79. Metacentric.**—At Art. 61, it was stated that the term *metacentre* is only strictly applicable to the point $M$ when the angle of inclination from the upright position is indefinitely small. In the same way, if the ship is floating at any finite angle of inclination with regard to the upright position, and then be further inclined through an indefinitely small angle, the point where the verticals, through the centre of buoyancy, in these conditions, intersect, will be in a curve termed the "*metacentric*." In other words, while the *metacentre* is the centre of curvature, at the origin, of the locus of centres of buoyancy, *i.e.*, at the point where it cuts the vertical through the centre of buoyancy when the ship is upright, the *metacentric* is the locus of the centres of curvature corresponding to the different points in the locus of the centres of buoyancy as the ship is inclined. Hence the *metacentric* is the locus of the metacentres, the latter term being applied to the centres of curvature of the locus of centres of buoyancy in every condition of the ship, including the upright one. This is not a strictly accurate use of the term, as will be seen by our previous definition, but it has gradually crept into use, and it is now very common to speak of the *metacentric* as the "locus of metacentres." In the following pages, we shall always refer to it as the *metacentric*.

In order to determine the form of this curve, or the position of the point in it equivalent to any finite angle of heel, two operations are necessary. In the first place, we have to find the height of this point above the centre of buoyancy at that inclination, that is, the length of the radius of curvature at that inclination; and in the second place, we have to find the position of the centre of buoyancy, that is, the point in the curve of buoyancy corresponding to the given inclination.

The length of the radius of curvature is found in a similar manner to that in which the height of metacentre above the centre of buoyancy in the upright position is obtained; only, in this case, the moment of inertia of two unequal planes must be calculated, instead of one symmetrically divided plane, as before. (See Arts. 63 and 64, also Table I.) The position of the inclined water plane is found in the manner described at Art. 68 and Table II. The displacement is, of course, constant.

To obtain the position of the centre of buoyancy, we have merely to remember that as the ship is inclined, the centre of buoyancy becomes shifted in the same direction; and the line joining it with the centre of buoyancy in the upright position is parallel to the line joining the centres of the immersed and emerged wedges. Further, $BB_1$ (fig. 1, Plate XIII.) is equal to $\frac{BN}{\cos\theta}$ where $\theta$ is the angle of inclination; and the mode of determining the value of $BN$ for any angle is stated at Art. 70. Hence, having the height of a point in the metacentric measured from the corresponding centre of buoyancy, and having the position of the latter known, the whole metacentric can be drawn, by a repetition of the preceding processes, for as many other angles of inclination as may be found necessary to obtain a complete and fair curve.

From the preceding it will be seen that the metacentric is the evolute of the curve of buoyancy, and, consequently, the latter is the metacentric involute. (See Art. 77.)

In fig. 2, Plate XVI., $B_2BB_1$ is the curve of buoyancy, $B$ being the centre of buoyancy in the upright condition, $B_1$ the centre of buoyancy corresponding to the inclined water plane $W_1L_1$, while $B_2$ is the point corresponding to the same inclination in the opposite direction, the curve being thus symmetrical about $AP$. $M_1MM_2$ is the metacentric, $M$ being the true metacentre, and $M_1$ and $M_2$ the centres of curvature of the curve of buoyancy at the points $B_1$ and $B_2$, respectively. The curve $B_2BB_1$ is seen to be of an elliptical character, while the metacentric $M_1MM_2$ is a cusp of which $MP$ is a tangent.*

**80. Longitudinal Metacentre.**—A definition of the *longitudinal metacentre* was given in Art. 60, at the commencement of this chapter. The method of obtaining this point is based upon the same principles as those by which we have found the position of the transverse metacentre. There are, however, certain differences in the two cases, due to the form of ships, which cause modifications in the actual calculations; so that it is necessary we should examine the longitudinal metacentre separately.

The first point of difference that we notice is, that whereas the transverse curve of flotation is cut symmetrically by the longitudinal vertical middle line plane of the ship, so that we have no occasion to determine the transverse position of the centre of flotation;† in the case now under consideration, owing to the two ends of the ship being unlike, we have no means of determining that point without actual calculation.

The next point of difference is seen in the fact that, as we still continue to use the ordinates of the load water plane, in order to determine its moment of inertia, and as that moment of inertia must be calculated about a transverse axis through the centre of flotation, we must adopt a different arithmetical process in calculating it, as the ordinates are now parallel instead of perpendicular to the axis.

Also, that as we do not know where the centre of flotation is until it is calculated, and as it is found convenient to make the calculation simultaneously with that for the moment of inertia, it is usual to first calculate the latter about an assumed axis (generally the middle ordinate), and then transfer the moment of inertia to the centre of flotation. (See Art. 75.)

---

\* For further details regarding the *metacentric* and the *curve of buoyancy*, the student is referred to an interesting paper on the subject by Messrs. White and John, to be found in Vol. XII. of the *Transactions of the Institution of Naval Architects*.

† In Art. 75, it was shown that every small angular displacement of a ship from the upright position takes place about an axis traversing the centre of flotation.

The moment of inertia of a plane figure relatively to one of its ordinates is calculated as follows:—

*Multiply each ordinate by its proper multiplier, according to Simpson's Rule; then multiply each of the products by the square of the number of whole intervals that the ordinate in question is distant from the ordinate taken as an axis of moments; multiply the Algebraical sum of these products by one-third of the cube of a whole interval: the product will be the moment of inertia required.*

If the centre of flotation is previously known, then the moment of inertia should be calculated about an axis, parallel to the ordinates, through that point; but if its position is not known, the middle ordinate is a convenient axis about which to calculate. Having obtained the moment of inertia about that axis, subtract from it the product of the area of the water plane into the square of the distance of the centre of flotation (as found in the course of the calculation) from the chosen axis; the remainder will be the required moment of inertia about the centre of flotation, and this being divided by the displacement in cubic feet, will give the height of the longitudinal metacentre above the centre of buoyancy.

**81. Longitudinal Metacentre Calculation Explained.**— On Table I., under the heading "Metacentres" and "Longitudinal," will be seen a calculation of the longitudinal metacentre which we will now explain.

The column headed "functions of ordinates," contains the products of the ordinates of the load water plane, and the respective Simpson's multipliers. The next column contains the several multipliers for moments, according to the positions of the respective ordinates, with regard to No. 6, about which the moment of inertia is calculated. It will be remembered that we must use the squares of these distances, in order to get the functions for moment of inertia; but it is found convenient to use these several multipliers twice instead of their squares once, as by so doing we have in the third column a series of functions for moments by which we can obtain the centre of gravity of the load water plane, i.e., the centre of flotation, to which point the moment of inertia has afterwards to be transferred. At the foot of the third column will be seen the calculation for the centre of gravity of the load water plane, which is found to be 3·5 feet abaft No. 6 ordinate, in this case. An explanation of this work is given in Art. 25.

In the fifth column are ranged the several functions for moment of inertia about No. 6 ordinate, and their sum is given at the foot. As will be seen, this is multiplied in three operations by one-third the cube of the longitudinal interval, according to the rule. The half area of the load water plane is then multiplied by $3·5^2$, and the result being deducted from that previously obtained, gives the moment of inertia of the half plane about the centre of flotation, which is then multiplied by 2 for the whole moment of inertia. Dividing by 35, we have the result in foot-tons, and then dividing by the displacement expressed in tons we obtain 181·71 ft., the height of the longitudinal metacentre above the centre of buoyancy. The latter being already found to be at 3·95 ft. below the load water line, the difference between 181·71 ft. and 3·95 ft. is 177·76 ft., the height of the longitudinal metacentre above the load water line.

**82. Longitudinal Metacentric Surface Stability.**—This is rarely obtained, being of little use to the naval designer. As, however, it shows that portion of the longitudinal stability of the vessel at a small inclination, which is due to her form, it is deserving of a passing notice. The same considerations apply in this case as were dwelt upon when discussing transverse metacentric surface stability. If the angle of inclination, that is, the *pitch* or *scend* be very small, say about 1 or 2 degrees, then calling the displacement $D$, the angle of pitch $\theta$, and $BM$ the height of longitudinal metacentre above centre buoyancy, the moment of longitudinal metacentric surface stability at that angle is

$$D \times BM \sin \theta \quad \ldots \ldots \ldots \ldots \ldots \ldots (I)$$

If the centre of gravity of the vessel coincides with the point $B$, the above is the *whole moment* of longitudinal metacentric stability at that angle; ordinarily, a deduction has to be made from expression (I) for the actual longitudinal stability; but this will be considered in the next chapter.

As the longitudinal inclinations of a ship are usually very small, compared with the transverse, and therefore of far less importance when considering her safety or efficient working, it is not customary to calculate the longitudinal stability by any other than the metacentric method; so that when it is desired to know the effect on the trim which is due to adding or shifting weights, and so altering the form of the immersed body of the ship, it is usual to determine the height of the longitudinal metacentre in the condition the ship is at the time of the change, and use that result in making the calculation. Should the change of immersion or trim be considerable, so as to alter the height of the longitudinal metacentre, then the height of the latter, when the ship is at the new draught of water, is used. This subject will be considered more fully in the next chapter.

**83. Comparative Surface Stability of different Vessels.**—The moments of the surface stabilities of vessels having load water planes of similar form, but of different size (*i.e.*, when it only requires an alteration in the scale of the drawing to make the load water planes identical), are proportional *to their lengths and the cubes of their breadths*. This follows from the considerations in the former portions of this chapter.

Again, since the displacements of the vessels are proportional *to their lengths, breadths and mean draughts of water*, therefore the heights of their metacentres above their centres of buoyancy are proportional *to the squares of the breadths divided by the mean draughts of water*.

# PART II.

## CALCULATIONS RELATING TO THE WEIGHTS AND CENTRES OF GRAVITY OF SHIPS.

### CHAPTER III.

#### STABILITY AND TRIM.

*Centre of Gravity—Metacentric Statical Stability—Exact Calculations of Statical and Dynamical Stability—To find the Centre of Gravity by Experiment—Specimen Calculation—Alteration of Trim by Shifting Weights—Moment to alter Trim one inch—Alteration of Trim by adding a Weight—When Weight is inconsiderable—When considerable—Effect on Trim by admission of Water in different ways—Effect on Stability by moving a Weight—By adding or removing a Weight—By admitting Water in different ways.*

**84. General Considerations.**—Hitherto we have discussed the statical and dynamical qualities of a vessel as affected by her form, without considering the effects due to the centre of gravity of the weight of the vessel and her contents not being situated at the centre of buoyancy; hence our investigations have been chiefly of a geometrical character. In this division of the subject, we purpose considering the modifications of the preceding results due to the floating body, being composed of a great number of parts, having different specific gravities, and irregularly disposed within the shell whose form invests it with the qualities we have already examined.

We will commence by assuming, for the present, that the vessel has a certain known weight, and that the position of the centre of gravity of that weight is known. This weight is the sum total of the weights of all the items composing the hull and equipment of the vessel; and its centre of gravity is that of all these weights, each acting at its own centre of gravity wherever it is situated. The manner of calculating the total weight and determining the position of its centre of gravity will be shown in the next chapter.

**85. Centre of Gravity.**—It was stated in Art. 4, that a body floating in a liquid, in a state of equilibrium, displaces a volume of the liquid whose weight is exactly equal to that of the body. We will now show that not only is this so, but that the centre of gravity of the floating body must be in the same vertical line as the centre of gravity (*i.e.*, centre of buoyancy) of the liquid displaced; and if the body is at any time floating in such a position that these conditions are not fulfilled, it is not in a state of equilibrium, but will seek to float in such a position that the centres of gravity of the body and of the displaced liquid are in a vertical line.

Fig. 1, Plate XVII., represents a transverse section of a body floating in water, $W_1 L_1$ being the load water line when in a certain inclined position: $G$ is the centre of gravity of the body, and $B_1$ that of the water displaced. When in this position the weight of the floating body acts vertically downwards, in the direction of the line $GP_1$, perpendicular to $W_1 L_1$; also the resultant upward pressure of the surrounding fluid acts vertically upwards through the centre of gravity $B_1$ of the displaced water along the line $B_1 M$. Since the weight of the body and that of the fluid are necessarily equal, each of these forces is equal to $D$, the weight of the displaced water. Through $G$ draw $GZ$ perpendicular to $B_1 M$, then these two equal forces constitute a couple, whose arm is $GZ$, the tendency of which, as shown by the arrows, is evidently to turn the floating body in such a way that $L_1$ approaches $L$, and $W_1$ approaches $W$. When that happens, the line $MB$ coincides with $MB_1$, and $GZ$ becomes zero; hence the couple vanishes. Should $W_1$, then, pass $W$, and be above it, and therefore $L_1$ be below $L$, there will exist a couple, whose arm will be on the other side of $MB$, tending to make $WL$ and $W_1 L_1$ also $MB$ and $MB_1$ again coincide; and so there will be no equilibrium while $GZ$ has any value. Hence $B_1$ must be in the line $BM$ for the body to float at rest. This

4B H

proves the statement for positions of the floating body, as shown in a transverse section; fig. 2, Plate XVII., shows the same longitudinally, the same reasoning being applicable in both cases; and so it may be proved for any deviations in skew directions (*i.e.*, between direct transverse and longitudinal inclinations of the floating body), that to obtain equilibrium it is necessary $B$ and $G$ shall be in the same vertical line.

But there is yet another condition which must be fulfilled before the body will float in stable equilibrium. In figs. 1 and 2, Plate XVII., $G$ is shown between $M$ and $B$, but it does not necessarily follow that it always occupies that relative position, although in a well-designed ship it is essential that it should do so, as we shall now see. Referring to fig. 1, Plate XVIII. (which is exaggerated in order to illustrate more clearly), it will be seen that $G$ is above $M$, and therefore $GZ$ is on the opposite side of $MB$ to that where it is seen in fig. 1, Plate XVII., when the ship is heeled in the same direction. As a result of this position of $G$, the couple is found to act in a contrary direction to that in the latter case, tending, in the present example, to cause the ship to incline still farther from, instead of restoring it to the upright position. The couple, in this case, is evidently an *upsetting* one, instead of a *righting* couple, as in Plate XVII. As already said, it is only in an ill-designed or badly stowed ship that this can occur, nevertheless it is necessary to notice the result of such a position of $G$, as although when the vessel is upright, and $GP$ and $MB_1$ coincide with $MB$, the arm of the couple $GZ$ vanishes, and the vessel is in a state of equilibrium; yet when she is inclined but to the slightest extent, an upsetting couple is produced which tends to increase the ship's heel, and finally upset her. When the ship is floating at rest, perfectly upright, with $G$ in the position, relatively to $B$, shown by fig. 1, Plate XVIII., she is said to be in a state of *unstable equilibrium*, and, when inclined ever so slightly, continues to heel until she upsets; in the event of the water not being able to get inside, she will incline until she arrives in such a position that the centre of gravity is below her metacentre, when she will be in a state of stable equilibrium. Hence the necessary conditions for a body to float at rest in a state of stable equilibrium are:—

1. That she shall displace a volume of water whose weight is equal to that of the body.
2. That the centre of gravity of the body and that of the displacement shall be in the same vertical line.
3. That the centre of gravity of the body shall be below the metacentre.

In Plates XVII. and fig. 1, Plate XVIII., the angles $BMB_1$ are shown of considerable amplitude, in order to obtain a distinct figure; the term metacentre just employed is, however, used in its exact signification, the extent of the inclination not affecting the truth of the proposition.

The derivation of the term "metacentre" is at once suggested by the preceding considerations, as it means the limit beyond which the ship's centre of gravity may not rise, in order to have stable equilibrium.

**86. Metacentric Statical Stability.**—In the last chapter we investigated expressions for that part of a ship's statical stability which is due to her form, *i.e.*, *her surface statical stability*. Two modes of obtaining this were obtained, one being inexact, except for very small angles of heel, and useful only as a means of instituting comparisons between vessels of a similar type; this was termed *metacentric surface statical stability*. Another and exact method was also investigated, whereby the surface statical stability could be found for any finite angle of heel. We now purpose considering what modifications in these results are necessary, owing to the vessel having the attribute of weight, which may be considered as centred or acting at a certain point which is not the centre of buoyancy. First, then, we will direct our attention to *metacentric statical stability*. At Art. 62, it was shown that the moment of surface stability is $D \times BN$, or $D \times BM \sin BMB_1$ (see fig. 1, Plate XVIII.), this being true at the angle $BMB_1$ when that angle is very small. It is based upon the assumption that $M$ (the actual metacentre) is unaltered in height above the load water line when the ship is inclined to that angle, and hence the expression is termed the "metacentric surface statical stability."

But the actual moment of statical stability, whether calculated by the metacentric or by the exact method, will differ from this according to the position of the centre of gravity of the ship. If that centre of gravity is above the centre of buoyancy the moment is less, and if below, it is greater than the moment of surface stability.

In fig. 2, Plate XVIII., $G$ is the centre of gravity in its usual position, viz., a little below the load water line, and therefore between the metacentre and centre of buoyancy. Through $G$ draw $GP$ perpendicular to the new water line $W_1 L_1$, cutting $BN$ at $O$, also draw $GZ$ perpendicular to $MB_1$. Now, as already seen, the moment due to the vessel's form, tending to restore the ship to the upright position, is $D \times BN$; but as the weight of the ship acts at $G$ instead of $B$, and in the direction of the vertical line $GP$, directly the ship is inclined from the upright position to that shown, there is an upsetting moment $D^* \times BO$ brought into play. Hence the resultant righting moment is the difference between the righting moment $D \times BN$ (due to the form of the body immersed), and the upsetting moment $D \times BO$, which is equal to $D(BN - BO) = D \times GZ$; and this is the moment of statical stability at the angle $BMB_1$, as found by the metacentric method. It will be at once seen that at the same angle of inclination the resultant righting moment becomes greater as $G$ approaches $B$, and decreases as $G$ approaches $M$.

We will now see what happens when $G$ is below $B$. Still referring to the figure: $G_1$ is the centre of gravity, and the perpendicular $BO_1$ upon the vertical $G_1 P_1$ is now on the other side of $MB$. Hence in this case both the moment due to form and that to the centre of gravity not coinciding with the centre of buoyancy are of a righting tendency, and thus the total moment of statical stability is $D(BN + BO_1) = D \times G_1 Z_1$.

Next consider the case when $G$ is about $M$, as shown by $G_2$ in the same figure. Here the righting moment due to form is $D \times BN$ as before, but the upsetting moment due to $G_2$ not coinciding with $B$ is $D \times BO_2$, which is in excess of the righting moment by the moment $D \times NO_2 = D \times G_2 Z_2$. Hence in this case the total moment is negative, and the ship is con-

* $D$ being equal to $W$ the weight of the ship.

sequently in a state of unstable equilibrium when upright, and continues to heel when slightly inclined until she upsets.

**87. Use of the Metacentric Method.**—The moment of statical stability determined by the process described in the preceding article is based upon the assumption that, for the inclination considered, $M$ remains at a constant distance from $G$. As stated at Art. 66, this is practically true in vessels of ordinary form up to an inclination of from 10 to 15 degrees; but as the method does not take into account the form of the body, except as regards the moment of inertia of the load water plane and the total displacement, the result for greater angles is incorrect, the error for some little distance being usually on the safe side. But with vessels of low freeboard, such as monitors, or if there be any irregularity of form above or below the load water line, the metacentric method affords us no information regarding the stability of the vessel except as regards the initial righting moment. It does, however, afford a valuable means of predicating the stability of a vessel by comparing the moment so found—or usually the distance $GM$—with that of another vessel of similar type. Hence it is usual in preparing a design to determine as nearly as is possible in the early stages of the work the positions of $M$ and $G$, so that the designer may, by paying at the same time due attention to the height of the vessel's side and its form, be guided in obtaining the required stability; the exact extent of which, at every finite angle of inclination, up to the upsetting point, can be only discovered by a laborious process (see Arts. 70 and 131) when the design is more fully matured.

Until the last few years, it has not been usual even in H.M. Service to calculate the statical stability by any other than the metacentric method, as in consequence of the similarity in the types of the ships then built, and the experience acquired regarding them, it was possible to obtain the qualities required by merely knowing the initial statical qualities of the ship when inclined. As we shall see hereafter, it was found almost as undesirable for the distance $GM$ to be very great as it was to be small; for in the former case the vessel laboured very heavily in a cross sea, while in the latter she was crank. A usual value was from 3 to 5 feet in large vessels, and rather more for those of the smaller size, the maximum value being about 6 feet.

The conditions of a ship for war, and one for mercantile purposes, as regards calculating their stabilities, are very different. The weights carried by the former and their positions are nearly constant, and can be anticipated in the design; but the cargo of a merchant ship is of a very varying character. Hence it is impossible to fix the position of the centre of gravity of the latter, or to say what value of $GM$ she will have. The metacentric method is usually adopted, and such a value of $BM$ is chosen, as has been found safe and desirable in other ships. The stevedore is depended upon to stow the cargo in the best method, so as to ensure that the ship shall be stable and roll easily.

**88. Exact Calculations of Statical Stability.**—In Arts. 67 to 70, we investigated an exact method of determining surface statical stability at any finite angle of inclination by calculating the moments of the transferred wedge. This being that portion of the resultant statical stability which is due to the vessel's form, we have, therefore, the same correction to make as before in determining the real statical stability. At Art. 67, it is shown that, at any angle, $D \times BN = V + HK$

$$\text{or } BN = \frac{V \times HK}{D}$$

where $D$ is known, and $V \times HK$ is the moment of the wedges as calculated at Art. 70. Hence having $BN$ known, and $BO = BG \sin BMB_1$ also known, $GZ$ the lever of statical stability is found as before, and thus the moment $D \times GZ$ is determined.

**89. Dynamical Stability.**—At Art. 72, the moment of dynamical surface stability was shown to be equal to $V(EH + IK)$ see fig. 1, Plate XVI.; this being the work due to the depression of the centre of buoyancy in the course of heeling the ship to the angle $BMB_1$. We will now find the whole dynamical stability, which is the work performed in both raising the centre of gravity and depressing the centre of buoyancy, and is therefore the product of displacement into the difference of level of her centres of gravity and buoyancy produced by heeling.

Referring to fig. 1, Plate XVI., it will be seen that its value is

$$D(ZB_1 - GB),$$

$Z$ being the foot of the perpendicular from $G$ upon $MB_1$. But $ZN = GB \cos BMB_1$; hence,

$$\text{Dynamical stability} = D(GB \cos BMB_1 + NB_1 - GB)$$
$$= D(NB_1 - GB \text{ versin } BMB_1).$$

In the specimen calculation shown by Table II., and explained at Art. 73, $D \times V(EH + IK)$ or $D \times NB_1$ has been shown in that case to be equal to $5976 \times \cdot 45$ foot-tons of mechanical work. The known position of $G$ in this ship is such that $GB = 8\cdot 529$ feet, and the versed sine of 16 degrees is $\cdot 0387$.

Hence, GB versin $GMB_1 = 8\cdot 529 \times \cdot 0387 = \cdot 33$;

and, therefore, the dynamical stability at that angle is

$5976 (\cdot 45 - \cdot 33) = 5976 \times \cdot 12 = 717\cdot 1$ foot-tons of mechanical work.

The following *approximation* has been given for the dynamical stability at a given angle of heel:—*Multiply the displacement by the height of the metacentre above the centre of gravity and by the versed sine of the angle of heel.*

The value of a knowledge of the dynamical stability of a ship will be apparent when we consider the question of sails and sail power. For as the wind does not always exert a steady pressure upon the sails such as would be counteracted by a statical moment, but often strikes them in sudden gusts, causing the vessel to suddenly heel over, it is desirable to know the dynamical stability of the ship, and so ensure that it requires the expenditure of a sufficient amount of mechanical work to incline her to an angle which is within the limits of her maximum stability. So that while a knowledge of the statical stability of a ship is very necessary in order that she may be known to be capable of resisting a steady heeling force and of returning to the upright position when inclined to a considerable angle, yet as she is oftener under the influence of dynamical than statical moments, it is of great importance that her dynamical qualities should be known.

**90. Experimental Method of Finding the Centre of Gravity.**—The importance which is attached to the position of this point in a ship has already been dwelt upon. Hitherto, however, we have used an assumed position in our investigations; we will now see how its whereabouts is determined experimentally after the ship is built and equipped. It should be first remarked that although it is impossible, or nearly so, to determine the exact position of the centre of gravity before the vessel is built, yet that position is approximately known in every vessel designed for the Royal Navy before the drawings are put into the builder's hands. This knowledge is sometimes obtained by comparison with a ship already built and the position of whose centre of gravity is known, if that ship is similar to the one designed; due allowances being made for the differences which may exist. Or else a detailed calculation is made, such as will be referred to in Chap. IV., and if this calculation is performed with care by an experienced person, and the work checked by another, or if two independent calculations be made by two calculators, the result is found to be very trustworthy, especially as regards the vertical position of the centre of gravity. In every case, the centre of gravity is determined by experiment after the vessel is built, and the results thus obtained prove most valuable criterions by which to judge the accuracy of the results obtained by calculation for other and similar ships.

The method by experiment is founded on that rule in statics which is stated at Art. 61, which may be thus expressed: If the centre of gravity of any part of a body be shifted in a given direction through a given distance, the centre of gravity of the whole body is shifted in a parallel direction through a distance smaller than the given distance, in the same proportion that the weight of the shifted part is smaller than the weight of the whole body.

In fig. 1, Plate XIX., $M$ represents the metacentre, the position of which has already been calculated. $MP$ is the upright axis, and it is therefore known that the centre of gravity is somewhere in that line; we have to find its depth below the point $M$.

Let $a$ be the centre of gravity of any heavy body of weight $W$ resting in the position shown when the vessel is upright, and let that body be now shifted across the deck to the other side of the ship, so that $b$ is the new position of its centre of gravity. The ship will consequently heel over to a certain angle which may be accurately measured. Let $PMP_1$ be that angle, so that the new centre of gravity is now somewhere in the line $MP_1$; also, call the displacement $D$.

Through $M$ draw $MT$ parallel to $ab$, and of such a length that $\frac{MT}{ab} = \frac{W}{D}$; and through $T$ draw $TG_1$ parallel to $MG$, cutting $MP_1$ at the point $G_1$; this point will be the new centre of gravity of the whole vessel. Through $G_1$ draw $G_1G$ parallel to $ab_1$, then $G$ will be the original centre of gravity of the vessel when upright.

$$\text{Since } \frac{MT}{ab} = \frac{W}{D}$$
$$\therefore \quad MT = \frac{W}{D} ab = GG_1$$

But $MG = GG_1 \cot BMB_1 = \frac{W}{D} ab \cot BMB_1$.

Hence, having the angle $BMB_1$ determined by experiment, $MG$ is readily found.

In performing the experiment, it is necessary that several precautions should be observed. The ship should be floating in still water as in a basin or dock, and it is desirable that the weather should be calm, as otherwise the pressure of the wind upon the side of the ship would produce an error in the calculation. Should there be any wind, the ship should be placed so that it will blow in the direction of her length. An accurate account should be taken, immediately before the experiment, of the positions of such portions of the ship as are not in their proper position; also of the items of the hull or equipment that are not on board, and the positions and weights of materials not belonging to the ship which are on board at the time. The hold should be pumped dry before the experiment; loose materials, such as coal, should be prevented from shifting, and the crew should be made to remain perfectly steady at their proper posts while the inclination is being observed. It is also necessary to measure the inclination of the ship by plumb lines at two or three positions in her length, say at the fore, main, and after hatches (if the ship is so constructed that vertical lines through these can reach the keelson), and take the mean of the inclinations so observed, as it does not necessarily happen that the ship inclines about a longitudinal axis, although if the centre of gravity of the ballast* is placed in the same transverse section of the ship as that containing the centre of buoyancy, the inclination should be the same throughout. As already stated, it is desirable that the ballast or other weights used in inclining the ship should at first be so placed that the ship is upright throughout her length. This is generally done by placing equal weights on each side of the ship in such positions that the above result is attained. The draught of water forward and aft is then observed, and from this the displacement, position of centre of buoyancy, and the height of metacentre at the time of the experiment can be calculated. The positions of the centres of gravity of the weights are now carefully measured, after which the ship is inclined by shifting them across the deck in different ways.

In the example which we shall presently give, it will be seen that the order of procedure is as follows:—The whole of the ballast on one side is first transferred to the other side of the ship, and the distance through which its centre of gravity is moved is carefully measured; when the ship ceases to oscillate the inclination is observed. Next, the weights are restored to their original position, when the ship should again be upright. If she is not, the slight deviation is recorded. This completes the first experiment. The ballast is then moved over to the other side of the deck so as to incline her in an opposite direction to that in the first experiment, and when the distance through which its centre of gravity is shifted has been carefully measured, and the ship is at rest, the inclination is again observed. The weights are once more restored to their original positions, when the ship should again be upright; if she is not, the deviation is recorded. This completes the second experiment. Should these experiments give slightly different values of $MG$, as is usually the case, the mean of the two is taken as correct. In order to reduce to a minimum the errors in the experiments, which result from the ship not being perfectly steady, or by reason of the distances through which the centres of gravity of the weights are moved not being accurately measured, etc., it is now usual to make at least four experiments, and sometimes

* Pig-iron ballast is the most convenient weight to employ when performing this experiment.

as many as six; this being done by shifting first a half and then the whole of the ballast on one side to the other, and afterwards doing the same on the other side of the ship. It is easy to see that by varying the quantity of ballast moved, or the distance moved through, several experiments may be made; and that by increasing the number of observations the resulting average value of $GM$ approaches more nearly to the truth.

**91. Specimen Calculation of $GM$ by Experiment.**—The example we are about to give was furnished by Mr. F. K. Barnes to the Institution of Naval Architects in 1866, and is contained in Vol. VII. of the Transactions of that Society.

The *Valiant* was inclined in the Steam Basin at Portsmouth on the 28th July 1865.

*Wind.*—Slight breeze, blowing in the direction of the fore and aft axis of the ship.

*The Ship* had her lower masts and topmasts on end, was rigged completely, had lower yards in place, gaffs in place, topsail yards on the caps, top-gallant masts struck; one top-gallant yard was lashed up the lower rigging, and the other against inside berthing above upper deck; spare spars on deck; spare screw on upper deck, forward (weight $3\frac{1}{2}$ tons); anchors stowed; chain in lockers and gangers in place; guns run out on main and upper decks; shot stowed round hatchways, not any in lockers; boom boats stowed, the other boats not on board; sails not on board; bowsprit in place, and jib-boom run in.

*Ballast for Experiment.*—100 tons of pig-iron ballast was placed on the upper deck, 50 tons on each side; stowed from the fore side of the after capstan to the fore side of the funnel.

*Men on Board during Experiments.*—60 labourers, to move the ballast, etc., and 47 artificers employed in various parts of the ship; also, 11 men of the ship's company.

*Coals on Board during Experiments.*—Coal in fore bunkers stowed up to deck; in after bunkers, up to deck nearly in one corner. Total weight about 120 tons.

*Draught of Water during Experiment.*—

    Forward, ..........................22 ft. $7\frac{1}{4}$ in.
    Aft, ...................... .....24 ft. $9\frac{3}{4}$ in.
    Mean, ................... ..........23 ft. $8\frac{1}{2}$ in.
    Displacement,......................6019·6 tons.

*In the First Experiment.*—The ship was inclined by moving 50 tons of ballast through 39 ft. 6 in., from starboard to port, which gave an inclination of $25\frac{1}{2}$ inches by fore plumb, and $24\frac{1}{4}$ by after one.

The ship plumbed well when the ballast was restored to its original position.*

*In the Second Experiment.*—The ship was inclined by moving 50 tons of ballast through 39 ft. 6 in., from the port side to starboard. Inclination in 25 feet was $24\frac{3}{4}$ inches by fore plumb, 25 inches by after one.

Taking the mean of the inclinations, as taken from the two plumbs in each experiment, we have

$$GM = \frac{W}{D} ab \cot BMB_1. \quad \text{(See fig. 1, Plate XIX.)}$$

$$= \frac{50}{6019 \cdot 6} \times 39 \cdot 5 \times \frac{4 \times 25 \times 12}{25\frac{1}{2} + 25\frac{1}{4} + 24\frac{3}{4} + 25} = 3 \cdot 917 \text{ feet.}$$

The separate values of $GM$ found by the two experiments are 3·879 ft. and 3·956 ft., the mean of these being 3·917 ft., as above.

The following values of $GM$, as found by the experiments, in four other iron-clad ships of H.M. fleet, are given by Mr. Barnes in the same paper:—

*Minotaur*, .................................2·293 feet.
*Warrior*, .........  ...................4·449 ,,
*Achilles*, ........................ ........2·556 ,,
*Prince Consort*,.....................6·535 ,,

Having made the necessary corrections in order to obtain the value of $GM$ *when the ballast is removed, the ships are at their load draughts, and in proper sea going condition*, the following are the results:—

*Valiant*, ...............................4·610 feet.
*Minotaur*, ...............................3·879 ,,
*Warrior*, ...............................4·678 ,,
*Achilles*, ... ...............................3·088 ,,
*Prince Consort*,.....................6·010 ,,

which results, as we shall see hereafter, afford valuable means of comparing not only the stabilities of the several ships, but also their rolling tendencies and their general efficiency as gun platforms. We may first remark in passing that the value of $GM$ for the *Achilles* is rather below the average, while that for the *Prince Consort* is considerably above. Indeed, as a matter of fact, the height of metacentre, above

---

* It will be seen that in these experiments only two plumbs were employed; it is, however, now customary to use three, as stated in the text.

centre of gravity, differs very little for well-designed war vessels of all sizes, being about $3\frac{1}{2}$ to $4\frac{1}{2}$ feet, and, in general, is greatest in the smallest vessels.

In vessels for which that height is exactly the same, the moments of stability at equal angles of heel are obviously proportional to the displacements.

**92. Position of Centre of Gravity, Longitudinally.**—It is perhaps unnecessary to state that the longitudinal position of the centre of gravity, when the ship is floating at rest, is at once found by observing the draught of water, and then calculating the longitudinal position of the centre of buoyancy from the ship's drawings to that water line; the centre of gravity will, of course, be in the transverse vertical section which contains the centre of buoyancy. Knowing that the centre of gravity is in the longitudinal vertical middle line plane of the ship, when she is floating upright, and having found its vertical and longitudinal position, the point is fully determined.

**93. Alteration of Trim due to Shifting Weights already on Board.**—The effect upon the trim of a ship, caused by shifting weights already on board in a longitudinal direction, will now occupy our attention. In fig. 2, Plate XIX., $G$ is the centre of gravity, and $B$ the centre of buoyancy of a ship floating in equilibrium at the load water line $WL$. The displacement $D$ is known, also the value of $BM$, $M$ being considered fixed during the small alteration of trim that we shall consider. A weight $P$, already on board, is shifted forward through a distance $d$, so that the ship then floats at the line $W_1 L_1$, intersecting $WL$ at the point $S$; and the two water lines intersect the fore and after perpendiculars of the ship at the points $W$, $W_1$, and $L$, $L_1$, respectively. It is required to find the lengths $WW_1$ and $LL_1$, which together constitute the alteration in trim.

$$P \times d = D \times GG_1,$$

where $GG_1$ is the distance which the centre of gravity of the ship is moved forward by shifting the weight $P$. As the point $M$ is considered fixed, a perpendicular to $W_1 L_1$ through $G_1$ also passes through $M$. The inclination being small, the point $S$ is a very close approximation to the centre of gravity of the load water plane.

Suppose a foot and ton to be the units of measurement and weight.

Since the angles $WSW_1$, $LSL_1$, and $GMG_1$ are equal, we have by the property of similar triangles,

$$\frac{WS}{WW_1} = \frac{LS}{LL_1} = \frac{MG}{GG_1}$$

$$\therefore \frac{WS + SL}{WW_1 + LL_1} = \frac{WL}{WW_1 + LL_1} = \frac{MG}{GG_1}.$$

But

$$GG_1 = \frac{P \times d}{D}.$$

Hence

$$\frac{WL}{WW_1 + LL_1} = \frac{MG \times D}{P \times d},$$

and

$$WW_1 + LL_1 = \frac{WL(P \times d)}{MG \times D} \quad \ldots\ldots\ldots\ldots\ldots(1)$$

But the terms on the right-hand side of this equation are all known, hence the total alteration of trim, viz., $WW_1 + LL_1$ is also determined.

To find the separate values of $WW_1$ and $LL_1$, we have—

$$WS : LS = WW_1 : LL_1$$

$$\frac{SL}{WS + SL} = \frac{LL_1}{WW_1 + LL_1}$$

and from (1) $\quad \dfrac{SL}{WL} = \dfrac{LL_1 (MG \times D)}{WL (P \times d)}$,

hence

$$LL_1 = \frac{SL(P \times d)}{MG \times D} \quad \ldots\ldots\ldots\ldots\ldots(2)$$

Similarly,

$$WW_1 = \frac{SW(P \times d)}{MG \times D}, \quad \ldots\ldots\ldots\ldots\ldots(3)$$

and as $SL$ and $SW$ are known by reference to the displacement sheet, the values of $LL_1$ and $WW_1$ are determined. If $S$ is at the middle of the length between perpendiculars, then

$$SL = SW = \frac{WL}{2},$$

hence

$$LL_1 = WW_1 = \frac{WL(P \times d)}{2MG \times D}.$$

MOMENT TO ALTER TRIM ONE INCH.   127

As an Example,* suppose $WL = 150$ ft., $MG = 177\cdot41$ ft., $D = 620\cdot158$ tons; also, let $WS = 73$ ft., and $LS = 77$ ft. Let a weight of 61·1 tons be moved forward a distance of 10 ft.; then $P = 61\cdot1$ tons, and $d = 10$ ft.

In this case,
$$LL_1 = \frac{77 \times 61\cdot1 \times 10}{620\cdot158 \times 177\cdot41} = \frac{77}{180} \text{ ft.} = 5\tfrac{2}{15} \text{ in.}$$
$$WW_1 = \frac{73 \times 61\cdot1 \times 10}{620\cdot158 \times 177\cdot41} = \frac{73}{180} \text{ ft.} = 4\tfrac{13}{15} \text{ in.}$$

and
$$WW_1 + LL_1 = 5\tfrac{2}{15} + 4\tfrac{13}{15} = 10 \text{ in.}$$

Hence the original draught of water being......
$\begin{cases} 10 \text{ ft. } 0 \text{ in. forward.} \\ 12 \text{ ft. } 0 \text{ in. aft.} \end{cases}$

The new draught is ............
$\begin{cases} 10 \text{ ft. } 0 \text{ in.} + 5\tfrac{2}{15} \text{ in.} = 10 \text{ ft. } 5\tfrac{2}{15} \text{ in. forward.} \\ 12 \text{ ft. } 0 \text{ in.} - 4\tfrac{13}{15} \text{ in.} = 11 \text{ ft. } 7\tfrac{2}{15} \text{ in. aft.} \end{cases}$

**94. Moment to alter Trim one inch.**—It is usual in H.M. service to calculate upon the ordinary displacement sheet the moment required to alter the trim one inch, the method of obtaining which depends upon the investigation just gone through.

In this case $WW_1 + LL_1 = 1$ in. $= \tfrac{1}{12}$ foot.

Hence the equation,
$$\frac{WL}{WW_1 + LL_1} = \frac{MG \times D}{P \times d}$$

becomes
$$P \times d = \frac{MG \times D}{12 \times WL}$$

Using the values in the displacement sheet (Table I.)
$$P \times d = \frac{177\cdot41 \times 620\cdot158}{12 \times 150} = 61\cdot1 \text{ foot-tons.}$$

Which is the moment required to alter the trim of this ship by one inch when she is floating at her load water line. Hence knowing this moment to alter trim, we are at once in a position to say what effect the shifting a weight, already on board, in a horizontal direction has upon the trim of the ship. It must, however, be remembered that if the shifted moment is sufficient to cause a very considerable alteration of trim,

* These values, except $WS$ and $SL$, are taken from the Displacement Sheet, Table I.

the value of $MG$ will change, owing to the different form and area of the load water plane; in that case an approximation to the trim is first found, then the value of $GM$ is calculated for the new water plane, and by this the moment to alter trim at the approximate line is obtained. The alteration of trim found by using this new value will give a very good approximation to the actual line. The trim found by using the moment calculated for the load water line is, however, usually sufficiently correct for all purposes in actual practice.

**95. Effect on the Trim by adding a Weight.**—I. *If the weight is inconsiderable.*—Let $P$ be the weight added, and $l$ be its distance in a horizontal direction from the transverse section containing the centre of gravity of the load water plane. Also let $F$ be the moment to alter trim one inch, and $T$ be the tons per inch immersion. Then $\frac{P}{T}$ is the extra immersion in inches. Suppose, first, that the weight $P$ is placed in the transverse section which contains the centre of gravity of the load water plane, then the ship will sink to a parallel depth of $\frac{P}{T}$ inches; for the horizontal moment of the added weight about the transverse plane, containing the centre of gravity of the ship, is the same as the moment of the added displacement about that plane. But in this case the weight $P$ is placed at a horizontal distance $l$ from that position; hence the alteration of trim is due to a moment of $P \times l$. Since $P$ is small compared with $D$, it is not considered sufficient to increase $MG$ or the displacement very considerably, hence we have

$$\frac{P \times l}{F} = \text{alteration of trim in inches,}$$

and

$$\frac{P \times l}{2F} = WW_1 = LL_1 \text{ approximately.}$$

Hence if the distance $l$ is measured on the fore side of the centre of gravity of the load water plane, then calling the original draught of water

$\begin{cases} \text{Forward} = X_2 \\ \text{Aft} \quad\quad = Y_2 \end{cases}$ and the new draught $\begin{cases} \text{Forward} = X_1 \\ \text{Aft} \quad\quad = Y_1 \end{cases}$

we have approximately

$$X_1 = X + \frac{P}{T} + \frac{P \times l}{2F}$$
$$Y_1 = Y + \frac{P}{T} - \frac{P \times l}{2F}.$$

In the example already considered (see Table I.), suppose $l = 61\cdot1$ ft., and $P = 10$ tons; also taking $T = 7\cdot65$ tons, and $F = 61\cdot1$ foot tons, as there given, the values of $X$ and $Y$ are 10 ft. and 12 ft., respectively.

$$X_1 = 10 \text{ ft. } 0 \text{ in. } + \frac{10}{7\cdot65} \text{ in. } + \frac{10 \times 61\cdot1}{2 \times 61\cdot1} \text{ in. } = 10 \text{ ft. } 6\tfrac{1}{4} \text{ in. forward}$$
$$Y_1 = 12 \text{ ft. } 0 \text{ in. } + \frac{10}{7\cdot65} \text{ in. } - \frac{10 \times 61\cdot1}{2 \times 61\cdot1} \text{ in. } = 11 \text{ ft. } 8\tfrac{1}{4} \text{ in. aft.}$$

If instead of taking $WW_1 = LL_1 = \frac{P \times l}{2F}$ we used their exact values, due to the centre of gravity of the load water plane being abaft the middle of the length between perpendiculars. Then, as already seen,

$$X_1 = 10 \text{ ft. } + 1\tfrac{1}{4} \text{ in. } + 4\tfrac{13}{15} \text{ in. } = 10 \text{ ft. } 6\tfrac{1}{15} \text{ in. forward}$$
$$Y_1 = 12 \text{ ft. } + 1\tfrac{1}{4} \text{ in. } - 5\tfrac{2}{15} \text{ in. } = 11 \text{ ft. } 8\tfrac{11}{15} \text{ in. aft.}$$

II. *If the weight is not inconsiderable.*—In this case we are not justified in assuming that $MG$ (fig. 2, Plate XIX.) remains unaltered, or that $D + P$ is not materially greater than $D$. We will commence by supposing that the weight is momentarily placed in the transverse plane which contains the centres of gravity of the load water line; then the ship commences to sink parallel to her former draught. But as she gets deeper in the water two things happen—in the first place, the centre of gravity of the successive load water planes move away from the cross section containing that at the load draught, owing to the alterations in the forms of the planes; and in the second place, the areas of these planes alter (usually by increasing), and so cause the tons per inch of immersion to vary. Hence we have to find the position of the centre of gravity of the water plane at which the vessel floats in equilibrium, and the mean tons per inch of immersion between the original and final load water planes (it being still assumed that the weight is placed momentarily, as already stated). These are found by a process which is necessarily tentative, and which we now proceed to examine. $T$ being the tons per inch at the load draught, and $P$ the weight added; $\frac{P}{T}$ is approximately the depth of immersion. Draw a line on the sheer draught parallel to the load water line, and at a distance $\frac{P}{T}$ inches above it, and calculate the area and the position of the centre of gravity of this line. In making the calculation for the new water plane, we obtain the tons per inch at the new immersion; this latter may, however, be found very nearly by continuing the curve of tons per inch to the required draught by means of a penning batten. Having these two extreme values of the tons per inch, a mean value may be found, especially if the curve is referred to. Let $T_1$ be the new value, then $\frac{P}{T_1}$ will be a close approximation to the actual mean distance the vessel sinks in the water. Let $c$ be the distance of the centre of gravity of original load water plane from the transverse section containing the centre of gravity of the ship, and $c_1$ be the distance of the new centre of gravity, as just found. Draw a line on the sheer draught joining these points, then by bisecting the portion of this line between the original load water line and the line distant $\frac{P}{T_1}$ from it, we get a good approximation to the position of the centre of buoyancy of the added displacement. Call the distance of this point from the transverse plane containing the centre of gravity of the ship $c_2$; then $P(c_2 - c)$ is the moment to alter trim due to the form of the ship between the new and original load water planes; it being still assumed that the weight $P$ is placed momentarily in the transverse plane containing the centre of gravity of the original load water plane. This moment is usually an upward after one, as the form of the vessel above the load water line is generally fuller aft than it is forward, it is thus equivalent to placing a weight $P$ at a distance $c_2 - c$ on the fore side of the centre of gravity of load water plane, or a downward fore moment.

But instead of the weight being placed as assumed, suppose it really situated at a distance $l$, say, on the fore side of the centre of gravity of the load water plane. Now to find the additional effect on the trim when in this position, we must determine the new value of $GM$. This will evidently differ from the original value to an extent governed by three conditions, viz., 1st, the difference in the length of $BM$ due to an altered load water plane, and an increased displacement; 2nd, an altered depth of $B$ below the original load water plane; and 3rd, the altered vertical position of the centre of gravity. The 1st and 2nd conditions will together fix the change in the height of $M$ above the original load water line, and, taken in connection with the altered position of $G$, with regard to that line, will give the new value of $GM$.

Two points must here be noticed, one of which is that it is always desirable to refer all vertical measurements to the original load water line, as by so doing mistakes are prevented; the second is, that in finding the value of $BM$, and the distance of $B$ from the water line, we suppose the new load water plane is parallel to the original. We are compelled at present to do this, as we do not know the actual trim; but as the moments of inertia of the assumed and real lines do not usually differ widely, and as the height of $B$ is generally very little affected by the supposition, we are enabled in this way to get a good approximation to the moment for altering trim at the new line, and by the aid of this the new load water line can be closely approximated to. When this approximate trim is found, the moment to alter trim can be found from that line, and if it differs much from that assumed, we can make a closer approximation to the real trim. It is thus seen that, as already remarked, the process is tentative; nevertheless, as the form of a ship's body does not alter very considerably within the limits due to shifting or placing ordinary portable weights on board, a very close approximation can be found to the real trim without continuing the process beyond that indicated above.

The preceding remarks will have almost sufficiently explained the work involved in finding the change of draught and trim due to placing a weight on board. We have first the new $BM$ to find by using the parallel draught due to the weight being assumed to be placed at the centre of gravity of the load water line. To do this we have to perform the work already described at Art. 66, using the ordinates of the assumed parallel line. Next we have to find the new distance of $B$ below the original load water line. The ship evidently sinks until the additional displacement is equal to the weight added. The centre of buoyancy of this added displacement will be nearly midway between the two parallel water lines, being rather nearer the new line than the old one. Let $D$ be the original displacement; $P$ the weight added; $l$ the distance of $B$ below original water line; $p$ the distance of centre of buoyancy of added displacement above that line, as just found; and $x$ the distance of the new centre of buoyancy from the same line. Then

$$x(D+P) = D \times l - P \times d$$
$$x = \frac{Dl - Pd}{D+P}.$$

If $M_1 B_1$ is the new value of $MB$, then $M_1 B_1 - x$ is the height of $M_1$ above the original load water line.

We have now to find the new position of $G$, which is evidently determined in the same way as that of $B$, it being known at what distance, above or below, the original water line the added weight is placed. In this way a new value of $GM$ is found: term it $G_1 M_1$. From this new value we determine the new value of the moment to alter trim, using $P + D$ instead of $D$. We then proceed as before by calculating the moment, either before or abaft, of the added weight in its true position about the centre of gravity of the new load water plane; this moment being divided by the "tons to alter trim," gives the alteration of trim in inches, which must be set off in the manner already explained. If the alteration of trim is considerable, enough to affect the height of $M_1$ above $B_1$, or $B_1$ below the original load water line, then a repetition of the preceding work must be gone through, using now the trim just found.

When the alteration of trim, as affected by shifting the weight to its true position, is found, we must make the allowance due to the change in position of the centre of gravity of the water plane, as found in the early stage of the question; i.e., the change of trim due to a fore moment of $P(c_2 - c)$.

## EFFECT ON THE TRIM BY ADDING A WEIGHT.

As an example, suppose $D = 4000$ tons, $P = 100$ tons, $T_1 = 20$ tons. Then $\dfrac{P}{T_1} = \dfrac{100}{20} = 5$ in. the added immersion.

Let $B_1 M_1$ at the new line, as found by calculation, be 210 ft., and let the B of 4000 tons be at 8 ft. beneath the load water line. Then

$$x = \frac{4000 \times 8 - 100 \times 2}{4000 + 100} = 7.8 \text{ ft.}$$

which is the distance of $B_1$ below the original load water line. Hence $210 - 7.8 = 202.2$ ft. the height of $M_1$ above that line.

Suppose $G$ to be originally at the water line, and, by adding the weight, to rise to ·2 above that line; then $M_1 G_1$ is $202.2 - 2 = 200$ ft.

The ship is, say, 200 ft. between perpendiculars. Then

$$\frac{M_1 G_1 \times (P + D)}{12 \times WL} = \frac{200 \times 4100}{12 \times 200} = 341.6 \text{ foot-tons,}$$

which is the moment to alter trim one inch at the assumed line.

Let the weight $P$ be now placed in its true position, viz., at 71·3 ft. abaft the centre of gravity of the load water plane; also let the value $c_2 - c$ (the distance of the centre of buoyancy of the added displacement abaft the centre of gravity of the load water plane) be 3 ft.

Then $100 (71.3 - 3.0) = 6830$ foot-tons after moment. But the moment to alter trim one inch is 341·6 foot-tons, hence $\dfrac{6830}{341.6} = 20$ in. is the alteration of trim. Suppose this to be divided at the bow and stern in the ratio of 9:11. Then the alteration forward is 9 in. and aft 11 in. Moreover, the added immersion is 5 in.

If the draught of water, before the weight was placed on board, was

Forward,................. 18 ft.
Aft,........................ 20 ,,

Then the new draught will be

18 ft. + 5 in. − 9 in. = 17 ft. 8 in. forward
20 ft. + 5 in. + 11 in. = 21 ft. 4 in. aft.

This is, of course, a first approximation, but will not differ materially from the truth if the vessel is of ordinary form. If considered desirable, values of $GM$ and of the "tons to alter trim" at the newly found line can be calculated, and corrections made if they are found to differ materially from the values used.

**96. Effect on the Trim by admitting Water into the Ship.**—In considering this question, we will assume that the ship is divided into water-tight compartments by transverse bulkheads, so as to localise the water which is admitted; for, owing to the fluid property of the weight thus added, it would otherwise distribute itself over the inside of the ship until its level was parallel to that of the water surface outside. In this latter case there would be a change of trim due to the position which the centre of gravity of the admitted water would occupy, and to the altered position of the centre of buoyancy of the whole displacement; but as the case is rarely met with in practice, owing to the space occupied by the cargo or other contents of the vessel (causing the distribution of the admitted water to be very irregular and difficult of calculation), and to the usual presence of bulkheads, it is not necessary to dwell any further upon it.

There are three principal conditions in which a ship may be considered to be placed by the admission of water into her interior.

1. *When any compartment is filled with water which is not in communication with the sea.*

2. *When any compartment is partially filled with water which is not in communication with the sea.*

3. *When any compartment has water in it which is in free communication with, and which can rise to the level of the sea.*

We will now consider the *trim* of the ship in each of these three conditions.

1. In this case the water, being confined, cannot change its form or position, and hence has the same effect upon the trim of the ship as any solid body of the same weight, and in the same position. The water carried in tanks for the use of the crew or passengers, also any other liquid carried in barrels or tanks, are instances of this kind. A more general case is that of water ballast carried in cellular spaces, or such a compartment as an iron-cased magazine when

entirely flooded. The double bottoms and smaller compartments of a ship when fitted with an iron crown, and filled with water by flooding cocks, are also examples of this kind.

*When the iron crown of such a compartment is below the water level* the condition of communication with the sea does not affect the question, as the water being unable to alter its form or change its position, it may be considered either as a weight carried or a loss of an equivalent displacement at that part. (See *B*, fig. 1, Plate XX.)

2. In this case (see *D*, fig. 1, Plate XX.), the water being free to alter its form, and therefore its centre of gravity being free to move within certain limits, the problem becomes more complicated; and that, too, just in proportion to the horizontal area of the compartment containing the water. Still, as the weight remains constant, we are enabled by a tentative process to arrive at a close approximation to the alteration of trim produced; it being remembered that, in all these conditions, we imagine the ship to be floating at rest in still water when the compartment is partially filled. It will be easily seen that if we start by assuming the level of the water admitted to be parallel to that of the sea, we can determine the position of its centre of gravity in that position, and then, by the process described in the preceding Article, find the alteration of trim produced upon that supposition. Then if we draw a line, parallel to the new load water line, for the surface of the water in the compartment (taking care that the volume remains constant), and then find the alteration in trim due to shifting the centre of gravity of the water, the result will be a close approximation to the real trim. If the area of the compartment be large, compared with the size of the ship, it may be necessary to make a second or third correction; but this must be left to the discretion of the calculator.

Instances of the kind just named are found in the cases of bilge water, and ballast tanks or double bottoms when only partially filled. Grain or coal cargoes, when the hold is not filled and due precautions against shifting are not taken, are instances which approximate somewhat to that considered.

3. We have finally to consider a case (see *A* and *C*, fig. 1, Plate XX.) which has often occurred, and for which due

provision will be made in every properly constructed ship. It is such a case as occurs when water is admitted into one of the compartments of a ship by a hole in the bottom. Now it is evident that the trim is affected by such an accident in proportion as the compartment pierced is near either of the extremities of the ship. Consequently, in Her Majesty's ships the compartments at the bow and stern are made as small as is convenient, and when two consecutive transverse bulkheads near the extremities are not sufficiently close together, an iron water-tight flat, below the level of the water line, is fitted between the bulkheads so as to place the ship when pierced below that flat in the first condition considered in this Article (see $B$ fig. 1, Plate XX.), and, if pierced above, in a far less dangerous condition than if the flat were not there. In the case we are now considering ($A$ and $C$, fig. 1, Plate XX.) the water flows freely into the ship through an aperture in the side, and rises to the level of the sea. It may be that the whole compartment is filled to that level from the keel upwards, or the hole is above a water-tight flat; the principle is the same in both cases, the effects differing only in degree.

It will be seen that the ship is then in the same condition as if the displacement due to the volume of the admitted water were removed from that part of the immersed body at which the filled space is situated. If the whole compartment is filled from the keel to the surface of the sea ($C$, fig. 1, Plate XX.), the result is the same as if the ship consisted of two pieces distant from each other the length of the compartment, yet tied rigidly together by the decks and sides, and if the water is admitted above a water-tight flat (see $A$, fig. 1, Plate XX.), the two pieces are joined further by a buoyant block beneath the surface. In both cases the same considerations are involved—the weight carried, and therefore the displacement remain constant, the centre of buoyancy is shifted, while the moment of inertia of the load water line is diminished. The depth of immersion is, of course, increased, in order that the displacement may be the same as it was before the support due to the portion of the immersed body, now filled with water, was removed. We have given, then, the volume of the space filled as high as the original load water line, and the position of its centre of buoyancy, the area of the portion of the load water line included between the bounding bulkheads of the compartment, also the total displacement and the position of its centre of buoyancy before piercing the side of the compartment, to find the new trim and immersion. The solution of this problem is also necessarily a tentative one.

We have first to find the depth to which the ship sinks, supposing the centre of buoyancy of the admitted water is in the transverse section which contains the centre of gravity of the load water line; that is, supposing the ship sinks to a line parallel to the load line. Let $V$ = volume of water admitted as high as original load water line, $T$ = tons per inch of immersion at that line, found by neglecting the area of the load water plane between the bounding bulkheads of the compartment filled. Then $\frac{V}{T}$ is an approximation to the depth in inches through which the vessel sinks. If the "tons per inch" remain constant through the increased immersion, then $\frac{V}{T}$ is the exact depth; if not, a second approximation must be made by using the new line in a somewhat similar manner to that described in preceding Art. If the additional immersion is considerable, so as to alter the form of the load water plane, and therefore shift* its centre of gravity, the position of the latter must be computed, and the usual forward moment due to the fullness of the ship aft must be obtained in the manner likewise explained in the preceding Article. Let this be $V(c_2 - c)$, using the same symbols to indicate this movement of the centre of gravity of the plane as before. Now, considering the centre of buoyancy of the water admitted to be in its real position, viz., at a distance $l$ on the fore side (say) of the centre of gravity of the load water plane, we have $V \times l$ = the fore moment produced, and $\frac{V \times l}{D}$ = the distance the centre of buoyancy is moved forward.

Now, in order to determine the effect upon the trim due

---

* The centre of gravity of the load water plane is already shifted from the position it occupied prior to the loss of area between the bounding bulkheads of the compartment filled. It is with regard to these already shifted positions that we determine the new position due to extra immersion.

to a forward moment of $V \times l$, we must find the value of $F_1$ or the moment to alter trim one inch in the new condition, and hence we require the new value of $MG$. To do this, we must find the moment of inertia of the effective load water plane (*i.e.*, the new load water plane minus the part of it in the filled compartment), and then divide by $D$ in the ordinary way. For example, if in the ship whose longitudinal metacentre is calculated upon Table I. a compartment extending from ordinate 8 to ordinate 10 is filled with water so as to practically cut it off from the ship in the way we are considering, then, supposing the ordinates of the load water line to be unchanged, we should have to multiply the ordinates 13·8, 12·8, and 10·3 by Simpson's multipliers 1, 4, and 1, and then by the same multipliers for moments and moments of inertia as are used in the Table, and, finally, treat the sum of the functions similarly to those of the whole plane, and deduct the result from 112,693·68 (see Table I.), whereupon dividing the remainder by the displacement 620·58, which remains unaltered, the quotient would be the value of $BM$ in the new condition of the ship. The vertical position of $B$ has next to be found, to do which we must find the centre of buoyancy of the water in the compartment to the height of the original load water line; having found which, the new position of $B$, vertically, is determined in the manner described on page 132. From this the height of $M$ above $G$ is at once found, as the position of $G$ does not change. Having $MG$—the value of $F_1$ is found from the equation

$$F_1 = \frac{MG \times D}{12 \times WL}. \qquad \text{(See Art. 94, and fig. 2, Plate XIX.)}$$

where $WL$ is the length between perpendiculars.

But the total moment altering the trim is

$$V \times l + V(c_2 - c),$$

and thus the total alteration of trim in inches,

$$\frac{V \times l + V(c_2 - c)}{F_1},$$

which in ordinary cases, where the extra immersion is not very great, becomes

$$\frac{V \times l}{F_1}.$$

EFFECT ON STABILITY BY ADDING A WEIGHT. 139

The added immersion being $\dfrac{V}{T}$, then supposing the original draught of water to be

$$\text{Forward} = A.$$
$$\text{Aft} = B.$$

the new draught is (supposing the alteration to be equal forward and aft).

$$\text{Forward} = A + \dfrac{V}{T} + \dfrac{V \times l}{2F_1}$$
$$\text{Aft} = B + \dfrac{V}{T} - \dfrac{V \times l}{2F_1}.$$

Should the alteration of trim be considerable, it may be necessary to use the above result as a first approximation, and obtain the values of $F_1$ and $T$ for a new load line, starting with this approximate line as a basis. From this a sufficiently correct result for all practical purposes will be obtained.

**97. Effect on the Stability by moving a Weight already on Board.**—As the stability of a ship increases as the value of $MG$ increases, hence as the point $M$ remains constant while the draught and trim is unaltered, it is evident that by moving a weight, already on board, in a vertical direction, the value of $MG$, and therefore the stability, is increased if the weight is lowered and decreased if the weight is raised.

If, however, the weight is moved longitudinally as well as vertically, the height of $M$ above the water line will vary according to the form of the new load water plane and the alteration in the depth of the centre of buoyancy. Usually it requires a considerable moment to be produced by the longitudinal movement to cause any very appreciable difference in the height of $M$ above the load water plane; hence, practically, it is sufficient to say that the movement of a weight on board a ship increases or diminishes the stability according as the new position, occupied by the weight, is below or above the level of its original position.

**98. Effect on the Stability by adding or removing a Weight.**—If the weight added or removed is considerable, the surface stability must be calculated (see Art. 70) to the new load water line, the latter being determined by the method explained in Art. 95. Then the new position of the centre of gravity of the ship must be found, and the correction due to its position made in the manner shown in Art. 88, whereupon we have the actual statical stability in the new condition with the weight added or removed.

To find the new position of the centre of gravity—Let $d$ be the distance of the original position below the load water line, and $a$ the distance of the added weight $P$ below that line, then $d_1$ the distance of the new centre of gravity below the original load line is

$$d_1 = \frac{Dd + Pa}{D + P}.$$

For moderate alterations of lading, it is unnecessary to go through this laborious process, as there is an easier method of finding the alteration of stability with sufficient accuracy. This method, due to Mr. F. K. Barnes, we now proceed to give in the words of that gentleman.*

"Since the positions of the centres of gravity of ships are in general but roughly approximated to, it becomes important to be able to dispense with the knowledge of the exact position of the centre of gravity of a ship, and to compare the stability under given conditions with the stability under other conditions; the difference of the two cases being known.

"In fig. 2, Plate XX.—Let $WL$ represent the water line of a ship, $G$ her centre of gravity, $B$ her centre of buoyancy.

"Let the ship be now inclined about the fore and aft horizontal axis through an angle $I$. Let $B'$ be her new centre of buoyancy.

"Through $B'$ draw $B'M$ vertical, and cutting the original vertical through $B$ in the point $M$. Also through $B$ and $G$ draw $BP$ and $GZ$, respectively, perpendicular to $B'M$.

"Then if $W$ represent the displacement of the ship—

$$\begin{aligned} \text{Stability} &= W \times GZ \\ &= W \times GM \sin I \\ &= W \times (BM - BG) \sin I \\ &= W.BM \sin I - W.BG \sin I. \end{aligned}$$

"Now $W.BM \sin I = W.BP = b.A.$, where $A$ represents the volume of either of the wedges of immersion or emersion, and $b$ the distance between the centres of gravity of these wedges.

* See *Shipbuilding, Theoretical and Practical*, p. 54.

## EFFECT ON STABILITY BY ADDING A WEIGHT.    141

"Suppose the ship to be once more upright; and let a weight $w$ (the same unit being taken as for the displacement $W$) be placed on board of her, causing her to sink in the water until $W_1 L_1$ becomes the new water line.

"Let the distance of the common centre of gravity of the weight or weights $w$ added, above the original centre of buoyancy, be represented by $a$.

"Let also $c$ represent the distance of the centre of gravity of the additional displacement, above the original centre of buoyancy.

"Let $B_1$ and $G_1$ represent the new centres of buoyancy and gravity, respectively, of the ship.

"Let the ship be now inclined as before, about a fore and aft axis, through the angle $I$. The centre of buoyancy is found at a point $B'_1$.

"Through $B'_1$ draw $B'_1 M_1$ vertical, cutting the original vertical $BGM$ in $M_1$; and through $B_1$ and $G_1$ draw $B_1 P_1$ and $G_1 Z_1$, respectively, perpendicular to $B'_1 M_1$.

"The stability is now represented by—

$$(W + w) G_1 Z_1 = (W + w) G_1 M_1 \sin I$$
$$= (W + w) (B_1 M_1 - B_1 G_1) \sin I$$
$$= (W + w) B_1 M_1 \sin I - (W + w) B_1 G_1 \sin I \ldots\ldots (A)$$

"But $(W + w)(B_1 M_1 \sin I) = (W + w) B_1 P_1 = b_1 A_1$, where $A_1$ represents the volume of either of the wedges of immersion or emersion, corresponding to the water line $W_1 L_1$, and $b_1$ represents the distance between the centres of gravity of those wedges.

Again $B_1 G_1 = BG + GG_1 - BB_1$;

$\therefore (W + w) B_1 G_1 = W.BG + w.BG + (W + w) GG_1 - (W + w) BB_1$.

But $w.BG + (W + w) GG_1 =$ the moment of the weights added ($w$) about the original centre of buoyancy $= wa$.

Also $(W + w) BB_1 =$ the moment of the additional displacement about the original centre of buoyancy $= wc$.

"Substituting these values for their respective quantities in equation (A); the stability of the ship at the inclination $I$ corresponding to the water line $W_1 L_1$—

$$= b_1 A_1 - W.BG \sin I - w (a - c) \sin I \ldots\ldots\ldots (B)$$

"The stability corresponding to the water line $WL$, when the inclination of the ship is $I$ from the upright position—

$$= bA - W.BG \sin I \ldots\ldots\ldots\ldots\ldots (C)$$

"Subtracting equation (C) from (B) it is found that the difference of the stabilities of the ship under the conditions above stated—

$$= b_1 A_1 - b A - w (a - c) \sin I \dots\dots\dots\dots\dots(D)$$

"Ships are commonly of such a form in the neighbourhood of the load water line, that, with a slight increase in the draught of water, the form of the new load water section is nearly the same as that of the original load water section.

"Also if the ship be inclined about a fore and aft axis, through the same angle, the wedges of immersion respectively corresponding to the two draughts of water will be very nearly the same; that is, see equation (D),

$b_1 A_1$ is practically equal to $bA$;

and the difference in the stability of the ship at the two draughts of water becomes $= - w (a - c) \sin I$.

"Consequently, if the centre of gravity of the weights added be situated in the same horizontal plane as the centre of gravity of the additional displacement (that contained between the water lines $W_1 L_1$ and $WL$), in which case $a = c$, the stability of the ship will be the same at the two draughts of water.

"If the centre of gravity of the weights added be above the centre of gravity of the additional displacement, i.e., if $a$ be greater than $c$, the stability will be diminished by the quantity $w (a - c) \sin I$. If the centre of gravity of the weights added be below that of the additional displacement, in which case $c$ is greater than $a$, the stability is increased by the quantity $w (c - a) \sin I$.

"If $c - a = GM$, the height of the metacentre above the centre of gravity will not be altered by the additional lading."

The author then proceeds to show that, "In a ship floating at a given draught of water, if some of her weights have to be removed, the alteration in the stability by the removal of the weights can also be ascertained in the same manner." The following are the results obtained:

"If the ship be of such a form as to give

$$bA = b_1 A_1.$$

Then $w (a - c) \sin I$ will represent the increase in the stability by the removal of the weights. That is, when $a$ is greater than $c$, or the centre of gravity of the weights removed is situated above the centre of gravity of the diminished displacement (between $W_1L_1$ and $WL$), the stability of the ship is increased by the removal of the weights.

"When the centre of gravity of the weights removed is situated in the same horizontal plane as that of the diminished displacement, the stability is the same as it was before the weights were removed.

"When the centre of gravity of the weights removed is situated below that of the diminished displacement, in which case $c$ is greater than $a$, the stability of the ship is diminished, by the removal of the weights $w$, by the quantity $w(c-a)\sin I$. If $c - a = GM$, the height of the metacentre above the centre of gravity is not altered by the removal of the weights."

As already stated, when the weight or weights added cause the ship to sink to such a depth that there is a material alteration in the form of the load water plane, and hence in the forms of the wedges of immersion and emersion, it becomes a laborious task to calculate the stability in the new condition. As, however, it is not so much the actual stability that is required as the relation between the altered and the original stabilities, an easy method of determining this alteration has been suggested by Mr. F. K. Barnes.* This method we will now state in the author's words:—

"In ships of a common form the ratio of the stability of one ship to that of another will be always substantially the same for ordinary equal inclinations, and nearly the same as the ratio of their stabilities when the inclination is evanescent. In the latter case the points in which the verticals through the centres of buoyancy corresponding to the inclined positions cut the original verticals through the centres of buoyancy corresponding to the upright position, are the metacentres.

"Referring to fig. 2, Plate XX., suppose the angle $I$ to be exceedingly small; then the points $M$ and $M_1$ are the metacentres corresponding to the water lines $WL$ and $W_1L_1$, respectively.

"Using the same notation as before, and taking the case

* *Shipbuilding, Theoretical and Practical*, p. 56.

where the weights $w$ (measured in cubic feet of sea-water), are put on board of the ship whose displacement in cubic feet of sea-water is $W$—

The stability corresponding to the water line $WL$

$$= W (BM - BG) \sin I,$$

and the stability corresponding to the water line $W_1 L_1$ is

$$= (W+w)(B_1 M - B_1 G_1) \sin I,$$

and these may be represented relatively by

$$W.BM - W.BG \text{ and}$$
$$(W+w) B_1 M_1 - (W+w) B_1 G_1, \text{ respectively.}$$

"Now $W.BM$ may be obtained from the table used for calculating the height of the metacentre corresponding to the water line $WL$. (See Table I.)

"Let this quantity be represented by $M$.

"Also $(W+w) B_1 M_1$ may be taken from the table in which was calculated the height of the metacentre corresponding to the water line $W_1 L_1$. Let this quantity be represented by $M_1$, then as before:

$$B_1 G_1 = BG + GG_1 - BB_1$$
$$\text{and } (W+w)B_1 G_1 = W.BG + w.BG + (W+w)GG_1 - (W+w)BB_1$$
$$= W.BG + w(a-c),$$

where $a$ is the distance of the centre of gravity of the additional weights $w$ put on board above the original centre of buoyancy; and $c$ is the distance of the centre of gravity of the displacement between the water lines $WL$ and $W_1 L_1$ above the original centre of buoyancy.

"The stability of the ship in the two conditions may therefore be represented by

$$M - W.BG,$$
$$\text{and } M_1 - W.BG - w(a-c) \text{ respectively,}$$

and the alteration in the stability, by the addition of the weights, may be represented by

$$M_1 - M - w(a-c).$$

"And if the position of $G$ be known or assumed, the proportionate loss or gain of stability will be readily found."

**99. Effect on the Stability by admitting Water into the Ship.**—In considering this question we must make the same assumptions with regard to the division of the ship into water-tight compartments, as when considering the effect on the trim (see Art. 96), with the further addition of longitudinal divisions which do not affect the principles involved in calculating the trim or longitudinal stability.

I. If the water is admitted into a compartment with a water-tight crown so as to fill it, then if the crown is always below the level of the sea, whether the water in the compartment is in free communication with the sea or not, its effect upon the stability is the same as that of any solid body of the same weight whose centre of gravity is similarly situated. (See preceding Article.)

II. If the compartment is not filled, and the water is not in free communication with the sea, the centre of gravity of the water moves towards the same direction as that to which the ship is inclined, and thus the upsetting moment due to the position of the centre of gravity of the weights in the ship is increased. The determination of this upsetting moment at any angle of heel involves a calculation of the moment due to the position of the weights previously in the ship added to the upsetting moment due to the weight and position of the centre of gravity of the water in the hold when at that angle. The positions of $B$ and $M$ will also be affected by the increased immersion, and thus the surface stability at the particular angle must also be calculated anew.

An instructive method of considering the question is to determine the initial stability of the ship in the case under notice. A comparison of this with the initial stability, as determined by the metacentric method in the normal condition of the ship without water in the compartment, will give a criterion whereby the stability of the ship may be judged. Any investigation of this kind, however, neglects the dynamical effect of the rolling of the water from side to side, which causes the ship to heel over farther than a statical consideration of the question would provide for; the dynamical effect being, indeed, the great source of danger in any case of shifting cargoes of a fluid or semi-fluid character. This dynamical effect is beyond the reach of prior calculation, as the period of the vessel's rolling cannot be predicted with certainty.

To determine the value of $GM$ in a case of this kind, we

may proceed as follows:—Fig. 3, Plate XX., shows a transverse section of a ship which is supposed to be inclined through a small angle $\theta$, the figure being purposely exaggerated for the sake of clearness. $WL$ is the upright and $W_1L_1$ the inclined load water planes when the water is in the ship; the angle being supposed to be small, these planes are similar in form and of equal area. $wl$ is the surface of the water in the hold when the ship is upright, and $w_1l_1$ is its inclined surface. The whole displacement is termed $D$, and $d$ is the volume of the water in the hold. The centre of buoyancy of the former is shown at $B$, and of the latter at $b$, while their positions in the inclined condition are shown at $B_1$ and $b_1$ respectively. $M$ is the metacentre obtained by a perpendicular from $B_1$, and $m$ that obtained by a perpendicular from $b_1$ in the inclined conditions. It will be remembered that a small angle of inclination is being considered. The centre of gravity of the ship is shown at $G$.

Using the symbol $\propto$ to represent the expression "varies as," we find

$$\text{Moment of stability at angle } \theta \propto (D.GM - dGm)$$
$$\propto D(BM - BG) - d(bm - bG)$$
$$\propto D.BM - d.bm - (D.BG - d.bG).$$

But using the expression $I_1$ to represent the moment of inertia of the load water plane, and $I_2$ that of the plane of the surface of the water in the hold, we have

$$D.BM = I_1$$
$$\text{and } d.bm = I_2$$
$$\text{also } D.BG - d.bG = (D-d)\beta G,$$

where $\beta$ is the centre of buoyancy of the displacement between $WL$ and $wl$.

$$\text{Hence moment of stability} \propto I_1 - I_2 - (D-d)\beta G$$
$$\text{and the virtual } \overline{GM} = \frac{I_1 - I_2}{D - d} - \beta G.$$

The moment of stability at an angle $\theta$, so small that $m$ and $M$ may be considered fixed, is

$$\overline{GM}(D-d) \sin \theta.$$

It is obvious that this investigation affords only as much information as can be obtained by the use of the metacentric method; besides which, the water in the hold being

# EFFECT ON THE STABILITY BY ADMITTING WATER.

free to move, the actual stability at a small angle of heel will be less than the above unless the vessel is inclined very slowly.

III. If the compartment is filled with water to the level of the sea—with which it is in free communication by means of a hole in the bottom, and its motion as the ship heels is not constrained by a water-tight crown, but its surface is always at the same level as that of the sea—then the ship is in the same condition as if the portion of the immersed body between the bounding bulkheads was removed, and support due to the displacement of that portion taken away (see Art. 96). In this case the ship sinks deeper into the water until the volume of displaced water above the original water line, outside the bounding bulkheads, is equal to the volume of displacement lost by admitting water into the compartment.

In a paper read before the Institution of Naval Architects, in the year 1867, Mr. F. K. Barnes has investigated the effects on the stability of a vessel, of which the transverse vertical sections are all equal rectangles, due to filling watertight compartments with water, using different ratios between the depth or draught of water and the breadth of the vessel. These investigations are of three kinds, viz., for compartments bounded by transverse and longitudinal water-tight bulkheads, and by horizontal water-tight flats. As the paper is too lengthy for complete insertion, we will content ourselves with stating the results arrived at therein. It must be remembered that in each case the compartment is supposed to be quite empty before the water is admitted—that being the most unfavourable supposition—also that the thickness of the sides and frames are neglected, these being supposed to be of iron. The centre of gravity is also assumed to be above the centre of buoyancy, as is the case in nearly all ships.

*First*, when a ship is divided into water-tight compartments by transverse vertical bulkheads, the distance between which are $\frac{1}{100}$, $\frac{1}{10}$, $\frac{1}{4}$, and $\frac{1}{2}$ the length of the ship—a separate result being obtained for each case.

"When the breadth is equal to the depth, and to twice the depth, the height of the metacentre above the under side of keel is greater after the compartment is injured than it was before. Consequently, also, the stability of the ship is in all these cases greater after the compartment is injured than it was before. It follows, therefore, that if sufficient freeboard be given to such ships to admit of their immersion being increased to the extent due to the volume of any one or more of its compartments, they will be quite safe when the compartments are injured.

"It also follows that ships of the above form and relative proportions would be lost by going down bodily in the water and losing their freeboard, and not from losing their stability and turning over.

"The same remark is practically applicable to the case in which the breadth is equal to three times the depth.

"Where the breadth is equal to four times the depth, the metacentre falls slightly between the limits taken; but it rises again as the bulkheads are placed nearer the extremities of the ship, *i.e.*, when they are more than half the length of the ship apart.

"As the breadth increases above this in proportion to the depth, the relative depression of the metacentre by injury to the compartments will be increased; but it must be borne in mind that in such cases the metacentre, before injury to the compartments, would be exceedingly high.

"The *Second case* is that of an iron ship divided into watertight compartments by longitudinal vertical bulkheads." Two bulkheads are chosen, each being taken at the several distances of $\frac{1}{100}$, $\frac{1}{10}$, $\frac{1}{4}$, and $\frac{1}{2}$* the breadth of the ship, measuring from her side, and a communication is assumed to be "made from side to side, so that when the compartment on one side is filled, the compartment on the other side is also filled." The results are as follow:—"Where the breadth is equal to the depth, the height of the metacentre above the bottom of the vessel is greater after the compartments are filled than it was before; and since, from the suppositions we have made, the centre of gravity of the ship itself is unaltered, the ship, if stable before the compartments are filled, will be more stable after they are filled.

"When the breadth is equal to twice the draught of water,

---

* When the bulkheads are each at one-half the breadth of the vessel from the side, they coincide at the middle line, and thus the vessel is filled with water. The centre of buoyancy and metacentre then coincide at an infinite distance above the keel.

the metacentre descends when the vertical longitudinal bulkhead is very close to the ship's side, and it reaches its lowest position when the bulkheads are fixed somewhere between one-fourth and one-tenth of the ship's breadth from the ship's side.

"From this position, as the bulkheads are placed nearer to the middle line, the metacentre continually rises as they approach the middle line. The same remarks apply when the breadth is equal to four times the draught of water; but the lowest position of the metacentre will not be reached until the bulkheads are relatively much nearer to the middle line than when the breadth of the ship is equal to twice the draught of water."

The *Third case* is that of a ship divided into water-tight compartments by horizontal flats, each compartment being made to communicate with the upper deck of the ship by means of small water-tight trunks.

The simplest condition is when a compartment between any two horizontal flats becomes suddenly filled with water. This case has already been considered.

"If any of the lower compartments of such a ship were to become filled, it is evident that the stability would always be greater after the compartment was filled than it was before, and would increase with the size of the compartment, and also with the distance of its centre of gravity below the water."

The case remaining "is that in which a ship, divided into water-tight compartments by horizontal flats, has one of these compartments only slightly injured." We have already referred to this condition; the results which Mr. Barnes has investigated are as follows:—

"When the upper surface of a horizontal flat, situated at the load water section in a ship of the usual form (of which the centre of gravity is above the centre of buoyancy), becomes covered only to a slight depth with water, the ship will not swim with its longitudinal diametrical plane vertical, since the equilibrium of the ship when that plane is vertical is one of instability.

"The same is also true of a ship with its sides vertical throughout, at whatever height the water-tight flat, which is covered with water, may be situated, provided the centre of gravity is above the centre of buoyancy; and more generally still when, under similar circumstances, the moment of inertia of the plane of the surface of the water on any deck about a longitudinal axis is equal to or greater than that of the load water section about its longitudinal axis.

"Such ships, in the condition above described, would generally have two positions of stable equilibrium, one on each side of what is the upright position before the water is on the deck, and the inclination of the two positions of equilibrium to the upright position would increase with the quantity of water on the deck."

# CHAPTER IV.

## CALCULATIONS OF THE WEIGHTS AND CENTRES OF GRAVITY OF SHIPS.

*Preliminary Calculations:* Approximation to Weight of Hull—To Centre of Gravity—To Centre of Buoyancy—To value of GM. *Detailed Calculations:* Armour — Backing — Deck Plating — Bottom Plating—Expansion of Bottom—Bottom Planking—Deck Beams—Plating—Flats—Bulkheads—Transverse Framing Method with Curves—Longitudinal Frames—Fittings.

**100. Arithmetical Calculations of the Weights and Centres of Gravity of Ships.**—When a ship is built, equipped, and afloat, her weight is accurately determined by calculating the weight of the volume of water displaced by the ship when floating at the observed draught of water. The sheer draught used in this calculation should be copied from the mould loft floor, as the lines there drawn represent the actual form of the ship with greater accuracy than the lines on the construction sheer draught. To ensure still greater accuracy, the form of the body is sometimes copied from the ship when on the building slip, or when in dock; but owing to the difficulty of "taking off" the ship in this way, and the liability to error in the process, the lines on the mould loft floor are generally employed, the work being simpler, and the result usually as accurate.

The centre of gravity of the ship being in the transverse section of the ship which contains the centre of buoyancy, and the position of the latter having been calculated from the drawings just referred to (see Table I.), the longitudinal position of the former is therefore at once known.

The vertical position of the centre of gravity is found by the method described at Art. 90.

If the ship is incomplete when the draught of water is observed, and the experiments made, or if it is desired to obtain her weight and the position of her centre of gravity, when any of the items of the equipment are removed, the new displacement, and the new position of the centre of gravity are found by the methods described in the preceding chapter.

In this chapter we propose considering the method of calculating the weight and position of the centre of gravity of a ship from her drawings *before she is built*, or even the design is given to the builder; in order to ensure that she shall float at the required draught and trim, and have the requisite stability when equipped and afloat.

**101. Preliminary Calculations.**—We may here remark that in the earliest stages of a design it is necessary that the designer should know, approximately, the weight of the proposed ship, and the position of its centre of gravity. This is not the place to notice the considerations which influence the naval architect in deciding upon the protection, armament, speed, stability, etc., necessary for the ship of war; or the accommodation for passengers, cargo space, speed, etc., for the merchant ship which he is designing. Even the ratio of length to breadth, and the most suitable draught of water are also questions which involve considerations of such importance, and demand so much space, that due justice could not be done to them in the limits of this small volume. Indeed, it rarely becomes the duty of the naval architect to make a thorough investigation of these principles in fixing upon his dimensions, for he is usually aided by the experience obtained from other vessels which partake, in some respect or another, of the characteristics of the intended vessel. Even the question of the scantlings employed in the construction, upon which the weight entirely depends, is usually settled by reference to other vessels whose behaviour at sea is known, and whose strength has been proved; although the skilful designer is always on the alert to make such improvements in the sizes and arrangements of the materials employed as shall reduce the weight, while the strength of the vessel is at least retained at its original amount. In the merchant navy the scantlings are usually fixed by the Rules of Lloyd's Register of Shipping, or of the Liverpool Registry.

In explaining the manner in which the designer proceeds to determine approximately the weight of a ship that he is about to design, and the position of its centre of gravity we will take the case of an ironclad ship, as that will include all the considerations that ever occur in any vessel whatever.

Let us suppose then that it is required to design an ironclad vessel for any special kind of service, and that by the aid of experience already acquired, it is believed that a certain number of guns, protected by a certain thickness of armour and backing, with armoured decks of a specified thickness, also ammunition, stores of all kinds, engines and boilers to give the required speed, and coals enough to last a certain time at that speed, can be carried by a ship of a certain length, breadth, and draught of water, having lines sufficiently fine to render the required speed possible, and sufficiently stable to be seaworthy and safe. We have to discover whether such a belief is accurate.

The question of engines, boilers, coals, fineness of lines, and speed, will be considered in Part V.; but at present we will take it for granted that these are determined, and it remains to be discovered whether the weights can be carried upon the trial displacement, and whether their common centre of gravity is suitably situated for the required stability and trim.

The question of scantlings can be readily settled by reference to specifications of ships of similar character already built, making any alterations suggested by experience, or rendered necessary by circumstances.

The available displacement is approximately found by multiplying together the proposed length, breadth, mean draught of water, and a co-efficient of fineness of displacement thought suitable for a vessel of the kind being designed, in order to attain the required speed. A Table of these co-efficients for typical vessels is given in Art. 59.

For the purposes of calculation it is desirable to divide the total weights in a ship into two divisions, viz., *hull* and *equipment*. The former includes all that composes the ship proper, without masts, rigging, anchors, cables, etc. The latter consists, as the name implies, of the stores and outfit, including provisions, rigging, guns, ammunition, and cargo. The *hull* of an ironclad is again subdivided into the *hull proper* and *armour*. The former consists of the structural parts of the ship, and the latter of the protective material, such as armour plates, backing, and protective deck plating. The *hull proper* is the first element whose weight and centre of gravity is calculated. This is generally the largest item of the total weight even in an ironclad ship, while in a merchant vessel it includes everything but the equipment.

**102. Approximation to Weight of Hull.**—An excellent approximation to the weight of hull proper is obtained by means of a comparison with the corresponding weight in a vessel of similar description and scantlings already built; the latter being, of course, found by deducting from the displacement at any draught those weights which do not belong to the hull proper. This approximation is found by multiplying the girth of each vessel around the upper deck, sides, and bottom, at midships, by her length on the load water line; then use the ratio: As the girth of the vessel already built is to the girth of the proposed vessel, so is the weight of hull proper in the former to that required of the latter. In the case of an armoured vessel, or one in which items occur which do not occur in the vessel whose weight — neglecting the equipment — is known; or when there are fittings or weights of any kind in the construction of the known ship which will not be required in that proposed; it is usual to calculate the weights of these portions in the case selected and deduct them from the total weight of the hull, and then, using this weight, by the aid of the ratio just referred to, the weight of the corresponding portion of the structure of the proposed vessel may be approximately found. For instance, in the case of an armoured ship whose weight it is required to determine approximately in the early stage of a design. Suppose the total weight of another ironclad ship of rather different dimensions, but of about the same scantlings as that which is to be designed is known. First, deduct from the total displacement all the weights constituting the equipment; and the remainder will be the weight of the hull of the ship. Next calculate the weights of armour, backing, protective deck plating, and any other portions of the ship which do not belong to the hull proper, and deduct these; the remainder will be a weight of hull which can be used for comparison. Obtain the products of the lengths and girths in the two cases, viz., those of the known ship and of the design, and by means of the ratio thus found determine the weight of hull proper in the proposed ship. Whereupon knowing the extent and thickness of armour, backing, etc., proposed for the intended ship, their weights can be calculated, and then when added to the approximate weight of hull proper, found by using the ratio, the total weight of the hull is determined. By adding to this the weights required for equipping the ship for her intended service, the total displacement which is necessary to float the proposed vessel, at the draught of water fixed upon, is at once known. By comparing this result with the displacement already found, we are able to discover whether the designer's intentions are feasible, and if the displacement is not enough, we have then to find how much the ship must be either lengthened widened, deepened, or the lines filled out, according to circumstances, in order to get the necessary displacement; or how the weight of the hull or equipment may be reduced.

**103. Approximation to position of Centre of Gravity.**— While making the preceding preliminary calculations for the approximate weight of hull of the proposed ship, we might at the same time have determined, approximately, the position of its centre of gravity. The methods and artifices adopted in making the several calculations will be referred to hereafter in this chapter; we are now merely pointing out the means by which approximate results may be found, which will be sufficiently correct to enable the designer to proceed with the drawings, etc., of the vessel, without having to make any considerable alterations or modifications when the results of the detailed calculations are known.

The position of the centre of gravity of the somewhat similar ship is supposed to be known, so that having her drawings before him, the calculator is able to determine pretty accurately the positions of the centres of gravity of the several items of the equipment, also of the armour, backing, protective deck plating, etc., which he removes from the ship in order to reduce her to a state whereby a comparison may be instituted with a similar part of the intended ship. By this means the height of centre of gravity above the under side of keel,* also its longitudinal position with reference to the middle of her length on the load water line, may be found in the stripped and therefore comparable state. Then for the height of the centre of gravity of the similar portion of the intended ship above the under side of keel institute this ratio: As the depth of the known vessel from upper deck to under side of keel is to the depth, similarly measured, in the design, so is the height of centre of gravity above keel in the known vessel to the similar height in the design. Also for the longitudinal position of the centre of gravity: As the length on the load water line of the known ship is to the length, similarly measured, of the design, so is the distance, on the fore or after side of the middle of the length, of the centre of gravity in the known vessel to the similar distance in the design. It may be remarked in passing that this centre of gravity is almost invariably abaft the middle of the length on the load water line. It is necessary that the two vessels should have about the same trim, or else this ratio will not be useful. As already remarked, these are merely approximate positions; but they are generally very trustworthy. By taking into account the vertical and longitudinal positions of the centres of gravity of the armour, backing, etc., also of the items of the equipment, the vertical and longitudinal positions of the centre of gravity of the complete ship is approximately found.

**104. Approximate position of Centre of Buoyancy.**—In order that the preceding knowledge may be useful to the designer, it is necessary that the position of the centre of buoyancy of his design may also be approximately known; for unless the centres of gravity and buoyancy are in the same transverse section, the ship will not float at the intended trim.

For the longitudinal position of the centre of buoyancy, a similar method may be used as for the centre of gravity: As the length, on the load water line, of the known ship is to the distance of the centre of buoyancy from the middle of the length, so is the length on the load water line of the design to the position of its centre of buoyancy with regard to the middle of its length. Should the centres of gravity

* By the term keel, as employed in this chapter, must be understood a flat keel plate, as of an ironclad, unless it is otherwise stated.

and buoyancy not be in the same section, then it shows that either the form of the body must be altered, or else that weights on board must be so shifted as to produce a change of moment, in the required direction, equal to the product of the displacement and the distance between the two centres. In this case also it is necessary that the ships should have similar trims. For the vertical position of the centre of buoyancy: As the mean draught of the known ship is to the height of its centre of buoyancy above under side of keel, so is the mean draught of design to the similar height of its centre of buoyancy. It need hardly be remarked that this method will not give a good approximation unless the bodies of the two vessels are tolerably similar.

105. **Approximate Value of** $GM$.—If it be desired to push our approximate calculations still further, and find the stability which the new ship may be expected to have, the value of $GM$ may be approximately found in the following manner:—Draw a load water line, by the aid of the length, breadth, and co-efficient of fineness given; and then calculate its moment of inertia about the middle line axis, as explained at Art. 66. Divide this result by the approximate displacement, the quotient will be an approximate value of $BM$; and the approximate positions of $B$ and $G$ having been already determined, a good idea of the value of $GM$ is thus found. $D \times GM \sin \theta$, will be a very good approximation to the moment of statical stability, when $\theta$ is less than 15 degrees.

106. **Detailed Calculations — Defensive Materials.—** I. **Armour Plating, Weight of.**—This is the heaviest and at the same time one of the simplest items of a ship's hull to calculate. Except when fitted under the counter, it has usually either a flat or a developable surface. Being of such thick and heavy material, great accuracy is necessary in taking the measurements; consequently, the form of the portion of the vessel that is covered with armour should be carefully copied from the sheer draught. An expansion of the armour surface should be made, and the edges of the strakes of plating as well as the butts of the plates drawn thereon. The thickness of each plate should be marked on the expansion. It is hardly possible that the arrangement of butts

made by the calculator should agree exactly with that afterwards adopted at the ship; nevertheless, the difference will not, in general, be sufficient to introduce any error of importance. It is desirable that a copy of this expansion should be furnished to the builder, in order that the arrangement adopted at the ship shall agree, as closely as circumstances will permit, with that originally contemplated. In constructing this expansion, it is desirable that the load water line should be developed straight thereon, for convenience in calculating the vertical position of the centre of gravity. The expansion will usually be of a very simple character, so that it is not necessary to explain the mode of preparing it; especially as the question of making an expansion of a ship's surface will be explained in Art. 111.

The average weight of a cubic foot of iron being 480 lbs., the weight of each plate, or an area of uniform thickness, is easily found by multiplying 40 lbs. by the number of inches the armour plate is thick, the result being the weight per square foot of the plating of that thickness. To the result so found must be added a percentage for the points of the bolts and the nuts; this percentage varies from about 2 per cent. for plates of 9 in. thick and upwards, to 5 per cent. for plates of 4 in.

**107. Armour Plating, Centre of Gravity of.**—In calculating the positions of the centres of gravity of the component parts of a ship's hull, it is desirable to measure vertical distances from the load water line, and horizontal distances from the midship section. With regard to the armour plating, for the sake of greater simplicity and accuracy it is recommended that all the measurements for moments be taken from the sheer draught, and not from the expansion drawing. To do this the edges and butts should be drawn upon the sheer plan, and the butts at the bow and stern marked upon the half-breadth plan. Transverse armour bulkheads should be drawn, with their edges and butts, in the body plan. If this be done the distances of the centres of the plates, both vertically and longitudinally, from the lines of reference can be readily measured. The weights and distances of the centres of gravity of the plates, both vertically and longitudinally, are then entered upon a tabular form (as shown by

Table III.), together with those of the other items in the hull, in order to obtain the total result.

**108. II. Backing behind Armour—Weight and Centre of Gravity of.**—These are obtained in a similar manner to that stated for the armour in the preceding Article, except that the cubic contents of the several thicknesses of backing are calculated, and not the superficies. A weight of 56 lbs. per cubic foot is usually allowed for teak; this weight including the bolts used in securing the backing. It should be remarked, however, that although 54 lbs. is often allowed, yet when the teak is not well seasoned 60 lbs. is nearer the truth.

**109. III. Protective Deck Plating** is a very considerable item as regards weight in the construction of recent iron-clad ships.

As this is not a treatise on practical shipbuilding, we will not examine the purpose for which this plating is put into the ship; we have merely to take the drawings which show such protective deck plating, and estimate its weight and the position of its centre of gravity. This is very readily done, as the area and longitudinal position of the centre of gravity of a surface of uniform thickness is at once found by the use of Simpson's Rule. If there is any sheer in the deck, or round up to the beam, the vertical position of the centre of gravity of a surface of uniform thickness is found by multiplying each ordinate of the area by the vertical distance of its centre of gravity from the load water line; the sum of the products being divided by the sum of the ordinates will give the distance of the centre of gravity of the whole surface from the line in question. If different parts of a deck have different thicknesses of plating, the sum of the moments of the different thicknesses, divided by the total weight, gives the vertical position of the common centre of gravity. It is, however, desirable to make a separate entry in the tabular form for each thickness of plating. Deck plating of one inch thick and upwards may be usually considered as being fitted for protective purposes in contradistinction to the plating which is laid upon the beams for purely structural purposes.

The preceding remark is made in order that the calculator may be able to properly classify his results; as armour, backing, and protective deck plating do not constitute part of the hull proper, but are rather the mail or defensive burden which the ship has to carry. This distinction is necessary, inasmuch as in preparing a design, a principal object is to carry the equipment and protective material as economically as possible, consistent with the necessary strength. Besides this, as already mentioned, it is not possible to estimate the weight of one vessel from that of another, or institute comparisons between the efficiency, in this respect, of different ships without knowing the weight of the material composing the hull proper, separately from that of the weights carried. The weights of the protective materials in unmasted ironclads now in existence in the Royal Navy range from about 50 to 70 per cent. of the weights of the structural materials, while in full-rigged ironclads the percentages range from about 22 to 38.

110. **Structural Weights—Bottom Plating.**—This is the heaviest element in the hull of an iron ship, whether for war or mercantile purposes; its preponderance over the other elements being more marked in the latter than in the former. By the term bottom plating we include not only that part of the shell of the ship that is below the water, but also the plating of the ship's side, except the armour already considered. It must, however, be remarked that whereas in merchant ships and unarmoured ships generally, the mode of plating the side and bottom is the same; in iron-clad vessels, the side plating is generally flush, while the bottom is lap jointed.

There are two principal methods of calculating the weight of a ship's bottom and side plating, viz., by means of an expansion drawing and by measurement from the sheer draught. The second is by far the preferable course, both as regards the weight and centre of gravity; for owing to the undevelopable nature of the surface it is impossible to obtain a sufficiently good approximation to the area, also the vertical position of the centre of gravity cannot be easily calculated from such a drawing. The method by measurement is therefore that generally used, one or two different modes of procedure being adopted, as we shall show presently. We will, however, first show how expansion drawings of a ship's bottom are constructed.

111. **Expansion of Bottom.**—The best method is by cut-

ting and fitting a sheet of thin and flexible paper so as **to** exactly cover the surface of a model of the ship. This method is not possible without the model, and as that is not usually made in the early stages of a design, we may pass it over without further notice. It is, however, evident that the result, so far as the area is concerned, is very accurate, and the centre of gravity may be readily and correctly calculated from the model itself, if the edges of the plates are drawn thereon.

For an approximation to the expansion of the surface the following method is often adopted:—Draw a number of diagonal lines\* in the body plan of the sheer draught, about the same distance apart at the midship section as the level lines, the diagonal lines being as nearly as possible square to the square stations. Draw in the half-breadth plans the rabatments of these lines. Then bend some narrow strips of paper around these lines, and mark upon the strips the intersections of the several square stations, also the stem and stern post. Next, bend some narrow strips around the square stations in the body, and mark upon them the intersections of the several diagonal lines, also the middle line of the keel. Then draw a straight line on a sheet of paper to represent the middle line of keel, and set off upon it the positions of the several square stations. Pin the keel extremity of each square station strip of paper to the position of that square station on the keel line. Next, pin the first diagonal strip of paper to the midship section strip, with the corresponding points on them together, and keep the midship section strip square to the keel line. Also, pin the diagonal strip to the other square station strips with the respective points coincident, the whole being pinned to the sheet of paper and drawing board. Proceed similarly with the other diagonal strips, observing that it will be necessary to bend and distort the square station (except the midship station) and diagonal strips in order that the respective spots on both may coincide and lie flat on the paper. When all the strips are pinned down, a pencil line drawn round the boundaries will then inclose an approximation to the area of the bottom. Pencil lines drawn against the sides of the square station strips will

\* Level lines are often used instead of diagonal lines.

show the positions of the respective square stations when the bottom is approximately developed in this way.

In No. 3 of the *Annual* of the Royal School of Naval Architecture will be found a method of making an expansion of a ship's bottom suggested, we believe, by Mr. Crossland, one of the chief constructors of the Navy. In explaining his method the writer says:—

"The ordinary mode of making an expansion of the bottom plating or planking—for obtaining the area of its surface, which consists of taking the lengths of a series of level lines, and of a series of transverse sections, and making their intersections meet on a flat surface by means of two sets of strips of paper—is a very troublesome business, and the process is not correct in principle. The water lines and sections, if traced on the model, would divide the surface into a number of four-sided figures, having their sides inclined at different angles. To represent any one of those figures on a flat surface it would be necessary to measure the lengths of the four sides, and at least one of the angles between them. In the usual way of making the expansion, the sides are correctly measured, but no means are adopted for obtaining the angle referred to. The angles in the expanded drawing are determined by making all the quadrilaterals fit into one another and form one continuous area. And these angles do not correspond to those on the surface of the model. In my opinion, an approximation of the area may be drawn out in the form of an expansion which is as nearly correct as an ordinary drawing can be made, and on a perfectly obvious and simple plan.

"For instance, let $ab$ and $cd$ (fig. 1, Plate XXI.) be two sections. Draw $bc$ and $ad$ as nearly perpendicular as possible to both sections, at such a distance apart that $ab$ and $cd$ may be regarded as nearly straight lines. Then these lines, when traced on the surface of the model, will be very nearly perpendicular to each other. To find the area of the inclosed space, therefore, it will be only necessary to obtain the lengths of $bc$ and $ad$, and then construct the figure thus: Make (in fig. 2) $AD=$ true length of $ad$; draw $AB$ and $DC$ perpendicular to $AD$; make $AB=ab$, and $DC=cd$; join $BC$. This figure will represent very nearly the area (not the form) of the surface, inclosed by the four lines on the model.

"To apply this to the curved surface of a ship, draw in the body a series of curved lines, at convenient distances, square to the sections at the other points of intersection, as shown in fig. 1, Plate XXI. Then run off the true lengths of these lines as bent diagonals. Then begin with the lowest, and set off on the stations the square breadths of the lowest strip. Draw a line through the point thus obtained, and apply the lengths of the first diagonal on this line, starting from the midship section, and setting off the expanded positions of the stations. A second set of breadths must be set off from these points perpendicular to the line just drawn, and a new line through the second line of points so got. The length of the second expanded line must be set off on the line last drawn and the intersections of the sections marked as before. This will add to the drawing the area of the second strip of the bottom, counting from below. This operation must, of course, be repeated till the whole expansion is completed. A water line can be put upon this expansion, observing by measuring its distance above or below any of the curved diagonals in the body, and transferring these measurements to the expansion, as shown in fig. 2. The nature of the construction will be understood by comparing the points lettered in the figs.

$$AD = ad.$$
$$AB = ab.$$
$$DC = dc.$$
$$CB = cb.$$

"Fig. 3 on the same Plate represents the expansion of the bent diagonals. The area of this expansion up to the water line is 538·7 square feet. The area of the same, calculated by taking the mean girth and multiplying by the length, is 533·7 square feet."

The writer further says:—

"This method of constructing the area of the bottom is applicable to any ordinary form of bottom," and in his opinion "it does not involve more labour than the usual plan," which has already been described.

When an expansion drawing is made, the several strakes of plating can be shown upon it, also their thicknesses, whereupon the weight can be found by the ordinary rules of mensuration. It is obviously impossible to calculate the position of the centre of gravity from an expansion.

**112. Calculation for Area of Bottom Plating without an Expansion.**—The method usually adopted for calculating the weight and the position of the centre of gravity of the plating on a ship's sides and bottom is by measurement taken from the sheer draught, as we shall now proceed to explain.

We shall assume that the plating is in zones or belts of different thicknesses; and, moreover, that the thicknesses of some of the belts are varied towards the extremities of the ship. We will suppose that the boundaries of these belts of plating are drawn in the body plan (see fig. 1, Plate XXII.)

Two modes of procedure may then be adopted, viz., either to calculate the weight and position of the centre of gravity of each area with uniform thickness; or else to commence by finding the weight and centre of gravity of the whole surface, supposing it to consist of plating of the minimum thickness. If the latter method is adopted, we have to add the result of the calculation for the weight and centre of gravity of the surface (except that part which is of the minimum thickness), supposing it to be of a thickness equal to the difference between the minimum and next thickness. And so on by successively clothing the surface until the whole plating is accounted for, the weight and moment (both vertically and longitudinally) of the bottom plating is obtained.

Suppose the area of the whole surface is required: Carefully measure the girths of the plating at all the square stations, add them together, and divide the sum by the number of girths, the quotient will be the mean transverse girth of the plating. Run off in the half-breadth plan a number of rabatted diagonal lines, as explained in Art. 111, and measure the length of each one of them. Add the lengths together, divide the sum by the number of diagonal lines employed, the quotient will be the mean longitudinal girth. Multiply the mean transverse by the mean longitudinal girth, and the product is an approximation to the area of the bottom.

Should the area of a belt or zone of plating be required, the girths of the portions of the square stations included in the belt are measured, and the mean breadth of the belt thus obtained; while the mean lengths of the diagonal lines on the belt is taken as the mean length of the belt. Their product is the area of the belt. Having the area of the surface of any thickness of plating, its weight is found by allowing 480 lbs. per cubic foot which gives 40 lbs. per square foot for 1 in. plating, 30 lbs. for $\frac{3}{4}$ in., 20 lbs. for $\frac{1}{2}$ in., and so on for other thicknesses. A percentage must be added to this result to allow for the butts, laps, and liners; the percentage varying with the thickness of the plating. On Table IV. will be found a list of the percentages for different thicknesses; should the lengths or breadths of the plates employed differ from those by which this list of percentages was prepared, a correction must be made for the laps and butts, it being evident that the proportionate weights of the latter diminish as the lengths and breadths of the plates increase. The above percentage having been added, about 3 per cent more is added to the whole, in order to allow for the heads and clenches of the rivets.

### 113. Calculation for Centre of Gravity of Bottom Plating.

—I. *Longitudinally.*—The longitudinal position of the centre of gravity of bottom plating is found in the manner we are about to explain. Whether the first or second mode of calculating the weight of the bottom plating is adopted, in either case the method of calculating the longitudinal position of the centre of gravity, which we are about to describe, may be used, the results giving either the longitudinal positions of the centres of gravity of the whole surface, considered as of the minimum thickness, also of the surfaces of the added layers; or else the centre of gravity, longitudinally, of each area having a uniform thickness. For instance, referring to fig. 1, Plate XXII., we may find the longitudinal position of the centre of gravity of the whole area of the bottom, considering it to be $\frac{1}{2}''$ thick, also of the area $DEOEF$ considered $\frac{1}{4}''$ thick; of $GHOHK$ considered $\frac{1}{8}''$ thick; of $LMOMN$ considered $\frac{1}{8}''$ thick; of $DLRP$ considered $\frac{1}{4}''$ thick; and $KSTN$ considered $\frac{1}{8}''$ thick.

Or, again, we may find the longitudinal position of the centre of gravity of each of the belts or zones, $ABEFC$, $PEHKF$, $QHMTS$, $LMOMN$, $DLRP$, $KSTN$ (see fig. 1, Plate XXII.). In either case, having the weight of each piece or area, and the longitudinal position of its centre of gravity, the longitudinal position of the centre of gravity of the whole is easily found.

To find the position (longitudinally) of the centre of gravity of the whole or part of the area of a ship's bottom: Measure the transverse girths as for the area; multiply each girth by the number representing the order of its position on either side of the square station of reference, or that about which moments are taken, and divide the Algebraical sum of the products by the sum of the girths; the quotient, multiplied by the common interval between the square stations at which the girths are measured, gives the distance of the centre of gravity from the square station of reference. The centre of gravity is, of course, on that side of the square station which has the excess of moment.

For instance, referring to fig. 1, Plate XXII., to find the centre of gravity of the whole surface of the bottom, supposing it to be of uniform thickness. Suppose the girths to be as below; then for the longitudinal position of the centre of gravity:—

| Number of Square Station. | Half girth. | Multipliers for Leverage. | Products. |
|---|---|---|---|
| No. 1, - - - | 25·2 | 6 | 151·2 |
| ,, 2, - - - | 28·4 | 5 | 142·0 |
| ,, 3, - - - | 31·3 | 4 | 125·2 |
| ,, 4, - - - | 33·5 | 3 | 100·5 |
| ,, 5, - - - | 35·0 | 2 | 70·0 |
| ,, 6, - - - | 35·5 | 1 | 35·5 |
| ,, 7, - - - | 35·8 | 0 | 624·4 |
| ,, 8, - - - | 35·8 | 1 | 35·8 |
| ,, 9, - - - | 35·6 | 2 | 71·2 |
| ,, 10, - - - | 35·1 | 3 | 105·3 |
| ,, 11, - - - | 34·0 | 4 | 136·0 |
| ,, 12, - - - | 34·2 | 5 | 171·0 |
| ,, 13, - - - | 30·0 | 6 | 180·0 |
| | 429·4 | | 699·3 |
| | | | 624·4 |
| | | | 429·4 )74·90 |
| | | | ·174 |

The common interval between the square stations is 20 ft.

∴ ·174 × 20 = 3·5 ft. abaft No. 7 station,

the position of the centre of gravity of the whole bottom, supposing it to be of uniform thickness. In a ship with a full midship section, and fine lines forward and aft, where there is much variation in the girths, greater accuracy will be obtained by affecting the half girths with Simpson's multipliers before using the multipliers for leverage, in the same way as we find the centre of gravity of a plane area.

There is a slight error admitted into the previous result, owing to an assumption upon which the method is based being somewhat erroneous. Fig. 2, Plate XXII., represents part of a half-breadth plan of a ship; referring to it we shall see that the area of bottom plating between consecutive square stations increases as we proceed from the midship section to forward and aft. Now in the method we have just explained, it is assumed that the girth of each station, say No. 2 in the figure, is a fixed multiple of the area embraced between a square station $BC$, half way between Nos.

1 and 2, and a square station $AD$, half way between Nos. 2 and 3. Now, as a matter of fact, as is seen, the ratio between the girth and the area is a varying one, the areas increasing, relatively, for some distance, as we proceed from midships in either direction. What makes the assumption at all trustworthy is, that we assume the midship section as our station of reference, and the obliquity of the surface of the bottom with regard to the planes of the square stations is nearly symmetrical on either side of *dead flat*. For instance, in ships of ordinary form, $A_1B_1$ is about equal to $AB$, and $E_1F_1$ to $EF$; and thus the excesses in area nearly balance one another. Experience shows that $A_1B_1$ and $E_1F_1$ are usually slightly in excess of $AB$ and $EF$ respectively, and hence the longitudinal position of the centre of gravity, as found by this method, is slightly on the fore side of the true position.

A modification of the preceding method is adopted when the water or diagonal lines of the fore and after bodies are very unlike. The breadth $XX_1$, equal to the room and space, is measured at the midship section, and is taken as the unit of breadth throughout. The lengths of $AB$, $FE$, etc., and $DC$ are measured; and the sum of the lengths divided by the number of measurements, gives the mean room and space, measured on the run of the bottom. This quantity, divided by the length $XX_1$, gives a multiple for the girth at station 2. Each girth is then multiplied by its multiple, and the results are used in the same way as the girths in the preceding description.

II. *Vertically.*—To find the vertical position of the centre of gravity of the whole surface of a ship's bottom, supposing it to be of plating uniformly thick; or to find the vertical position of the centre of gravity of any belt or zone of plating of uniform thickness.

Use the same square stations as before, and find the centre of gravity of the curve of each section, or that part of it included in the belt or zone of plating. To find the position of the centre of gravity of a curve proceed as follows: In fig. 1, Plate XXIII., $ACB$ is the form of square station No. 2. Bisect the curve at the point $C$, and join $AC$ and $BC$. Bisect $AC$ and $BC$ at the points $E$ and $G$ respectively, from which points draw $ED$ and $GF$ perpendiculars to $AC$

and $BC$, cutting the curves at the points $D$ and $F$. Take $DK = \frac{2}{5} * ED$ and $HF = \frac{2}{5} GF$, and join $HK$. Bisect $HK$ at $L$, which will be a close approximation to the centre of gravity of the curve $ACB$. Similarly, find by construction the centre of gravity of each of the other curves of the square stations (see $L_1$ for station 11). In order to test the accuracy of the constructions, a line should be passed through the centres of gravity in each body, and if these centres are correctly found, the lines will be fair curves, as shown by $OO$ and $O_1O_1$.

Next measure the vertical distance of each centre of gravity from the water line $WW$, as shown by $LM$, $L_1M_1$, and multiply the length of each girth by the distance of its centre of gravity from the water line, either above or below it. Divide the Algebraical sum of the products by the sum of the girths, and the result will give the distance of the centre of gravity of the whole surface from the load water line.

As an example, we will choose the case for which we have already found the longitudinal position of the centre of gravity.

| Number of Square Station. | Half Girths. | Vertical distances of CG from LWL. | | Products. | |
|---|---|---|---|---|---|
| | | Above. | Below. | Above. | Below. |
| No. 1, | 25·2 | ·5 | — | 12·6 | — |
| ,, 2, | 28·4 | — | 1·2 | — | 34·0 |
| ,, 3, | 31·3 | — | 2·5 | — | 78·3 |
| ,, 4, | 33·5 | — | 3·6 | — | 120·6 |
| ,, 5, | 35·0 | — | 4·2 | — | 147·0 |
| ,, 6, | 35·5 | — | 4·5 | — | 159·8 |
| ,, 7, | 35·8 | — | 4·6 | — | 165·0 |
| ,, 8, | 35·8 | — | 4·6 | — | 165·0 |
| ,, 9, | 35·6 | — | 4·5 | — | 160·2 |
| ,, 10, | 35·1 | — | 4·1 | — | 144·0 |
| ,, 11, | 34·0 | — | 3·0 | — | 102·0 |
| ,, 12, | 34·2 | — | 1·5 | — | 51·3 |
| ,, 13, | 30·0 | 1·2 | — | 36·0 | — |
| | 429·4 | | | 48·6 | 1327·2 |
| | | | | | 48·6 |
| | | | | | 1278·6 |

\* This fraction has been found by experience to be nearly true for sections of ordinary form.

$$\frac{1278\cdot 6}{429\cdot 4} = 2\cdot 98 \text{ feet}$$ = the distance of the centre of gravity of the plating on the bottom below the load water, the plating being supposed of uniform thickness.

It will be at once seen that this method can be applied in either of the modes already referred to by which the weight of the bottom plating is calculated. Having found the weight and vertical position of the centre of gravity of all the belts, zones, etc., of uniform thickness, the results are combined, and the total weight and moment found in the usual manner.

**114. Weight and Centre of Gravity of Sheathing, Bottom Planking, etc.**—These are found in a similar manner to that already described in the preceding Article.

The following is a list of the average weights per cubic foot of the different kinds of wood used in shipbuilding, also of the metals commonly employed:—

| | | | |
|---|---|---|---|
| Steel, | 490 lbs. | Oak, English, | 56 lbs. |
| Iron, Cast, | 444 ,, | ,, Italian, | 60 ,, |
| ,, Wrought, | 480 ,, | ,, African, | 60 ,, |
| Copper, | 550 ,, | ,, Dantzic, | 45 ,, |
| Lead, | 710 ,, | Fir, Dantzic, | 36 ,, |
| Zinc, | 440 ,, | ,, Riga, | 40 ,, |
| Brass, | 520 ,, | ,, Larch, | 44 ,, |
| Teak, | 52 ,, | ,, Red Pine, | 36 ,, |
| Honduras Mahogany, | 38 ,, | ,, Yellow Pine, | 34 ,, |
| Elm, | 53 ,, | Cork, | 16 ,, |

The various weights given above refer to timber in a fit condition to work into a ship. When green, or after being in the water some time, they will weigh about 10 per cent. heavier; on the other hand, when thoroughly dry, they will weigh in many cases 4 per cent. less.

In calculating the weight of wood work, it is usual to add a sufficient percentage to the weight per cubic foot, to allow for the fastenings. The percentage required will vary from about 3 to 4 per cent. for deck fastenings, and backing behind armour to as much as from 8 to 10 per cent., for sheathing on a ship's side and bottom when the fastenings are closely spaced.

**115. Deck Beams, Plating, and Flats.**—The weights of the beams, plating, and flat, for each deck, should be calculated successively, as, when the area of the surface of the deck is found, the weights of the beams, flat, etc., are readily obtained.

To find the area of a deck surface we proceed in the same way as when calculating that of a water plane, by dividing the length into a sufficient number of equal intervals, measuring the ordinates thereat, and then calculating the area by Simpson's Rule. The centre of gravity of the area should be found at the same time, in the same way as for a water plane.

**116. Beams.**—Having the area of the beam surface, the number of feet running of beams required for it is at once found by dividing the area by the spacing between the beams. No deduction is made for hatchways except when they are unusually large, as in the case of the boiler hatches on the lower decks of some ships. The carlings generally cover whatever is saved in beams by ordinary hatches, and it is usual to make a further allowance for carlings by adding a length of beam equal to that of the deck, and when the deck supports guns, it has been found by experience necessary to add twice the length of the deck for carlings. When, however, there are hatchways of considerable size, deductions must be made for them, more especially with regard to the longitudinal position of the centre of gravity of the beams. Hence, in such cases, instead of assuming the centre of gravity of the beams and carlings to coincide with that of the deck surface, the moment due to the absence of beams at such places must be deducted.

In addition to the allowance for carlings, the weight of the beam arms must be taken into account. In order to determine their exact weight, divide the area of the deck by its length, and the quotient will be the mean length of the beams. Calculate the weight of such a beam, and that of its arms, and find the ratio between them; this ratio, if used for the beams of the whole deck, will be found to amount to about 12 per cent. of their weight in ships of the Royal Navy, and about 6 to 8 per cent. in merchant ships. Table V. contains a list of the weights per lineal foot of the Butterly Co.'s Tee Bulb and Angle Beams, for which information we are indebted to the courtesy of the makers. Particulars are also given in the same Table for calculating the weights per foot of length of plate bulb, which is commonly used for beams. Table

VI. contains the weights of angle or T irons of the dimensions which usually occur in ships.

**117. Deck Flats.**—The area and centre of gravity of the beam surface are also those of the surface of the deck flat, when the latter is of uniform thickness and of the same material throughout. This is, of course, on the supposition that the flat extends to the surface of the outer plating. If the flat, as it usually does, stops against the reverse frame, or a gutter water-course, a strip of parallel width must be deducted on each side. Removing this parallel strip will not practically alter the position of the centre of gravity, and the slight change can be readily allowed for. Having the area of the surface, the volume of the flat in cubic feet is at once found, and its weight obtained. The additional weight due to certain strakes of plank being thicker or of harder wood than the others, also the weight due to the extra thickness of the waterways, must be taken into account with their effect, if any, upon the position of the centre of gravity. No deduction is made for hatchways of the ordinary size, but when they are of exceptional dimensions, as in the case of the boiler hatch in the lower decks of some ships, the areas are deducted, and the alteration in weight and moment due to them are allowed for. The reason for not making a deduction for the smaller hatchways is in consequence of the coamings, head-ledges, and gratings, which are not calculated, but are taken as about equal in weight to the deck flat which would be fitted if the hatchways were not there.

**118. Deck Plating and Stringers.**—These are calculated in a similar way to deck flats; the necessary percentage for edge strips and butt straps for the several thicknesses when worked in this way will be found in Table IV.

**119. Vertical Position of Centre of Gravity of Decks.**—Owing to the sheer usually given to decks, and the variable breadths of the deck at different positions in the curve of the sheer, it is not possible to measure direct from the profile of the ship the vertical distance of the centre of gravity of the deck from the water line. By experience, it is found that a very good approximation to the vertical position of the centre of gravity of the beams, deck plating, and flat of any deck is found by measuring one-third the half length of the ship on the fore side of the midship section, and measuring the distance from the water line to two-thirds the round of the beam above the beam at side line at that position. The beam at side line being at the upper surface of the beam, one-half the thickness of the deck must be added to this distance for the centre of gravity of the deck flat when the deck is above the load water line, and deducted when it is below. Similarly, about one-third the depth of the beam is added or subtracted, as the case may be, for the centre of gravity of the beams.

The more accurate method is to multiply the half breadth of the deck at each of the equidistant ordinates by the distance of the centre of gravity of the deck flat or beam at that ordinate from the load water line. Divide the sum of the products by the sum of the half breadths, and the quotient will be the distance of the centre of gravity of the whole deck from the water line.

120. **Transverse and Longitudinal Bulkheads.**— The areas of these are found from drawings of them by the aid of Simpson's Rule; and their centres of gravity by the same means. Knowing the weight per square foot of the material composing them, their total weights are readily found, after allowing for the butt straps and edge strips, by using the percentages for bulkhead work given in Table IV. Bulkheads are usually of thicker material at the bottom than at the top; consequently, the separate areas of the thick plating must be found, and the extra weight, due to the thickness in excess of that at the top, added. Also the effect of the extra thickness on the position of the centre of gravity must also be allowed for. The weight of angle or T iron stiffeners is found by dividing the area of the bulkhead by the spacing apart of the stiffeners, and multiplying the quotient by the weight per foot of the angle or T iron. Allowance must also be made for the angle irons connecting the bulkhead to the sides of the ship, which can be easily measured, and their weights then calculated by the use of Table VI.

It must be particularly noticed that in all riveted iron work, 3 per cent of the total weight of the material must be added, to allow for the heads and clenches of the rivets.

The bulkhead work is very considerable in the hold, embracing—besides the transverse bulkheads—the magazines, shell rooms, shaft passages, chain lockers, and often the store rooms; such of these as have iron crowns, stiffened by angle irons, are calculated similarly to the bulkheads.

**121. Transverse Framing.**—In a merchant vessel, the transverse framing is usually of uniform character throughout, each consisting of frame and reverse angle irons, and a floor plate. In an armour clad, the transverse framing is of a very variable character, that below the armour or submerged armour-deck being of a totally distinct character to that above. Also the frames behind the armour are different from either of the other kinds. The unarmoured ships of the Royal Navy, while not framed in so variable a way as the ironclads, have, nevertheless, framework of a more complex character than ordinary merchant ships. We will therefore consider the different classes of framing separately.

**122. Merchant Ship Frames.**—The midship section and specification contain instructions regarding the points of termination of the reverse angle irons and floor plates. With this data curves are drawn in the body plan representing the boundaries at which the angle irons and floor plates stop throughout the length of the ship. Equidistant stations, in sufficient number, are chosen, and a sketch made of the transverse frame at each of these sections, showing how it is constructed. The weight of angle irons (see Table VI.), and plates in each of these is carefully calculated, and the moment of the whole about the load water line determined. Two curves are then constructed, viz., one of weights, and the other of vertical moments. The curve of weights is drawn by setting off from a base line ordinates representing to scale the weights of the respective frames; the distance between the ordinates being that between the several stations drawn to some known scale. The area of this curve, found by Simpson's Rule, divided by the length of the base of the curve, and multiplied by the total number of frames, gives a function (according to the scale of the curve) of the total weight of the framing, and the centre of gravity of the area is that of the centre of gravity of the frames, longitudinally. An excellent test of the accuracy of the several calculations for the weights of the frames at the stations chosen is afforded by the batten when it is bent to pass through the extremities of the ordinates; if it refuses to pass fairly through these points, it shows that an error has been made in one or more of the calculations, the extent of which error is thus known, and we are aware in what part of the calculation to look for it.

The curve of vertical moments is drawn by setting off on the same ordinates lengths representing to scale the moments of the respective frames about the load water line. The area of this curve, divided by the area of the curve of weights, when both are reduced to the same scale, gives the distance of the centre of gravity of the frames from the load water line. It will frequently happen that some of the moments are positive, and others negative with regard to the water line, in that case some parts of the curve of moments will be above, and others below the base line. In finding the total moment, the smaller area is deducted from the larger, and the difference divided by the total area of the curve of weights, both being reduced to the same scale. The centre of gravity will be on that side of the water line upon which there is the excess of moment.

Whenever there are additional frames, as under the engines and boilers, or whenever these frames are of stronger and heavier make than elsewhere, a separate calculation should be made for the excess, both as regards weight and moment.

**123. Transverse Frames below Armour.**—The preceding description of the mode of calculating the weight and position of the centre of gravity of the transverse frames of a merchant ship, requires but little modification to be applicable to the transverse frames below armour of an ironclad; or to the transverse frames of an unarmoured ship.

In a ship of war with a double bottom, which armoured ships invariably have, there are at least three groups of frames, viz., those within, and those before and abaft the double bottom. All three of these contain frames of at least two kinds, viz., bracket and water-tight, and, in wake of the engines and boilers, solid pierced frames are usually fitted.

Transverse sections of the ship's framing have first to be constructed on paper, at intervals of about 16 ft. apart; these being at midships, at the extremities of the double bottom, at a few frame spaces from the stem and stern post, and at intermediate places. To construct these sections, the positions of the longitudinals given in the midship section are transferred to the body plan, and the sight edges of the longitudinals drawn in that plan in some such a way as they will be built in the ship. The scantlings and taper of the longitudinals, given in the specification, determine the depths of the frames, so that their inner edges may be thereby drawn. The sketches of the sections are first made as if they were all bracket frames, and the same sketches will serve for afterwards determining the weights of the solid and water-tight frames by making the necessary alteration in coloured pencil. The load water line must be drawn across each section.

When calculating the weights of the details of each frame, their moments about the load water line can also be obtained. Thus by putting the weights of plates and angle irons in one column, and the corresponding moments opposite to them in another, two summations give us the weight of a frame and its moment about the load water line. If the solid frames are numerous, the weights and vertical moments of several equidistant frames in the space where this variety occurs are also calculated in a similar manner; but if only a few of these frames are fitted, it will be sufficient to subsequently make a correction for the additional weight and moment due to the particular frame being constructed in this way. The water-tight frames being usually one-fourth or fifth of the whole number in the double bottom space, it is necessary to determine the additional weights and moments due to the frames calculated in that space being so constructed. Outside the double bottom, where they are less numerous, it is sufficient to subsequently make a correction, based upon the comparison discovered in calculating those within that space, for the additional weight and moments for these frames.

Curves can now be constructed in the same way as before, with the exception that now we have a greater number. Fig. 2, Plate XXIII. shows the curves of weight and moment for the transverse frames below armour of an iron-clad ship. The scales of these curves, which are drawn to one-eighth the usual size, are marked upon the Plate. The manner of using the curves was explained in the previous Article.

**124. More Extensive Application of Curves.**—While treating of the method of calculating weights and moments by the aid of curves, we may remark that the peculiarities of the framing of an iron-clad ship limits considerably the extent of their possible application. When all the frames are of the same character, and the beams, deck-flats, etc., are uniform, not only the weight and moment of the frames, but also those of the hull proper can be represented by two curves drawn in the following manner:—

The weight and moment of a section of a ship, including plating, planking, beams, and frames, for the length of a room and space, is calculated in a manner similar to that just described. The beams include their proportionate amount of carlings; the framing includes longitudinals, keel, keelsons, hold stringers, inner bottom, etc., and the plating includes its proportion of butt straps, laps, etc., all being computed for the length of the room and space. Transverse bulkheads, works in hold, fittings on decks and topsides, stem, sternpost, rudder and fittings, etc., cannot be included in the curve, as these being irregularly distributed, would produce such discontinuities as not only to prevent a curve from passing fairly through the points determined, but also to destroy that check on the accuracy of the calculation for each section, which is one of the great advantages of the method.

Sections are taken at equidistant intervals, if possible; about ten to fifteen sections should be taken in ordinary cases, according to the length of the ship, and where there is a long midship body one section will serve for a considerable length of that body. Curves are constructed from these results, as already described, and the total weights and moments determined therefrom. In calculating the weight at each section, care should be taken to make separate totals of the weights of plate, angle, beam, or other iron, and of the wood-work embraced therein, and to express the value of each of these in regular succession on each ordinate, so that if the weights of these several materials are afterwards required for the purpose of estimating the probable cost of the ship, they can be found by passing curves through the points on the ordinates for these items, and calculating the areas of the belts or spaces between the curves.

**125. Transverse Frames above and behind Armour.**—
The framing at these parts of an armoured ship is of a very simple character, and does not require special consideration after the preceding description. Neither is any separate explanation necessary regarding the manner of calculating the weight and position of the centre of gravity of the frames of unarmoured ships of the Royal Navy.

**126. Longitudinal Frames.**—The weight and moments of the longitudinal frames are found by first drawing both the sight and inner edges of these frames in the body plan, the necessary taper being found by reference to the specification. By considering the portions of each longitudinal in the double bottom, and before and abaft it separately, the calculation is much simplified. The length of the longitudinal, or a portion of it, is given very nearly by the length of a rabatted diagonal line, drawn as closely as possible to the longitudinal. When considered in separate pieces, with a little experience, a calculator is enabled to approximate, by inspection, very closely to the vertical position of the centre of gravity of each piece of these frames. Care must be taken to make the requisite deduction from the weight, in consequence of the man and lightening holes. These can generally be expressed in the form of a percentage determined for a certain length of a longitudinal, and applied for the others. The manner of calculating the longitudinal position of the centre of gravity is similar to that for a belt of bottom plating.

The preceding are the portions of the work which are of the greatest magnitude, and present the greatest difficulties to the calculator.

**127. Fittings.**—In calculating the weights of the numerous fittings in a ship, and the wood-work in the hold, considerable practical experience is necessary, in order to arrive at correct weights and moments. The fittings contained in a completed ship are far more considerable than a glance at a design would suggest. The only satisfactory way of getting at the weights of these items is by referring to the records of weights kept in building a similar ship, or one such that a comparison can be instituted. In the Royal Dockyards such records are kept, and they prove of invaluable service in the preparation of after designs on this account.

There is, however, an element of uncertainty necessarily inseparable from all calculations of the weights and centres of gravity of ships. Whatever care is taken in calculating the principal portions of the ship, and whatever accuracy is obtained so far, in the result, there still remains a considerable weight of work in the form of fittings, which it is almost impossible for the calculator to value accurately. These consist of anchor and boat fittings, works in connection with the rigging, and fittings of all kinds throughout the vessel, the nature of which varies with different ships, and the weight with different practical supervisors. It is well known that two ships built at different yards from the same drawings, will vary in immersion and trim, this being due, in a large degree, to the different opinions which shipbuilders form of the scantlings necessary for fittings whose dimensions are not specified. Some officers are heavy, and others light-handed in this respect. Again, materials such as cement, paint, oakum, pitch, etc., which amount to a great weight, will be used to a different extent by different workmen, and under different circumstances. On account of the difficulties attendant upon a calculation of these items, it is usual to base estimates thereon upon the quantities used in ships actually built. If the ships are of the same class and size, then the weights may be taken the same; but if different, then they must be varied proportionately to the respective differences which cause these variations in the two ships. For instance: cabins will vary with the complement of officers; mess tables and stools with that of the crew; paint with the products of the lengths and greatest transverse girths of the two ships; oakum with the dimensions of the decks and other caulked surfaces; boat fittings will vary with the number and weights of the boats; anchor fittings with the weight of the anchors and cables, and so on.

But while pointing out the elements of uncertainty that necessarily exist in all calculations of this class, it must be stated that these should not at all vitiate the result. For owing to these indeterminate items being distributed all over the ship, they should not materially affect the trim, nor the vertical position of the centre of gravity. The displacement should not be in error more than 1 to 2 per cent. in iron-clad ships, nor from 4 to 5 per cent. in small vessels, from these causes. It is usual to add about 3 to 5 per cent., the percentage being greatest in the smallest ships, of all weights in the hull except armour and other protective portions, to the result of the calculation, to cover items which may, perchance, be incorrectly estimated, or not taken into account at all. This percentage, being supposed uniformly distributed, is taken at the centre of gravity of the ship.

In making calculations, such as this chapter refers to, great care is necessary to prevent errors, sometimes of great magnitude, occurring. A mistake, slight in itself and easily made, will sometimes affect the result to such a degree as to ruin a ship built upon designs based thereon. It is consequently highly important that separate and independent calculations should be made by two persons, simultaneously if possible, and if not, one very soon after the other, and before the building of the vessel is materially advanced.

# CHAPTER V.

## CURVES OF STABILITY.

Metacentric Curves—Curves of Statical and Dynamical Stability—Specimen Calculations—The Body Plan—Measuring the Ordinates—Preliminary Tables—Combination Tables—Volumes and Moments of Assumed Wedges for Statical Stability—Area and Centre of Gravity of Inclined Water Plane—Statical Correction for Layer—For Appendages—Values of BN and GZ—Check Spot—Curve of Dynamical Stability—Dynamical Correction for Layer—For Appendages—Geometrical Method of Calculating Dynamical Stability — Curve of Statical Stability at Light Draught.

**128. Metacentric Curves.**—By *metacentric curve*, or *curve of metacentres*, is meant the curve passing through the extremities of ordinates, whose lengths are equal to the heights of the transverse metacentres above the underside of keel at successive parallel draughts of water. For instance, if by the method investigated at Arts. 63 to 66, the heights of $M$ above the underside of keel at successive parallel draughts of water be obtained, and set off to scale as ordinates; the abscissæ being the distances, to scale, between the respective water lines, then the curve passing through the extremities of these ordinates is the *metacentric curve* of the ship at that trim. It will be seen that these curves will vary slightly for the same ship at different trims; but in ships of ordinary form the characters of the curves will be substantially the same within the limits of alteration of trim which usually occur. It is usual to calculate and construct the metacentric curve of a ship at her usual load trim and parallel draughts, although as the ship lightens or deepens the trim will vary according to the form of the body, and the longitudinal position of the weights which are added or removed to increase or diminish the draught of water. There is thus an element of error admitted, and the curve does not really represent the actual positions of the point

$M$ at the several draughts of water. However, as the curve is not taken as representing the actual positions of $M$, but merely close approximations thereto (which they really are), and as it is only consulted within such small limits of the draught of water that no practical error can occur in vessels of ordinary form, it affords a valuable criterion whereby the tendency of the surface stability to increase or decrease at successive draughts may be discovered, and a sufficiently correct representation of the actual increase or decrease of surface stability at the small variations of draught which are commonly experienced when at sea.

In addition to the information afforded by these curves, with regard to the surface stability, they are rendered of more practical value by setting off upon the ordinate at any draught of water the position of the centre of gravity, as determined by experiment (see Art. 90), or as calculated for the ship at any time when floating at that draught. It need hardly be said that a ship may, at different times, float at the same mean draught of water, or even at the same trim and draught, and yet have the centre of gravity at a different height. However, the variations in the vertical position of the centre of gravity are usually very small in a ship of war at the same draught of water, and if a record be kept of the actual equipment or cargo on board at the time the experiment or calculation was made, a correction can readily be made for the true vertical position of the centre of gravity at any other time. Without the position of the centre of gravity being known at any draught, the metacentric curve merely shows the tendency to stability due to the vessel's form, but by carefully recording on the diagram the positions of the centre of gravity, at different draughts, which have been observed from time to time, it is very easy to fix, with tolerable accuracy, the positions of that point at intermediate or at closely adjacent draughts.

It will be seen that in order to set off the positions of the centre of gravity, so as to be of use in this way, it is necessary that the position of the water line with regard to the point $M$ at every draught of water should be represented on the diagram. This is done in a very simple and convenient manner by drawing the curve in the manner shown by fig. 1, Plate XXIV. A number of parallel lines are drawn at distances apart equal, to scale, to the distances between the water lines employed; and a line is drawn cutting these parallel lines at an angle of 45 degrees. Ordinates, perpendicular to the water lines, are drawn through the points of intersection of this line at 45 degrees with the several water lines; and the distances of the centres of buoyancy beneath the latter (obtained by previous calculation) are set off below the points of intersection of the diagonal line with the respective water lines, to the same scale as before, and a curve drawn through the points so obtained is called the *curve of centres of buoyancy*. The respective values of $BM$, $B_1M_1$, $B_2M_2$, etc., are then set off from these points $B$, $B_1$, $B_2$, etc., to the same scale, and a curve drawn through the points so obtained is termed the *metacentric curve*, or *curve of metacentres*. If it be required to know the value of $BM$ at any mean draught of water between the limits of the water lines used, the line representing that draught must be drawn in its proper position, to scale, and a perpendicular to the water lines drawn through the point of intersection of the line representing the draught of water with the line at 45 degrees; the distance on this line between the curve of metacentres and that of centres of buoyancy will be the value of $BM$ at that draught. If a moderately stiff penning batten is used in getting in the curves, the latter may be continued for a short distance on either side of the extreme water lines on the diagram, and so values of $BM$, at greater or less draughts of water than those employed in constructing the curves, may be obtained with a considerable degree of accuracy.

The reason for drawing the line at 45 degrees is evident, as by so doing not only is the curve of metacentres kept within the limits of a moderately small diagram, but the scale of the abscissæ thus becomes the same as the scale of the draughts of water and of the ordinates. The curves are also by this means constructed in such a way as to simplify the interpolation of intermediate water lines, and thus enables us at once to obtain the value of $BM$ at any intermediate draught of water.

It may be remarked that, for vessels of ordinary form, the

curve of centres of buoyancy is concave with regard to a horizontal line at the keel, being practically straight between the light and load lines, and making an angle which varies between 28 and 38 degrees with the horizontal. The curve of metacentres is usually of the character shown in the figure, the value of $BM$ usually increasing very rapidly as the draught diminishes. This is especially the case in vessels having a very flat floor; as the moment of inertia of the water plane remains very considerable while the displacement becomes almost zero. If, however, the vessel has a very rising or a hollow floor, the curve of metacentres is flatter, being, indeed, in some cases slightly concave with regard to the water lines in the diagram. The old gun brigs of H.M. Navy are examples of ships having this kind of curve; at least, within the limits of draught between which the curve is usually constructed. (See fig. 2, Plate XXIV.)

It is usual in H.M. Service to construct these curves on the scale of half an inch to a foot.

In fig. 1, Plate XXIV., the points $G$, $G_1$, $G_2$, etc., represent the positions of the centre of gravity as found at different times when the ship was at those draughts of water, or as calculated from the known position at some particular draught. The values $GM$, $G_1 M_1$, $G_2 M_2$, are measures of the leverage of statical stability at the load, second, and third water lines respectively. In the case shown by fig. 1, $G_1 M_1$ is about equal to $GM$; this is very often the case, as near the load draught the position of $G$, with regard to the load water line rising somewhat, the few weights, such as coals or stores, removed to reduce the draught, being generally a little below the centre of gravity, while at the same time the metacentric curve at that point is usually nearly parallel to the water lines. As the ship lightens still more the point $G$ continues to rise, while the metacentre curve still remains nearly flat. This continues until $G$ rises slower than the curve, and then the value of $GM$ increases, as shown by $G_4 M_4$ at the fifth water line. It must, however, be remembered that as the moment of statical stability at a small angle of inclination $\theta$ is $D \times GM \sin \theta$, that moment is usually greatest at or about the load draught, owing to the value of $D$ being greater than at the lesser draughts.

It is perhaps necessary to remind the student that these curves are only useful for determining the metacentric statical stability, as the values of $BM$ are absolutely true only for an infinitely small angle of heel. However, in ships of ordinary form, they afford sufficient data for determining the statical stability up to 10 or 15 degrees of inclination, correctly enough for all practical purposes.

Fig. 2, Plate XXIV., shows metacentric diagrams for different ships, which may be taken as types of the various forms met with in practice.

**129. Curves of Statical Stability.**—In Arts. 70 and 73, we showed how the statical and dynamical surface stability of a ship can be calculated at any given angle of heel. If the values of $BN$ (see fig. 1, Plate XVI.), for successive angles of heel between the upright position and that inclination at which $BN$ becomes zero, are set off to scale as ordinates from a base line, the abscissæ of which represent to scale the angular intervals chosen, then a curve passed through the extremities of these ordinates would be termed a "*curve of statical surface stability.*" Similarly, if the ordinates are drawn to scale, so as to represent the successive values of $NB_1 - AB$ versin $\theta - A_1 A_2$, the abscissæ being as before, a curve passed through the extremities of the ordinates would be a "*curve of dynamical surface stability.*" Such curves, however, would not be of much practical use, as they would merely indicate the tendency to stability due to the vessel's form alone. Hence, while they would represent the possible qualities of the ship, no information would be afforded regarding her actual qualities. Nevertheless, the fact must not be lost sight of that to a very large degree the range of a vessel's stability is governed by her form, and no disposition of weights in a badly formed ship will compensate for that badness of form. Indeed, the limits within which the position of the weights in a war ship are necessarily restricted render the form of the vessel an element of the greatest importance in regard to the range and magnitude of her stability.

At Art. 86, it was shown that when the centre of gravity is above the centre of buoyancy (its usual position), $BG$ sin $\theta$ must be deducted from the value of $BN$ (the lever of surface statical stability), in order to obtain the actual righting lever at that angle. If the centre of gravity is below the centre of buoyancy, $BG \sin \theta$ must be added. The conventional expression for $BN \pm BG \sin \theta$ is $GZ$ (see fig 1, Plate XVI.). As will be seen by reference to fig. 2, Plate XVIII., for the same value of $BN$, there may be any number of different values of $GZ$, both positive and negative, between the possible lowest and highest positions of $G$ in the ship; so that, while a curve of *surface* statical stability may show considerable amplitude and range, yet if $G$ is above $M$, there will be no statical stability at all, but a continually increasing upsetting couple. Again, if $BN$ for any angle be so small as to represent comparatively small surface stability, yet if $G$ is sufficiently low in the ship, the actual stability may be considerable up to a large angle of inclination. But, as already stated, in a war ship such exaggerated positions of $G$ are impossible, and in a merchant vessel, if the stability is secured by a very low centre of weight in the lading, the behaviour of such a vessel as regards rolling and straining is very unsatisfactory. In every case the stability should be chiefly obtained by form, and the centre of gravity should be as near as possible to the load water line. We shall consider these points more minutely in a future chapter.

The length of $GZ$ at any angle being the lever of statical stability at that inclination, if ordinates be set off from a base line so as to represent to scale the successive values of $GZ$ at the different angles of heel between the upright position and 90 degrees, the abscissæ representing to scale the angular intervals between the inclinations at which $GZ$ is calculated, then a curve passed through the extremities of these ordinates is termed a "*curve of statical stability.*" When this curve is drawn, the length of the ordinate at the point on the base line corresponding with any given angle—read by the proper scale—multiplied by the displacement, gives the moment of the righting or upsetting couple at that angle. The units employed are usually a foot and a ton. In constructing the curve, positive values of $GZ$ are set off above the base line, and negative values below.

Plate XXV. shows curves of statical stability for the several classes of ships named; these may be regarded as types of the various kinds of curves that occur in practice.

An examination of these curves will prove very instructive to an experienced eye, as they reveal certain important facts in connection with the form of the ship, and height of the centre of gravity, and enable the naval architect to predict with certainty regarding the power of the ship to stand up under sail. Table VII. contains specimen calculations for ordinates of a curve of statical stability which are similar to the calculations for the surface statical stability at a finite angle which are given in Table II. The calculations shown in Table VII. are extracted from the appendix to the paper by Messrs. White and John, contained in Vol. XII. of the *Transactions of the Institution of Naval Architects*, which paper has already been referred to; and the work in them is arranged in the manner usually adopted when calculating the stability at a number of successive angles for the purpose of constructing a curve of statical stability. As the calculations for the curve of dynamical stability are included in the same Tables, we will defer our explanation of them until we have briefly alluded to these curves. Plate XXVI. shows the body plan of the vessel to which these curves relate.

**130. Curves of Dynamical Stability.**—In Art. 72 it was shown that the dynamical surface stability at any angle $\theta$ is equal to $D(NB_1 - AB \text{ versin } \theta - A_2A_1)$, (see fig. 1, Plate XVI.); and in Art. 89 the dynamical stability at that angle was found to be $D(NB_1 - GB \text{ versin } \theta)$. The object of the calculation for the ordinate of the curve of dynamical stability at any angle is to find the value of $NB_1$ at that angle, and from this is deducted the product of the constant value $GB$ (which is determined by the position of the centre of gravity), and the variable quantity versin $\theta$, the difference being the whole distance that the centre of buoyancy is depressed and the centre of gravity elevated in inclining the ship over to that angle. Thus $D(NB_1 - GB \text{ versin } \theta)$ is the mechanical work performed in inclining the ship. We have repeated these explanations, already given in Chap. III., in order that the student may readily follow what we have now to say regarding the curve of dynamical stability. The curve is constructed in the ordinary way. Having the values of $D(NB_1 - GB \text{ versin } \theta)$ for a number of successive angles of heel; these values are set off to scale as ordinates from a base line, the abscissæ of which represent to scale the angular distances between the inclinations at which ordinates are obtained. A curve drawn through the extremities of the ordinates is a *curve of dynamical stability*. If it be required to know the work performed in inclining the ship to any intermediate angle between those calculated, the ordinate to the curve from the point on the base representing the position of that angle is measured with the proper scale, and the product of the length of the ordinate and the displacement of the ship is the total work performed. Plate XXVII. shows some curves of dynamical stability. The ordinates continually increase until the statical heeling moment becomes zero, after which, as the ship no longer offers resistance to heeling, but rather seeks to incline still farther, the work performed is negative, and the ordinates begin to diminish. The curve of dynamical stability crosses the base line at a point corresponding with such an angle that the work performed in inclining the ship to her angle of vanishing statical stability has been equalled by the work which would have been required to prevent her inclining from that point to the angle referred to.

The dynamical stability at any angle being the total work performed in heeling the ship to that angle, it is therefore the sum of the infinite number of moments of statical stability at all the infinitely close intermediate angles between that position and when upright. In other words, the dynamical stability at any angle is the integral of the statical stability. This is graphically represented in a very intelligible manner by the area of the curve of statical stability included between the origin of the curve and its ordinate at the angle in question. Thus, the dynamical stability at any angle may be readily calculated from the curve of statical stability, by simply finding the area of the portion of that curve up to the given angle, by means of Simpson's Rule, and multiplying the result by the displacement.

Expressed algebraically, if $M$ = the statical stability at any angle $\theta$, and $U$ the dynamical stability,

$$\text{Then } U = \int M \, d\theta.$$

We shall presently show how the work of such a calculation is performed. It is, however, necessary to first explain the ordinary calculations for the curves of statical and dynamical stability given in Table VII.

**131. Specimen Calculations for Curves of Statical and Dynamical Stability.—I. The Body Plan.**—The first operation when proceeding to calculate the curve of stability of a ship is to prepare a suitable body plan. In the first place, the stations must be perpendicular to the load water line in order that the water lines may appear straight in the body plan. This is the invariable mode of preparing sheer draughts at the Admiralty, and the practice is very common in merchant yards. The stations should be from about one-twelfth to one-fourteenth of the length of the vessel apart, and, at the extremities, one or two stations at half intervals should be drawn. If the body is a full one, two such stations should be drawn at each extremity; but if the lines are of the ordinary character, one at each end will be sufficient (see Plate XXVI.). In drawing these stations, the form of the section should be completed across the uppermost continuous deck, the upper line being drawn to the round of that deck. Whenever there are recesses or embrasures in the side of the ship, water-tight elevations, such as breastworks, raised central batteries, etc., the section through such should show their exact external form. It is further necessary to have carefully drawn sheer and half-breadth plans, showing the forms of all irregularities as they appear in those plans, in order that their volumes, moments, etc., may be accurately calculated. In drawing the stations when there are any such irregularities of the deck and side as have been mentioned, it is the usual and by far the best way to draw the sections as if the side and deck were continuous, and first calculate to the continuous lines. The corrections due to the irregularities are afterwards treated as "appendages," as likewise are the portions of the bow and stern before and abaft the extreme stations.

Having these plans ready, the next thing to be done is to draw the radiating lines representing the load water plane at equiangular inclinations, on the supposition that all these water planes pass through the longitudinal axis of the upright load water plane. The magnitude of the angular interval is generally governed by that of the angle with the upright water plane which is made by the water plane when the ship is so inclined that the edge of the upper deck at amidships is just at the surface of the water. This is chosen as one of the angles at which the stability is calculated; for as the edge of the deck is a point of considerable discontinuity in the surface of the ship, it is desirable to make it what is termed a "stop point in the integration," when applying Simpson's Rule. This will be further explained presently. In the example shown by Plate XXVI., this angle is seen to be 32 degrees, and in order that a water plane at that angle may be multiplied by 1, in affecting the water planes by the multipliers—

$$1\ .\ 4\ .\ 1\ .$$
$$1\ .\ 4\ .\ 1,\ \text{etc.}$$

it is necessary that 32 degrees should be divided into an even number of intervals, to produce an odd number of ordinates. 16 degrees would be too large an interval, but 8 degrees does very well. Hence three radiating lines are drawn right across the body, both above and below the upright load water plane at 8 degrees apart. The remainder of the 90 degrees is divided up into multiples of 8 degrees, the last being 88 degrees, and radiating lines drawn as before. In order to reduce the error which is necessarily occasioned by applying Simpson's Rule to a surface so discontinuous as that of the side and deck of a ship, at the edge of the deck, it is usual to draw an intermediate plane at a half interval, just above the edge of the deck, as shown at 32 degrees in the Plate.

132. II. **Measuring the Ordinates.**—We have next to measure off the ordinates of the different water planes, and enter them upon the **Preliminary Tables.** The numbers of the sections are written down in the first column of each of these tables, and the lengths of the ordinates in the second column.

The ordinates for the load water plane are the same as would be inserted in a displacement sheet. Those of the water plane at 8 degrees for the immersed wedge are obtained by keeping one extremity of the scale at the point from which the lines radiate, and reading off the intersections of the stations of the fore and after bodies with the line at 8 degrees *above* the upright water plane, and those for the emerged wedge by reading off the intersections of the stations of the fore and after bodies with the line at 8 degrees *below* the upright water plane. This process is performed separately for every angle, it being observed that where the radiating lines cut the deck the distances must be measured to such intersections; also remembering what has been already said, that the projections beyond and depressions beneath the continuous surface are afterwards treated as appendages, and thus the intersections of the radiating planes must be considered at where the boundary of the section would be if the irregularity did not exist. It will be observed that, in the tables, we have given the measurements and calculations up to 32 degrees only, the remainder of the calculation being omitted from want of space, and because the portion given sufficiently illustrates the method of arranging the work in the calculations.

133. III. **Preliminary Tables.**—The Preliminary Tables will be found to be arranged very similar to that shown in Table II., only that no notice is now taken of the longitudinal moments of the wedges, it being no part of the present calculation to determine the effect of a transverse heel upon the longitudinal trim of the ship. In every other respect, except the relative position of the tables for immersed and emerged wedges, the arrangement is the same. It will however be noticed that in the Preliminary Tables now under consideration, the division by 3—peculiar to Simpson's 1st Rule—is made in order to at once reduce the number of figures as much as possible, and thus make the remainder of the work less laborious. Also, the summation of the *functions of cubes* is there made, in order that the calculation for the total moments of the wedges may be proceeded with at once on the subsequent calculation.

134. IV. **Combination Tables** is the name given to the subsequent calculations just alluded to. Their object is to determine from the sums of the functions of the ordinates, and those of their squares and cubes, the volumes and moments of the assumed wedges of immersion and emersion, also the area and the position of the centre of gravity of the

assumed inclined water plane. By these are found the thickness, volume, and centre of gravity of the "layer" of displacement, which is added or removed in order to obtain the true volumes of the wedges, and the actual position of the inclined water plane. In this way the correction in moment is made, which is necessary owing to the water plane being assumed to pass through the longitudinal axis of the upright water plane. These results, together with the corrections due to appendages, before the value of $GZ$ at any angle can be determined, completes the work of the Combination Table. We will now consider these operations in detail.

135. V. **Volumes of Assumed Wedges.**—The sums of the functions of the squares of the ordinates of each of the radiating planes contained in the wedges of immersion and emersion having been found in the Preliminary Table, and divided by 3, as already mentioned; these values are inserted in the proper column in the Combination Table (see Table VII.), in the row corresponding to the number of degrees which the radiating plane is inclined to the upright water plane. They are then affected by the proper Simpson's Multiplier, and these new functions are added together. This is done for each wedge. The lesser result is then deducted from the greater, and the remainder is a function of the excess in volume of one assumed wedge over the other. The difference is divided by 2, according to the rule given at Art. 49, and then after being multiplied by the longitudinal interval, and one-third the angular interval in circular measure, the result is the excess in volume of one wedge over the other.

136. VI. **Moments of Assumed Wedges for Statical Stability.**—We have next to determine the sum of the moments of the assumed wedges about the longitudinal middle line plane of the ship. The sums of the functions of cubes of ordinates for both the immersed and emerged wedges, already divided by 3 on the Preliminary Table, are inserted in their respective rows, and affected by Simpson's Multipliers. The products resulting are then multiplied by the cosines of the inclinations of the respective radial planes with the inclined water plane, this latter being now perpendicular to the longitudinal middle line plane of the ship. The sum of the new products is multiplied by one-third the angular

interval in circular measure, and again by the longitudinal interval between the ordinates, the result is the moment of the assumed wedges for statical stability. Corrections have to be made before the moment of the true wedges is determined.

137. VII. **Area of Inclined Water Plane.**—We have next to find the area of the inclined water plane, as the excess in volume of one wedge over the other, divided by this area, gives the thickness of the layer, which must be added or removed, in order that wedges of equal volume shall remain. The area of the inclined water plane is readily found from the sums of the functions of the ordinates of the portion of the water plane belonging to each wedge, which have already been found in the Preliminary Table. The sum of these functions (already divided by 3), multiplied by the longitudinal interval, gives the total area of the water plane in question. The excess in volume of one wedge over the other, divided by this area, gives a very close approximation to the thickness of the layer which must be added or removed. If the wedge of immersion is the greater of the two, the layer is removed, and *vice versa*. It will be readily seen that half the thickness of the layer must be a very close approximation to the vertical position of its centre of gravity.

138. VIII. **Centre of Gravity of Inclined Water Plane.**—The distance of the centre of gravity of the inclined water plane from the longitudinal axis of the upright water plane is a sufficiently close approximation to the distance of the centre of gravity of the layer from that point when the layer is not very thick. To find the distance of the centre of gravity of the inclined water plane from the point in question, we must find the difference in the moments of the two sides of that plane about the longitudinal axis of the upright water plane, and divide that difference by the area of the inclined water plane. The difference of the moments of the two sides of that plane are found by taking the difference between the halves of the sums of the functions of the squares of the ordinates of the two sides, and multiplying it by the longitudinal interval; the sums having been already divided by 3. This resultant moment, divided by the area of the inclined water plane, gives the distance of its centre of gravity from

the axis about which moments were taken. The centre of gravity will, of course, be towards that side which has the excess of moment. As already mentioned, the distance of the centre of gravity of the layer from the longitudinal middle line plane approximates very closely to the distance thus found, when the layer is not very thick. Should, however, the layer be so thick that, in the judgment of the calculator, the distance of the centre of gravity of the inclined water plane from the axis is not a sufficiently good approximation to the true distance of the centre of gravity of the layer from that axis, a closer approximation may be obtained in the following manner: Draw the actual inclined water line upon the body plan, so that the drawing will then contain the upper and lower bounding planes of the layer. Calculate the distance of the centre of gravity of the true inclined water plane from the middle line of the body in the same way as the distance of the centre of gravity of the assumed inclined water plane has been obtained; and mark the positions of these two centres of gravity upon the body plan. Join the two points, and bisect the joining line; the perpendicular distance of the point of bisection from the middle line of the body will be a close approximation to the distance required.

139. IX. **Statical Correction for Layer.**—The assumed position of the inclined water plane being in error, and a layer of displacement having to be added or removed; in other words, volume having to be transferred from one wedge to the other, in order to make them equal, we have now to determine the necessary correction in moment due to this assumption. This correction obviously consists of the moment of the excess of volume about the longitudinal middle line plane, or, in other words, the product of the excess into the distance of the centre of gravity of the layer from the axis of the upright water plane. If the centre of gravity of the layer lies toward that side for which the assumed wedge is the greater, then deduct the correction; if it lies toward the opposite side, add the correction.

140. X. **Statical Correction for Appendages.**—In addition to the correction just referred to, other corrections have frequently to be made in consequence of appendages not having

hitherto been taken into account in the calculation. The nature of some of these appendages has already been referred to in Art. 131, others occur very often at the bow and stern of the ship beyond the extreme ordinates. In every case the volume of the portion of the appendage included in every angle of inclination, both as regards the immersed and emerged wedges, must be calculated. It is generally possible to guess very closely to the position of the centres of gravity of an appendage, and the moment of the latter is found by multiplying its volume by the distance from the axis of the upright water plane of a perpendicular from the centre of gravity of the appendage upon the inclined water plane. If the appendage adds to the volume of either of the wedges, the moment due to it must be added when making the correction; but if the appendage is a negative one, produced by an embrasure or some other recess in the side, the moment due to it must be deducted.

Corrections in the thickness of the layer, and in the area and position of the centre of gravity of the inclined water plane have also to be frequently made in consequence of appendages which were not previously taken into account. Care must be taken to include the correction due to the appendages, both in the excess in volume of one wedge over the other, and in the excess in moment of area of one side of the inclined water plane over that of the other side, before determining the *correction for layer*, referred to in the preceding Article. The way in which these several corrections are included in the calculation is shown on the Combination Table for 32 degrees.

141. XI. **Values of $BN$ and $GZ$.**—The various corrections having been made for the moments of the wedges, the corrected moment is divided by the displacement in cubic feet, the result being the value of $BN$ (see fig. 2, Plate XVIII.), for the reasons given at Art. 88.

From this $BG\sin\theta$ has to be deducted, $\theta$ being the angle of inclination, the remainder is the value of $GZ$ for that angle. The values of $GZ$ for successive angles of inclination are the ordinates of the curve of statical stability.

The ordinates of a curve of stability are usually drawn to a scale of one quarter of an inch for every tenth part of a foot in the value of $GZ$, and the abscissæ to a scale of one quarter of an inch for every degree of inclination.

142. XII. Check Spot at 90 Degrees.—As a check upon the accuracy of the curve, it is usual to calculate the value of $GZ$ at an angle of 90 degrees\* by an independent method. This is very desirable, as the figures in the several Combination Tables being copied from one to the other, an error made in one table will be repeated throughout all those which follow, unless great care is taken. The method we are about to explain is very simple, and the work may be rapidly performed. Should there be an error in the curve, this separate calculation will be sure to discover it, and whether error is discovered or not, the satisfaction derived from the check is worth the trouble involved in the work of making it.

Referring to fig. 1, Plate XXVIII., the body plan there shown is that of a ship which is heeled over to an angle of 90 degrees with the usual upright position; so that the new water line is $W_1 L_1$. Suppose $B_1$ to be the position of the centre of buoyancy when inclined at that angle, then the couple, tending to right the ship or upset her still farther, is $D \times GZ$ where $GZ$ is (as usual) the perpendicular from the centre of gravity upon the vertical through the new centre of buoyancy. If the vertical, through the new centre of buoyancy, cuts the middle line of the ship on the side of $G$, farthest from the upright water line, then the couple is an upsetting one, and the value of $GZ$ is negative. This case is shown by Plate XXVIII. If the vertical is on the other side of $G$, the couple is a righting one, and the value of $GZ$ is positive.

The problem to be solved is to find the position of $B_1$, with regard to the upright water plane $WL$, that is, the distance $ZA$; we are not concerned with its distance from the middle line of the ship. In order to determine the value of $ZA$, the easiest way is to use the curve of tons per inch of

---

\* This is in an ordinary case when $GZ$ has neither a large positive nor a large negative value at that angle; in the case of a ship of low freeboard, whose range of stability does not exceed, say, 60 degrees, a check spot is found at an angle near that at which the stability is found to vanish.

immersion. From this curve can be readily calculated the areas of the half water planes as high as the load line, and if there is no discontinuity in the side of the ship, the curve can be accurately continued to the upper deck by simply bending a batten to the curve already drawn, and allowing its extremity to spring fairly. If this cannot be relied upon for the portion of the ship above the load water line, a water line above the load line should be run off in the half-breadth plan, and its area and tons per inch calculated. With this additional data, the curve can be continued to the upper deck. Next, water lines should be drawn in the body plan above the load line, the same distance apart as those already used in calculating the curve of tons per inch. This will leave an appendage between the upper water line and the deck. Should this appendage be inconveniently large, it will be better to draw in a new set of water lines, commencing at the upper deck at side on the midship section, and drawing them equidistant. The half areas of these water lines are at once found from the curve of tons per inch.

It will be observed that in using these half areas we are supposing that $AP$ is the load water plane when the ship is inclined. Should there be a layer, it is allowed for afterwards.

By means of the half areas of water planes, the displacement and position of the centre of buoyancy of the ship, supposing her to float at the line $PA$, are readily found by Simpson's Rule, and by taking moments in the usual way. Allowance must then be made for the appendage above the highest water line, and at other parts of the ship, according to the circumstances of the case; and after taking everything into account, the total displacement to the line $AP$ is found, and the distance of the centre of buoyancy of that displacement from either of the water lines.

Should the displacement so found be less than that of the ship, it shows that she will sink deeper, and therefore a layer has to be added; should the displacement, however, be greater, the contrary is indicated.

We will suppose the usual case, viz., that the total displacement is greater than that of the ship when floating at the line $AP$. We have then to calculate the area of the vertical longitudinal middle line plane of the ship from the keel to upper deck. Divide the difference between the displacements, expressed in cubic feet, by the area thus found, and the result will be a close approximation to the thickness of the layer $AA_1$. Should $AA_1$ be sufficiently large to cause the water line $W_1L_1$ to differ in area much from the middle line plane $AP$, the actual area of $W_1L_1$ should be found, and a correction made in the value of $AA_1$. The distance of the centre of buoyancy of the layer from the line $WL$ is readily found, and the correction in the position of the centre of buoyancy of the whole displacement with regard to $WL$ can then be made. The value of $AG$ being thus found, the distance $GZ$ is at once known for an inclination of 90 degrees. If the work is accurately performed, and the curve of stability correctly drawn, the value of $GZ$ will agree with the ordinate of the curve at that angle.

**143. Curve of Dynamical Stability.**—The same Preliminary Tables are used as for the curve of statical stability. The Combination Tables given on Table VII. show on the right hand side the separate work for the curve of dynamical stability. As will be seen, the additional work consists in multiplying the products of the sums of functions of cubes by the *sines* instead of the *cosines* of the inclinations which the radiating planes make with the plane at the particular angle under consideration. The reason for this course of procedure is explained at Art. 51. The sum of the results of these multiplications is divided by 3, and then by the proper fraction of the angular interval, according to the particular rule for integration which is adopted. This is again multiplied by the longitudinal interval, after which the corrections for the appendages and layer have to be made.

*The correction for appendages* is obtained by using the volumes of appendages obtained for the statical curve. The moment of an appendage for dynamical stability is found by multiplying its volume by the perpendicular distance of its centre of gravity from the inclined water plane, at the angle under consideration. If the appendage is a positive one, *i.e.*, a projection on the surface of the ship, the correction must be an additive one in all cases; and if it consists of an indent, such as an embrasure, etc., the correction is a subtractive one.

*The correction for the layer* has now to be made. The manner of finding the thickness of the layer is given at Art. 137. For all practical purposes, the centre of gravity of the layer may be taken at the middle of its thickness; hence to find the dynamical correction, the volume of the layer is multiplied by half its thickness, and this correction is *always* a subtractive one.

These corrections having been made, the result is divided by the volume of displacement in cubic feet, and the result is the value of $B_1 N$ for that angle. We have only to deduct from this the value of $BG$ versin $\theta$ ($\theta$ being the angle under consideration), and the result is the lever of dynamical stability, or the distance through which the displacement is lifted in inclining the ship from the upright position to that angle. The curve of dynamical stability is constructed with these ordinates similarly to the curve of statical stability. Plate XXVIII., fig. 2, shows the curves of statical and dynamical stability of the ship shown by Plate XXVI., the calculations for which are made in Table VII.

**144. Geometrical Mode of Calculating Dynamical Stability.**—At Art. 130, we indicated the method by which the curve of dynamical stability is calculated and constructed from the curve of statical stability. As we there stated, the dynamical stability at any angle is the integral of the statical stability; or the area of the curve of statical stability included between the origin of the curve and its ordinate at the angle in question. The process of geometrical integration was explained at Art. 42. In order to apply the method there explained to finding the area of a curve of statical stability, it must be remembered that the abscissæ of such a curve cannot be measured with a scale in the same way as the ordinates; for while the latter are drawn to some specific scale, the former merely inform the calculator regarding the number of degrees whose circular measure has to be taken into account.

For instance, suppose the ordinate of the curve of dynamical stability at 40 degrees be required for the ship whose curve of statical stability is given in fig. 2, Plate XXVIII. The problem before us is to find the area of the curved surface $ABC$, the lengths of the ordinates in feet being shown by the

## STABILITY AT LIGHT DRAUGHT.

scale on the diagram, and the common interval is the circular measure of 10 degrees. Hence we proceed as follows:—

|  |  |  |
|---|---|---|
| 0° | 0 × 1 = | 0 |
| 10° | ·5 × 4 = | 2·0 |
| 20° | 1·2 × 2 = | 2·4 |
| 30° | 2·1 × 4 = | 8·4 |
| 40° | 2·8 × 1 = | 2·8 |

$$3)\overline{15·6}$$
$$\overline{5·2}$$

The circular measure of 10 degrees is ·1746.
∴ ·1746 × 5·2 = ·908.

Hence ·908 feet is the length of $CD$, the ordinate at 40 degrees of the curve of dynamical stability. The ordinates of this curve will continue to increase until that angle of inclination is attained, at which the statical stability vanishes; when the dynamical stability will be a maximum. After this the ordinates diminish until a point is attained, at which the area of the curve of statical stability below the base line is equal to that above it—when the dynamical stability will be zero. The work done by the ship herself in completing the capsize is then equal to the work done to incline her before the point of vanishing stability was attained—or where she commenced to offer opposition to returning to the upright position rather than to being inclined still farther.

145. **Curve of Statical Stability at Light Draught.**—If a ship when at sea always floated at the same mean draught of water—even although the trim varied somewhat—the curve of stability at the load draught and trim would represent the condition of the ship in that respect, with a sufficient degree of accuracy for all useful purposes. But it happens that the longer a ship is at sea the less her mean immersion becomes, until all consumable stores are gone. In the case of a steam ship this condition is still further affected by burning the coals, and the boilers and engine condensers being emptied of their water. It need hardly be pointed out that in this "ordinary light condition," as it is termed in the Royal Navy, the curve of stability of the ship is very different to that in the load condition. The alteration in the

curve is due to two causes—1st, to the change in the position of the centre of gravity; and 2nd, to the change in the relative forms of the portions of the body that are in the water and out of it.

The "ordinary light condition" is that condition in which a ship has—

    1. The boilers empty.
    2. The fresh water tanks empty.
    3. All provisions consumed.
    4. No water in the engine condensers.
    5. All coals consumed.
    6. All consumable stores used.

The consumable stores referred to are taken as one-half of the weights of the engineers', gunner's, carpenter's, and boatswain's stores. This is, of course, a very improbable condition; but as it represents the worst conceivable condition, it is desirable to know the curve of stability at such a time, for then we are aware what are the limits of its phases between the load and the lightest probable draughts of water.

In most vessels the removal of the weights above named, causes the centre of gravity of the ship to rise, with regard to the underside of keel. Consequently, in ordinary cases the range of the curve of stability will be less in the light than in the load condition. If, however, the vessel in the load condition has a very low freeboard, it is quite possible that the increase of freeboard, due to the removal of the weights, will more than compensate for the raising of the centre of gravity, especially if the weights removed were originally stowed tolerably high in the vessel. In any case, the curve of stability is not so much reduced in a ship of low as in one of high freeboard by placing her in the usual light condition.

Having the curve of stability in the load condition, the curve in the light condition may be deduced from it by the following method, without going through all the labour of calculating a separate curve by independent means.

The first thing to be done in this calculation is to find the centre of gravity of the ship when the weights already named are removed. The mode of doing this is shown at page 140.

The corrections to be made in the known curve are of a twofold character, as already stated, viz., that due to the change of mean draught; and that due to the vertical rise of the centre of gravity. The alteration of trim is not taken into account, it being found by experience that the curve is not affected by the small changes of this kind that usually occur. The weight of the stores removed from the ship, divided by the "tons per inch of immersion" at the load draught, gives a first approximation to the distance between the load and light water lines. A mean between the tons per inch of immersion at the light line thus found, and the load tons per inch gives a very close approximation to the real tons per inch of immersion to be used. It is, perhaps, hardly necessary to say that the tons per inch at the assumed light line is found by reference to the "curve of tons per inch of immersion" (see Art. 39). The weight removed, divided by the mean tons per inch, gives the actual distance of the light line below the load line in the body plan. In fig. 1 of Plate XXIX., $WL$ is the load line, and $W_1L_1$ is the light line thus found for a certain assumed case; the layer of displacement between $WL$ and $W_1L_1$ being equal to the weight of the consumable stores.

Let $D$ = the total displacement of the fully-equipped vessel, and $d$ = the weight removed; also let $D_1$ = the light displacement. Then
$$D_1 + d = D.$$
In the figure, $G$ is the position of the centre of gravity of the fully-equipped ship, and $G_1$ is the centre of gravity of the ship in the light condition, so that the centre of gravity has risen through the distance $GG_1$.

Now suppose the vessel inclined through an angle $\theta$; it is required to determine the length of the arm of the righting couple at that angle, in order to construct the curve of stability for the lightened ship; it being known that $GZ$ is the length of the arm at that angle in the load condition.

From the original calculation for the curve of stability of the fully-equipped ship, the position of the load water line in the inclined condition at the angle $\theta$ is known. Let $wl$ be that line. Again, the area of a plane $hh_1$, passing through the middle point $A$, and inclined at the angle $\theta$, was also found in the original calculation. Thus a first approximation to the distance of the inclined light line $w_1l_1$, below the inclined load line $wl$, is at once found by dividing the displacement $d$ of the layer by the area of the plane $hh_1$. This distance is termed the "thickness of the layer." If it be desired, the actual volume of this layer, and the distance of its centre of gravity from the line $AR$, drawn through $A$, perpendicular to $hh_1$, can be found by calculating the areas and centres of gravity of equidistant sections of the layer, and integrating them by Simpson's Rule in the ordinary way. If the volume is found unequal to $d$, corrections may then be made in the value of $t$—the thickness of the layer—until a perfect equality results. Such a calculation is, however, never needed in practice for finding the statical stability, as there cannot be an appreciable error in the perpendicular distance of the centre of gravity of the layer from the line $AR$, if we assume that the centre of gravity of a plane, midway between $wl$ and $w_1l_1$, is also the centre of gravity of the layer. This assumption is commonly made in these calculations.

Let $a$ be the perpendicular distance of the centre of gravity $C$ of the layer, found in this way, from the line $AR$. Also let $BN$ be the perpendicular from the upright centre of buoyancy $B$ of the fully-equipped ship upon $B_1M$, the vertical through the centre of buoyancy when the ship is inclined through an angle $\theta$; and let $BN_1$ be the perpendicular upon $B_2M_1$, the vertical through $B_2$, the centre of buoyancy of the lightened ship at the same angle.

Then $BN - BA \sin \theta = RN$,
and $a + (BN - BA \sin \theta) = CA + RN$.

Consequently, taking moments about $MB_1$, we have

$$d\{a + (BN - BA \sin \theta)\} = D_1 \times NN_1,$$
$$\text{or} \quad NN_1 = \frac{d\{a + (BN - BA \sin \theta)\}}{D_1}$$

It should here be remarked that it often happens that the line $B_1M$, and sometimes the point $C$, are on different sides of $AR$ at different angles of heel; and so the signs in the expression

$$\{a + (BN - BA \sin \theta)\}$$

should be carefully considered for each angle.

Having the value of $NN_1$, we know that of $BN_1$

Since $BN_1 = BN + NN_1$

for $BN$ is found from the original stability calculation. Again, it should be remarked that the signs of this expression should be carefully noticed for every angle of heel, as $M_1B_2$ may at some angles be on the other side of $MB_1$.

Having $BN_1$ we know the value of $G_1Z_1$, since

$$G_1Z_1 = BN_1 - BG_1 \sin \theta.$$

The value of $BN_1$ should be calculated for each of the angles of heel at which the value of $GZ$ was found in the original stability calculation for the load condition; in order that the value of $G_1Z_1$ may be found for the same angles.

Fig. 2, Plate XXIX., shows two curves of statical stability for the same vessel, one being in the load, and the other in the light condition. The effect of removing the stores already enumerated, in the case of an ordinary ship, upon the height and extent of the curve is shown by this figure. In this example the maximum value of $GZ$ is about 3·5 ft., and this is attained at an angle of 51 degrees; the stability vanishing at 86 degrees. In the light condition the maximum value of $G_1Z_1$ is attained at an inclination of 54 degrees, being then 3 ft.; while the stability vanishes at 79 degrees. Two facts will be noticed here, viz., 1st, that owing to the greater freeboard in the light condition, the maximum stability is attained at an inclination of 3 degrees greater than when she is fully equipped, although owing to the centre of gravity being raised, the leverage is 6 in. less; 2nd, that owing to the elevation of the centre of gravity when the ship is light, the stability vanishes at an inclination of 7 degrees less than when fully equipped.

By a similar process the curve of stability can be found when the ship is floating at a deeper draught than that for which the original curve was calculated.

# CHAPTER VI.

## WAVES AND ROLLING.

Still Water Rolling—The Revolving Pendulum—Isochronous and Free Oscillations—The Equivalent Pendulum—Radius of Gyration—Period of Still Water Rolling—Winging out the Weights—Pitching—Still Water Resistances to Rolling—Dipping—Period of Dipping—Waves: their Forms—Motion—Form of Surface—Motion of Wave Surface and Sub-surfaces—Sub-surfaces of Uniform Pressure—Resultant Pressure—Effective Wave Surface—Internal Structure of a Wave—Period of a Wave—Rules and Formulæ for Waves—Passive Rolling—Rolling in a Sea-way—Stiffness—Steadiness—Periods of Oscillations of certain Ships.

**146. Still Water Rolling.**—When a ship, floating in still water, has been forcibly inclined out of her normal or upright position of equilibrium, a certain force is required to retain her in the inclined condition. If that force is suddenly removed, she at once seeks to restore the statical equilibrium that had been thus destroyed. In returning to the normal position a certain amount of mechanical work is accumulated which carries the ship beyond the upright position to an angle of inclination on the opposite side. If the return motion of the ship is unresisted, the angle to which she inclines on the opposite side of the upright position is the same as that at which she was inclined before the force which kept her there was removed. The ship then commences a return motion which results in an oscillation of the same amplitude as before; and so the rolling continues *ad infinitum*. This hypothetical case is termed "*unresisted rolling in still water*." It need hardly be stated that the friction of the water on the ship's bottom, the irregularities of her form, and the resistance of the atmosphere, all tend to diminish the force which causes the motion, and therefore continually reduce the amplitude of the oscillation until the ship ultimately arrives at a state of rest in her normal position of uprightness.

The similarity between the cases of a ship and a simple pendulum is obvious. There is, however, this difference between them, that whereas the pendulum oscillates about a certain fixed point, a ship when rolling oscillates about a point which travels in a certain path, governed by the form of the vessel, and the position of her centre of gravity.

The study of *unresisted rolling* is instructive only in so far as we can gather from it the principles which govern the rolling of a ship under the circumstances which actually occur. By the application of the principles which regulate the motion of a pendulum, we are enabled to determine many facts regarding the rolling of ships, on the supposition that their oscillations are unrestrained. The actual amount of resistance offered to that motion in a real case is difficult, and, in fact, impossible, to determine by calculation beforehand; but by taking account of the time which elapses before the ship comes to a state of rest, the resistance can be experimentally determined. This resistance has not only the effect of finally extinguishing the rolling motion, but also of diminishing the extent of rolling and lengthening the periodic time. The late Professor Rankine has proved that the fluid resistances offered to a vessel's motion, in the form of friction, and by volumes of water being set in motion by the keel, bilge keels, and sharp parts of the body, cause the extent of rolling to be diminished nearly in geometrical progression, at a rate increasing with the amount of resistance, and diminishing with the increase of the vessel's moment of inertia. Also that the period of the oscillation is increased to an extent which would follow if the radius of gyration were increased in a particular ratio, which ratio varies directly as the amount of resistance exerted, and inversely as the distance which the metacentre is above the centre of gravity.

Such rolling as we have been considering, wherein the ship is supposed to be floating in still water, and merely under the influence of the resistances we have named, is termed "*free rolling*." Even this case, including as it does more usual conditions than those we started with, is still never met with in practice; at least to such an extent as to render it worthy of our consideration upon its own merits only. The cases of rolling which are of the greatest importance, by reason of their general occurrence, are those of a ship among waves, where, in addition to the resistances already named, the motion of the vessel is further influenced by that of the particles of water in which she floats. The rolling motion communicated to a ship by waves is termed "*forced rolling*," and the movements of the ship are termed "*forced oscillation.*" We will first discuss the question of *free rolling*, in order that we may be able to establish certain principles to guide us in dealing with the complex—and as yet scarcely understood—problem of forced oscillations, and the compound motions of a ship among waves.

**147. The Revolving Pendulum.**—In considering the oscillations of ships it is convenient to compare them to the motion of a *revolving pendulum*,* and express the rolling properties of the ship in terms of those of an *equivalent revolving pendulum* whose time of revolution is the same as the period of the ship's oscillation. It should be here observed that by the *period* of the oscillation is meant the time occupied by a complete or double oscillation which brings the body back to the same position and condition as when it started.

The principles of the pendulum are discussed in every treatise on dynamics, consequently we do not propose to consider them here, but shall content ourselves with merely stating the results of such investigations and taking them as demonstrated.

When a body is constrained to revolve in a circle with a uniform speed, the deflecting force which impresses a circular instead of a rectilinear motion is equal to

$$\frac{Wv^2}{gr}$$

where $W$ = the weight of the body, $v$ = its velocity, $r$ = the radius of the circle, and $g$ the accumulating force of gravity (32·2).

If $A$ represents the angular velocity in circular measure,

then $v = Ar$,

and the deflecting force expressed in these terms =

$$\frac{WA^2r^2}{gr} = \frac{WA^2r}{32 \cdot 2}.$$

* Such as the governor of a steam engine.

It is usually more convenient to express the speed of revolution by means of revolutions per second. Let $S =$ the number of revolutions per second. Then $A = 2\pi S$, and the deflecting force =

$$\frac{4WS^2\pi^2 r}{g} = \frac{WS^2 r}{\cdot 8154}.$$

If $S =$ the number of revolutions per minute, the above expression becomes

$$\frac{WS^2 r}{2935}.$$

In fig. 1, Plate **XXX.**, $CA$ represents a revolving pendulum consisting of a weight $C$ hung from the point $A$, and swinging round the vertical axis $AB$, in a circle whose radius is $CB$.

$AB$ is the height of the pendulum, which, therefore, diminishes as the angle $CAB$ increases.

If a force is communicated to the weight, it is by means of the rod or string $AC$; hence the tension of that string or rod is equal to the sum of the weight and the deflecting force. Therefore, if $P =$ deflecting force, and $W =$ weight,

$$P : W = CB : AB;$$

$$\text{But } P = \frac{WS^2 r}{\cdot 8154} = \frac{WS^2 \times CB}{\cdot 8154}$$

$$\therefore AB = \frac{W \times CB}{P} = \frac{W \times \cdot 8154 \times P}{P \times W \times S^2}$$

$$AB = \frac{\cdot 8154}{S^2}.$$

This result may be represented by the following rules:—

I. To find the height in feet of a revolving pendulum which makes a given number of revolutions per second: *Divide ·8154 by the square of the number of revolutions per second; or divide 2935 by the square of the number of revolutions per minute.*

II. To find the number of revolutions made in a given time by a revolving pendulum of a given height: *Divide ·8154 by the height in feet, and the square root of the quotient gives the number of revolutions per second; or, divide 2935 by the height in feet and the square root of the quotient gives the number of revolutions per minute.*

**148. Isochronous Oscillations.**—When the period of the oscillation of a body is the same, whether the oscillation be large or small, the oscillation is said to be isochronous. On the supposition that the rolling motion of a ship is of this character, the height of its equivalent pendulum may be found by means of the following ratio; it being observed that the necessary condition of isochronous rolling is that the righting moment of the ship shall be proportional to the angle at which she is inclined.*

Let $M$ = the righting moment at an angle $\theta$,
  ,,   $I$ = the moment of inertia of the ship,
  ,,   $h$ = the height of equivalent pendulum;
Then, $M : I = \theta : h$;
$$\therefore h = \frac{M}{I \times \theta} \quad \quad \quad \quad \quad (A)$$

Having the value of $h$, the number of oscillations per second or minute may be found by the Rules given in the preceding Article.

By means of formula (A) the height of the equivalent pendulum may be found for oscillations not exceeding 10 degrees each way, or for a total amplitude of 20 degrees; as up to this inclination the righting couple is generally almost proportional to the angle of heel. In the following remarks the oscillations of ships will be treated as isochronous, as the error thus introduced is so slight as not to be of any practical importance, provided the oscillation does not exceed 15 or 20 degrees each way.

Professor Rankine has shown in a paper read before the Institution of Naval Architects in 1864, that the conditions for an isochronous rolling ship is, that "the metacentric evolute is the involute of a circle described about the centre of gravity and through the metacentre; and, consequently, the metacentric involute is the involute of the involute of that circle." In other words, the metacentric (see Art. 79) is the involute of a circle passing through the metacentre, and whose centre is the centre of gravity, so that the curve of buoyancy (see Art. 77) is the involute of the involute of that

---

* From this it is evident that the curve of stability is a straight line up to that angle of inclination at which the rolling ceases to be isochronous.

circle. It is evident that for small inclinations this condition is practically fulfilled in all cases.

**149. Free Oscillations.**—A ship is capable of three kinds of free oscillations, viz., *rolling*, or oscillation about a longitudinal axis; *pitching*, or oscillation about a transverse axis; and *dipping*, or vertical oscillation with regard to the surface of still water.

**150. Axis of Rotation.**—Rolling, when not accompanied by pitching nor dipping, is performed about a longitudinal axis. Instead, however, of this axis being fixed, like the point of suspension of a pendulum, it has a motion which, in the case of unresisted or free rolling, such as we are now considering, is easily determined. Suppose the surface of flotation (see Art. 74) and the surface of the still water to become rigid without friction, so that the former may roll or slide freely upon the latter without being interfered with by the body of the vessel, but only subjected to the forces of weight and buoyancy acting through their respective centres. The condition is then exactly analogous to that of a ship rolling freely in still water and influenced by the resistances which actually occur in such a case. We have simply the case of a smooth solid body without weight rolling upon a smooth horizontal plane under the action of certain forces.

In fig. 2, Plate XXX., the transverse section of a ship is shown, of which $HP$ is the middle line, and $WL$ the load water line in the upright condition. The ship is shown inclined, so that $W_1L_1$ is the new load water line. $FAF_1$ is a transverse section of the surface of flotation, $S$ being the point of contact of the curve of flotation with the inclined position of the water line $W_1L_1$. The ship is therefore supposed to be in such a condition that its rigid surface of flotation $FAF_1$ is rolling upon the rigid surface of the water. Being under the influence of forces which act vertically, the motion of the centre of gravity must be in a vertical direction; consequently, at any instant, the axis about which the body is rotating will be found in a horizontal line $GO$. Again, the instantaneous direction of motion of the point of contact of the surface of flotation with the water surface must be along the plane of the latter, and therefore its motion is horizontal. From this, it follows that the instantaneous axis must be in the line $SO$ drawn through the point of contact perpendicular to the water plane. Having $GO$ and $SO$ the co-ordinates of the point, therefore $O$ is the position of the instantaneous axis corresponding to the inclined position of the ship shown in the figure. By tracing the locus of the point $O$, it will be found to be a curve of the character $O_1GO$ passing through the centre of gravity.

**151. Relation between a Ship and her Equivalent Pendulum.**—In Art. 148 we stated that

$$h = \frac{M}{I \times \theta}.$$

But the value of $I$—or the moment of inertia of a ship about a longitudinal axis—is equal to her displacement, multiplied by the square of her transverse radius of gyration. This follows from the principles of moments of inertia enunciated at Art. 52. Expressed algebraically this will be

$$I = D \times k^2,$$

$k$ being the length of the radius of gyration. Also the moment of the righting couple is very nearly equal to the displacement multiplied by the height of metacentre above centre of gravity, multiplied by the angle of heel in circular measure. Expressed algebraically—

$$M = D \times GM \times \theta.$$
$$\text{But} \quad h = \frac{M}{I \times \theta}$$
$$= \frac{D \times GM \times \theta}{D \times k^2 \times \theta}$$
$$= \frac{GM}{k^2} = \frac{m}{k^2}, \text{ putting } m \text{ for GM.}$$

Hence we have the following rule:—

*Divide the square of the ship's transverse radius of gyration by the height of her metacentre about her centre of gravity; the quotient will be the height of her equivalent pendulum for rolling.*

By Rule II., Art. 147, we have, calling $T$ the time in

seconds in which the complete roll from port to starboard is made,

$$T = \sqrt{\frac{h}{\cdot 815}}$$
$$= \sqrt{\frac{k^2}{\cdot 815\,m}}.$$

**152. Geometrical Method of finding $h$.**—Professor Rankine has given a simple geometrical construction for finding the height of the equivalent pendulum. In fig. 3, Plate XXX., let $G$ represent the ship's centre of gravity, and $M$ her metacentre. Perpendicular to $GM$ draw $GR$ equal to the transverse radius of gyration. Join $MR$; and perpendicular to it draw $RP$, cutting $MG$ produced in $P$: $GP$ will be the height of the equivalent pendulum required.

Professor Rankine also adds the following: To represent a *compound pendulum*, which shall have not only the same period of oscillation with the ship, but the same statical and dynamical stability, proceed as follows:—About $M$ (fig. 3, Plate XXX.), with a radius equal to $GR$, draw a circular arc, cutting the straight line $RG$ in two points $B, B$, equidistant from $G$. Conceive that $MBB$ represents a light triangular frame, hung from the point $M$; and that it is loaded by having *one half of the weight of the ship* concentrated at each of the points $B, B$; the triangular frame, so suspended and loaded, will be the compound pendulum required.

**153. To find the Radius of Gyration.**—It is a very difficult problem to determine the radius of gyration of a ship by measurement and calculation. The hull and equipment consist of so many items of different form and specific gravity that the task is impracticable. But by experiment, after the ship is built and equipped, the length of the radius of gyration is readily determined from the observed period of the ship's free rolling. The length being once determined for any ship, a very close approximation can be made for that of another ship of similar character by simply making allowance for the differences in the weights and positions of the principal elements in the hull and equipment. In this way the designer is able to predict with tolerable accuracy the length of the radius of gyration of a new design, provided he knows its length in another ship of similar form and construction.

The experiment for finding the length of the radius of gyration is conducted in the following manner: The ship, floating in still water, is forcibly inclined through a moderate angle, say 5 to 10 degrees, and then allowed to roll freely. The number of double rolls, or complete oscillations from side to side, in a convenient interval of time is then counted, and the time, divided by the number, gives the period of rolling.

I. *Multiply the square of the period in seconds by ·815, and the result will be the height of the equivalent pendulum in feet.*

II. *Multiply the height of the equivalent pendulum by the height of the ship's metacentre above her centre of gravity; the product will be the square of her radius of gyration.*

If $T$ = the period of rolling as observed. Then, using the nomenclature already adopted in this chapter, Rule I. will be expressed thus—

$$h = ·815\, T^2$$

and Rule II.

$$k^2 = mh$$
$$= ·815\, mT^2.$$

The first formulæ agrees with Rule I. of Art 147, while the second is identical with the formulæ already given in Art. 151.

**154. Regulation of the Period of Rolling.**—A glance at the expression for the period of free rolling

$$T = \sqrt{\frac{k^2}{·815\, m}}$$

shows that $T$ increases as $k$ increases, but diminishes as $m$ becomes greater. From this we see that to increase the period of rolling either or both of two expedients may be adopted; the length of the radius of gyration may be increased; the distance between the centre of gravity and metacentre may be diminished; or both of these changes may be made. The reverse of these alterations, of course, produces a contrary effect. The radius of gyration is increased in length by what is termed "winging out the weights," *i.e.*, by spreading out the principal weights farther from the middle line of the ship. Consequently, placing armour on the sides of ships increases the period of rolling considerably beyond what it would be if the same weights were distributed uniformly as in unarmoured ships. As we shall see hereafter, there is an advantage to be obtained in a ship's behaviour among waves by increasing her period of rolling, and, consequently, the system of armour plating the sides of ships lends itself very usefully in attaining that end.

The distance between the metacentre and centre of gravity may be diminished or increased by changes in both the form and stowage of the ship. Widening the ship at the load water line, or fineing the form below, raises the metacentre with regard to the underside of keel, and *vice versa*. Also giving a rising floor raises the centre of buoyancy with regard to the underside of keel; and giving a flat floor or barge-like form to the body lowers the centre of buoyancy. By combining these two sets of changes, it is possible to raise or depress the metacentre with regard to the water line or underside of keel. But changes in form are not so readily accomplished as changes in stowage, as the shape of the vessel is usually influenced by other considerations than those of stability or rolling. So that we may say the period of rolling of a ship is diminished by raising the centre of gravity, and *vice versa*.

It is, however, obvious that a reduction in the value of $GM$ (or $m$ in our formulæ), causes a loss of stability, and it may happen that the value of $m$, which is best adapted for slow and steady rolling, is too small to ensure the requisite stability in a low-sided or heavily-rigged ship. Consequently, the best mode, if practicable, of increasing the period of a ship's rolling is to increase the length of the radius of gyration, which is accomplished by "winging out the weight."

155. **Effect of "Winging out the Weights."**—Suppose a pair of equal weights to be originally situated with their centres of gravity at equal distances on opposite sides of the longitudinal vertical middle line plane of the vessel, and that they are shifted out at greater, but still equal, distances in a horizontal direction from that plane; to find the increase in the length of the ship's radius of gyration.

*From the square of the new distance of the centre of gravity of either weight from the middle line, subtract the square of the original distance; multiply the remainder by the sum of the shifted weights, and divide by the displacement; the square root of the quotient will be the increase of the ship's transverse radius of gyration.*

Expressed algebraically—

Let $D$ = displacement.
" $W$ = each weight.
" $l$ = original distance of the $G$ of each weight from middle line.
" $l_1$ = new distance of the $G$ of each weight from middle line.
" $k$ = original radius of gyration.
" $K$ = new radius of gyration.

$$\text{Then } K - k = \left\{ \frac{2W(l^2 - l_1^2)}{D} \right\}^{\frac{1}{2}}$$

$$\text{Hence } K = k + \left\{ \frac{2W(l^2 - l_1^2)}{D} \right\}^{\frac{1}{2}}$$

**156. Pitching.**—As *rolling* is the name given to the transverse oscillations of a ship about a longitudinal axis, so *pitching* designates the longitudinal rolling about a transverse axis.

The same principles are involved in the two kinds of oscillation, between which there may be any number of directions in which oscillations may take place. In point of fact, direct rolling or pitching are rarely observed, as even in still water one motion gives rise to the other, owing to the difference in the forms of the wedges of immersion and emersion. The oscillatory motion of a ship is generally in a diagonal direction.

The term *pitching*, as here employed, denotes the complete or double oscillation, but in practice the lowering of the bow and raising of the stem is spoken of as pitching, the other half of the oscillation, which consists of raising the bow and lowering the stern, is termed *scending*.

The principles which regulate the pitching oscillations, and the rules applying to them, are the same as for rolling, and therefore do not require separate treatment. Instead of the height of the transverse metacentre above the centre of gravity, that of the longitudinal metacentre is substituted; and instead of the transverse radius of gyration we use the longitudinal radius; the latter being a quantity which, if calculated, would be found by multiplying each weight in the ship by the square of its distance from a transverse axis through the centre of gravity, adding together the products, dividing by the displacement, and taking the square root of the quotient.

**157. Regulation of Period of Pitching.**—As we shall see hereafter, it is generally desirable that the period of a ship's pitching should be as short as possible, or, in other words, that she should be "lively." As in the cases of rolling there are two modes of producing this, viz., by shortening the length of the longitudinal radius of gyration, or by increasing the height of the longitudinal metacentre above the centre of gravity. There are difficulties in the way of making a change in the period by the latter course of procedure. In the first place, the height of a ship's longitudinal metacentre above her centre of gravity is usually so great that a very considerable lowering of the centre of gravity would be necessary in order to produce an appreciable change. And, secondly, an increase in the height of the longitudinal metacentre above the centre of buoyancy is only effected by filling out the lines at the bow or stern; and as by so doing the speed is considerably reduced, it is evident that there are great objections to that course. The only practicable manner then of producing "liveliness" in pitching, is by stowing the principal weights as close lengthwise to the centre of gravity of the ship as possible.

**158. Still Water Resistance to Rolling.**—Hitherto we have supposed no resistance to be offered by the water to a ship's oscillatory motions; we shall now consider the effect of the *passive resistances* of the water upon the surface of the ship's bottom. By such resistance we do not include the statical forces which tend to right or upset a vessel, but the resistances to her motion whatever the direction of that motion may be. The observed effect of passive resistance upon free rolling is to diminish the amplitude of the roll and cause the oscillations to gradually diminish in extent and finally become extinguished.

The resistance of a fluid to the motion of a body immersed in it consists of two parts: one of these is the effect of the resistance of the fluid particles to sliding past each other, and the other is the waste of mechanical work in producing eddies in the fluid.

The first of these is proportional to the velocity of the motion of the body, and the second is proportional to the square of that velocity.

These resistances vary with the form and nature of the surface of the ship's bottom. It is evident that the tendency to reduce the extent of roll, and to increase the period of rolling, is greater when the ship has a rising floor, deep keel and bilge keels, than if she had a flat floor, rounded bilges, and an absence of keels.

The experiment by which the length of the transverse radius of gyration is determined also furnishes the data for determining the resistance, if the "rate of extinction" of the rolling is observed at the same time. Professor Rankine, in a paper communicated to the Institution of Naval Architects in 1864, says:—" By means of suitable experiments on the rolling of a ship in smooth water two quantities may be determined: *the square of her radius of gyration*, and a quantity which may be called the *leverage of keel-resistance;* being the length of the lever at which the whole weight of the ship would have to act, in order to exert a moment equal to the moment of the resistance opposed by the water to the keel, when the angular velocity of rolling is unity.

" I. Let the ship be forcibly heeled over, and set free to roll; observe the periodic time of rolling by counting the complete oscillations or *double rolls* in a certain number of seconds; observe also the greatest angle of heel at the commencement of the experiment, and also after the lapse of a certain time in seconds, taking care to measure those angles by observations of fixed objects, or by an instrument of the gyroscope kind (like that invented by Prof. Piazzi Smyth),[*] and not by a plummet or level.

" II. Divide the hyperbolic logarithm of the ratio in which the original angle of heel exceeds the diminished angle, by the time in seconds (or the common logarithm by the time in seconds × ·4343), the quotient will be a number which we may call the *exponent.*

---

[*] Mr. W. Froude, F.R.S., has invented a very ingenious apparatus which is superior to the gyroscope in point of accuracy, and which automatically records the motion of the vessel. See *Trans. Institution of Naval Architects*, 1873, p. 179.

"III. To find what the periodic time would be in the absence of keel resistance: Multiply the square of the actual periodic time of a double roll in seconds and fraction of a second, by the square of the *exponent* above mentioned, and divide the product by 39·48 ($4\pi^2$), to the quotient add 1, then by that sum divide the square of the actual periodic time, the result will be the *square of the periodic time of unresisted rolling*.

"IV. Multiply the square of the periodic time of unresisted rolling by the constant ·815 $\left(\frac{g}{4\pi^2}\text{ in feet}\right)$, the product will be the length of the *corresponding simple pendulum* in feet.

"V. Multiply that length by the height of the ship's metacentre above her centre of gravity; the product will be the *square of her radius of gyration*.

"VI. Multiply the square of the radius of gyration by the *exponent* (Rule II.), and divide by 16·1 $\left(\frac{g}{2}\text{ in feet}\right)$; the quotient will be the *leverage of keel resistance* in feet.

"Experiments and calculations of the kind just described are most likely to give accurate and consistent results at moderate angles of heel (say not exceeding about 10 degrees), for it is only under that condition that the resistance to rolling can be treated as approximately proportional to the angular velocity of rolling. The test whether the angles of heel are small enough is simply their diminishing sensibly in geometrical progression."

Professor Rankine was of opinion that the efficiency of bilge keels was very doubtful, but Mr. Froude found by experiments made with two vessels, each of over 1000 tons displacement, one of which was without bilge keels, while the other had a pair, each 100 feet long and 3 feet 6 inches wide, that the rolling of the vessel with bilge keels was barely half that of the other, although both vessels were loaded to oscillate in the same time, and were nearly alike in form.

**159. Dipping** is the name given to the vertical oscillatory motion of a ship which is produced by rolling and pitching. On this account it has been termed a *secondary oscillation;* pitching, when produced by rolling, being another instance of an oscillation produced by another oscillation.

*Dipping produced by rolling* results from the form of the vessel's body in the neighbourhood of the water line being such that when the vessel is inclined the centre of gravity is at a greater or less distance from the water surface than when she is upright. If the side of the vessel flares out above the water, the inclined water plane cuts the original in a straight line on that side of the vertical longitudinal middle line plane towards which the ship is inclined, and thus the centre of gravity is at a greater distance from the surface of the water than when the ship is upright. Consequently, mechanical work in opposition to gravity is performed in the inclination, equal to the whole weight of the ship multiplied by the distance through which the centre of gravity is raised, and vertical oscillatory motion is set up by the dynamical effect of the fall due to gravity which follows. Such a motion is undesirable, and can occur to an injurious extent only in a badly formed vessel such as we have described. Fig. 2, Plate XVI., illustrates the kind of section which produces such uneasiness; the vertical motion being due to the distance which the axis of level motion (see Art. 76) is above the centre of gravity. In well stowed ships the centre of gravity is generally near the load water line; consequently, in order to secure a steady motion when rolling, the form of the sections of the body should be such that the axis of level motion is near the load water line. When that axis traverses the centre of gravity, the latter point is, of course, immovable, and the ship has no vertical motion at all.

*Dipping produced by pitching* is influenced by the same principles as already mentioned, which in this case may be expressed thus: Dipping is produced by pitching when the centre of gravity of the load water plane is not in the same transverse section as the centre of buoyancy.

160. **Period of Dipping.**—The period of a ship's dipping oscillations is usually shorter than those of pitching, and much shorter than those of rolling. Should the periodic time of dipping be about half that of rolling, the extent of the alternate dipping and rising goes on increasing until the acceleration is balanced by the resistance of the water, and then it becomes permanent so long as rolling continues. In such cases the axis of level motion no longer keeps at a con-

stant height above the water surface, but acquires a vertical oscillatory motion also, and the centre of gravity attains its greatest elevation about a quarter of a period after the instant of greatest heel. Consequently, every particle in the ship, above and below the centre of gravity, describes a curve thus: ∞.

**161. Waves.**—Before the principles which regulate the motions of a vessel when floating among waves can be discovered, it is first necessary to know the character and laws of wave motion.

Waves are of two principal kinds, which may be styled: *solitary* and *gregarious*. The tidal wave, and the wave which is raised by the bow of a ship when she is in motion, are instances of the *solitary* wave. The common sea-wave, familiar to all who will read this book, is an instance of the *gregarious* wave. The waves which follow a paddle steamer are other examples of the same kind. In the case of the solitary wave, we have a body of water heaped upon the surface of the sea, and wholly above the level of the latter; while in the case of the common sea-wave the level of still water is very nearly midway between the highest and lowest points in the surface of the wave.

**162. Wave Form.**—In the ordinary sea-wave, the form alone has a translatory motion; the particles of water merely revolving in orbits of a certain character while the wave is passing. The particles may also have a translatory motion, but if so it is altogether independent of the wave forces, and is due to currents of some kind. In the case of the *solitary* wave, however, each particle comes to a state of rest at a short distance in advance of its original position.

The waves which we have to consider are those of the ordinary kind, in which wave follows wave in a continuous succession. The surface of the sea, when disturbed by wind, assumes an undulatory form, which, while the wind is blowing, is of a rather complex character, consisting as it does of waves superposed upon waves, the shorter upon the longer. The smaller irregularities of the surface do not, however, affect the problem that we have to discuss, as they do not generally have a very marked effect upon a floating body of the dimensions of a ship; at least, not anything approaching to the same degree as the main undulatory sweep forming the wave proper. We shall consider the wave to be of the character exhibited by a "ground swell" after a storm, when the wind has subsided.

The summit of a wave is termed the "*crest*," and the lowest point in its surface is termed the "*trough*." The "*height*" of a wave is the vertical distance from *crest* to *trough*. The greatest height which has been accurately measured in the open sea is 30 ft.; but there can be little doubt that during storms in the Atlantic, waves are sometimes engendered which exceed that height. The level of still water is, as we have said, nearly midway between crest and trough. If a transverse section of the wave surface is a curve of sines, the bed of still water is just midway; but if, as is generally assumed, the curvature is trochoidal, the level of still water is rather nearer the trough than the crest. The *length* of the wave is the horizontal distance between consecutive crests or consecutive troughs. The greatest length which has been accurately measured is 500 feet.

**163. Wave Motion.**—The changes of form which the surface of water undergoes when waves are traversing it, shows that there must necessarily be, at least, a vertical motion among the particles. Closer observations show that there is also a backward and forward motion among the particles of water. The exact character of the combined vertical and horizontal motions of a particle of water in a wave is not fully understood, but experimental researches go to show that in deep water, *i.e.*, water sufficiently deep to prevent any resistance to wave motion being offered by the surface of the bottom, the backward and forward motion is equal to the vertical motion, and it would therefore appear that each particle of water has a circular orbit. In shallow water the horizontal motion is greater than the vertical, the difference increasing as the water shallows, and thus the particles in this case have orbital motion of a flattened oval character. Assuming, then, that each particle of water in the wave revolves in a circular orbit, it follows that the combined effect of this motion, with the translatory motion of the wave form, causes the surface to assume a curvature of which a transverse section will be either a trochoid, curve of sines, or some other curve of that family.

Theories on this subject have, in some cases, been based upon a supposition that the curve is that of the trochoid, and in others that it is a curve of sines. General support seems to be given to the former hypothesis, which we shall therefore adopt, especially as by so doing several phenomena pertaining to wave motion are more readily accounted for thereby.

In consequence of the nature of the motions among the particles which generate the ordinary sea-wave, the latter has been styled the *oscillatory wave*.

**164. Form of Wave Surface.**—We shall consider the wave to be in deep water, and therefore that the motions of the particles are unaffected by the sea bottom. Professor Rankine fixes the minimum depth of what can be thus considered as deep water at five-twelfths the length of the wave.

In Plate XXXI., consider a straight line $C_0, C_6$ to represent the length of a wave. Divide the line $C_0, C_6$ into any number of equal parts, say six, at the points $C_1, C_2, C_3$, etc., and let the points $C_0, C_1, C_2$, etc., be the centres of the orbits of seven particles on the surface of the wave. With each of these points as a centre, and with a radius equal to half the height of the wave, sweep circles. Let the particle in the middle orbit be at the crest of the wave, then the particles on the orbits whose centres are $C_0$ and $C_6$ will be in the trough, and will, in fact, be in similar positions. Through $C_3$ draw $C_3, P_3$ upwards, perpendicular to $C_0, C_6$, and at $C_0$ and $C_6$ draw $C_0 P_0$ and $C_6 P_6$ perpendiculars downwards to meet the arcs of the circles. Then $P_3$ will be a particle on the crest, also $P_0$ and $P_6$ will be particles in consecutive troughs of the wave. Since $P_0$ is at the lowest part of its orbit, and $P_3$ at the highest, the particles in the circles whose centres are $C_1$ and $C_2$ will be at intermediate positions in their orbits. Also since $C_0 C_1 = C_1 C_2 = C_2 C_3$, and because there are 180 degrees between the positions of $P_0$ and $P_3$, therefore $P_1$ is at 60 degrees, and $P_2$ at 120 degrees from the position of $P_0$. Similarly, $P_4$ and $P_5$ are at 60 degrees and 120 degrees respectively from $P_3$. Thus $P_0, P_1, P_2, P_3$, etc., are points in the surface of a wave of length $C_0 C_6$, and height equal to $2\, C_3 P_3$.

It is perhaps unnecessary to state that the curve, traced by a point which is within or without the circumference of a circle that rolls upon a straight line, is a *trochoid;* hence the surface of a wave, when generated in this way, has a trochoidal curvature.

If a circle be swept with either of the points $C_0$, $C_1$, etc., as a centre, and with a radius bearing the ratio to the length of the wave of about 7 : 22, then the circumference of this circle will be equal to the length of the wave. Let $A_3 B_3$ be the diameter of this circle. Draw $A_0 A_6$ touching the circle and parallel to $C_0 C_6$. Through $C_0$, $C_1$, $C_2$, etc., draw perpendiculars, meeting $A_0 A_6$ at the points $A_0$, $A_1$, $A_2$, etc., so that $A_0 A_6$ is the length of the wave, then the curve of the wave surface is traced out by the point $P_3$ as the large circle rolls upon the line $A_0 A_6$ from $A_0$ to $A_6$. Between each pair of consecutive points $A_0$, $A_1$, $A_2$, etc., the tracing point $P$ revolves through an arc of 60 degrees.

**165. Motion of Wave Surface.**—Suppose, at any instant, the positions of former horizontally equidistant particles are as shown by $P_0$, $P_1$, $P_2$, etc. (Plate XXXI.), and that the motion of the wave, and, therefore, of the rolling circle, is that indicated by the arrow at the top of the figure. Suppose the rolling circle to move from $A_3$ to $A_4$, then each of the particles represented by the points $P_0$, $P_1$, $P_2$, etc., will move through an arc of 60 degrees in the direction shown by the curved arrows, and the wave surface will then be as shown by the ticked line.

By observing this motion of the particles, and the change in the position of the wave which accompanies it, the following facts will be noted: A particle in the trough of the wave is moving backwards, on the front slope upwards, on the crest forwards, and on the back slope downwards.

**166. Form and Motion of Sub-Surfaces.**—The motion of the particles of water for the whole depth to which the wave influence extends is of the same character as at the surface, but the extent of the motion diminishes very rapidly in going downwards. The length of the wave remains constant to whatever depth its influence extends, but the radii of the

orbits of the particles diminish in geometrical progression.*
The curve marked $P'_0$, $P'_1$, $P'_2$, $P'_3$, etc. (Plate XXXI.), is the
form of a transverse section of the surface in which particles,
at that depth below the original level of the water, move.
This curve is likewise trochoidal, but much flatter than the
surface curve. The motion is similar to that at the surface.

**167. Sub-Surfaces of Uniform Pressure.**—The surfaces of
horizontal layers of water, when the latter is still, are surfaces
of uniform pressure. The same condition of equilibrium is
preserved when the particles of water are in their orbital
motion, the surfaces which were originally level being now
of a trochoidal form; $P'_0$, $P'_1$, $P'_2$, etc. (Plate XXXI.), is
such a surface. The trochoidal character merges into a plane
at that depth where the water below is uninfluenced by the
passing wave.

**168. Direction of the Resultant Pressure.**—In order that
the resultant of the pressures on a particle at the surface
of a fluid should be in a certain line, it is necessary that the
surface should be at right angles to that line. In still water,
the resultant line being necessarily perpendicular, the surface
is necessarily level. In undulating water, the resultant has
that amount of obliquity which the motion of the particles
prescribe, and therefore the surface must of necessity be as much
out of level as the resultant is out of perpendicular. Consequently, the resultant of the forces acting upon a particle of
water at the surface of a wave is perpendicular to a tangent
to the water line at that point. In other words, whatever
tendency a body floating on the surface of a wave—*i.e.*, but
slightly immersed in the wave—has to keep its axis of equilibrium vertical in still water, is exerted to keep it normal
to the surface of the wave.

**169. Effective Wave Surface.**—Each of the particles of
water at every sub-surface of uniform pressure is under the influence of two forces, viz., gravity and a rotating force, which
have a resultant acting, as we have seen, normal to the subsurface. Hence a body floating in the wave is under the
influence of the resultant forces at every sub-surface it meets.

---

* This law is based upon the necessary geometrical continuity of
the wave water; a proof of it by Mr. C. W. Merrifield, F.R.S., is given
in No. 3 of the *Annual of the Royal School of Naval Architecture*.

These forces act in different directions; there are an infinite number of the resultant forces—one for each of the infinite number of sub-surfaces—between the water surface and the keel, and the directions of the resultants vary continuously between that of the surface normal and the normal to the lowest sub-surface. It was for some time assumed that the resultant pressure due to all these resultant forces acted through the centre of gravity of the ship's displacement, and that it was the resultant force acting on a particle in the sub-surface of uniform pressure passing through the centre of buoyancy; the particle being supposed to be at the centre of buoyancy. Hence the sub-surface of uniform pressure passing through the centre of buoyancy was considered to be the *effective wave surface*, and the curvature of its trochoid gave the effective wave slope at any point in that surface.

In a paper communicated to the Institution of Naval Architects, in 1873, Mr. Froude has shown that, except in special cases, this is not so. He says: "Independently of, and besides that which may be called the normalising force, inherent in the wave slope, impressed on a stable floating body which rests upon it, the floating body may be so shaped as to experience from the molecular forces, on which the internal structure of the wave depends, a separate force of rotation, the operation of which is dependent on the elevation of the centre of gravity, and which may thus modify to almost any assignable extent the effect of the general normalising force." The investigation is a somewhat lengthy one, but it goes to show that the position of the effective wave surface varies with the form, dimensions, and position of the centre of gravity of the weights of the ship. Mr. Froude says: "We might, if we pleased, so proportion and weight a ship of this form,\* that in waves of a certain proportionate dimension she would experience no disturbing force in the waves passed under her." He shows that the effective wave surface may in some cases pass through the underside of the keel, and be even wholly below the vessel. For further particulars on this subject the student is referred to Vol. XIV. of the *Transactions of the Institution of Naval Architects*, page 96, *et. seq.* We

---

\* The form here referred to is somewhat similar to that of a Thames barge.

may, however, remark that the dimensions of a ship are generally so small compared with that of the whole body of water set in motion by the passing wave, that for ordinary calculations the surface of the wave is usually assumed to be the effective wave surface.

170. **Internal Structure of a Wave.**—Suppose a body of still water to be divided into cubical blocks by an imaginary series of horizontal and vertical planes, each set being equidistant, then a section of the block made by a vertical plane, perpendicular to both of the sets of dividing planes, will be divided into a series of equal rectangles. Now, suppose a trochoidal wave to traverse this block of water in the direction of the section, each of the particles of water in that section will have a circular motion in the plane of the section, and at any instant the figures which were previously rectangles will now be distorted, the distortion occurring as far below the surface as the wave influence extends, and diminishing as we proceed downwards. In Plate XXXII., the curved lines shown are originally vertical and horizontal planes as they appear in the section we have made. Particles which were in plane surfaces of equal pressure are now in trochoidal surfaces of equal pressure, and particles which were originally in vertical lines are now in lines which are inclined to the vertical at the surface, and each sub-surface at practically the same angle that the surface and respective sub-surface is inclined to the horizontal at that point. The area of a figure, such as $P^d P_1^d P_1^e P^e$, is equal to the area of the rectangle, bounded by the corresponding vertical and horizontal lines when the water was still, and thus such a figure shows the amount of distortion which a block of water at any part undergoes when the wave is passing. Considering the spaces between the vertical dividing planes it will be observed that, as the crest of the wave approaches a vertical column of water the latter lengthens and narrows, while, as the crest passes, it shortens and widens; in both cases the quantity of water remaining the same. Between these two positions the columns have a swaying motion like the stalks in a cornfield as the wind passes over them, with this difference, that the columns of water undergo alterations of length and thickness in addition to the bend in their form. This motion of the

columns of water and change in form of the blocks into which a wave may be supposed to be divided is very interesting, as by observing it we are enabled to judge of the character of the impressed forces upon a ship or other floating body immersed in the wave; for the conditions of dynamical equilibrium are such that the floating body seeks to conform to the same laws of motion which govern the particles displaced by the body. This may be seen by placing a board or raft upon the surface of the wave as at $A$, Plate XXXII., the motion of the wave in the direction shown causes the board to follow in the direction of the surface particles, as indicated by the curved arrow. If, however, the board were very thin and weightless, having no stability, so that it would float edgewise as at $B$, it would follow the motion of the originally vertical column of water in which it floats, and therefore the direction of its motion would be opposite to that of the board at $A$. By combining the two, as shown at $C$, the one motion modifies the other, and the position of the compound float at any moment will be somewhere midway between those which would have been occupied by the flat and vertical boards if floating separately.

The condition of the midship body of a ship as low as the bilge is similar to that of the raft $A$, and the condition of the keel, sharp parts of the floor, deadwood, stem, and stern post, is analogous to that of the board $B$. Hence the ship is under two sets of forces, each of which tends to modify the effect of the other. It is thus seen how important is a knowledge of the internal structure or mechanism of a wave, in order to determine the character of the form and arrangement of the weights in a ship which is required to be seaworthy when floating in that wave.

**171. Period of a Wave.**—As we have already said, the length of a wave is the horizontal distance between consecutive crests or hollows. The period of a wave is the time which a wave-length occupies in passing a given point.

When the particles composing a wave revolve uniformly in circular orbits, the only forces acting upon them are the centrifugal and that of gravity. Now the normal to a trochoid at any point passes through the point of contact of the rolling circle with the straight line under which it rolls.

Hence the conditions of equilibrium in a trochoidal wave are satisfied if the radius of the rolling circle bears the same ratio to that of the orbit of any particle as gravity bears to the centrifugal acceleration of that particle.

Let T be the periodic time.
,, $r =$ the radius of the orbit of a surface particle.
,, $R =$ the radius of the orbit of rolling circle.

Then if $v$ is the velocity of the particle

$$v = \frac{2\pi r}{T},$$

and the centrifugal acceleration is

$$\frac{v^2}{r} = \frac{4\pi^2 r}{T^2}.$$

But $\quad R : r = g : \frac{4\pi^2 r}{T^2}$

whence $\quad R = \frac{T^2 g}{4\pi^2},$

which is the expression for the length of a revolving pendulum, whose time is $T$, as shown at Art. 147.

The wave length is, of course, $= 2\pi R$

$$= \frac{T^2 g}{2\pi},$$

and the number of waves which pass a particular spot in a given time $t$ is

$$\frac{t}{T} = \frac{t}{2\pi}\sqrt{\frac{g}{R}}.$$

The speed of the wave's advance is found by dividing the total length of these waves by $t$,

$$= \frac{1}{t} \times \frac{t}{2\pi}\sqrt{\frac{g}{R}} \times 2\pi R$$
$$= \sqrt{gR}.$$

Also since

$$R = \frac{T^2 g}{4\pi^2}$$
$$\therefore T = 2\pi \sqrt{\frac{R}{g}}$$

which is the periodic time of the wave.

**172. Rules and Formulæ for Waves.**—The following rules for waves in *deep water* are given in Rankine's Shipbuilding, and may be deduced from the preceding investigations:—

I. Height of equivalent pendulum (or radius of rolling circle) in feet—

$$= \frac{T^2 g}{4\pi^2} = \cdot 8154\, T^2;$$

where $T$ represents the periodic time of the wave in seconds.

II. Length of wave in feet

$$= 2\pi R = 6 \cdot 2832 \times R$$
$$= 6 \cdot 2832 \times \text{equivalent pendulum}$$
$$\text{or} = 6 \cdot 2832 \times \cdot 8154\, T^2$$
$$\therefore L = 5 \cdot 1233\, T^2,$$

where $L$ is the length of the wave, and, like $R$, is expressed in feet, while $T$ is expressed in seconds.

Also, if $V$ = the velocity of advance of the wave in feet per second—

$$V = \sqrt{gR}$$
$$V^2 = gR$$
$$R = \frac{V^2}{g}$$
$$\text{and } L = 2\pi R = \frac{2\pi V^2}{g} = \frac{V^2}{5 \cdot 1233}.$$
$$\text{Again, } L = V \times T.$$

III. Since $L$, the length of wave in feet, $= \frac{V^2}{5 \cdot 1233}$, and since it is also $= V \times T$.

$$\therefore V \times T = \frac{V^2}{5 \cdot 1233},$$
$$\text{and } V = 5 \cdot 1233 \times T.$$
$$\text{Again, } V = \sqrt{gR}$$
$$= \sqrt{\{32 \cdot 2 \times \text{equivalent pendulum.}\}}$$

Also since

$$L = \frac{V^2}{5 \cdot 1233}$$
$$\therefore V = \sqrt{\{5 \cdot 1233 \times L\}}$$

Once more; since

$$L = V \times T$$
$$\therefore V = \frac{L}{T}.$$

IV. Velocity of advance of wave in knots

$$= \frac{V}{1\cdot 688} = V_1.$$

V. Velocity of advance of wave in miles an hour

$$= V_1 \times 1\cdot 151.$$

VI. Sine of steepest slope of surface of wave $= \frac{r}{R}$ (approximately).

If $h =$ the length of wave,
then $h = 2r$,
and sine of steepest slop $= \frac{h}{2R}$.

Also since

$$2\pi R = L,$$
$$\therefore R = \frac{L}{2\pi}$$

and sine of steepest slope $= \frac{h \times \pi}{L}$.

$$= \frac{3\cdot 1416 \times h}{L}.$$

(The angle of slope in degrees is roughly equal to $\frac{180\,h}{L}$).

VII. The velocity $v$ of the particles at the surface

$$= V \times \text{sine of steepest slope of surface.}$$

The following rules are not deducible from any investigations we have given, but are stated by Professor Rankine as the results of more intricate calculations, such as are beyond the scope of this work; we, however, append the results in the words of Professor Rankine.

VIII. "To find the ratio in which the orbits and velocities of the particles are diminished at a given depth below the surface: Divide the given depth by the equivalent pendulum; the natural number answering to the quotient in a table of hyperbolic logarithms will be the reciprocal of the ratio required.

"The following approximate rule is very nearly correct:

"The orbits and velocities of the particles of water are diminished by *one-half*, for each additional depth below the surface equal to *one-ninth of a wave-length*. For example:—

Depths in fractions of a wave-length: 0, $\frac{1}{9}$, $\frac{2}{9}$, $\frac{3}{9}$, etc.
Proportionate velocities and diameters: 1, $\frac{1}{2}$, $\frac{1}{4}$, $\frac{1}{8}$, etc.

IX. "To find how high the centre of the orbit of a given particle is above the level of that particle in still water: Divide the square of the diameter of the orbit by eight times the equivalent pendulum of the waves; or divide the square of the velocity of the particle in feet per second by 64·4, for the height in feet.

X. "To find the mechanical energy in a layer of water agitated by wave motion: Multiply the weight of the layer by twice the height at which the centres of the orbits of its particles stand above the positions of these particles when the water is still.

"One-half of this energy consists in motion, and the other half in elevation.

XI. "To find the mechanical energy of a mass of water of a given horizontal area and unlimited depth, agitated by waves: Multiply the area by *one-sixteenth* part of the square of the height of the waves, and by the heaviness of the fluid (64 lbs. per cubic foot for sea water).

XII. "To find the mechanical energy of *one wave-length* of a layer of water of a given breadth and thickness: Multiply together the breadth and thickness of the layer, the square of the diameter of the orbits of the particles in it, the heaviness of the fluid and the constant, $1·5708 = \left(\frac{\pi}{2}\right)$."

Table VIII. contains a list of the *periods* and *lengths* of waves in deep water, arranged according to their velocities in knots. This table is the work of Professor Rankine.

**173. Rolling of a Ship among Waves.**—Having thus considered the character and properties of sea waves, we will now proceed to discuss the rolling motion of a ship when in what is termed a "sea-way," *i.e.*, when floating among the waves that are met with in the open sea in deep water.

**174. Passive Heaving.**—As we have already remarked, every particle of a body floating in water undergoing wave motion is under the influence of the same forces as would act upon the water it displaces, and thus, if the dimensions of the floating body are indefinitely small, it will revolve in the same orbit as the surface particles. Suppose a ship to be in the same condition as the surface particle, that is, suppose her to be without stability, so that her centre of gravity, metacentre, and centre of buoyancy coincide at one point; also, suppose the distortion in the configuration of the water as the wave passes to be neglected, then such a ship has no tendency to oscillate freely in still water, and when among waves, under the above limitation, every particle in the ship would move in the same orbit as the particles in the effective wave surface. Such a case as this is, necessarily, never met with, yet in every vessel there is a tendency for her centre of gravity, and, indeed, every particle in her, to move in such a way; and they really would do so were there not other forces tending to modify that motion. *Passive heaving* is the name given to this rotatory motion which the waves tend to impress upon a ship. When the horizontal component of this heaving motion takes place with different velocities, or in opposite directions, at the bow and stern, the vessel swerves from side to side, and is said to "yaw." The forces producing this motion are greatest when the vessel's course is inclined to the direction of the waves. She then "yaws" from the wind in mounting the crest, and towards the wind when descending into the trough.

175. **Passive Rolling.**—We will now consider the ship floating amid waves to have *very great stability but small inertia;* that is to say, her tendency to maintain her upright position when in still water is very great, and her equivalent pendulum very short. Such a ship will seek to keep her axis of equilibrium in the direction of a normal to the effective wave surface throughout the whole period of the passing wave. This tendency will be modified to some extent by the change in the position and shape of the originally vertical columns of water, which will cause the vessel to deviate somewhat at any instant from a truly normal position. The successive positions occupied by that axis causes the vessel to roll, the period of the oscillation being equal to that of the wave, while its amplitude is governed by the slope of the effective wave surface. This is termed *passive or forced rolling*.

If the vessel is floating on the surface, and therefore not influenced by the change in the configuration of the water as the wave passes, it will float like the raft shown at *A*, Plate XXXII., with its surface a tangent to that of the wave, and therefore its axis of equilibrium normal to the wave surface.

If, however, the vessel floats deeply in the wave, it is also under the influence of the forces which cause a change in the direction and form of the originally vertical columns of water. For instance, a thin, light board of little inertia and no stability, if floating upright on its edge in still water, will follow the direction of the originally vertical columns of water as a wave passes, as shown by *B*, Plate XXXII., and therefore roll against the waves. A ship may be considered as a case analagous to that of a raft and vertical board combined, and so, as already explained, the instantaneous position of a ship of great stability and small inertia, floating among waves, deviates somewhat from the true normal to the effective wave surface.

The tendency of a ship to roll with the waves, and with her axis of equilibrium normal to the effective wave surface, is due to gravity, centrifugal force, and pressure, and is termed *stiffness*.

The action on the bottom which tends to make her roll against the waves like the board *B*, is called *keel resistance*. Professor Rankine and Mr. Froude have shown "that there is an essential difference between the two sets of forces before mentioned, in consequence of which, though conflicting, they are not directly opposed, viz., That the stiffness is an active force which tends not only to prevent the ship from deviating from a position upright to the effective wave surface, but to restore her to that position after she has left it, with a force proportional to her deviation; while the keel resistance is merely a passive force, opposing the deviation of the ship from the position of the originally vertical columns of water with a force depending, not on that deviation, but on the velocity of the relative motion of the ship and the particles of water, and not tending to restore the ship to any definite position. Hence those two kinds of forces cannot directly counteract, but only modify, each other's effects."

176. **Rolling in a Sea-way.**—From the preceding it will be seen that the actual rolling motion of a ship is compounded

of the passive rolling, due to the wave period and slope, and of her free oscillations, the character of which is governed by her stability, keel resistance, inertia, and the varied resistances caused by eddies, etc., in the fluid, which can be determined only by experiment.

The problem of determining the properties of this complex motion is a very intricate one. All we know upon the subject at present is due to the experimental researches and mathematical applications of Mr. Froude, F.R.S. Many theories, more or less ingenious, have been propounded at different times by mathematicians and naval architects, but nothing certain can be obtained without making such careful experimental researches as those to which Mr. Froude has devoted so many years of his life. The late Professor Rankine successfully applied his great mathematical skill to the solution of many of the most intricate problems in this branch of physical science. But it rests with experimental philosophers such as Mr. Froude, and the careful observations of naval officers, to solve problems, concerning which the data we possess is still very meagre. The subject is gradually becoming clearer and our knowledge more certain, but at this stage of the inquiry, and in a book such as this, it is not desirable to look closely into the investigations which have hitherto been made. Although a great deal of light has been thrown upon the subject during the last fifteen years, yet even now the mathematics of the question are based upon suppositions which remain to be verified, and some of which are known to be only approximately correct.

An eminent authority, who signed himself J. C. in the *Annual of the Royal School of Naval Architecture for* 1872, referring to the question of stability in connection with a ship's rolling, after calling attention to the number of inaccuracies which exist in the present state of the theory on this subject, says: "At present I do not see a way to overcome these objections and difficulties, nor should I regard either method of investigation as affording trustworthy means of calculating the precise amount of stability which would be required for new designs. The only safe guide in this matter is, in my opinion, found in experience with successful ships, and in designing new vessels it appears desirable to provide that amount and range of stability which have been proved sufficient in ships that have been thoroughly tried."

Notwithstanding the uncertainty existing on the subject which prevents us from assigning exact quantitative values, yet the qualitative conditions are sufficiently well understood, and enough experiments have been verified, to enable certain rules to be laid down for the guidance of the naval architect in determining the stability, inertia, keel resistance, etc., which it is necessary a ship should possess in order to behave well in a sea-way.

We have already said that the actual rolling of an ordinary ship in a sea-way is composed of two sets of oscillations, viz., those due to the period of the waves, and those due to the form of the vessel and the arrangement of her weights.

Suppose, then, a vessel in still water, rolling without resistance at the rate of $n$ oscillations per minute, and a series of waves to pass her in a direction perpendicular to her length at the rate of $n$ waves per minute, the first wave meeting her at the commencement of an oscillation. It is evident that the period of the set of oscillation set up by the waves being the same as those of the ship in still water, each wave as it passes gives an impulse which adds to the amplitude of the oscillations, until at last the ship rolls completely over. At sea the oscillations would be first set up by the waves, and if the period of the ship's unresisted oscillation accorded with them, each wave would add to the rolling motion communicated by its predecessors. From this we see that it is highly undesirable that the wave period and that of the ship's free rolling should coincide; and, in order that the forced rolling among waves may not be frequent and considerable, it is desirable to lengthen the period of free rolling when in still water as much as possible.

The mathematics of the problem of a ship's rolling are of a too lengthy and difficult a character for insertion in a work of this kind. The whole subject is thoroughly investigated in the volumes of the *Transactions of the Institution of Naval Architects*, especially those of 1861, 1863, and 1864, to which the student who requires more complete information is referred. We will content ourselves here by giving a summary of the results arrived at.

I. The permanent rolling motion of a vessel having very great stability, and very little keel resistance, is governed by the motion of the effective wave surface like the raft $A$, in Plates XXXII. and XXXIII. Such a vessel will roll with the waves, at the rate of one oscillation for every wave period, being upright when on the crest and in the trough of the wave, while the inclination between these points will vary with the slope of the effective wave surface; her angle of heel at any point being the slope of the effective wave surface at that point. Thus the greatest angle of heel is equal to the greatest slope.

II. When the period of a ship's unresisted rolling in still water is to the period of the waves as $\sqrt{2}$ is to 1, the permanent rolling is wholly governed by the motion of the originally vertical columns of water, and the ship will roll against the wave similarly to the board $B$, in Plates XXXII. and XXXIII., making one oscillation per wave period. In this case the ship is upright when on the crest and trough of the wave, and her inclination between these positions varies with the slope of the surface of the wave; the inclination of the vessel to the vertical at any point being practically equal to the slope of the wave at that point.

III. When the period of a ship's unresisted rolling in still water bears to the period of the wave a lesser ratio than $\sqrt{2}:1$, she is upright before the crest and trough of the wave pass her, see $C_0$, $C_2$, and $C_4$, Plate XXXIII., and her greatest angle of heel is *greater* than the greatest slope of the effective wave surface. See $C_1$ and $C_3$ in the same Plate.

IV. When the period of a ship's unresisted rolling is equal to that of the waves, the greatest angle of permanent rolling occurs. The less the keel resistance the more the angle of roll exceeds the slope of the waves, and when the keel resistance is zero, the rolling becomes infinite; or, in other words, the ship turns right over.

V. When the period of a ship's unresisted rolling bears to the period of the waves a greater ratio than $\sqrt{2}:1$, she is upright after the crests and troughs of the waves pass her, as shown by $D_0$, $D_2$, and $D_4$, Plate XXXIII., and her greatest angle of heel is less than the greatest slope of the waves, as shown by $D_1$ and $D_3$.

**177. Stiffness and Steadiness.**—We have already defined *stiffness* as that quality of a vessel, due to great stability, which causes her to seek to accompany the motions of the effective wave surface, with her axis of equilibrium normal to that surface. A period of free rolling, much less than that of passive rolling, gives great *stiffness*, as seen in the preceding Article.

*Steadiness* is the tendency of a vessel to keep truly upright in a sea-way. Hence a ship that is very stable is not likely to be very steady, unless there are special features in the design, such as large bilge keels, or a certain form of the body or arrangement of the weights.

A period of free rolling exceeding $\sqrt{2}$ times that of passive rolling is favourable to steadiness, provided that period of free rolling is produced by winging out the weights and increasing the inertia of the ship, and not by reducing the stability to an insufficient amount.

The action of the water on a deep keel, bilge keels, a sharp floor, or fine extremities below water, tends to diminish the rolling produced by the period of the waves and that of the ship's free oscillations coinciding or being nearly equal. It must, however, be noticed that when the period of free rolling is very long the deep keel, bilge keel, etc., have a contrary effect.

The motion of the vessel through the water is conducive to steadiness if her course is near to the wind, and *vice versa*. A deep draught of water is also favourable in many respects to steadiness. It should also be remarked that a steady pressure of wind on the sails is very conducive to a steady motion.

As a result of what has gone before, we see that a ship should only have that amount of stability which is essential for her safety, as an excess of stability tends to make the vessel roll rapidly, and to synchronise with the periods of the waves she is likely to meet. If, however, great stability must necessarily be given to a ship her stiffness should be reduced, and therefore her steadiness promoted, by winging out her weights, so as to lengthen the period of her free oscillations. Attention should also be given to the form of the vessel's body in the neighbourhood of the water line, so that the axis of level motion may not be far above the centre of gravity.

178. **Periods of Oscillations of Certain Ships.**—The subjoined Table gives the periods of the oscillations of certain typical ships in the English, French, and American Navies. The particulars would be more complete if we knew the lengths of the radii of gyration; but as the moment of stability up to about 10 or 15 degrees can be expressed with tolerable accuracy for most ships by the form $GM \sin \theta$, we include in the list the values of $GM$ for these vessels. The connection between those values and the periods of rolling will be noticed; although in the absence of particulars concerning the moments of inertia of the ships the relations are not in every case very clear.

| Class of Vessel. | Value of GM. | Period of Double Roll. |
|---|---|---|
| | ft. | seconds. |
| French two-decked iron-clad ship *Magenta*, | 3·25 | 14·6 |
| French armoured frigates, of *Flandre* class, | 4·25 | 12·0 |
| English ironclad, *Prince Consort*, | 6·00 | 10·3 |
| ,, modern ironclad, of *Sultan* type, | 2·75 | 17·7 |
| *Devastation*, | 4·00 | 13·5 |
| American *Miantonomoh*, | 14·00 | 5·4 |
| French corvette, | 3·25 | 11·5 |
| English wood frigate, | 3·75 | 10·5 |
| ,, sloop, | 3·50 | 7·5 |

# PART III.

## CALCULATIONS RELATING TO THE STRENGTH OF SHIPS.

---

### CHAPTER VII.

#### LOCAL STRENGTH.

Definitions—Properties of Bodies under Stress—Intensity of Stress—Classes of Stress—Local Stresses—Diameters and Spacing of Rivets—Butt Straps—Edge Connections—Strengths of Butt Straps—Strength of a Shift of Plates—Strength of Pillars—Beams—Shearing Stress—Bending Moment—Bending Moments and Shearing Stresses for various kinds of Loading and modes of Support—Resistance to Bending—Specimen Calculations—The Deflections of Beams—Examples—Strength of Bent Pillars—Twisting Moments.

**179. General Considerations.**—In no department of Naval Architecture has such great advances been made during late years as in that relating to the combination of materials, so as to obtain the greatest strength with the least weight. This has been chiefly due to the introduction of iron as a material for ship construction, and the strides which have been made in the manufacture of that metal in forms suited for ship construction. Improvements have also been made in the construction of wood ships, whereby it has been possible to build them of great length, and render them sufficiently rigid to resist the great vibration and the straining effects produced by powerful engines. These improvements, however, have consisted more in the form of iron strengthenings efficiently disposed, than in a superior mode of combining the wooden components of the hull. In fact, the characteristic feature of ship construction during the past twenty years has been the superseding of wood in favour of iron. True it is that owing to the rapid fouling of the bottoms of iron ships, which up to the present time it has been found impossible to prevent for any considerable period, wood ships are still preferred for certain trades. Nevertheless, we believe it is only where iron and coal are relatively dear that ships constructed wholly of wood are built in any considerable number. In other places, ships which are required to make long voyages are sometimes built on the composite system, wherein all the advantages of the metal-sheathed wooden bottoms are obtained, combined with the superior lightness and strength which are found in framing of iron. In the Royal Navy, large vessels which are required to keep the sea for a considerable time, without going into dock to have their bottoms cleaned, are built of iron, in order to obtain the strength which that material affords when well combined, while the iron bottoms are sheathed with wood and then with copper, zinc, or Muntz's metal, in order to obtain the same freedom from fouling which is found in wooden ships. From this it will be seen that in considering the strength of ships, our attention should be chiefly directed to the combinations of iron. This we shall keep in view throughout the following remarks.

**180. Definitions.**—In explaining the meanings of certain terms, which we shall have occasion to employ, we shall closely follow the definitions used by the late Professor Rankine, than whom no one has contributed more to the science of the strength of materials as applied to shipbuilding.

*Elasticity* is that property of a body by which it retains, and seeks to retain, a certain determinate volume and figure at a given pressure and temperature.

*Stress* means the intensity of the force which tends to alter the form of a solid body; it is also the equal and opposite resistance offered by the body to the change of form.

*Strain* is the measure of the alteration of form which a solid body undergoes when under the influence of a given stress.

*Properties of bodies under stress.*—The shape of a body when not under the influence of a stress is its *unstrained* or *free shape.* A body becomes strained under the influence of a stress, and if upon the removal of the stress it returns to its unstrained form, it is said to be *perfectly elastic;* if it remains of the strained form, or only partially recovers its original form, it is said to be *imperfectly elastic, soft, ductile,* or *plastic.* No bodies are perfectly elastic, but for many the imperfection of elasticity below certain limits of stress is so small as to be of no importance in practice.

*Set* is the permanent strain or alteration of shape which remains in an imperfectly elastic body after a stress has been removed.

*Stiffness* is measured by the intensity of the stress required to produce a certain fixed quantity of strain.

*Pliability* is the inverse of *stiffness*, and is measured by the quantity of strain produced by a certain fixed stress.

*Strength* is the utmost amount of stress which a solid body can bear without breaking.

*Elastic strength* is the utmost amount of stress which a body can bear without set.

*Proof strength* is the utmost stress which a body can bear without suffering any diminution of its stiffness and strength. A stress exceeding the proof strength of the material, although it may not produce instant fracture, produces fracture eventually by long continued application and frequent repetition.

*Working strength* is the utmost stress to which it is considered safe to subject a body during its ordinary use as part of a structure.

*Ultimate strength* is the stress required to produce fracture in some specified way.

*Factors of safety* are of three kinds:—

I. The ratio in which the breaking load exceeds the proof load.

II. The ratio in which the breaking load exceeds the working load.

III. The ratio in which the proof load exceeds the working load.

Unless otherwise stated—when the term "factor of safety" is used—it is to be understood in the second of these senses.

The following Table, due to the late Professor Rankine, gives examples of those factors which occur in practice.

# DEFINITIONS.

## EXAMPLES OF FACTORS OF SAFETY.

| MATERIAL. | Breaking Load ÷ Proof Load. | Breaking Load ÷ Working Load. | Proof Load ÷ Working Load. | REMARKS. |
|---|---|---|---|---|
| Strongest steel, ....... | 1½ | ... | ... | ... |
| Ordinary steel and wrought iron, ....... | 2 | 3 | 1½ | Steady loads |
| Do. do...... | 2 | 4 to 6 | 2 to 3 | Moving ,, |
| Wrought iron riveted structures, .......... | 3 | 6 | 2 | |
| Wrought iron boilers, | 2 | 8 | 4 | ... |
| Cast iron, ............... | 2 to 3 | 3 to 4 | about 1½ | Steady ,, |
| Do. .............. | 3 | 6 to 8 | 2 to 2¾ | Moving ,, |
| Timber, average, ..... | 3 | about 10 | 3½ | ... |

*Ultimate strain* is the utmost strain or alteration of shape which a body can bear without breaking.

*Proof strain* is the utmost strain which a body can bear without injury.

*Spring* or *Resilience* is the quantity of work or mechanical energy which is required to produce the proof strain, and is one-half of the product of the proof stress of the body by its proof strain.

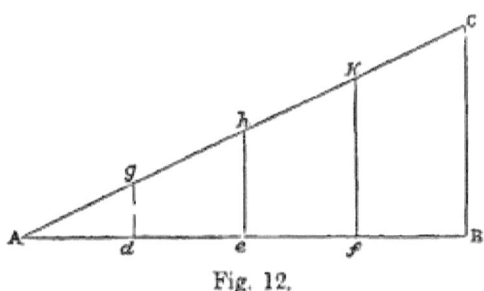

Fig. 12.

In explanation of the above, it may be remarked that, as the body suffers no injury, the strain produced by any stress, up to and including the proof stress, is about proportional to that stress. In fig. 12, AB is the proof stress, and the ordinate BC the proof strain. A$d$, A$e$, A$f$, are other stresses to which $dg$, $eh$, and $fk$ are corresponding strains, so that A$ghk$C is a straight line.* Now, the whole work done by the stresses in producing the strains between A and BC is evidently the area of the triangle ABC or $\dfrac{AB \times BC}{2}$, which is, therefore, the amount of work which must be applied to produce the strain BC.

**181. Measure of Direct Strain.**—When a body is under the influence of an extensive or compressive stress, such as a pull or thrust, so as to produce a certain strain, then the ratio of the amount of strain to the original length of the body strained is termed the *measure of direct strain*. In testing the proof strength of iron or steel it is usual to make two marks on the test sample six inches apart, then when the piece is broken the distance between the marks is again measured, and the amount of strain is thus determined. The ratio of the strain to six inches is the measure of the direct breaking strain. Should the body be tested only to the proof strain, then the ratio is the measure of the direct proof strain. If the body is under a compressive stress, the ratio of the contraction to the original length would also be the measure of direct strain.

Supposing a length of six inches to stretch to six-and-a-quarter inches, then the extension would be $\frac{1}{24} = \cdot 0416$. This is true whether the breaking strain be reached or not. In order to form a better idea of the qualities of the material subjected to the stress, the amount of direct strain produced by each pound on the square inch of direct stress is calculated, this being termed the *direct extensibility* or *compressibility* of the body, as the case may be. For instance, suppose a direct stress of 44,800 pounds on the square inch stretches a bar six inches long until it measures six-and-a-quarter inches, then

$$\tfrac{1}{24} \times \tfrac{1}{44800} = \tfrac{1}{1075200} = \cdot 00000093,$$

which is the *extensibility* of the material under experiment. The term *pliability* is used to comprehend both *extensibility* and *compressibility*.

In most substances the extensibility and compressibility are nearly uniform and equal to each other for stresses not exceeding the proof stress. When the proof stress is exceeded the

* This is nearly true for most materials.

pliability increases very rapidly, and the fact of its doing so in any test is a proof that the stress is great enough to weaken the material.

**Modulus of Elasticity.**—If the stress does not exceed the proof stress, then the reciprocal of the direct pliability is termed the *modulus of elasticity*. For instance, suppose a pull of 22,400 pounds per square inch causes a bar of iron to lengthen by $\frac{1}{1300}$ of its original length, then $22,400 \times 1300 = 31,120,000$ pounds per square inch is the modulus of elasticity of the iron in question. In this example the proof stress is not reached, and thus the modulus is far greater than would be given by the reciprocal of the direct pliability in the preceding case where the material is supposed to have broken under the stress.

Table IX. gives values of the modulus of elasticity of different substances as found by experiment, and recorded in Professor Rankine's "*Useful Rules and Tables.*"

**Intensity of Stress** means the amount of stress in units of force, divided by the number of units of area in the surface, over which it acts. For instance, if a bar whose section is 1 square foot be subjected to a direct pull of $64\frac{1}{4}$ tons, then, calling 1 square inch the unit of area, and 1 lb. the unit of force, the intensity of the stress is $\frac{143920}{144} = 1000$.

**Classes of Stress.**—There are three principal kinds of simple stresses, viz.:—

    I. *Thrust* or *Compression*.
    II. *Pull* or *Tension*.
    III. *Shear* or *Tangential Stress*.

The *first* is such as acts upon a vertical pillar supporting a load, the *second* such as acts upon a rod hanging vertically and supporting a load at its extremity, and the *third* is such as acts upon a rivet connecting two lap-jointed plates when the plates are being pulled asunder or pushed over each other by forces acting along their common surfaces.

Besides the above there are certain compound stresses, the principal of which are—

    I. *Twisting*.
    II. *Tranverse* or *Bending*.

The former of these is such as an engine shaft is subjected to, and the latter is represented by a loaded beam.

There are many combinations of these which occur, but their effects may be generally investigated by resolving them into their elementary stresses.

**182. Local and Structural Strengths.**—In considering the principles regulating the strength of materials as applied to shipbuilding, we shall divide the stresses to which a vessel may be subjected into two classes, viz.: first, *Local Stresses;* and second, *Structural Stresses.*

The first of these divisions will include the strength of riveted joints and other connections which unite the innumerable pieces of which a ship's hull is composed, also the power to resist local stresses possessed by different parts of the structure, such as pillars, beams, etc.

The second division will relate to the qualities necessary to insure the requisite strength in the whole structure, considered as one piece, so that it may be able to resist the stresses to which the ship is liable.

**183. Local Stresses.**—The hull of an iron ship is composed of a great number of plates and angle-irons which are joined together with rivets. The plates are either lapped over each other in order to connect them, or else they are united by means of other pieces of plate in the form of *straps* and *strips.* The name of *straps* is given to the pieces of plate which join the butts of plates while those which join the edges are called *strips.* Angle-irons (when not welded together) are joined by short angle-iron straps, and plates are riveted to angle-irons by causing one of the flanges of the latter to lie against the face of the plate. But in all these modes of disposing the parts joined together rivets are the joining mediums. For the characteristics of the several kinds of rivets employed, see the work on *Practical Naval Architecture* in this Series.

In estimating the strength of a riveted joint, we assume the force to be in the form of a pull or thrust acting in the plane of the surfaces in contact and square to the joint. Under these circumstances the tendency is to shear the rivets or else break one of the plates joined, or the joining strap if any is used. In order that the joint may be efficient it is a necessary condition that the resistance of the rivets to shearing, and that of the plates to breaking, should be equal; for, as the strength of the whole is that of its weakest part, any excess of strength at one point over another is of no value. A riveted joint can never be so strong as a continuous plate; but as the plates composing a ship are mostly weakened by holes, elsewhere than at their butts, in order to connect them to the other parts of the structure, we have to get a joint whose strength approximates closely to that of the plates at their weakest section; and to insure that the riveting is of such a character, and so arranged at that joint, that there is no more tendency of the rivets to shear than of the iron between the rivet holes to break, and *vice versa*.

In order to make such a calculation, and thereby arrange the riveting, it is necessary that we should know the resistance per unit of area which iron offers to breaking by extension or compression, and which a rivet offers to shearing. These resistances vary with the quality of the materials. The Admiralty standard of tensile strength for $BB$ iron is 22 tons per square inch in the direction of the grain, and 18 tons per square inch across the grain. Iron of $B$ quality is required to stand tests of 20 and 17 tons with and across the grain respectively. Wrought iron offers about $\frac{4}{5}$ the resistance to compression that it does to extension. The resistance of rivets to shearing is about the same as the tensile strength of iron of the same quality. For instance, the shearing strength of a $\frac{3}{4}$-inch rivet of Lowmoor or Bowling iron is about 10 tons, which is equal to $22\frac{1}{2}$ tons to the square inch. Although the best Admiralty iron is required to stand a tensile strain of 22 tons to the square inch before breaking, it must nevertheless be remembered that the strength of this iron in the vicinity of the rivet holes is reduced by the punching process to about 18 tons per square inch, which is the value we shall employ when referring to punched work.

**184. Diameters of Rivets.**—The first thing to be considered when joining iron plates together is the diameter of the rivet to be used. This is fixed by two considerations: First, the minimum size of the hole that can be punched in a plate of the given thickness;* and second, the rivet must be of such a diameter that it shall be on the point of shearing just before

---

* This only applies to punched holes; when drilled, as in the best boiler work, the size of the rivet is not influenced by this consideration.

the iron between the rivet and the butt of the plate is being forced out.

The first of these conditions is the lesser in point of importance, seeing that a hole can be punched readily, provided its diameter is at least equal to the thickness of the plate.

With regard to the second condition, it must be remembered that joints have usually to be watertight, to insure which, the rivet must not be far away from the butt or edge of the plate, or else the joint cannot be caulked; the usual practice is to place the rivet rather more than its own diameter from the edge.

Let $d$ = diameter of the rivet,
$t$ = thickness of the plate

to find the maximum ratio between $d$ and $t$. Since the shearing strength of a $\frac{3}{4}$ in. rivet = 10 tons. Therefore the shearing strength of a rivet $d$ inches in diameter

$$= \frac{160}{9} d^2 \text{ tons.}$$

Let the strength of the iron in the wake of the holes be 18 tons per square inch.

Stress required to force out the bearing surface—

$$= 18 \times 2dt = 36dt \text{ tons.}$$

Supposing the rivet on the point of shearing when the iron is on the point of bursting out in front of the rivet; then

$$\frac{160}{9} d^2 = 36dt$$
$$160d = 324t$$
or $\quad d : t :: 2 : 1$.

From which we see that the diameter of the rivet should never be more than twice the thickness of the plate. This result is followed out in practice; and the experience of our best shipbuilders has led them to adopt a tolerably uniform ratio of $d$ to $t$ for each thickness of plate. The following Table shows the diameters of the rivets for the several thicknesses of plate, as required by Lloyd's and the Liverpool Rules, also the practice of H.M. Dockyards. The sizes are given in sixteenths of an inch:—

## TABLE OF DIAMETERS OF RIVETS FOR DIFFERENT THICKNESSES OF PLATES.

| Thicknesses of Plates. | Diameters of Rivets. | | |
|---|---|---|---|
| | Lloyd's Rules. | Liverpool Rules. | H.M. Dockyards. |
| 5  | 10 | 8  | 8  |
| 6  | 10 | 10 | 10 |
| 7  | 10 | 10 | 12 |
| 8  | 12 | 12 | 12 |
| 9  | 12 | 12 | 14 |
| 10 | 12 | 13 | 14 |
| 11 | 14 | 14 | 14 |
| 12 | 14 | 14 | 16 |
| 13 | 14 | 15 | 16 |
| 14 | 16 | 16 | 18 |
| 15 | 16 | 17 | 18 |
| 16 | 16 | 18 | 18 |

As will be seen by reference to this Table, it is found in practice desirable to use a larger rivet in proportion to the thickness of the plate when the latter is small than when it is large. We have already shown that the rivet should never have a greater diameter than is equal to twice the thickness of the plate, and we see by the Table that Lloyd's Rules require $\frac{5}{8}$ in. rivets for $\frac{5}{16}$ in. plates. Other practices do not differ materially from this. But when the plate is 1 in. thick the diameter of the rivet is 1 in., by Lloyd's Rules, and $1\frac{1}{8}$ in. by the Liverpool and Admiralty Rules. In investigating the strengths of riveted joints, we shall use the diameters required by Lloyd's Rules, as they are those most commonly adopted, and do not deviate materially from other practices.

**185. Spacing of Rivets.**—In spacing rivets, we are often limited by the necessary conditions for the work being watertight. In order to secure this quality it is requisite that the rivets shall be sufficiently close together, and near the edge of the plating to enable the joint to be caulked, and then remain rigid when subjected to water pressure, or any other stress to which it is liable. It is evident that if the plates are thin the rivets should be closer together, in order to make the joint watertight, than when the plates are thick; but on no account should the rivets be so close to the edge as to cause the resistance offered by the iron between the rivet hole and the edge of the plate to be inferior to the shearing strength of the rivet; nor should the rivet holes be punched so close together as to seriously cripple the iron between the rivet holes. As we have already said, the ordinary practice is to punch the holes rather more than the diameter of the rivet from the edge of the plate. With regard, however, to the spacing of the rivets (or the "pitch," as it is sometimes termed), in order to secure watertightness, it is found by experiment that the holes should not be more than $3\frac{1}{2}$ diameters of the rivet from centre to centre in very thin plates, and about $4\frac{1}{2}$ to 5 diameters in plates of the ordinary thickness employed in the bottoms and sides of ships. The diameter of the rivet is fixed by the thickness of the plate, in accordance with the Table given in Art. 184.

Lloyd's Rules require a spacing of $4\frac{1}{2}$ diameters; the Liverpool Register requires 4 diameters; while the Admiralty practice is to space the rivets $4\frac{1}{2}$ to 5 diameters apart in edges and butts of bottom and bulkhead plating, and 5 to 6 diameters apart in watertight work elsewhere.

Calculations based solely upon the necessary equality between the tensile strength of the iron left between the punched holes and the shearing strength of the rivet, give results which differ materially from the above practices when the joints and butts are single riveted, and show a somewhat smaller pitch for double riveted work than is commonly practiced in ship work. Such calculations are based upon the assumption, to a considerable extent borne out by experiment, that the tensile strength of $BB$ iron, after being punched for watertight work, is 18 tons to the square inch instead of 22 tons, as in the unwounded material; also that the shearing strength of a rivet is 22 tons per square inch of its sectional area.

We will now make such an investigation for a *single riveted joint* connecting two plates.

Let $t$ = the thickness of either of the plates in inches.
,, $d$ = the diameter of the rivet in inches.
,, $p$ = the pitch of the rivets in inches.
Then $p - d$ = distance between consecutive rivet holes,
and $(p - d)t$ = sectional area of the iron between these holes.

Also $\dfrac{\pi d^2}{4}$ = sectional area of a rivet.

## SPACING OF RIVETS.

Assume 22 tons per square inch to be the shearing strength of a rivet; and 18 tons per square inch to be the tensile strength of the iron in the line of rivet holes after punching. Then, in order that the rivet shall be on the point of shearing, just as either of the plates is about to break between the rivet holes, we have—

$$\frac{22\pi d^2}{4} = 18t(p-d)$$

$$\text{or} \quad p = d + \frac{11\pi d^2}{36t}$$

$$= d + \cdot 96\frac{d^2}{t}.$$

To apply this result to a specified case, suppose the plates connected to be each $\frac{1}{2}$ in. thick, and the rivets therefore $\frac{3}{4}$ in. in diameter (see Table in Art 184). Then—

$$p = \tfrac{3}{4} + 1\cdot 08 = 1\cdot 83 \text{ in.}$$
$$\text{or} \quad 1\cdot 83 \times \tfrac{4}{3} = 2\cdot 44 \text{ diameters,}$$

instead of 4 to 5 diameters, as is the common practice in ship work.

Next suppose the joint to be *double riveted*. Then the strength of either of the plates in the line of rivet holes remains the same, while the resistance to shearing is doubled.

$$\text{Hence} \quad 11\pi d^2 = 18t(p-d)$$

$$\text{or} \quad p = d + \frac{11\pi d^2}{18t}$$

$$= d + 1\cdot 92\frac{d^2}{t}$$

Applying this, again, to the case of $\frac{1}{2}$ in. plates and $\frac{3}{4}$ in. rivets, we have—

$$v = \cdot 75 + 2\cdot 16 = 2\cdot 91 \text{ in.}$$
$$\text{or} \quad 2\cdot 91 \times \tfrac{4}{3} = 3\cdot 88 \text{ diameters.}$$

which is rather less than the spacing adopted in practice.

If the joint were *treble riveted*, we should have

$$p = \cdot 75 + 3\cdot 24 = 3\cdot 99 \text{ in.}$$
$$\text{or} \quad 3\cdot 99 \times \tfrac{4}{3} = 5\cdot 32 \text{ diameters.}$$

which is a spacing rather in excess of what is desirable for watertight work.

These results would seem to indicate that the ordinary pitch is too open for single riveted work, but on the other hand it must be remembered that single riveting is never adopted for butt straps in cases where great strength is required. The result for double riveted work is rather below the ordinary practice, in which it would appear that the rivets are not so strong as the iron between the holes. It is, however, rather significant that in all the cases on record of an iron ship breaking, the fracture—when it takes place at the joints and butts—is almost invariably produced by the iron breaking between the rivet holes; and cases in which the rivets have been sheared are very rare. If the holes in the plates were exactly opposite to each other in all cases, and the riveting well performed, it is very probable that 22 tons per square inch is a fair allowance for the resistance to shearing; but with the drift punch, used so often as it unfortunately is, it is impossible to insure that the intended diameter of the rivet will not be exceeded. Besides this, it seems very likely, considering the frictional resistance to separation which is offered by the surfaces of the plates in contact when pressed together by the contraction of the rivet in cooling, that the allowance of 22 tons per square inch of rivet section does not represent the total resistance to fracture by shearing.

186. **Number of Rows of Rivets.**—As we have already indicated, the object of the shipbuilder in arranging the rivets of the butts of bottom plating, stringers, deck plating, etc., is not to unite the plates so as to make the connection as nearly as possible equal in strength to the plates themselves, but to make the strength at the joint at least equal to that at the weakest section of the plate elsewhere, as, for instance, where it is riveted to the frames, beams, etc. Any stronger connection is unnecessary. Also, in joining the edges of adjacent plates, it must be remembered that the frames and beams assist the edge fastenings in uniting the plates of bottom and deck respectively. Consequently, the edges of plating have never more than a double row of rivets, while sometimes three and even four rows are put in the butt straps. The usual practice is to put double riveting in both edges and butts, but in some cases the edges are single, while the butts are double, riveted. Mr. J. Scott Russell has built some ships with single riveted edges and butts, but these vessels were constructed on the longitudinal principle, wherein both

the edge and butt riveting are succoured—the former by the transverse, and the latter by the longitudinal, framing. It will thus be seen that in arranging the local fastenings at any part of a ship, attention must be given to the mode of construction, in order that the strength of the connection may not be much, if at all, in excess of the strength of the parts connected, such additional strength being, of course, unnecessary.

187. **Butt Straps.**—Butt straps are of two kinds—*single* and *double*. Single butt straps are usually of the same thickness as the plates they connect, but in some cases they have been made a little thicker. Double butt straps are fitted one on each side of the plates joined, and the thickness of each strap is made about $\frac{1}{16}$ to $\frac{1}{8}$ inch more than the half thickness of the plates, in order that one or both of the straps may not break by the iron being forced away in front of the rivets. As we have said, the riveting in butt straps is of different kinds, as *single, double, treble,* etc. The riveting is also arranged in two different styles, viz., *chain* and *zig-zag;* in each of these styles some of the rivets are at times omitted in order to obtain more uniform strength. The question of watertightness, or otherwise, considerably modifies the spacing and the omission, or the contrary, of any of the rivets.

Plate XXXIV. shows specimens of the different kinds of riveting employed in butt straps. *A, B,* and *C* are single, double, and treble chain riveted straps respectively. *D* and *E* are respectively double and treble zig-zag riveted straps. *F, G,* and *K* are specimens of treble chain riveted straps with rivets omitted where they are not necessary for caulking, while *H* is a treble zig-zag riveted strap with rivets omitted for the same reason. *L* and *M* are sections of double riveted single and double straps respectively.

Single butt straps are usually employed to connect plates already weakened by holes, or in cases where very great longitudinal strength is not required, while double butt straps are used in order to obtain as nearly as possible the same strength as in the unpierced plate. There is often some inconsistency in their use in ships: as, for instance, a watertight longitudinal is weakened by holes in the wake of the watertight frame as much as the other longitudinals; yet while single butt straps, double riveted, serve for the latter, double butt straps, sometimes treble riveted, are used in the former. There is more reason for the use of double butt straps in a vertical keel, as in that case the loss of strength due to the close pitch of the riveting which connects it to the watertight frames is restored by the double angle-irons at the bottom of the keel and by an additional flat keel plate. It is perhaps hardly necessary to say that the advantage in the use of a double butt strap is that every rivet must be sheared twice that would only be sheared once in breaking the joint having a single strap.

The relative merits of *chain* and *zig-zag* riveting (see Plate XXXIV.) appears to be more a question of experiment than calculation, depending as it does upon the relative binding and frictional resistances between the surfaces of the plates joined; also, the relative watertightness of the joints and the relative strengths of the iron in the neighbourhood of the punched holes. Apart from these considerations, the whole question resolves itself into one of putting enough rivets to get shearing resistance equal to the tensile strength of the iron between the holes, and this is altogether independent of the pattern which the rivets assume when worked.

**188. Edge Connections.**—These are of two kinds—lap and jump joints. In Plate XXXV., $A$, $B$, and $C$ are specimens of lap joints, while $D$, $E$, and $F$ show the jump joint edge connections, and $G$ and $H$ show sections of the two. As will be seen, the weight of the material used in joining the plates is twice as much for the same kind of riveting in the jump as compared with the lap joints, while the resistance offered to a pull is the same in each case. The jump joints, when the edges are closely fitted, offer far greater resistance to compressive stresses; for while the edges are in contact, there is no tendency whatever to shear the rivets. As, however, the pulling stresses on side plating are the most frequent, and as the power to resist these constitutes the actual strength of the connection, the jump joint connections are not used for strengthening purposes so much as to get a flush surface. Jump jointed work is usually found in deck plating, inner bottoms, and topside plating of war ships. $A$, in Plate XXXV., shows a single riveted lap, $B$ a double chain riveted lap, and $C$ a double zig-zag riveted lap; while $D$, $E$, and $F$

are respectively single, double chain, and double zig-zag riveted jump joints.

**189. Strength of Butt Straps.**—This subject has already been briefly considered in Art. 185; we now propose to discuss the question somewhat more in detail. As will be seen by what has already been said, the strength of any riveted joint cannot exceed that due to the iron left between the row of rivet holes nearest the butt or edge of either of the plates connected, unless some of the rivets are omitted in that row and not in the others, which is a case we do not propose to consider at present. Assume 18 tons per square inch to be the tensile strength of the iron between the rivet holes, and consider the portion of the butt connection which extends from midway between two consecutive rivets to midway between the next two (*i.e.*, from $aa$ to $bb$, figs. 1, 2, and 4, Plate XXXVI.).

Using the same nomenclature as in Art. 185, we have for the strength of the iron in either of the plates through the line of rivet holes nearest the butt

$$= 18 t (p - d).$$

Hence if $p$ and $d$ have the same values in all the butt connections, the strengths of the latter are equal so far as the plates are concerned. But $d$ has a constant value for each value of $t$ in ship work, hence the only variation in the strength of the plates which can occur must be due to the pitch of the rivets. If the ratio of $p$ to $p - d$ is as 4 to 3, that is, if $\frac{p-d}{p} = \frac{3}{4}$, then the strength of the plate through the line of holes is three-fourths that of the plate elsewhere, supposing the iron not to be impaired by punching. Making allowance for the tensile strength of the iron being reduced from 22 tons to 18 tons per square inch, then the fraction which the strength of the pierced is of the unpierced plate is $\frac{3}{4} \times \frac{18}{22} = \frac{27}{44} = \cdot 61$. This is the maximum "*efficiency*" which any butt connection can have in which the rivets are spaced four diameters from centre to centre, and the strength of the plate is reduced from 22 to 18 tons per square inch by punching.

But this "*efficiency*" can only exist when the shearing strength of the rivet or rivets is at least equal to the tensile strength of the iron between the holes. If the one rivet is equal to the strength of the plate between consecutive holes, double riveting is unnecessary when the pitch is four diameters; and, if adopted, the pitch must be increased in order to obtain the requisite equality. To a greater degree the same remark applies to treble riveting.

The area of the rivet section is $\frac{\pi d^2}{2}$, and its shearing strength has been assumed to be 22 tons per square inch. Hence, $\frac{11\pi d^2}{2}$ is the strength of the rivet in the single riveted butt.

$$\therefore \frac{11\pi d^2}{2} = 18t(p-d)$$

where $p = 4d$ and $t$ is constant

hence $11\pi d^2 = 108td$

$$d = \frac{108t}{11\pi} = 3\cdot12 t.$$

Which shows that in order for a single riveted butt strap, with rivets spaced four diameters apart, to have an efficiency of ·61, the diameter of the rivet must be 3·12 times the thickness of the plate. The impracticability of this condition has been already shown. We have proved that under no circumstances should the diameter of the rivet be more than twice the thickness of the plate; and we have also shown that it is a necessary condition that the rivet should not be less than its diameter from the edge of the plate. Suppose the thickness of the plate to be ½ inch, it would require a rivet rather more than 1½ inches in diameter, and placed at rather more than 1½ inch from the edge of the plate, in order that the efficiency of the joint may be ·61. The impossibility of caulking the joint and other practical difficulties quite preclude such a large rivet from being used.

The universal size of rivet used for ½ inch plates is ¾ inch, and a pitch of four diameters would cause these rivets to be spaced three inches from centre to centre.

Substituting these figures in the expression for the strength of the rivet, we have

$$\frac{11\pi d^2}{2} = \frac{11}{2} \times \pi \times \frac{9}{16} = \frac{99}{32}\pi = 9\cdot72 \text{ tons,}$$

and for the strength of the iron between the rivet holes we have

$$18 \times \tfrac{1}{2} \times (3 - \tfrac{3}{4}) = 20\cdot 25 \text{ tons,}$$

which shows that the rivet is not half so strong as the plates joined, and that the efficiency of the joint is really

$$\frac{9\cdot 72}{20\cdot 25} \times \cdot 61 = \cdot 3 \text{ nearly.}$$

Had there been two rows of rivets, then the strength of the rivets would have been $2 \times 9\cdot 72 = 19\cdot 44$ tons, and the efficiency of the joint would then have been

$$\frac{19\cdot 44}{20\cdot 25} \times \cdot 61 = \cdot 59 \text{ nearly.}$$

The efficiency of a single riveted butt connection with a four diameter spacing cannot thus exceed ·3, nor that of a double riveted butt exceed ·59, if the plates are $\tfrac{1}{2}$ inch thick and the rivets $\tfrac{3}{4}$ inch in diameter.* Had we started with $\tfrac{1}{4}$ inch plates and $\tfrac{1}{2}$ inch rivets, we should have obtained an efficiency of ·39 for single riveting, and ·61 for double riveting; the rivets in the case of double riveting being stronger than the plate. But had we started with a 1 inch plate and a 1 inch rivet, the efficiency when single riveted would have been scarcely ·2, and when double riveted only ·39. Indeed, it would require three rows of rivets before the strength of the riveting would at all approach that of the iron between the holes.

These investigations point to the following conclusions in regard to single butt connections, when rivets are used of the diameters given in the Table on p. 247 :—

1. That a closer pitch should be adopted in single than in double riveted butts; and in double than in treble riveted butts.

2. That with a 4 diameter pitch the efficiency of a single riveted butt joint is very small, especially when the plates are thick.

3. That with a 4 diameter pitch the efficiency of a double riveted butt joint is about at the maximum for that pitch when the plates are not more than $\tfrac{1}{2}$ inch thick, and the value of the strap may be improved by increasing the spacing to

* This is upon the supposition that punching the plate reduces its tensile strength from 22 tons to 13 tons per square inch.

4½ diameters in the case of very thin plates, if that pitch will permit of satisfactory caulking. But the efficiency is very low when thick plates are used; and at least three complete rows of rivets are necessary in order to obtain the efficiency due to the pitch.

4. That other things being the same it is desirable to put larger rivets in plates of more than ¾ inch in thickness than are now commonly used.

It will be observed by referring to figs. 1, 2, and 4 of Plate XXXVI., that if the rivets are the stronger, the fracture will take place as follows:—In fig. 1, by either the plates or the strap breaking through either of the lines of holes $xx$ or $yy$; in figs. 2 and 4 by one of the plates breaking through the line of holes $x_1 x_1$ or $y_1 y_1$, or the strap breaking through either $xx$ or $yy$. If, however, the rivets are the weaker, the fracture will occur by all the rivets shearing on one side of the butt. It is evident that the fracture will never take place by the plate or strap breaking along either of the middle rows of rivets on the two sides of the butt (see fig. 4), as in addition to fracturing the plate or strap (which are as strong there as through the other lines of rivet holes), a row of rivets must also be sheared to break the connection.

The efficiency of the single strap connection might be considerably increased by using four rows of rivets—or quadruple riveting—and omitting alternate rivets in the rows nearest the butt and the edges of the strap (see fig. 3, Plate XXXVI.). It is hardly necessary to say that the efficiency of the strap, with a pitch of four diameters, would not be at all increased by using four entire rows, as the strength of the plates in the lines of rivet holes would still remain the same.

Considering a breadth equal to two rivet spacings (see fig. 3), and reckoning the tensile strength of the iron between the widely spaced rivet holes at 20 tons per square inch, we have for the strength of the plate

$$20t(2p - d),$$

and for the strength of the rivets

$$33\pi d^2.$$

If $t = \frac{1}{2}$, $d = \frac{7}{8}$, and $p = 3$,
then the strength of the plate $= 10 \times 5\frac{1}{4} = 52.5$ tons,
and of the rivets $= 58.3$ tons.

The efficiency of the joint is nearly ·8; but this butt strap cannot be caulked.

In cases where it is desired to obtain a higher efficiency than is possible with a single strap having a four diameter pitch, double butt straps are often employed; the advantage of using which is found in the fact that the rivets must be sheared twice instead of once, as in the single strap; the strength of the plate between the holes remaining the same as before, unless alternate rivets are omitted. By this double shear the efficiency of the strap becomes that due to the pitch, or $\frac{p}{p-d}$; no reduction occurring by reason of the relative weakness of the rivets, as is the case with single and, generally, with double riveted single straps. In order to obtain an equality of strength between the plates and straps through the lines of rivet holes, the straps should each be one-half the thickness of the plates. But in practice it is usual to make the straps rather more than half—say by one-sixteenth to one-eighth of an inch—as in that way the size of the rivet employed is not so disproportionate to the thickness of the strap, and it is not then necessary to allow so much distance between the outer rows of rivets and the edges of the straps, in order to prevent one of the latter breaking away in front of the rivets. It is unnecessary to investigate the strengths of single or double riveted double straps when no rivets are omitted, as the strength of the rivets is nearly doubled, and hence in excess of the strength of the plates or straps through the lines of rivet holes. The efficiency of the double riveted double strap might, however, be increased by reducing the size of the rivets, and keeping the spacing the same. In this way, if the straps are each rather more than $\frac{1}{4}$ inch thick, the rivets $\frac{5}{8}$ inch, and the spacing 3 inches, we should have for the strength of either of the plates or of the two straps—

$$18t(p-d) = 9 \times 2\tfrac{3}{8} = 21 \cdot 4 \text{ tons,}$$

and the strength of the rivets

$$22\pi d^2 = 27 \text{ tons.}$$

The efficiency of this connection is ·65.

The advantage of double butt straps is, however, chiefly found when at least treble riveting is used, and certain rivets are omitted. It must, however, be remembered that it is impossible to get a caulk when these rivets are omitted; but that is unimportant, for joints of such an efficiency are not usually required where water-tight work is essential. By referring to fig. 5, Plate XXXVI., it will be seen that the butt connection there shown may be broken in five different ways, viz.:—(1) By a plate breaking through either of the rows of rivet holes $yy$ or $y_1y_1$; (2) by the two straps breaking through either of the rows of rivet holes $xx$ or $x_1x_1$; (3) by all the rivets shearing on one side of the butt; (4) by a plate breaking through either of the rows of rivet holes $zz$ or $z_1z_1$, and shearing the rivets in the line $xx$ or $x_1x_1$; (5) by the straps breaking through either of the rows of rivet holes $zz$ or $z_1z_1$, and shearing the rivets in the line $yy$ or $y_1y_1$. The weakest of these modes of fracture is evidently that which would occur, and which fixes the strength of the strap.

In investigating the resistances to fracture by each of these modes, we shall assume the pitch to be 4 diameters, where alternate rivets are not omitted; and, therefore, 8 diameters elsewhere. We shall also consider the diameters of the rivets to be in accordance with Lloyd's Rules, and the thickness of each strap to be nine-sixteenths of the thickness of the plates joined. Considering a length of the strap equal to twice the pitch of rivets, we have the strength by

1st mode of fracture $= 20t(2p - d)$

2nd ,, ,, $= \dfrac{9}{8} \times 20t(2p - d) = \dfrac{45t}{2}(2p - d)$

3rd ,, ,, $= 4 \times \dfrac{22\pi d^2}{4} \times 2 = 44\pi d^2$

4th ,, ,, $= 18t(2p - 2d) + \dfrac{22\pi d^2}{4} \times 2 = 36t(p - d) + 11\pi d^2$

5th ,, ,, $= \dfrac{9}{8} \times 18t(2p - 2d) + \dfrac{22\pi d^2}{4} \times 2 = \dfrac{81}{2}t(2p - d) + 11\pi d^2$

Assume $t = \frac{1}{2}$, $d = \frac{3}{4}$, $p = 3$.

Then strength by

1st mode $= 10(6 - \frac{3}{4})$ $= 51\cdot25$ tons

2nd ,, $= \dfrac{45}{4}(6 - \frac{3}{4})$ $= 59$ ,,

3rd ,, $= 4 \times 20$ $= 80$ ,,

4th ,, $= 18(3 - \frac{3}{4}) + 20 = 60\cdot5$ ,,

5th ,, $= \dfrac{81}{4}(3 - \frac{3}{4}) + 20 = 65\cdot6$ ,,

The strength of this connection is therefore 51·25 tons; and since the strength of the unpierced plate is

$$2p \times t \times 22 = 66 \text{ tons,}$$

the efficiency of the strap is $\dfrac{51 \cdot 25}{66} = \cdot 78$.

Had we started with the supposition that the iron between the rivet holes—when the latter are spaced 6 inches apart—was uninjured by punching, the efficiency of the strap would have been $\frac{5}{6} = \cdot 83$.

A greater uniformity in the strengths of the strap by the several modes of fracture would have been obtained had the pitch been a little greater.

In the above investigation it will again be seen that the maximum strength of any connection by single or double butt straps, however riveted, is the strength of the plate in either of the lines of rivets $yy$ or $y_1 y_1$, and thus the strongest strap connection is that wherein there is only one rivet in that line; it being assumed that the total number of rivets in the straps is sufficient, and that the strap or straps are of the proper thickness. Mr. E. J. Reed, in his *Shipbuilding in Iron and Steel*, has given the particulars of a calculation made by Mr. N. Barnaby, the present Director of Naval Construction, of the stresses required to fracture a butt strap, the form and riveting of which are based upon the principles just referred to.

"The plates united to form the tie are $\frac{15}{16}$ inch thick and 24 inches wide, with double butt straps each $\frac{9}{16}$ inch thick, riveted with 1 inch rivets, arranged as shown by $a$ in Plate XXXVII., it being obvious that the use of extra thickness in the butt straps must in this case be resorted to, because the strength of the straps through the line of holes next the butt has to be made equal to the strength of the plate through the single rivet hole. The ordinary rule observed in shipbuilding is carried into effect here, all the rivet holes being a diameter clear of the edges and butts. The tensile strength of the unpunched plate is assumed to be 22 tons per square inch of section, and hence it follows that we have—

Breaking strength of the unpunched tie $= 24'' \times \frac{15}{16}'' \times 22$ tons $= 330$ tons.

"The butt may be fractured by breaking either the plate or the butt straps, and shearing the rivets. There are altogether ten modes of fracture which we propose to examine, commencing with those in which the *plate* is broken, observing that although the plates or straps might break in other ways, these ten modes appear sufficient for the present investigation, as they apparently comprise all the weakest cases. In these investigations we shall take the double shearing strength of a 1 inch rivet at 32 tons. The simplest mode of fracture is that illustrated by $b$, Plate XXXVII., where the plate has been broken through the single rivet hole. As there is only this one hole in the breadth of the plate, it will be fair to assume that the iron in the line of fracture retains its full strength of 22 tons per square inch. The effective breadth of the plate is reduced by the rivet hole to 23 inches, and we consequently have for Mode I:—

$$\text{Breaking strength} = 23'' \times 1\tfrac{3}{8}'' \times 22 \text{ tons} = 316 \text{ tons}.$$

"A second mode of fracture is shown by $c$ in Plate XXXVII., where the plate has been broken across two rivet holes, and the single rivet has been sheared twice. In this case also it may be fairly assumed that the tensile strength of the iron in the line of fracture is almost unchanged by the punching of the two holes. The effective breadth of the plate is reduced to 22 inches by the two rivet holes, and we thus obtain Mode II.:—

$$\begin{aligned}\text{Breaking strength of plate} &= 22'' \times 1\tfrac{3}{8}'' \times 22 \text{ tons} = 303 \text{ tons}\\ \text{Added for double shear of one rivet,} &\ldots\ldots\ldots\ldots = \phantom{0}32 \text{ ,,}\\ \text{Total breaking strength,} &\ldots\ldots\ldots = \overline{335} \text{ ,,}\end{aligned}$$

"A third mode of fracture is given in $d$, Plate XXXVII., where the plate has been broken through three rivet holes, and three rivets have been sheared twice. In this case the tensile strength of the iron in the line of fracture may be considered to have been reduced to 20 tons per square inch. The effective breadth of the plate is 21 inches, and we have for Mode III.:—

$$\begin{aligned}\text{Breaking strength of plate} &= 21'' \times 1\tfrac{3}{8}'' \times 20 \text{ tons} = 263 \text{ tons}\\ \text{Added for double shear of three rivets,} &\ldots\ldots\ldots = \phantom{0}96 \text{ ,,}\\ \text{Total breaking strength,} &\ldots\ldots\ldots = \overline{359} \text{ ,,}\end{aligned}$$

"A fourth mode of fracture is illustrated by $e$, Plate XXXVII., where the plate has been broken through the row of rivet holes nearest the butt, and the remaining six rivets on that side of the butt have been sheared twice. Here, as the pitch of the rivets is about 4 diameters, it will be proper to take 18 tons as the tensile strength of the iron in the line of fracture. The effective breadth of the plate is reduced to 19 inches, and we obtain for Mode IV.:—

$$\begin{aligned}\text{Breaking strength of plate} &= 19'' \times 1\tfrac{3}{8}'' \times 18 \text{ tons} = 214 \text{ tons}\\ \text{Added for double shear of six rivets,} &\ldots\ldots\ldots\ldots = 192 \text{ ,,}\\ \text{Total breaking strength,} &\ldots\ldots\ldots = \overline{406} \text{ ,,}\end{aligned}$$

"A fifth mode of fracture consists in shearing twice the eleven rivets on one side of the butt, and this gives for Mode V.:—

$$\text{Breaking strength} = 11 \times 32 = 352 \text{ tons}.$$

"Before proceeding to consider the other cases of fracture in which the *straps* are broken across, it may be well to state that we shall assume 18 tons per square inch to be the tensile strength of the iron in all the lines of fracture, the breadth of the straps being proportioned in such a manner as to bring all the rivets within a diameter of the edges, as before described.

"A sixth mode of fracture is illustrated by $f$, Plate XXXVII., where the straps have been broken across the single rivet hole, and the remaining ten rivets on that side of the butt have been sheared twice. Remembering that there are double straps, each $\frac{9}{16}$ inch thick, and that the effective breadth of the straps along the line of fracture is 2 inches, we obtain for Mode VI.:—

Breaking strength of straps $= 2 \times 2'' \times \frac{9}{16}'' \times 18$ tons $= 41$ tons
Added for double shear of ten rivets, ............... $= 320$ ,,

Total breaking strength, ......... $= 361$ ,,

"A seventh mode of fracture is shown by $g$, Plate XXXVII., where the straps have been broken through two rivet holes, and the eight rivets between the fracture and the butt have been sheared twice. The total breadth of the strap at this part is 8 inches, and its effective breadth is therefore 6 inches, thus giving for Mode VII.:—

Breaking strength of straps $= 2 \times 6'' \times \frac{9}{16}'' \times 18$ tons $= 122$ tons
Add for double shear of eight rivets, ............... $= 256$ ,,

Total breaking strength, ......... $= 378$ ,,

"An eighth mode of fracture is given in $h$, Plate XXXVII., where the straps have been broken through three rivet holes, and the five rivets nearest the butt have been sheared twice. The total breadth of the strap is here 12 inches, and the effective breadth 9 inches; we thus obtain for Mode VIII.:—

Breaking strength of straps $= 2 \times 9'' \times \frac{9}{16}'' \times 18$ tons $= 182$ tons
Added for double shear of five rivets, ............... $= 160$ ,,

Total breaking strength, ......... $= 342$ ,,

"Another mode of fracture is shown by $k$, Plate XXXVII., where the straps have been broken through the five holes nearest the butt. The effective breadth of the strap is here 19 inches, and we obtain for Mode IX.:—

Breaking strength $= 2 \times 19'' \times \frac{9}{16}'' \times 18$ tons $= 385$ tons.

"The remaining mode of fracture is shown by $l$, Plate XXXVII., where the straps have been broken, as in Mode VIII., and the plate has been broken through the line of holes nearest the butt; we thus have for Mode X.:—

Breaking strength of straps as in Mode VIII. $= 182$ tons
,, ,, plate as in Mode IV. $= 214$ ,,

Total breaking strength, ...... $= 396$ ,,

"It will be seen from these results that in all the various modes of fracture, except the first, the breaking strength is greater than the strength of the unpunched tie plate, and that the strength of the butt is, consequently, less than the strength of the tie by one rivet hole only."

**190. Strength of a Shift of Plates.**—In investigating the efficiency of plate connections at their butts and edges, the most profitable method is to consider a complete shift of plating, *i.e.*, the strength in the weakest section of butted plates and the plates which intervene between two consecutive butts in the same transverse section. Apart from other lines of relative weakness, the strength of such a section will vary with the number of "passing strakes," *i.e.*, the number of strakes between consecutive butts in that section. Adjacent strakes being always butted at some multiple of the frame or beam spacing apart, and the lengths of the plates being limited to the capabilities of the rolling mills, or the price the builder is willing to pay, the problem of obtaining the best shift of butts has excited some ingenuity. In these attempts two things have been arrived at, one being to get a maximum number of passing strakes between consecutive butts in the same transverse section; and the other being to prevent the butts of adjacent strakes being so close together as to make a weak step-shaped section, or, in other words, to prevent the plating breaking along these adjacent butts and the edge riveting between them. Plate XXXVIII. shows specimens of different shifts of butts that have been adopted. Fig. 1 is termed the brick shift, for reasons which are obvious; this method was common when it was difficult to get plates long enough for any other arrangement. Fig. 2 is the diagonal shift in common use on our principal shipbuilding rivers. Figs. 3, 4, etc., are other shifts which have been adopted in vessels for the Royal Navy.

We will now investigate the strength of a diagonal shift of butts, such as is shown by fig. 2, Plate XXXVIII. In this arrangement there are two passing strakes between consecutive butts, hence it will be necessary to calculate the strength of the butted plate in conjunction with the plate above and the plate below it. As the outer plates in the case we are about to consider are narrower than the inner, in order to give an appearance of uniform width on the outside; and as the butt straps of the inner strakes are the same width as the plates, while those of the outer are less by twice the lap; it is evident that, in investigating the strength of the shift, we must consider two cases: (1) an outer strake butt in connection with the inner strake on either side of it; and (2) an inner strake butt in connection with the outer strake on either side.

Plate XXXIX. shows a portion of the bottom plating of an iron vessel, $a$ and $c$ being outer, and $b$ and $d$ inner strakes. We will first investigate the strength of the strakes $b$, $c$, and $d$, taken together, and then that of the strakes $a$, $b$, and $c$, taken together.

The plates and butt straps are all $\frac{1}{2}$ inch thick, and the outer strakes are 3 feet 3 inches wide, while the inner strakes are 4 feet wide; the breadth of the lap being $4\frac{1}{2}$ inches. The rivets are $\frac{3}{4}$ inch in diameter, and spaced as shown on the Plate.

First, then, considering the three strakes, $b$, $c$, and $d$, the middle one of which is butted as shown. Neglecting the rivet holes at the water-tight frames, which will be alluded to presently, there are six possible modes of fracture:—

1. By the plates being broken through the line of rivet holes of the frame $AB$; the line of fracture is shown.

2. By the plates $b$ and $d$, and the butt strap of $c$ breaking in the manner shown by the line $XX$; the plates breaking through edge rivets, and the butt strap in the row of rivets $EF$ nearest the butt.

3. By the plates $b$ and $d$ breaking in the line $XX$, as before, but all the rivets on one side of the butt shearing instead of the butt strap breaking in the line $EF$.

4. By the plates $b$ and $d$ breaking through the line of the frame rivets $AB$; and the edge rivets between the butt and the frame, also the rivets on one side of the butt strap being sheared.

5. By the plates $b$ and $d$ breaking along the line of holes $AB$, as before, and the edge rivets between the butt and the frame being sheared, also the butt strap being broken in the line of holes $EF$.

6. By the plates $b$ and $d$ breaking as before in the line $AB$, and then the edge rivets between $AB$ and $GH$ being sheared, and the plate $c$ broken in the line of rivet holes $GH$.

The strength of unpunched iron will be taken at 22 tons per square inch, and this will be employed when a plate is broken across through its edge rivets; elsewhere, owing to the punching, a tensile strength of 18 tons per square inch will be used. The single shearing strength of a $\frac{3}{4}''$ rivet will be taken at 10 tons.

*First Mode.*

Length of plates $b$, $c$, and $d$, broken $= \overset{\text{ft.}}{4} + \overset{\text{ft.}}{3} \overset{\text{in.}}{3} + \overset{\text{ft.}}{4} = \overset{\text{ft.}}{11} \overset{\text{in.}}{3}$

Deduct for rivet holes in line $AB = 29 \times \frac{3}{4} = \frac{87}{4} = \underline{1 \quad 9\frac{3}{4}}$

$\phantom{Deduct for rivet holes in line AB = 29 \times \frac{3}{4} = \frac{87}{4} = } 9 \quad 5\frac{1}{4} = 113\cdot25$ sq. in.

Area of section $= 113\cdot25 \times \cdot5 = 56\cdot625$ sq. in.
Breaking stress $= 56\cdot625 \times 18 = 1019$ tons.

*Second Mode.*

Length of plates $b$ and $d$ broken .................. $= \overset{\text{ft.}}{4} + \overset{\text{ft.}}{4} = \overset{\text{ft.}}{8} \overset{\text{in.}}{0}$
Deduct for rivet holes in line $XX$ ............ $= 8 \times \frac{3}{4} = \underline{0 \quad 6}$
$\phantom{Deduct for rivet holes in line XX = 8 \times \frac{3}{4} = } 7 \quad 6 = 90$ in.

Area of section ... $= 90 \times \cdot5 = 45$ sq. in.
Breaking stress of plates ... $= 45 \times 22 = 990$ tons.
Length of butt strap broken $= \overset{\text{ft.}}{2} \quad \overset{\text{in.}}{6}$
Deduct for rivet holes $9 \times \frac{3}{4} = \underline{0 \quad 6\frac{3}{4}}$
$\phantom{Deduct for rivet holes 9 \times \frac{3}{4} = } 1 \quad 11\frac{1}{4} = 23\cdot25$ in.

Area of section $= 23\cdot25 \times \cdot5 = 11\cdot625$ sq. in.
Breaking stress of butt strap $= 11\cdot625 \times 18 = \phantom{0}209$ tons.
Add for plates, .......... ..................... $= \phantom{0}990$ ,,
$\phantom{xxxxxxxxxxxxx}$ Total ............... ................ $\overline{1199}$ ,,

*Third Mode.*

Breaking stress of plates $b$ and $d$ (as before), ............... $= \phantom{0}990$ tons
Shearing strength of rivets on one side of the $\Big\}$ $= 18 \times 10 = \phantom{0}180$ ,,
$\phantom{xxx}$ butt strap, ..................................... 
$\phantom{xxxxxxxxxxxxx}$ Total ........................................ $\overline{1170}$ ,,

*Fourth Mode.*

Length of plates $b$ and $d$ broken, ............... $= \overset{\text{ft.}}{4} + \overset{\text{ft.}}{4} = \overset{\text{ft.}}{8} \overset{\text{in.}}{0}$
Deduct for rivets in line $AB$ ............$20 \times \frac{3}{4} = \phantom{0}15 = \underline{1 \quad 3}$
$\phantom{xxxxxxxxxxxxxxxxxxxxxxxxxxxxxxxxxxxxx} 6 \quad 9 = 81$ in.

Area of section ... $= 81 \times \cdot5 = 40\cdot5$ sq. in.
Breaking stress, ...................$= 40\cdot5 \times 18 = \phantom{0}729$ tons
Shearing strength of rivets in $\Big\}$ $= 46 \times 10 = \phantom{0}460$ ,,
$\phantom{xxx}$ edges and butt strap, .........
$\phantom{xxxxxxxxxxxxx}$ Total ........................................ $\overline{1189}$ ,,

### Fifth Mode.

Breaking stress of plates $b$ and $d$ (as before), ............... = 729 tons
Breaking stress of butt strap (as before), .................. = 209 ,,
Shearing strength of rivets between AB and EF, ................................. } $= 28 \times 10 =$ 280 ,,
  Total................................................ 1218 ,,

### Sixth Mode.

Breaking stress of plates $b$ and $d$ (as before)............. = 729 tons.
Length of plate $c$ broken, ................................ = 3 ft. 3 in.
Deduct for rivets in plate $c$ .............. $13 \times \tfrac{3}{4} = \dfrac{39}{4} =$ 0 ft. 9¾ in.
                                                      ────────
                                                      2  5¼ = 29¼ in.

  Area of section... = 29·25 + ·5 = 14·625 sq. in.
  Breaking stress of section = 14·625 × 18 ....... = 263 tons
  Shearing strength of edge rivets between AB and GH,............. } = 20 × 10 = 200 ,,
  Add for plates $b$ and $d$,............................ = 729 ,,
    Total................................................ 1192 ,,

These results show a tolerable uniformity of strength, the butt connection being stronger than the plates themselves in the line of rivets connecting them to the bracket frames. The close riveting in the water-tight frame (see Plate XXXIX.), would render a section thereat much weaker than elsewhere, were it not that the strength is restored by means of the wide liners $s\,s$, having a row of rivets on each side of the frame.

We will next investigate the strength of the butted plate $b$ in connection with the plates $a$ and $c$ on either side of it. It is unnecessary to again particularise the several possible modes of fracture, as they are similar to those already considered for the other butt connection.

### First Mode.

Length of plates $a$, $b$, and $c$, broken = 3 ft. 3 in. + 4 ft. 3 in. + 3 ft. 3 in. = 10 ft. 6 in.
Deduct for rivet holes in line CD........ = 28 × ¾ = 21 = 1  9
                                                       ────────
                                                       8  9 = 105 in.

  Area of section...... = 105 × ·5 = 52·5 sq. in.
  Breaking stress ..... = 52·5 × 18 = 945 tons.

### Second Mode.

Length of plates $a$ and $c$, broken.... ... $= \begin{matrix}\text{ft. in.}\\3\ \ 3\end{matrix} + \begin{matrix}\text{ft. in.}\\3\ \ 3\end{matrix} = \begin{matrix}\text{ft. in.}\\6\ \ 6\end{matrix}$

Deduct for rivet holes in the line $X_1 X_1$ ....... $= 10 \times \tfrac{3}{4} = \underline{\ \ 7\tfrac{1}{2}\ }$

$\qquad\qquad\qquad\qquad\qquad\qquad\qquad\qquad 5\ \ 10\tfrac{1}{2} = 70\tfrac{1}{2}$ in.

Area of section $= 70\cdot 5 \times \cdot 5 = 35\cdot 25$ sq. in.

Breaking stress of plates $= 35\cdot 25 \times 22 = 775$ tons.

Length of butt strap broken $= \begin{matrix}\text{ft. in.}\\4\ \ 0\end{matrix}$

Deduct for rivet holes $16 \times \tfrac{3}{4} = \underline{1\ \ 0}$

$\qquad\qquad\qquad\qquad\qquad\qquad 3\ \ 0 = 36$ in.

Area of section of strap $= 36 \times \cdot 5 = 18$ sq. in.

Breaking stress of strap $= 18 \times 18 = 324$ tons

Add for plates........................ $= \underline{775}$ ,,

$\qquad\qquad$ Total.................... $1099$ ,,

### Third Mode.

Breaking stress of plates $a$ and $c$, as before.................. $= 775$ tons.

Shearing stress of rivets on one side of the strap $= 32 \times 10 = \underline{320}$ ,,

$\qquad\qquad\qquad$ Total....................................... $1095$ ,,

### Fourth Mode.

Length of plates $a$ and $c$, broken.. $= \begin{matrix}\text{ft. in.}\\3\ \ 3\end{matrix} + \begin{matrix}\text{ft. in.}\\3\ \ 3\end{matrix} = \begin{matrix}\text{ft. in.}\\6\ \ 6\end{matrix}$

Deduct for rivets in line CD......... $= 18 \times \tfrac{3}{4} = 0\ \ 13\tfrac{1}{2} = \underline{1\ \ 1\tfrac{1}{2}}$

$\qquad\qquad\qquad\qquad\qquad\qquad\qquad\quad 5\ \ 4\tfrac{1}{2} = 64\tfrac{1}{2}$ in.

Area of section ............... $= 64\cdot 5 \times \cdot 5 = 32\cdot 25$ sq. in.

Breaking stress.............. $= 32\cdot 25 \times 18 = 580$ tons

Shearing strength of rivets $\big\}$ $= 52 \times 10 = \underline{520}$ ,,
in edges and butt straps

$\qquad\qquad$ Total....................... $1100$ ,,

### Fifth Mode.

Breaking stress of plates $a$ and $c$, as before ................. $= 580$ tons

Breaking stress of butt strap, as before ...................... $= 324$ ,,

Shearing strength of edge rivets between CD $\big\}$ $= 28 \times 10 = \underline{280}$ ,,
and KL...........................................

$\qquad\qquad$ Total.................... $1184$ ,,

### Sixth Mode.

Breaking stress of plates $a$ and $c$, as before.................. $= 580$ tons

Length of plate $b$, broken........................... $= \begin{matrix}\text{ft. in.}\\4\ \ 0\end{matrix}$

Deduct for rivets, ......... ............... $16 \times \tfrac{3}{4} = \underline{1\ \ 0}$

$\qquad\qquad\qquad\qquad\qquad\qquad 3\ \ 0 = 36$ inches.

Area of section........................ $= 36 \times \cdot 5 = 18$ sq. in.

Breaking stress of section............. $= 18 \times 18 = 324$ tons

Shearing strength of edge rivets $\big\}$ $= 20 \times 10 = 200$ ,,
between CD and MN.............

Add for plates $a$ and $c$........................... $= \underline{580}$ ,,

$\qquad\qquad$ Total......,................. $1104$ ,,

**191. Strength of Pillars.**—We now approach a subject regarding which we are not able to arrive at such exact conclusions as when considering the strength of combinations of plates subjected to tensile stresses. This is due to the fact that the resistance of any material in the form of a pillar to compressive forces is of a compound character, and it is impossible to predicate with accuracy in what particular mode rupture will take place. We are therefore, to a great extent, obliged to investigate the subject experimentally with different materials, made into pillars of different proportions both as regards sectional area and ratio of length to diameter.

The resistance to compression, when the limit of proof stress is not exceeded, is about the same as the resistance to extension, and is expressed by the same modulus of elasticity. When that limit is exceeded, the irregular alterations undergone by the figure of the substance render the precise determination of the resistance to compression difficult, if not impossible. *Crushing* may take place (1) by the material *splitting* into fragments, separated by smooth surfaces whose general direction is parallel to that of the crushing force; (2) by one part of the material *shearing* or *sliding* over the other; (3) by *bulging* or *lateral swelling* and *spreading;* (4) by *buckling* or *crippling;* and (5) by *cross breaking.*

The 1st and 2nd modes of crushing are exemplified by such materials as glass and hard earthenware; the 2nd by cast iron, stone, etc.; the 3rd by wrought iron; the 4th by timber, wrought iron, and bars longer than those which give way by bulging; while the 5th is the mode of fracture of pillars in which the length greatly exceeds the diameter. It is caused by the pillar first yielding sideways and then being broken as a beam.

Competent authorities have stated that, in order to determine the true resistance of substances to compression, experiments should be made on blocks the proportion of whose length to diameter is not less than 3 to 2.

In wrought iron the resistance to the direct crushing of short blocks is from $\frac{2}{3}$ to $\frac{4}{5}$ the tenacity, and the resistance of most kinds of timber to crushing when dry is from $\frac{1}{2}$ to $\frac{2}{3}$, while that of cast iron is six times the tenacity.

Pillars whose lengths exceed their diameters in considerable proportions, such as is always the case in a ship, do not give way by crushing, but by bending sideways and breaking across, being crushed at one side of the pillar and torn asunder at the other side. Professor Rankine says,* "There does not yet exist any complete theory of this phenomenon. The formulæ which have been provisionally adopted are founded on a mode of investigation partly theoretical and partly empirical." He then gives an investigation from which results the following:—

Let P = the load on a long pillar,
,, S = its sectional area,

then one part $p_1$ of the intensity of the greatest stress is simply—

$$p_1 = \frac{P}{S}.$$

Another part is that which arises from bending, which will take place in that direction in which the pillar is most flexible, that is, in the direction of its least diameter, if the diameters are unequal:—

Let $h$ = that diameter,
,, $b$ = the diameter perpendicular to it,
,, $l$ = the length of the pillar;
also, let $p_2$ = the greatest stress produced by bending,

then $p_2 \propto \dfrac{Pl^2}{Sh^2} \propto p_1 \dfrac{l^2}{h^2}$;

that is, *the additional stress due to bending is to the stress due to direct pressure in a ratio which increases as the square of the proportion in which the length of the pillar exceeds the least diameter.*

Let $f$ be a co-efficient of strength representing the whole intensity of the greatest stress on the material of the pillar, then

$$f = p_1 + p_2 = \frac{P}{S}\left(1 + a\frac{l^2}{h^2}\right) \quad \text{................(1)}$$

in which $a$ is a constant co-efficient to be determined by experiment.

Hence the following is the strength of a long pillar:—

$$P = \frac{fS}{1 + a\dfrac{l^2}{h^2}} \quad \text{................(2)}$$

* *Applied Mechanics*, p. 360.

The following values of $f$ and $a$ are given for the ultimate strength of pillars *fixed at the ends* by flat heads and heels.

| MATERIAL. | Modulus $f$. lbs. per sq. in. | Multiplier $a$. | Form of Pillar. |
|---|---|---|---|
| Cast iron, | 80,000 | $\frac{1}{400}$ * | Hollow cylinder. |
| Wrought iron, | 36,000 | $\frac{1}{3000}$ * | Solid rectangle. |
| ,, ,, | ... | $\frac{1}{3000}$ | Thin square tube or cell. |
| ,, ,, | ... | $\frac{1}{2250}$ | Solid cylinder. |
| ,, ,, | ... | $\frac{1}{1500}$ | Thin cylindrical tube. |
| ,, ,, | ... | $\frac{1}{1500}$ | Angle-iron. |
| ,, ,, | ... | $\frac{1}{1500}$ | Cross-shaped section. |
| Timber (average), | 6,500 | $\frac{1}{750}$ * | Solid rectangle. |

For pillars *jointed at both ends*, multiply the values of $a$ given in the Table by 4.

For pillars *fixed at one end and jointed at the other*, multiply the values of $a$ given in the Table by 2.

In using the preceding formulæ for pillars, the following factors of safety should be employed: for cast iron, 8; wrought iron, 6; and timber, 10.

**192. Beams.**—A beam is a combination of material so placed in the structure that it supports a load at one or more points in its length, while it is itself supported at one or more other points. The direction of the load being in the same line as that in which the supporting force acts (the directions being usually vertical), a mechanical couple is set up which tends to rack or shear, and to bend the beam. We will consider some of the ordinary cases of a horizontal beam subject to the influence of vertical parallel forces, these consisting of the load or loads acting downwards, and the supporting reaction or reactions acting upwards.

*Firstly,* Take the case of a weightless beam $AB$ supported at its ends $A$ and $B$, and loaded at an intermediate point $C$

---

* These three values of $a$ are the results of experiments; the others have been inferred from the second by the probable supposition that they are proportional to the flexibility.

(fig. 1, Plate XL.); $W$ is the given load, also $P$ and $P_1$ are the required supporting forces—

Then $W = P + P_1;$ .................(1)

also $P \times AB = W \times BC,$ ...............(2)

and $P_1 \times AB = W \times AC.$ ...............(3)

From (2) $P = W \times \dfrac{BC}{AB};$ ...............(4)

from (3) $P_1 = W \times \dfrac{AC}{AB}$ ...............(5)

*Secondly,* Take the case of a weightless beam $AB$ loaded at a point $A$, fixed at the point $B$, and supported at an intermediate point $C$. Let $W$ be the load at $A$, $W_1$ the required downward force at $B$, necessary to hold the beam in place, and $P$ the required supporting force at $C$.

Then $W = P - W_1;$ ...............(1)

also $P \times CB = W \times AB,$ ...............(2)

and $W_1 \times CB = W \times AC.$ ...............(3)

From (2) $P = W \times \dfrac{AB}{CB};$ ...............(4)

from (3) $W_1 = W \times \dfrac{AC}{CB}$ ...............(5)

From this we will proceed to show how to determine the *shearing stress* and *bending moment* at any given cross section of the beam.

**193. Shearing Stress.**—The shearing stress at any cross section of the beam $AB$ (fig. 1, Plate XL.), between the points $A$ and $C$ is equal to the force $P$, while the shearing stress at any cross section between $C$ and $B$ is equal to the force $P_1$. Similarly, the shearing stress at any cross section between $A$ and $C$ (fig. 2, Plate XL.) is equal to the load $W$; and that at any cross section between $B$ and $C$ is equal to the load $W_1$.

The tendency of these shearing stresses is to rack or distort the beam; the racking action upon the two parts of each beam into which the point $C$ divides it being opposite in direction.

*If the beam is loaded at several points in its length,* as at

$C$, $D$, $E$, $F$, etc. (fig. 3, Plate XL.), and supported at the ends as at $A$ and $B$. The magnitude of the resultant load is

$$W_1 + W_2 + W_3 + W_4 + W_5 + W_6 = W_x \text{ say.}$$

Also

$$W_x \times AX = W_1 \times AC + W_2 \times AD + W_3 \times AE + W_4 \times AF + W_5 \times AG + W_6 \times AH.$$

Therefore

$$AX = \frac{W_1 \times AC + W_2 \times AD + W_3 \times AE + W_4 \times AF + W_5 \times AG + W_6 \times AH}{W_1 + W_2 + W_3 + W_4 + W_5 + W_6}$$

which gives the point of application $X$ of the resultant load. Hence having the magnitude of $W_x$, and the distance of the point $X$ from $A$ or $B$, we are able, as before, to find the values of $P_1$ and $P_2$.

We can now determine the shearing stress on any division of this beam. The shearing stress at any cross section in the division $AC$ is equal to the force $P_1$; that at any cross section in the division $CD$ is $P_1 - W_1$; at any division in $DE$ it is $P_1 - W_1 - W_2$, and so on. In general terms, *the shearing stress on any division of this beam is the resultant of the forces acting upon the beam between that division and either extremity.* It must be particularly noticed that to find this resultant the forces are distinguished as positive and negative, according to their direction, so that by their successive subtraction the shearing stresses at the different divisions are found one after another. In carrying out this process, a point will at length be reached where the load is greater than the shearing stress on the previous division, so that the shearing stress on the next division is negative. Such a point is seen in $X$, fig. 3, Plate XL., the direction of the racking action being reversed there. The remaining shearing stresses are found by adding, instead of subtracting, the successive loads, the stresses so found being negative, or contrary in direction to the positive shearing stresses on the other side of the point $X$.

194. **Bending Moment.**—Besides the shearing action just alluded to, the load upon a beam, supported at each end, tends to bend it so that it assumes a convex form on the side towards which the direction of the load acts. For instance, the tendency of the beam, shown by fig. 1, Plate XL, is to become arched in some such a manner as is shown by

the ticked line, the points $A$ and $B$ where the beam rests being, of course, fixed. Again, the beam shown by fig. 2, Plate XL., which is fixed at a point between two loads, bends in a contrary direction, the point $C$ being stationary, and the convexity as shown by the ticked lines. In both cases the bending is produced by a drooping of the portions at which the loads are placed.

The magnitude of the bending moment at any cross section of either end of the beam is equal to the product of the force at that end of the beam, between which and the point $C$ the section is situated, into the distance of the section from that end. For instance, the bending moment at any section $D$ of the beam (fig. 1, Plate XL.) between $A$ and $C$ is equal to $P \times AD$. That at $C$ is equal to $P \times AC$, which, as we already know, is equal to $P_1 \times BC$, and that is consequently the maximum bending moment. It is important to notice here that this is the point of reverse racking, and where the shearing stress is zero. From what has been said it follows that the bending moments at $A$ and $B$ are zero.

Referring to fig. 2, Plate XL., the bending moment at $D$ is equal to $W \times AD$, and consequently the maximum bending moment is at $C$, where $W \times AC = W_1 \times BC$; also that the bending moments at $A$ and $B$ are zero.

From these two cases it will be seen that the same results follow, both for shearing stresses and bending moments, whether the beam rests at each end, and is loaded at an intermediate point, or is loaded at each end and rests at an intermediate point; also that the direction of the convexity is always in that of the intermediate force.

When the beam is loaded at several intermediate points, as in fig. 3, Plate XL., the bending moment at $A$ is zero, that at $C$ is equal to $P_1 \times AC$; at the point $D$ it is $P_1 \times AC + (P_1 - W_1)CD$; also at the point $E$ the bending moment is $P_1 \times AC + (P_1 - W_1)CD + (P_1 - W_1 - W_2)DE$, and so on. At the point $X$ where the shearing stress is zero, and the racking force changes direction, the bending moment is at a maximum, for the same result is found as if we started from $B$. By starting from $A$, as above, and computing the bending moment at $B$, we shall find it to be zero, in consequence of the shearing stress at $F$, viz., $P_1 - W_1 - W_2 - W_3 - W_4$, and all the succeeding stresses being negative, and $X$ being the point where the resultant load acts.

The general rule for calculating the bending moment at a cross section through any given loaded point of a beam is as follows:—*Multiply each shearing stress by the length of the division on which it acts, then the bending moment at any given loaded point is equal to the algebraical sum of the products corresponding to the divisions which lie between that point and either end of the beam.*

**195. Numerical Example.**—For the distances $AC$, $CD$, $DE$, $EF$, etc., in fig. 3, Plate XL., substitute the following lengths in feet, viz., 4, 4, 5, 6, 5, 3, and 3 feet respectively; also for $W_1$, $W_2$, $W_3$, $W_4$, etc., substitute in tons as follows: 2, 5, 3, 4, 6, 1, respectively. (See fig. 4, Plate XL.)

Taking moments about the extremities of the beam—

$$P_1 = \frac{1 \times 3 + 6 \times 6 + 4 \times 11 + 3 \times 17 + 5 \times 22 + 2 \times 26}{4+4+5+6+5+3+3}$$

$$= \frac{3+36+44+51+110+52}{30} = \frac{296}{30} = 9\tfrac{16}{30} \text{ tons}$$

$$P_2 = \frac{2 \times 4 + 5 \times 8 + 3 \times 13 + 4 \times 19 + 6 \times 24 + 1 \times 27}{4+4+5+6+5+3+3}$$

$$= \frac{8+40+39+76+144+27}{30} = \frac{334}{30} = 11\tfrac{2}{15} \text{ tons.}$$

Also $\quad AX = \dfrac{296}{2+5+3+4+6+1} = \dfrac{296}{21} = 14\tfrac{2}{21}$ feet

$\quad\quad BX = \dfrac{334}{2+5+3+4+6+1} = \dfrac{334}{21} = 15\tfrac{19}{21}$ ,,

*Then for the shearing stresses—*       tons.

| | |
|---|---|
| Shearing stress on division $AC$, ........ | $+\ 9\tfrac{13}{15} = P_1$ |
| Load at $C$, ........................... | $-\ 2$ |
| Shearing stress on division $CD$, ........ | $+\ 7\tfrac{13}{15}$ |
| Load at $D$, ........................... | $-\ 5$ |
| Shearing stress on division $DE$, ........ | $+\ 2\tfrac{13}{15}$ |
| Load at $E$, ........................... | $-\ 3$ |

                                        racking action reversed at X.

| | |
|---|---|
| Shearing stress on division $EF$, ........ | $-\ \tfrac{2}{15}$ |
| Load at $F$, ........................... | $-\ 4$ |
| Shearing stress on division $FG$, ........ | $-\ 4\tfrac{2}{15}$ |
| Load at $G$, ........................... | $-\ 6$ |
| Shearing stress on division $GH$, ........ | $-\ 10\tfrac{2}{15}$ |
| Load at $H$, ........................... | $-\ 1$ |
| Shearing stress on division $HB$, ........ | $-\ 11\tfrac{2}{15} = P_2$ |

274   THEORETICAL NAVAL ARCHITECTURE.

### NEXT FOR THE BENDING MOMENTS AT THE LOADED POINTS.

| Points. | Shearing Stress. | Length of Division. | Products. | Bending Moments. |
|---|---|---|---|---|
|  | tons. | feet. | oot-tons. | foot-tons. |
| A | ... | ... | ... | 0 |
|  | $+ 9\frac{3}{15}$ | 4 | $+39\frac{7}{15}$ | ... |
| C | ... | ... | ... | $39\frac{7}{15}$ |
|  | $+ 7\frac{13}{15}$ | 4 | $+31\frac{7}{15}$ | ... |
| D | ... | ... | ... | $70\frac{14}{15}$ |
|  | $+ 2\frac{13}{15}$ | 5 | $+14\frac{3}{15}$ | ... |
| E | ... | ... | ... | $85\frac{1}{15}$ greatest |
|  | $- \frac{3}{15}$ | 6 | $- 1\frac{3}{15}$ | ... at X. |
| F | ... | ... | ... | $84\frac{7}{15}$ |
|  | $- 4\frac{7}{15}$ | 5 | $- 20\frac{13}{15}$ | ... |
| G | ... | ... | ... | $63\frac{12}{15}$ |
|  | $- 10\frac{2}{15}$ | 3 | $- 30\frac{3}{15}$ | ... |
| H | ... | ... | ... | $33\frac{3}{15}$ |
|  | $- 11\frac{2}{15}$ | 3 | $- 33\frac{3}{15}$ | ... |
| B | ... | ... | ... | 0 |

**196. Graphical Representation of Preceding.**—Fig. 5, Plate XL., represents graphically the preceding results. The line $AB$ represents the beam shown by figs. 3 and 4. $C$, $D$, $E$, $F$, etc., are the same loaded points, and loaded similarly to those shown by fig. 4. An ordinate of length equal to $9\frac{3}{15}$ tons to some scale, drawn anywhere between the points $A$ and $C$, represents the shearing stress on that division. Similarly, an ordinate representing to scale $7\frac{13}{15}$ tons, may be drawn anywhere between $C$ and $D$, to indicate the shearing stress on any section of the division $CD$, and so on. Between $E$ and $F$, the shearing stress having changed sign, the ordinate will be drawn on the opposite side of the line $AB$, and so we proceed until an ordinate of length equal to $11\frac{2}{15}$ tons to scale represents the shearing stress on any section of the division $HB$ of the beam. By thus drawing an ordinate of the proper length at each extremity of each division, and joining the extremities of the ordinates, we get a series of rectangles, as shown in the figure. It will be at once seen that the bending moment at any of the loaded points is equal to the algebraical sum of the areas of the rectangles between that point and either extremity of the beam, treating the rectangles on one side of the line $AB$ as positive, and on the other side as negative. It is obvious that the areas of the rectangles on one side of the line are together equal to those on the other side. If we start from $A$ and draw ordinates from the points $C$, $D$, $E$, $F$, $G$, and $H$, each of which represents to some scale the algebraical sum of the areas between that point and $A$, we shall find that the lengths of these ordinates are as found in the preceding Article, viz., $39\frac{7}{15}$, $70\frac{4}{15}$, $85\frac{4}{15}$, $84\frac{7}{15}$, $63\frac{12}{15}$, and $33\frac{6}{15}$ tons respectively. If we join the extremities of these ordinates with straight lines, we are able to determine the bending moment at any cross section between the loaded points, by drawing an ordinate from that section to the line joining the extremities of the two adjacent ordinates, and measuring its length to the required scale. The reason we join the extremities with straight lines, and do not pass a curve through them, is because the bending moments vary between each pair of loaded points in proportion to the distance from the point we start from, and thus the variation is indicated by a straight line.

197. **Distributed Load.**—We will now consider the more general case met with in actual practice, viz., that of a load distributed continuously over the whole length of the beam, the latter being supported, as before, at the two ends. In considering the load in this case we will use its *intensity*, *i.e.*, the load in units of weight per unit of length of the span. This intensity varies continuously.

In fig. 1, Plate XLI., $AB$ is the axis of the beam, supported at $A$ and $B$; this is supposed to be loaded continuously with loads of varying intensity. Ordinates are drawn representing in length, to scale, the intensities of the loads at the points on the beam where the ordinates are situated, and a curve $ADFB$ is drawn through the extremities of these ordinates. This line is termed the *curve of loads.* By calculating the area of the space enclosed by this curve and the line $AB$, we have, to scale, the total load $W$ on the beam; also, the area $ADFEA$ represents to scale the total load on the length $AE$ of the beam.

*To determine the supporting pressures at the extremities $A$ and $B$:* find first the position, longitudinally, of the centre of gravity of the area $ADFB$; this will give the point $G$, which is the centre of gravity of all the loads on the beam. Having, then, the total load and the position of its centre of gravity, we know by the preceding investigations that the upward pressure $P$ at the point $A$ is

$$P = \frac{W \times GB}{AB},$$
$$\text{and that } P_1 = \frac{W \times AG}{AB}.$$

*Next, to find the shearing stresses.*—At the points $A$ and $B$ draw ordinates $AH$ and $BK$ in opposite directions, representing to scale the magnitudes of the two supporting forces $P$ and $P_1$. These are drawn in opposite directions, for, being the shearing stresses at the points $A$ and $B$, they act in contrary directions, one being considered positive and the other negative. For the shearing stress at any point in the span, say $C$: measure by Simpson's Rule, as before, the area of the space $ACD$, and deduct the result from the value of $P$, the remainder will be the shearing stress at $C$. Calculate in a similar manner the shearing stresses at a sufficient number of other points in the span, and set off ordinates representing to scale the magnitude of these stresses. At a certain point in the length these differences of the areas, starting from $A$, will become zero and then negative. Pass a curve $ALXK$ through the points so found; this is the *curve of shearing stresses*, and is such that, by drawing ordinates to it from any point in the axis of the beam, the length of that ordinate is, to scale, the magnitude of the shearing stress on the cross section at that point. The point $X$, where the curve of shearing stresses crosses the axis, is the point of reverse racking which was explained in Art. 193. The direction of the racking force at any section is shown by the position of the ordinate, either above or below the axis $AB$.

*To find the bending moments.*—The areas $AHX$ and $BXK$ are, of course, equal. Either of them represents to scale the magnitude of the bending moment at the point $X$, which is there at a maximum. The bending moment at any other cross section of the beam, say at $C$, is represented to scale by the area of $AHLC$ between that section and the extremity of the beam which is on the opposite side to it that $X$ is. If the cross section is on the other side of $X$, then the bending moment at that section is represented by the area of the space enclosed by an ordinate to the curve of shearing stresses at that point and that portion of the curve and axis which is on the side of the ordinate nearest the extremity $B$. By calculating the bending moments in this way at a sufficient number of points on $AB$, and drawing from those points ordinates representing to scale the magnitudes of the bending moments, a curve drawn through the extremities of these ordinates is termed the *curve of bending moments*, and is such that the bending moment at any cross section, say $C$, in the length of the beam is given to scale by the length of the ordinate $CM$ to the curve of bending moments from that point. The maximum ordinate is, of course, that from the point $X$ or $OX$, which represents to scale either of the equal areas $AHX$ or $BKX$.

**198. Distributed Load and Support.**—The case now to be considered is not met with in any local connection or support in the ship, but is represented by the ship herself when floating in the water. We consider it at this place rather than in the next chapter, in consequence of the intimate relation which the investigation bears to that just gone through. The loads considered consist of the weight of the ship and her cargo and equipment, the intensities of which are found in units of weight per unit of length of the ship, say in tons per foot of length. These intensities in a merchant vessel vary with a tolerable approach to continuity throughout the length of the ship. The supporting forces are the upward pressures of the water, their intensities being the displacements of the vessel in tons per foot of her length. Right forward and aft the weights carried are considerably in excess of the supporting pressures of the water. Proceeding towards midships the weights and pressures approach equality, after which the displacement per foot of length exceeds the weight, until about amidships a maximum difference is obtained. From thence to aft the conditions are reversed, so that there are two points of maximum excess of weight over support, one point of maximum excess of support over weight, and two points where the difference is zero. This is a common case; of course, instances may occur, as in an ironclad, where the differences are of another character. The differences of the intensities of weight and support having been found at a sufficient number of points in the length of the beam, as we now consider it, these differences are set off as ordinates at the proper points, being drawn above or below the axis of the beam according as the support is in excess of the weight or *vice versa*. A curve drawn through the extremities of the ordinates is termed the *curve of loads*. (See *CDEFG*, fig. 2, Plate XLI.)

We have now to consider the beam whose axis is $AB$ subjected to the influence of loads throughout the whole of its length, which loads vary continuously in their intensities; the intensity of the load at any point in its length being represented in magnitude by the length of the ordinate from the axis $AB$ to the curve of loads at that point. The direction of the load, whether upward or downward, is represented by the position of the ordinate, *i.e.*, whether above or below the axis. The loads at the extremities $A$ and $B$ act downward, and are represented in magnitude by the ordinates $AC$ and $BG$ respectively. At $D$ and $F$ the load is zero, and at $X$ the load is in the form of an upward pressure whose magnitude is represented by the ordinate $EX$.

As the ship is floating in equilibrium at a certain line, the sum of the upward forces must be equal to that of the downward forces; hence the areas of the figures $ACD$ and $FBG$ are together equal to the area $DEF$. For the same reason the moments of the upward and downward forces about a transverse axis, through the points $A$ or $B$, must be equal to each other. In other words, the sum of the moments of the areas $ACD$ and $FBG$ about an ordinate through either $A$ or $B$ will be equal to the moment of the area $DEF$ about that ordinate. Otherwise the trim of the vessel would be altered.

*To find the shearing stress at any point*, we construct a *curve of shearing stresses* from the curve of loads in the following manner:—The area of the curve of loads between any point and an extremity of the axis $AB$ is the shearing stress at that point; observing that portions of the area above the line $AB$ are considered positive, and those below negative. For it will be observed that the beam is now supported at the points $D$ and $F$, and therefore the shearing stresses are at a maximum at those points, while their racking actions are in contrary directions. Hence the shearing stress at the point $D$ is equal to the algebraical sum of all the loads on either side of it; that is, equal to the area $ACD$, or, which is the same thing, the area $DEF$ minus the area $FGB$. The ordinate $DH$, representing to scale either of those areas, is therefore the shearing stress at the point $D$. Similarly, the ordinate $FK$ which is drawn equal, to scale, to either the area $FGB$ or the area $DEF$ minus the area $ACD$, represents the shearing stress at the point $F$; being drawn below the axis to show that the racking action is of a contrary direction to that at $D$. At the point $X$ where the ordinate $EX$ to the curve of loads cuts off an area $DEX$ equal to the area $ADC$, and the area $EXF$ equal to the area $FBG$, the shearing stress is zero. Also at the points $A$ and $B$, where the area $ACD + FBG - DEF =$ zero, the shearing stresses are also zero. In this way, by constructing a sufficient number of ordinates, the *curve of shearing stresses* $AHXKB$ is drawn, whereby the shearing stress at any point in the length of the beam may be measured.

*To find the bending moment at any point*, we proceed as follows: Measure the area between an ordinate to the curve of shearing stresses at that point and that end of the beam between which and the point $X$ the given point is situated.

The point $X$ being the point of reverse racking, where the shearing stress is zero, is, as we have already shown, the point of maximum bending moment, the latter being equal to either of the areas $AHX$ or $BKX$. The bending moment at any point $D$ between $X$ and the extremity $A$ is, as before, equal to the area $AHD$, and so on. Similar conditions hold good on the side of $X$ towards the extremity $B$. By finding the bending moment in this way at a sufficient number of points in the axis $AB$, and setting up ordinates representing the results, to scale, a curve drawn through the extremities of the ordinates is termed the *curve of bending moments*, and is such that the bending moment at any intermediate point is found by measuring the length of the ordinate from that point to the curve.

**199. Algebraical expression for the preceding.**—Referring to fig. 1, Plate XLII., $APC$ is a curve of loads, and $AB$

the axis of the beam. Consider an indefinitely short length $dx$ of the beam, the load upon which is $P$, that is, $P$ is the intensity of the load on a length $dx$; then $F$, the shearing stress on that section or short length $dx$, is represented by the expression—

$$F = \int P dx \quad \text{...............................(1)}$$

the limits of the integration being between $A$ and the distance from $A$ to the section, along the axis $AB$.

Hence $\dfrac{dF}{dx} = P$ ........................................(2)

Again, referring to fig 2, on the same Plate, $AB$ is the axis of the beam, as before, and $AFC$ is the curve of shearing stresses. Suppose the shearing stress on a section of the beam distant $x$ from the point $A$ is $F$; also that the bending moment on that section is $M$. Then the bending moment on a section indefinitely near to it, or at a distance $x + dx$ from the point $A$, is $M + dM$. It is also equal to $M + Fdx$.

Hence $M + dM = M + Fdx$
$\therefore \quad dM = Fdx$
or $\dfrac{dM}{dx} = F$ ............................(3)
$\therefore \quad M = \int F dx.$ ........ ...............(4)

**200. Bending Moments and Shearing Stresses for various Modes of Loading, etc., considered Algebraically.**

1. *Beam fixed at one end and loaded at the other.*

Find the sectional area necessary for the flanges of an I-shaped beam 20 ft. long and 15 in. deep to support a ton weight at one of its ends, the other being fixed.

Working stress : tension = 4 tons, compression = 2 tons.

Figs. 3 and 4, Plate XLII., represent this beam : fig. 3 being an elevation, and fig. 4 a section. Consider the equilibrium of a section at $X$.

To preserve equilibrium there must be two equal forces $T$ and $H$ acting in the directions shown by the arrows; also a vertical force of 1 ton at the section. The horizontal forces are due to the extensive and compressive effect of the bending moment, while 1 ton is the uniform shearing stress.

# BENDING MOMENTS AND SHEARING STRESSES.

Let $x$ be the distance in inches of the section $X$ from the loaded extremity;

Then $T \times 15 = x \times 1$

$$T = \frac{x}{15}.$$

When $x = 240$ inches,

$$T = \frac{240}{15} = 16 \text{ tons of extension;}$$

also $H = 16$ tons of compression.

But 4 tons is the working extensive stress per sq. inch, and 2 tons is the working compressive stress per sq. inch;

$$\therefore \frac{16}{4} = 4 \text{ sq. inches area of CEFD,}$$

and $\frac{16}{2} = 8$ sq. inches area of GKLH.

The web $MOPN$ has to be simply strong enough to resist a shearing stress of 1 ton.

2. *Beam supported at its ends and loaded in the middle.*

A beam $AB$ (see fig. 5, Plate XLII.) is supported at its ends and loaded in the middle with 10 tons, find the bending moment and shearing stress at any point; also the maximum bending moment; the length of the beam being 20 feet.

Let $AB = 2a$. Consider any vertical section at $X$ distant $x$ from the middle point $O$ of the beam. Taking moments about that point

$$M = 5(a - x),$$

which increases as $x$ diminishes, and is therefore a maximum at $O$.

Hence $M = 5a = 5 \times 120 = 600$ inch tons.

The shearing stress at any cross section between $A$ and $O$, and between $B$ and $O$ is 5 tons.

3. *Beam supported at its ends and loaded uniformly.*

Supposing the beam 20 feet long, as before, and the total load to be 10 tons. Hence the intensity of the load is $\frac{1}{24}$ ton, the unit of length being one inch.

Consider the case generally, and then substitute the particular values. (See fig. 6, Plate XLII.)

Let $2a =$ length of beam in inches;
,, $w =$ intensity of load.
Shearing stress at $X = wa - w(a - x) = F$
$\therefore F = wx.$

Hence $F$ is greatest at the points of support where it is equal to $wa$, and diminishes to zero at the extremities of the beam. For the bending moment at $X$, taking moments about that point,

$$\begin{aligned} M &= wa(a-x) - w(a-x)\tfrac{1}{2}(a-x) \\ &= wa^2 - wax - \tfrac{1}{2}w(a^2 - 2ax + x^2) \\ &= \frac{wa^2 - wx^2}{2} = \frac{w}{2}(a^2 - x^2) \\ &= \frac{w}{2}(a-x)(a+x). \end{aligned}$$

The greatest bending moment is at the middle;

for $M = \dfrac{w}{2}(a^2 - x^2)$ is a maximum when $x = 0$,

in that case $M = \dfrac{wa^2}{2} = \tfrac{1}{24} \times \tfrac{1}{2} \times 14400 = 300$ inch-tons,

which is one-half the maximum bending moment when the whole load is concentrated at the middle, as shown by Example 2 in this Article.

Without pursuing these investigations any farther, we will now state in a tabular form the values of $M$ and $F$ for beams under various conditions, as given by Professor Rankine.

**201. Beams fixed at One End only.**—$x$ is the distance of the section from the fixed extremity, $c$ is the length of the projecting part of the beam.

| Example. | Shearing Force F. | | Bending Moment M. | |
|---|---|---|---|---|
| | Anywhere F. | Greatest $F_0$. | Anywhere M. | Greatest $M_0$. |
| I. Loaded at extreme end with W | $-W$ | $-W$ | $-(c-x)W$ | $-cW$ |
| II. Uniform load of intensity $w$, ....... | $-w(c-x)$ | $-wc$ | $-\dfrac{w(c-x)^2}{2}$ | $-\dfrac{wc^2}{2}$ |
| III. Uniform load of intensity $w$, and additional load at the extreme end $W_1$,................. | $-W_1 - w(c-x)$ | $-W_1 - wc$ | $-W_1(c-x)$ $-\dfrac{w(c-x)^2}{2}$ | $-W_1 c - \dfrac{wc^2}{2}$ |

*N.B.*—The negative signs indicate downward forces and

distances measured to the right, while positive signs indicate upward forces and distances measured to the left.

**202. Beams supported at Both Ends.**—$2c$ being the total span and $x$ the distance of the section from the middle point $O$ of the beam:—

| Example. | Shearing Force F. | | Bending Moment M. | |
|---|---|---|---|---|
| | Anywhere F. | Greatest $F_1$ or $F_2$. | Anywhere M. | Greatest $M_0$ or $M_y$. |
| IV. Single load $W$ in middle, ........ Left of $O$, ..... Right of $O$, ... | $\dfrac{W}{2}$ $-W$ | $\dfrac{W}{2}$ $-\dfrac{W}{2}$ | $\left.\begin{array}{c}\\ \dfrac{(c-x)W}{2} \\ \end{array}\right\}$ | $\dfrac{cW}{2}=M_0$ |
| V. Single load $W$ applied at $x_2$, .... Left of $x_2$, ..... Right of $x_2$, ... | $\dfrac{(c+x_2)W}{2c}$ $-\dfrac{(c-x_2)W}{2c}$ | $\dfrac{(c+x_2)W}{2c}$ $-\dfrac{(c-x_2)W}{2c}$ | $\dfrac{(c+x_2)(c-x)W}{2c}$ $\dfrac{(c-x_2)(c+x)W}{2c}$ | $\left.\begin{array}{c}\dfrac{(c_2^2-x_2^2)W}{2c} \\ =M_2 \text{ at } x_2\end{array}\right\}$ |
| VI. Uniform load of Intensity $w$, .. | $wx$ | $wc$ | $\dfrac{w(c^2-x^2)}{2}$ | $\dfrac{wc^2}{2}=M_0$ |

**203. Bending Moment in terms of Load and Length.**—The maximum bending moment may be conveniently expressed in terms of the *total load* $W$ and *unsupported length* $l$ of a beam by means of a formula whose general form is—

$$M_0 = mWl$$

where $m$ is a numerical factor.

For beams fixed at one end $l=c$; and for beams supported at both ends $l=2c=$ the span; for a uniform load $W=wl$. We then have the following values of the factor $m$:—

    I. Beam fixed at one end and loaded at the other.............. 1
    II. Beam fixed at one end and loaded uniformly................ ½
    IV. Beam supported at both ends and loaded in the middle... ¼
    V. Beam supported at both ends, loaded at $x_2$ from the middle.............................................. $\left.\right\} \frac{1}{4}\left(1-\dfrac{4x_2^2}{l^2}\right)$
    VI. Beam supported at both ends, uniformly loaded............ ⅛

## 284  THEORETICAL NAVAL ARCHITECTURE.

**204. Resistance to Bending.**—The observed effect of a load upon a beam is a tendency to flexure or bending, the form of the curvature being governed by the form of the beam and the mode of loading it. If the beam is of uniform section, and is subjected to a uniform bending moment, not exceeding the limits of elasticity of the material, the curvature will closely approximate to that of an arc of a circle.

Referring to Plate XLIII., fig. 1 represents a portion of a beam, a section of which is shown by fig. 2. Under the influence of a bending moment the beam assumes the form shown by fig. 3.* In this state there is a tendency to rupture, at the upper part of the beam by an extensive stress, and at the lower part by a compressive stress. Consequently, between the upper and lower sides there must be some layer which is neither stretched nor compressed. This layer is called the *neutral surface*, and the line in which it cuts any transverse section of the beam is termed the *neutral axis* of that section. Let $NN$, fig. 1, $N_1N_1$, fig. 3, be that neutral surface, and $N_2N_2$, fig. 2, the neutral axis. In fig. 1, $ab$ and $cd$ are two transverse sections of the beam, and are thus parallel to each other. When the beam is bent, these sections stand in the directions $a_1b_1$ and $c_1d_1$, being still normal to the upper and lower edges of the beam. Produce $a_1b_1$ and $c_1d_1$ to meet at the point $O$, then $O$ is the centre of curvature of the beam. We will now show that the neutral axis $N_2N_2$, fig. 2, passes through the centre of gravity of the section.

Consider the stress on a layer $PP$ in fig. 1. When the beam is bent this layer assumes the form $P_1P_1$, and it cuts the section of the beam in the line $P_4P_2$. If $N_2N_2$ does not pass through the centre of gravity of the section, draw the horizontal line $Sx$ passing through that point; we have now to show that $SN_2 = 0$. The section being symmetrical, draw the middle line $Sy$, and consider it to be the axis of $y$, and the line $Sx$ to be the axis of $x$ for rectangular co-ordinates:—

$$\text{Let } SP_2 = y,$$
$$\text{and } SN_2 = \bar{y};$$
$$\therefore P_2N_2 = y + \bar{y} = P_1N_1.$$

* The curvature is purposely exaggerated in order that the figure may be clear.

## RESISTANCE TO BENDING.   285

Now, $N_1N_1$ being the neutral surface, therefore $P_1P_1 - N_1N_1$ is the extension of the layer $PP$.

Call $ON_1$ (the radius of curvature of the beam) $\rho$

Then $\dfrac{P_1P_1}{\rho + y + \bar{y}} = \dfrac{N_1N_1}{\rho} = \dfrac{P_1P_1 - N_1N_1}{y + \bar{y}}$.

Let $x =$ the extension of the layer PP per unit of length,
and $p =$ the intensity of the resistance of that layer to extension;
also $E =$ modulus of elasticity of the material composing the beam.
Then $p = Ex$.

But $P_1P_1 - N_1N_1$ is the actual extension;

$\therefore P_1P_1 - N_1N_1 = x N_1N_1 = xNN$.

Again, $\dfrac{N_1N_1}{\rho} = \dfrac{P_1P_1 - N_1N_1}{y + \bar{y}}$,

$\therefore \dfrac{1}{\rho} = \dfrac{x}{y + \bar{y}} = \dfrac{p}{E(y + \bar{y})}$,

and $p = \dfrac{E}{\rho}(y + \bar{y})$.

We have now to find the value of $y + \bar{y}$.

Now, the stress on a small element of the layer $P_2 P_4$

$= p\,dx\,dy;$

$p$ may be here either positive or negative, *i.e.*, either an extensive or a compressive stress.

At the neutral axis

$$\int\int p\,dx\,dy = 0;$$

$$\therefore \dfrac{E}{\rho}\int\int (y + \bar{y})\,dx\,dy = 0;$$

Hence, $\int\int (y + \bar{y})\,dx\,dy = 0,$

and since $y$ passes through the centre of gravity of the section

$$\therefore \int\int y\,dx\,dy = 0 \text{ also.}$$

Hence, $\int\int \bar{y}\,dx\,dy = 0;$

or, $\bar{y}\int\int dx\,dy = 0;$ $\bar{y}$ being a constant;

$\therefore \bar{y} = 0,$

which shows that $SN_2 = 0;$

and, therefore, the centre of gravity of the section is in the neutral axis.

$$\text{But } p = \frac{E}{\rho}(y + \bar{y}).$$

$$\therefore \quad p = \frac{E}{\rho} y$$

$$\text{or} \quad \frac{p}{y} = \frac{E}{\rho},$$

and this, as we have already explained, is independent of the sign of $p$, and is true, therefore, for layers above and below the neutral axis.

Again, the stress upon a small element of a layer $P_4P_5$, is as we have shown $pdxdy$, and its moment about the axis of $x$ through the centre of gravity of the section is

$$pydxdy.$$

Let $M_x = $ the whole moment of the layer about that axis,

$$\text{then} \quad M_x = \int\int pydxdy$$
$$= \frac{E}{\rho} \int\int y^2 dxdy$$

But $\int\int y^2 dxdy =$ moment of inertia of a transverse section of the beam about the axis of $x$.

Let this be termed I,

$$\therefore \quad M_x = \frac{EI}{\rho}.$$

Similarly,

$$M_y = \int\int pxdxdy$$
$$= \frac{E}{\rho} \int\int xydxdy.$$

But $\int\int xydxdy$ is the product of inertia of the section about the axis of $x$ and $y$.

Denote this by K,

$$\therefore \quad M_y = \frac{EK}{\rho}.$$

In fig. 4, let $SR$ represent graphically the moment of inertia

$M_x$, and $SL$ represent $M_y$; then $SK$ represents the direction and magnitude of the resultant moment.

Let $M$ = this resultant moment,

then $M = \sqrt{M_x^2 + M_y^2}$

$= \dfrac{E}{\rho} \sqrt{I^2 + K^2}$

Hence $\dfrac{p}{y} = \dfrac{M}{\sqrt{I^2 + K^2}} = \dfrac{E}{\rho}$

also $\tan \theta = \dfrac{K}{I}$ gives the direction of the resultant axis SK.

When the stress is perpendicular, or in the line of the axis of $y$, as is the usual case, then $K = 0$, or, in other words, there is no tendency to bend the beam other than in a vertical plane;

$$\therefore \dfrac{p}{y} = \dfrac{M}{I} = \dfrac{E}{\rho}.$$

The stress on any layer of a beam may be calculated when its bending moment and the dimensions and shape of the section are known by one of these equations, viz.:—

$$\dfrac{p}{y} = \dfrac{M}{I};$$

and by the other

$$\dfrac{p}{y} = \dfrac{E}{\rho},$$

we are able to determine the radius of curvature when the modulus of elasticity is also known.

**205. Specimen Calculations.**—I. Consider the case of a beam of rectangular section, as in fig. 7, Plate XLII., under the influence of a bending moment $M$, to find the stress on any particle $P$ distant $PN$ from the neutral axis.

Let $A$ = area of the section,

,, $h$ = its depth,

so that $\dfrac{A}{h}$ is the breadth.

Let $PN = y$,

then $I = \dfrac{Ah^2}{12}$. (See page 80.)

Now, since $\dfrac{p}{y} = \dfrac{M}{I}$;

$\therefore \dfrac{p}{y} = \dfrac{12M}{Ah^2}$;

$p = \dfrac{12My}{Ah^2}$ ....................(A)

Suppose $h = 6$ inches and $A = 12$ square inches, so that the beam is 2 inches thick; also, take $M$ at 12 foot-tons = 144 inch-tons, and consider the point $P$ at the upper side of the beam, and therefore $y = \dfrac{h}{2} = 3$.

$$\text{then } p = \frac{12 \times 144 \times 3}{12 \times 36} = 12 \text{ tons.}$$

which is the tensile stress per square inch at the upper side of the beam. The section being rectangular, and therefore symmetrical about the neutral axis, the compressive stress per square inch at the under side of the beam is also 12 tons. Equation (A) shows that the value of $p$ varies with the distance of $P$ from the neutral axis.

II. Find the minimum radius of curvature of a bar whose section is 2 inches square, the stress being restricted to 9000 lbs. per square inch, and $E = 24{,}000{,}000$.

$$\text{Here } p = 9000$$
$$y = 1$$
$$E = 24000000$$
$$\frac{p}{y} = \frac{E}{\rho};$$
$$\therefore 9000 = \frac{24000000}{\rho},$$

and $\rho = 2666\tfrac{2}{3}$ in. $= 222$ ft. $2\tfrac{2}{3}$ in.,

which is the radius of curvature of the beam.

N.B.—*In the preceding investigations it has been assumed that the beam is bent in the arc of a circle; this is true only when the transverse dimensions are small compared with the length. It is also true only in this case up to the limits of elasticity of the material, beyond this the assumption is merely approximate.*

III. What must be the diameter of a circular bar 10 feet long, supported at both ends, and loaded at the middle, to carry a load of $31\tfrac{1}{2}$ tons; the greatest stress not to exceed 4 tons per square inch?

In this case the greatest bending moment is—

$$M = \frac{31\frac{1}{2} \times 10}{4} \times 12 \quad \text{(see Art. 203.)}$$

Now $\dfrac{p}{y} = \dfrac{M}{I}$

$$\therefore \frac{4}{r} = \frac{\dfrac{31\frac{1}{2} \times 10 \times 12}{4}}{\dfrac{\pi r^4}{4}}$$

$$\therefore r_3 = \frac{3780}{4\pi} = 300$$

$$r = \sqrt[3]{300} = 6.7 \text{ inches.}$$

**206. Beam of I-shaped Section.**—In the preceding examples of the application of the formulæ for finding the intensities of the stresses on sections of beams when loaded, also for determing their radii of curvature, we have chosen simple cases wherein the value of I is readily computed. Such examples as the foregoing do not occur frequently in actual practice, for the simple reason that the material in them would not be economically distributed. For as the stress is greatest at the greatest distance from the neutral axis, and is nothing at that axis, it is evident that with a given quantity of material, we should so form the section of the beam as to provide the greatest resistance where the greatest stress will occur. Besides this, in order to ensure that the beam shall bend in the direction of the bending moment, and not buckle or twist in such a way as to impair its efficiency, it is desirable to so dispose the material as to give sufficient lateral stiffness, and place the stiffening parts where they will also afford resistance to the greatest tensile and compressive forces. Also should the material be such as to offer different resistances to tensile and compressive stresses, the parts of the beam should be so disposed as to make the intensities of these stresses, as nearly as possible, uniform. Hence the I-shaped section in one or other of its modifications is that generally adopted for beams. The vertical portion of the beam is termed the *web*, and the two horizontal parts are known as the upper and lower *flanges*. Sometimes the beam is rolled in one piece, or welded in the form shown; but when its depth is considerable, the beam is made of a plate web, and double angle-irons at the upper and lower edges. Beams of sufficient strength, and very convenient form for ships, are made thus (see fig. 13), with a

Fig. 13.

bulb-shaped lower edge; these are known as **T**-*bulb*, *plate-bulb* and *angle-iron*, and *angle-bulb* beams. The flanges are formed at the upper edges to receive the fastenings of the deck, and the bulb at the lower edge is found to be sufficient to provide the necessary lateral stiffness at that part, and at the same time give, with the flanges, enough substance to the beam to resist the extensive or compressive stresses to which it is subjected.

*Specimen calculation for I-shaped beam.*—1. Consider the case of a beam having the two flanges equal (see fig. 8, Plate XLII.).

Let $A$ = area of section of each flange,
 ,,  $C$ = area of section of web,
 ,,  $h$ = distance from centre to centre of flanges.

Since the flanges are equal, the neutral axis of the section is midway between them, or at a distance of $\frac{h}{2}$ from the centre of either.

Moment of inertia of upper flange about neutral axis $= \dfrac{Ah^2}{4}$

,, ,, lower ,, ,, $= \dfrac{Ah^2}{4}$

,, ,, web ,, ,, $= \dfrac{Ch^2}{12}$

$$\therefore I = \frac{Ah^2}{2} + \frac{Ch^2}{12}$$
$$= \frac{h^2}{2}\left(A + \frac{C}{6}\right)$$

But $\dfrac{p}{y} = \dfrac{M}{I}$

Let $f$ = the working intensity of stress for the material in the beam—

then $p = f$
and $y = \dfrac{h}{2}$;

$$\therefore M = I \frac{2f}{h}$$
$$= hf\left(A + \frac{C}{6}\right).$$

And by substituting the values of $h$, $f$, $A$, and $C$, in any particular case, the working bending moment can be obtained.

2. Consider the case in which the flanges are not equal (see fig. 9, Plate XLII.)—

Let $A$ = area of section of upper flange,
 ,, $B$ = ,, ,, lower ,,
 ,, $C$ = ,, ,, web

We must first find the position of the neutral axis—

Let $y_1$ = distance of neutral axis from centre of B,
 ,, $y_2$ = ,, ,, ,, A,
 ,, $h = y_1 + y_2$ = distance between centres of A and B.

Taking moments about the neutral axis—

$$\text{then } Ay_2 + C\left(\frac{h}{2} - y_1\right) = By_1,$$

$$\text{or } Ay_2 + C\left(\frac{y_2 - y_1}{2}\right) = By_1.$$

Let $y_2 : y_1 = K :: 1$

Then $B = KA + \tfrac{1}{2}(K-1)C$ ........................(1)

By the aid of this equation we are able to arrange the portions of the section so that the neutral axis may be in any required position; that position being governed by the relative compressive and extensive resistances offered by the material.

Next, let $f_B$ and $f_A$ be the intensities of the working stresses which the material is able to bear in the lower and upper flanges, respectively,

$$\text{then } \frac{f_A}{y_2} = \frac{f_B}{y_1}$$

$$\text{and } f_A = K f_B$$

$$\text{But } \frac{p}{y} = \frac{M}{I}$$

$$\therefore \frac{M}{I} = \frac{f_A}{y_2} = \frac{f_B}{y_1}$$

$$= \frac{f_B + f_A}{y_1 + y_2} = \frac{f_B + f_A}{h} = \frac{f_B(1+K)}{h}$$

$$\therefore M = f_B(1+K)\frac{I}{h} \quad \text{........................(2)}$$

292   THEORETICAL NAVAL ARCHITECTURE.

We have now to find the moment of inertia of a transverse section of the beam about the neutral axis. This is evidently

$$I = Ay_2^2 + By_1^2 + \frac{1}{12}Ch^3 + \frac{C}{4}(y_2 - y_1)^2$$

$$\therefore I = h^2 \left\{ \frac{K^2 A}{(1+K)^2} + \frac{B}{(1+K)^2} + \frac{C}{12} + \frac{C}{4}\left(\frac{K-1}{1+K}\right)^2 \right\}$$

Substituting the value of $B$ given in equation (1), and then substituting this value of $I$ in equation (2), we have after reduction

$$M = f_B h \{ AK + \tfrac{1}{6}(2K - 1)C \} \quad \ldots \ldots \ldots \ldots \ldots (3)$$

*Numerical examples.*—1. The web of an I-beam is of the same area as the smaller flange; what should be the proportion between the flanges, in order that the intensities of the stresses upon them may be as 4 : 1?

By equation (1)

$$B = KA + \tfrac{1}{6}(K - 1)C$$

in this case,

$$K = 4$$
$$C = A$$
$$\therefore B = 4A + \tfrac{3}{6}A = 5\tfrac{1}{2}A.$$

2. Find the dimensions of a **T** wrought-iron beam 20 feet long, and 10 inches deep to support a load of 2 tons at the middle; the working intensities of stress being 3 tons for compression and 5 tons for extension.

Here $K = \tfrac{5}{3}$,

also $M = \dfrac{Wl}{4} = \dfrac{2 \times 240}{4} = 120$ inch tons.

But by equation (3)—

$$M = f_B h \{ AK + \tfrac{1}{6}(2K - 1)C \}$$

In this case—

$$A = 0$$
$$f_B = 3$$
$$f_A = 5 \text{ and } h = 10;$$
$$\therefore 120 = 3 \times 10 \{ \tfrac{1}{6}(\tfrac{10}{3} - 1)C \}$$

whence $C = \tfrac{32}{3} = 10\tfrac{2}{3}$ sq. inches.

By equation (1)—

$$B = KA + \tfrac{1}{6}(K - 1)C$$
$$= \tfrac{1}{6}(\tfrac{5}{3} - 1)C$$
$$= \tfrac{1}{9}C = 3\tfrac{1}{2} \text{ sq. inches.}$$

3. Find the maximum load which a wrought-iron beam of I-shaped section will support when uniformly distributed; the length of the beam being 10 feet; the area of each flange being 6 square inches—that of the web 4 square inches, and the depth from centre to centre of flange being 6 inches.

Here $M = \dfrac{Wl}{8} = \dfrac{120W}{8}$ inch tons.

$$\dfrac{p}{y} = \dfrac{M}{I}.$$

$$I = \dfrac{Ah^2}{4} + \dfrac{Bh^2}{4} + \dfrac{ch^2}{12}$$

where $A = B = 6$ square inches,
$C = 4$ square inches,
$h = 6$ inches.

Hence $I = \dfrac{6 \times 36}{2} + \dfrac{4 \times 36}{12} = 108 + 12 = 120$

$$\therefore \dfrac{p}{y} = \dfrac{\dfrac{120W}{8}}{120} = \dfrac{W}{8}$$

the value of $p$ for wrought-iron is 36,000

$$\dfrac{36000}{3} = \dfrac{W}{8}$$

$\therefore W = 96,000$ pounds $= 43$ tons nearly.

4. Find the maximum load in the above case when the area of each flange is 3 square inches. *Ans.* 52,800 lbs.

**207. The Deflections of Beams.**—The expression $\dfrac{p}{y} = \dfrac{E}{\rho}$, whereby the deflection or curvature of a beam when loaded may be calculated has been already obtained; we will now show how this expression is applied. As previously stated, the expression is only true when the curvature of the beam is that of a circular arc, and is approximately true when the curvature is not quite circular.

Let *AB*, in fig. 1, Plate XLIV., *be the axis of a beam, which is supposed to be fixed at A and loaded at B with a weight W.* Under these circumstances the centre line, or locus of the neutral axis *AB* assumes the curvature shown by $AB_1$. Consider any point $P$ in $AB$, and draw $PN$ perpendicular to it.

Let A be the origin of co-ordinates.
,, $PN = y$
,, $AN = x$.

Since $\rho$ is the radius of curvature of the arc $AB_1$

$$\frac{1}{\rho} = \frac{\frac{d^2y}{dx^2}}{\left\{1+\left(\frac{dy}{dx}\right)^2\right\}^{\frac{3}{2}}}$$

Now if $\rho$ be very great, as it usually is, then the inclination of the tangent to the arc is very small; hence $\frac{dy}{dx} = 0$.

and $\frac{1}{\rho} = \frac{d^2y}{dx^2}$.

But $\frac{p}{y} = \frac{M}{I} = \frac{E}{\rho}$,

$\therefore \frac{1}{\rho} = \frac{M}{E.I}$;

hence $\frac{d^2y}{dx^2} = \frac{M}{E.I}$

Now at the point $P$

$M = W \times BN$
$= W(a-x)$

where $a = AB$

$\therefore \frac{d^2y}{dx^2} = \frac{1}{\rho} = \frac{M}{E.I} = \frac{W(a-x)}{E.I}$

Integrating, we have

$$\frac{dy}{dx} = \frac{W\left(ax - \frac{x^2}{2}\right)}{E.I}$$

There is no constant in the integration; for when $x = o$ $\frac{dy}{dx} = o$. Making $x = a$, and calling $\frac{dy}{dx} = \tan i = i$ in the limit, where $i$ represents the deflection of the beam, we have

$$\tan i = \frac{Wa^2}{2E.I}$$

Hence the inclination or deflection varies as $a^2$, or as the square of the distance of the point $P$ from $A$. For the actual depression of the beam at any point, integrating again

$$y = \frac{W(\tfrac{1}{2}ax^2 - \tfrac{1}{6}x^3)}{E.I}$$

Again there is no constant, as the curve passes through the origin as before.

Making $x = a$ we have for the depression at the loaded extremity of the beam

$$y = \frac{Wa^3}{3E.I}$$

which varies as the cube of the distance from $B$ to $A$.

*Next, suppose the beam to be loaded uniformly and supported at its ends*, as in fig. 2, Plate XLIV. The same equations hold, and the origin is now at the centre of the beam.

Hence $\dfrac{d^2y}{dx^2} = \dfrac{M}{E.I}$.

But in this case

$M = \tfrac{1}{2}w(a^2 - x^2)$, where $w$ is the intensity of the load;

$$\therefore \frac{d^2y}{dx^2} = \frac{\tfrac{1}{2}w(a^2 - x^2)}{E.I}.$$

Integrating—

$$\frac{dy}{dx} = \frac{\tfrac{1}{2}w\left(a^2 x - \dfrac{x^3}{3}\right)}{E.I}$$

which gives the slope of the beam at any point.

When $x = a$, $\quad \dfrac{dy}{dx} = \dfrac{wa^3}{3E.I}$.

The second integration gives

$$y = \frac{\tfrac{1}{2}w\left(\dfrac{a^2 x^2}{2} - \dfrac{x^4}{12}\right)}{E.I}$$

When $x = a$

$$y = \frac{5wa^4}{24E.I}$$

*Next suppose the beam fixed at both ends, and loaded uniformly*, as in fig. 3, Plate XLIV. In this case there are two points of contrary flexure in the beam as at $C, C$. At these points $\rho = \infty$ hence $M = 0$, and the condition of the middle of the beam is the same as if the beam were supported at the points $CC$. Take $O$, the centre of the beam, as the origin. Let $OC = r$. Then the bending moment at the point $C$ is

$$M = \tfrac{1}{2}w(r^2 - x^2).$$

To find the deflection of the beam we must substitute this value in the equation

$$\frac{d^2y}{dx^2} = \frac{M}{E.I}$$

and integrate as before.

Thus
$$\frac{dy}{dx} = \frac{\tfrac{1}{2}w\left(r^2x - \dfrac{x^3}{3}\right)}{E.I}$$

and when $x = r$
$$\frac{dy}{dx} = \frac{wr^3}{3E.I}.$$

But $r$ is an unknown quantity.

Now, when $x = a$, or when the point is at the extremity of the beam

$$\text{then } \frac{dy}{dx} = 0$$

for the beam is horizontal at $A$ and $B$.

$$\text{But } \frac{dy}{dx} = \frac{\tfrac{1}{2}w\left(r^2x - \dfrac{x^3}{3}\right)}{E.I}$$

$$= \frac{\tfrac{1}{2}w\left(r^2a - \dfrac{a^3}{3}\right)}{E.I} = 0$$

$$\therefore 3r^2 = a^2$$

$$r = \frac{a}{\sqrt{3}}$$

But $M = \tfrac{1}{2}w(r^2 - x^2)$

$$= \tfrac{1}{2}w\left(\frac{a^2}{3} - x^2\right)$$

Proceeding by the same process as before we are able to obtain both the depression and the deflection; for

$$\frac{d^2y}{dx^2} = \frac{M}{E.I} = \frac{\frac{1}{2}w\left(\frac{a^2}{3} - x^2\right)}{E.I}$$

$$\therefore \frac{dy}{dx} = \frac{\frac{1}{2}w\left(\frac{a^2x}{3} - \frac{x^3}{3}\right)}{E.I}$$

when $x = a$ or $x = 0$ } then $\frac{dy}{dx} = $ { 0 as before, the beam being horizontal at A, B, and O.

when $x = \frac{a}{2}$ then $\frac{dy}{dx} = \frac{wa^3}{8E.I} = $ { the tangent of the inclination at $\frac{1}{4}$ the length of the beam.

when $x = \frac{a}{\sqrt{3}}$ then $\frac{dy}{dx} = \frac{w}{9} \frac{a^3}{\sqrt{3} E.I} = $ { the tangent of the inclination at the points C, C.

Again, since

$$\frac{dy}{dx} = \frac{\frac{1}{2}w\left(\frac{a^2x}{3} - \frac{x^3}{3}\right)}{E.I}$$

$$\therefore y = \frac{\frac{1}{2}w\left(\frac{a^2x^2}{6} - \frac{x^4}{12}\right)}{E.I}$$

When $x = a$

$$y = \frac{wa^4}{12E.I}$$

208. EXAMPLE 1.—Find the deflection of a wrought-iron bar whose section is one inch square, and whose length is 10 feet, when under its own weight; the weight of wrought-iron being 480 lbs. per cubic foot, and the modulus of elasticity 29,000,000; the bar being supported at its ends. (See fig. 2, Plate XLIV.)

$$M = \tfrac{1}{2}w(a^2 - x^2)$$
$$\frac{d^2y}{dx^2} = \frac{M}{E.I}$$
$$\tan i = \frac{dy}{dx} = \frac{\frac{1}{2}w\left(a^2x - \frac{x^3}{3}\right)}{E.I}$$
$$y = \frac{\frac{1}{2}w\left(\frac{a^2x^2}{2} - \frac{x^4}{12}\right)}{E.I}$$

when $x = a$

$$y = \frac{5wa^4}{24E.I}$$

In the foregoing,
$$y = PN$$
$$x = ON$$
$$a = OB = 60 \text{ inches}$$
$w =$ the weight of 1 cubic inch of iron $= \dfrac{480}{1728} = \dfrac{5}{18}$ lbs.

$$E = 29,000,000 \text{ lbs.}$$
$$I = \tfrac{1}{12}$$
$$y = \frac{5 \times \tfrac{5}{18} \times 12,960,000}{24 \times 29,000,000 \times \tfrac{1}{12}} = \cdot 31,$$

which is the deflection when $P$ is at $B$, that is, the greatest deflection of the beam.

For the inclination of the beam, substitute $a = 60$ inches in the equation for $\tan i$,

$$\text{then } \tan i = \frac{wa^3}{3E.I}$$

$$= \frac{\tfrac{5}{18} \times 216,000}{3 \times 29,000,000 \times \tfrac{1}{12}} = \cdot 008 = \text{tangent of the inclination of the beam at } A \text{ or } B \text{ to be horizontal.}$$

Having solved the problem, we will briefly notice one or two particulars of interest with reference to the question—

The deflection is $\dfrac{5wa^4}{24E.I}$.

Now $\dfrac{p}{y} = \dfrac{M}{I} = \dfrac{\tfrac{1}{2}wa^2}{I}$ in this case.

Let the greatest stress in a section of this beam be termed $f$; and for $y$ write $gh$; where $g$ is a certain fraction (for instance $g = \tfrac{1}{2}$ in a beam of symmetrical section), and $h =$ depth of the beam,

$$\text{then } \frac{p}{y} = \frac{f}{gh} = \frac{\tfrac{1}{2}wa^2}{I}$$

$$\therefore w = \frac{2If}{a^2 gh}.$$

But deflection $= \dfrac{5wa^4}{24E.I}$,

or, say, $d = \dfrac{5a^2 f}{12gh.E}$

$$\frac{d}{a} = \frac{5f}{12gE} \cdot \frac{a}{h}.$$

Now $f$, $g$, and $E$ are given quantities for any beam. It is thus seen that beams having a given ratio of deflection to span have also a corresponding ratio of depth to span, and *vice versa*. Hence in designing a beam for a uniform load, as in this case, we should choose such a ratio of depth to span as would give the necessary stiffness.

EXAMPLE 2.—A bar of cast-iron whose section is 1 inch square, and which is 54 inches long, is loaded in the middle with a weight of 336 lbs., the deflection was found to be 1·27 inches; find the modulus of elasticity of the bar.

Here $M = \tfrac{1}{2}W(a-x)$

$$\frac{d^2y}{dx^2} = \frac{M}{E.I} = \frac{\tfrac{1}{2}W(a-x)}{E.I}$$

$$\frac{dy}{dx} = \frac{\tfrac{1}{2}W\left(ax - \dfrac{x^2}{2}\right)}{E.I}$$

$$y = \frac{\tfrac{1}{2}W\left(\dfrac{ax^2}{2} - \dfrac{x^3}{6}\right)}{E.I}$$

when $x = a$ $\quad y = \dfrac{Wa^3}{6E.I} = y_1$

But $y_1 = 1\cdot 27$;

also $W = 336$,

and $I = \tfrac{1}{12}$,

$$\therefore \; 1\cdot 27 = \frac{336 \times 27^3}{6 \times \tfrac{1}{12} E} = \frac{336 \times 27^3}{\tfrac{1}{2} E}$$

$$E = \frac{672 \times 27^3}{1\cdot 27} = 10,414,944 \text{ lbs.}$$

By actual experiment in the above case it was found that the breaking load of the bar was 508 lbs., hence the trial load was two-thirds of the breaking load. This accounts for the low value of the modulus, the average value for cast-iron being 17,000,000. It ought not to have been tried beyond a load of 100 lbs., and then the modulus would have been much greater.

**209. Strength of Bent Pillars.**—The cases we are about to consider are such as davits, catheads, etc., which are subjected to a compound stress resulting from a compressive force and a bending moment.

1. Take the case of a bar bent into two arms at right angles to each other, one of which is fixed upright, and the other is therefore horizontal, the latter supporting a weight at its extremity (see fig. 4, Plate XLIV.).

Let $A$ be the area of a section of the upright bar at $P$, and let $b$ be the length of the horizontal arm, $W$ being the weight at its extremity.

The intensity $p$ of the compressive force at $P$ is

$$p = \frac{W}{A},$$

and the bending moment is

$$M = Wb.$$

This bending moment produces a stress whose intensity

$$p = \frac{My}{I} = \frac{Wby}{I}$$

at any point distant $y$ from the neutral axis of the section.

Thus the total effect of the load is the sum of these individual effects, and the actual intensity of the stress is

$$p = \frac{W}{A} + \frac{Wby}{I},$$

and the dimensions of the post are made such that $p$ shall not exceed a given amount.

If we consider the bending moment constant, the bar will be bent into an arc of a circle (see fig. 5, Plate XLIV.). Draw through the point $P$, $NPK$ perpendicular to $AN$. Then

$$M = W \cdot PK$$

when $PN$ is very small compared with $PK$, or when $PK$ is nearly equal to $B_1 C_1$.

When compression and bending are combined with extension,

$$p = \frac{H}{A} \pm \frac{My}{I};$$

where $H$ is the thrust on the pillar, and $M$ is the bending moment, either compressive or extensive, at the point considered.

Suppose the upright post to have a square section whose side is $h$, then

$$p = \frac{W}{A} + \frac{My}{I}$$
$$= \frac{W}{h^2} + \frac{Wb\frac{1}{2}h}{\frac{1}{12}h^4}$$
$$= \frac{W}{h^2}\left(1 + \frac{6b}{h}\right);$$

hence $W = \dfrac{ph^2}{1 + \dfrac{6b}{h}}$

from which equation, if $p$ is given, and $h$ and $b$ known, the load $W$ can be determined.

Next, for the stress at any point in the transverse section of bent bar (see fig. 6, Plate XLIV.),

$$p = \frac{H}{A} \pm \frac{My}{I}.$$

Now $H = W \sin \theta$;

$$\therefore p = \frac{W \sin \theta}{A} \pm \frac{My}{I},$$

from which $p$ is found by substitution, as before. When the stress is calculated for the compressed side of the bar, the positive sign is used, and *vice versa*.

**210. Twisting Moments.**—Moments of this kind have to be resisted by rudder heads, crank shafts, etc.

"The *twisting moment*, or moment of torsion, applied to a bar, is the moment of a pair of equal and opposite couples applied to two cross sections of the bar, in planes perpendicular to the axis of the bar, and tending to make the portion of the bar between the cross sections rotate in opposite directions about that axis." [*]

As the bar is uniform in figure, and the twisting moment is likewise uniform, the stresses on all cross sections of the bar are the same; also, if the bar is a circular cylinder, the stresses on all the particles at the same distance from the axis of the bar are the same.

In the bar shown by fig. 7, Plate XLIV. (where the two opposite couples are shown), suppose $C$ to be one side of a circular layer of an infinitely small thickness $dx$. The twisting moment causes the material in one face of the layer to be

[*] *Rankine's Applied Mechanics*, p. 353.

twisted through a small angle compared with the material in the other face. Let $di$ be this angle. Consider two particles, one on each surface, at the same distance $r$ from the axis of the cylinder, which points were originally opposite to each other; then the twisting moment causes them to be shifted from each other through a distance $r.di$. Hence the material in the layer between these two points is in a state of distortion in a plane perpendicular to the radius $r$.

This distortion may be expressed thus—

$$S = r.\frac{di}{dx},$$

and $S$ varies proportionally to the distance of the particle from the axis. There is thus a shearing stress at each point of the cross section at $C$, whose direction is perpendicular to the radius, and whose intensity is proportional to the distance of the point from the axis.

Let $q =$ this shearing stress,

$$q = Er.\frac{di}{dx}.\ *$$

*To determine the strength* of such a bar or axle let $p =$ the intensity of the shearing stress which the material of the bar is able to resist. This value may be either the *ultimate resistance, proof resistance*, or *working resistance*, according as the bar is to broken, tested, or used for working.

Let $r_1 =$ the external radius of the bar, then $p$ is the value of $q$ at the distance $r_1$ from the axis; or

$$\frac{p}{q} = \frac{r_1}{r}$$

$$q = \frac{pr}{r_1}.$$

Conceive the cross section $C$ to be divided into narrow concentric rings, the breadth of each being $dr$. Let $r$ be the *mean radius* of one of these rings, then its area $= 2\pi r dr$. The shearing stress is equal to

$$\frac{2\pi p r^2 dr}{r_1},$$

---

* E is the co-efficient of transverse elasticity; its value for wrought-iron is about 9,000,000 lbs. per square inch, while for cast-iron it is about 2,800,000 lbs., and for brass about 5,300,000 lbs.

and the leverage of this stress relatively to the axis of the cylinder is $r$. Hence the moment of the stress in this ring is equal to
$$\frac{2\pi p r^3 dr}{r_1},$$
and the moment of the stress on the whole section
$$M = \frac{2\pi p}{r_1} \int_0^{r_1} r^3 dr$$
$$= \frac{\pi p r_1^3}{2} = \text{moment of torsion.}$$

If the bar or axle is hollow, $r_0$ being the radius of the hollow, the integration will be between the limits
$$r = r_0 \text{ and } r = r_1;$$
$$\text{then } M = \frac{\pi p (r_1^4 - r_0^4)}{2 r_1}.$$

Substituting the value of $\pi$, and expressing the dimensions in terms of the diameters $d_0$ and $d_1$—

For a *solid* axle $M = \dfrac{p d_1^3}{5 \cdot 1}$.

For a *hollow* axle $M = \dfrac{p(d_1^4 - d_0^4)}{5 \cdot 1 d_1}$.

The following are working values of $p$:—

For cast-iron, ............... 5000 lbs. per square inch.
For wrought-iron, .........9000 lbs. ,, ,,

# CHAPTER VIII.

## STRUCTURAL STRENGTH.

STILL WATER STRESSES—Curve of Buoyancy—Of Weight of Hull—Of Lading—Of Weights—Of Loads—Of Shearing Stresses—Of Bending Moments—STRESSES AMONG WAVES—Curve of Buoyancy—Of Shearing Stresses and Bending Moments—Table of certain Maximum Bending Moments and Shearing Stresses—Application of preceding Results—Neutral Axis of a Ship—Equivalent Girder—Moment of Inertia of a Section—Specimen Calculation—Mr. John's Investigations.

**211. Structural Strength of Ships.**—Having considered the conditions of stress and strain of the several components of a ship's hull, we will now devote our attention to the ship as a whole, and examine the nature of the stresses to which she is subjected both in still water and when among waves of her own length. In each case we assume the ship to be floating in a state of equilibrium, so that the volume of displacement represents a weight of water equal to that of the ship.

**212. Still Water Stresses.**—Commencing, then, with the stresses which a ship has to resist when floating in still water. It will be readily seen that, although the weight of water displaced is equal to that of the ship and her contents, it by no means follows that this equality exists, in regard to the portion of the displacement and of the ship between any two transverse sections. Indeed, the contrary is the case; for at amidships the weight of water displaced by a given length of the ship is usually considerably in excess of the weights of that portion of the vessel and her contents. Consequently, at the extremities the weight of a certain length exceeds the displacement of that length. Between the part or parts of the vessel in which there is excess of buoyancy over weight, and the part or parts in which the weight exceeds the buoyancy, there are evidently sections of the ship at which the two are equal, and these are termed water-borne sections. It will thus be seen that a ship having two such water-borne sections, viz., one at each extremity of a certain length of the midship body, is in the condition of a beam supported at two points and subjected to vertical forces, those between the points being upward, and those on the other side of the points being downward. We have thus to consider a ship in the character of a beam loaded and supported in different ways, according to the form of the vessel and the arrangement of her stowage, or nature of her construction. We shall neglect all local considerations, and regard the materials of the ship as being combined in a proper manner, considering only the arrangement of the material and the scantlings employed, in order to discover whether these are sufficient to withstand the stresses whose intensities we shall calculate.

In Vols. I. and II. of *Naval Science* \* will be found the results of calculations of this kind, made upon certain of Her Majesty's ships selected as types of classes. These were calculated at the Admiralty; and having been published by Mr. Reed, after having been read before the Royal Society, we are enabled to refer to them in this work.

The resultant forces acting upon the vessel are the differences of two sets; one of which—the forces due to the buoyancy of the ship—acts upwards, and the other, due to the weight of the vessel, her engines, and lading, acts downwards. The differences of these forces are at some parts of the ship's length positive, *i.e.*, the downward forces are in excess; and at other parts the differences are negative, *i.e.*, the upward forces predominate. Again, at the water-borne sections the two are equal, as already mentioned.

The geometrical method, or method by curves, as explained in Articles 197, *et seq.*, of the last chapter, is adopted in these calculations.

**213. Curve of Buoyancy.**—This is the first and the most readily obtained curve. The ship's length is divided into intervals about 20 feet apart, and the areas of the cross sections of these, as high as the load water-line, are calculated. These areas may be readily obtained from the ordinary dis-

\* Edited by E. J. Reed, C.B., and Dr. Woolley.

placement sheet, taking the sections at the ordinates used in that calculation. Considering these sections as the sides of slices 1 foot in thickness, the displacement of each slice is at once obtained in tons by dividing its area by 35. These results are set up to scale as ordinates, to a base line representing the length of the ship on a convenient scale, say one quarter of an inch to a foot, and at the positions of the respective sections. A curve passed through the extremities of these ordinates is the *curve of buoyancy*. Such curves are denoted by the letters *DD*, etc., in figs. 1, 2, 3, and 4, Plate XLV., which show the curves of buoyancy for H.M. ships *Minotaur*, *Victoria and Albert*, *Bellerophon*, and *Audacious*. It is hardly necessary to say that the areas of these curves, allowing for the scale of the drawing, is the displacement of the ship. In other words, the curve of buoyancy is a curve of sectional areas, or a scale of displacement constructed from vertical instead of horizontal areas. (See Art. 38.)

214. **Curve of Weight of Hull.**—We next construct a *curve of weight of hull*. This is obtained by aid of the calculation explained at Art. 124. The weights of frame space lengths of the hull, at intervals of about the same distance apart as those used for the curve of buoyancy, are obtained, including the frames, beams, proportion of carlings, a frame space length of bottom plating, deck plating, stringers, deck flats, bulkheads, internal fittings, etc. These results are set up as ordinates on the same scale as the displacement ordinates, and from a base line of the same length as before. When armour is used in the construction of the ship in the form of batteries or bulkheads, it is necessary to set off the weights of the latter in the form of rectangles whose bases are equal to scale, to the lengths of the ship upon which the armour is placed, taking care to place them in their correct positions. It will frequently be impossible to pass a continuous curve through the extremities of the ordinates of the hull and the upper sides of these rectangles, in which case the curve must pass so as to include areas outside the rectangles equal to the areas lost by the curve being within the rectangles; taking care that the moments of the area of the curve about the base line and any ordinate are, respectively, the same as the moments of the curve of the hull proper

added to those of the rectangles about the base and that ordinate. (See the curves of weights of hull of the *Bellerophon* and *Audacious*, marked by the letters $H, H$, etc., in figs. 3 and 4 of Plate XLV.) The points, $PP$, and the curve in the vicinity of these points, indicate what we mean by the preceding explanation, it being remembered that there are armour-plated bulkheads and central batteries at those positions in the two ships. As there are usually greater discontinuities in the weights of the equipment and lading than in the weight of hull, and as the two curves of hull and contents are added together to obtain the *curve of weights*, it is desirable not to draw a curve such as $H H$, but add the ordinates and rectangles representing the hull to the ordinates and rectangles representing the weights of the equipment, etc., and then draw a curve in the manner already explained, which will be the *curve of weights*. (See Art. 216.)

**215. Curve of Lading.**—The weights of equipment, etc., carried by a ship, are very irregularly distributed as regards their intensity, and it is therefore impossible to consider the ship divided into blocks of a fixed length in determining a curve which shall represent in effect the distribution of these weights. Sometimes, as in the case of coal in a coal bunker, we have a heavy load occupying a length of about 100 feet; and again we have another heavy weight, as the chain cable in a locker, resting upon a very small length of the vessel. Hence, before constructing a *curve of lading* or *curve of equipment*, we must build upon the base line a series of rectangles, often one upon another, representing to scale the several weights carried in the ship in the form of engines, boilers, coals, stores, etc., and with bases equal to the lengths of the ship which they severally occupy, all being in their accurate position longitudinally. As already stated, it is desirable to add to these the ordinates representing, to the same scale, the weight of hull, and then draw a curve to represent the same statical effect as the diagram thus produced. The same method is adopted in drawing the curve as was described in the last Article. Great care must be taken to insure that the area of the space inclosed by the curve is the same as that of the space bounded by the limiting lines of the rectangles; also that the moments of the two are alike, both about any ordinate and about the base line.

**216. Curve of Weights.**—The curve just produced is termed the *curve of weights*, and its area is equal to the total weight of ship and contents, and therefore equal to the area of the curve of buoyancy. An ordinate of this curve, at any position in the length of the base, represents to scale the weight of a foot long of the hull and contents at that part of the vessel. These curves are marked $WW$, etc., in figs. 1, 2, 3, and 4 of Plate XLV. It will be noticed that these curves are drawn on the same side of the base as the curve of buoyancy, although the forces act in opposite directions. This is of no moment at present, and is merely done to show that the area of the curved space bounded by $DD$, etc., is equal to that bounded by $WW$, etc. Moreover, it should be remarked that, as each of the vessels is floating in equilibrium, the centres of gravity of these two curves for each ship will be on the same ordinate.

**217. Curve of Loads.**—This curve shows the total resultant force acting upon the vessel, the ordinate of it at any point in the length being, to scale, equal to the load per foot in length of the ship at that point, and its direction shows the character of the load, *i.e.*, whether upward or downward. The curve is obtained in the following manner:—The difference between the ordinate of the curve of buoyancy and that of the curve of weights at any point in the length of the vessel is set off as an ordinate of the curve of loads; if the ordinate of the curve of buoyancy is in excess, then the ordinate is measured upward, and *vice versa*. Figs. 1, 2, 3, and 4, Plate XLVI., show the curves of loads, marked $LLL$, etc., of the *Minotaur*, *Victoria and Albert*, *Bellerophon*, and *Audacious*. In the case of the second-named vessel (see fig. 2) this curve, commencing at the bow $A$, is below the axis $AB$, showing that the weights at that portion of the vessel are in excess of the buoyancy. The curve crosses the axis at $R_1$, where there is a waterborne section, and thus no load. Between $R_1$ and $R_2$ the curve is above the axis, showing that the buoyancy is there in excess of the weights; at $R_2$ there is another waterborne section. It will be observed that the curve of loads crosses the axis four times in all. The same remarks hold good with regard to figs. 3 and 4, but the curve of loads in the *Minotaur* (fig. 1) only crosses the axis twice.

As the ships are all floating in equilibrium, the sum of the upward forces is equal to that of the downward forces; hence the total area inclosed by the several loops of the curve of loads above the line $AB$ is equal to the total area of the loops below that line. Again, the common centre of gravity of all the loops is in the same ordinate as contains the centre of gravity and centre of buoyancy of the ship. The effect of the armoured bulkheads and battery of the *Audacious* is clearly shown in the curve of loads of that vessel (fig. 4) by the form of the centre loop below the axis, which indicates heavy weights centred at two points.

**218. Curve of Shearing Stresses.**—(See $VVV$, etc., figs. 1, 2, 3, and 4, Plate XLVI.) The curve of loads just described shows the manner in which the ship, considered as a beam, is loaded and supported. In figs. 2, 3, and 4 we have four points of support, and in fig. 1 we see two points of support. Starting, then, with the beam loaded in the manner shown by such a curve, we will proceed to construct a curve, the ordinate of which, at any point, shall be a measure of the shearing stress at that point, and shall also show the relative direction of that stress.

As was shown in Art. 193, the maximum intensities of the shearing stress are always found at the points of support. Also, in the same Art., it was shown that the shearing stress on any division of a beam so loaded is the resultant of the forces acting upon the beam between that division and either extremity. It was also explained that this shearing stress is the algebraical sum of all the forces acting upon the beam between that point and either extremity, the forces being distinguished as positive or negative according to their direction. Hence, to construct the *curve of shearing stresses* in any specific case, we proceed as follows:—Referring to the case of the *Minotaur* (fig. 1, Plate XLVI.), and commencing at the bow $A$; for the length of the ordinate of the curve at any point between $A$ and $R_1$ we find the area of the curve between the ordinate and the point $A$, and set off this area, to scale, upon the ordinate, which then represents the magnitude of the shearing stress at that point. In fig. 1 the ordinates are drawn below the axis at this end of the ship, consequently, after passing the point of reverse racking, the ordinates will be measured above the line. This is a matter of no importance, it being necessary only that the ordinates should have the correct *relative* sign. Still referring to fig. 1, it will be seen that the first point of maximum shearing stress is at the ordinate $R_1R_1$, through $R_1$, which represents to scale the area of the loop $ALR_1$, of the curve of loads. As the latter curve changes sign at the point $R_1$, the areas on the left of that point inclosed between it and any ordinate must be deducted from the area $R_1LA$, and then we arrive at $a$, the point of reverse racking. On the left of $a$ we can start afresh; and, to determine the shearing stress at any point between $a$ and $R$, we have simply to find the area of the curve of loads inclosed by an ordinate through the point and the point $a$, observing that this ordinate will be set off above $AB$. At $R_2$ we reach a second point of maximum shearing stress, and from thence the areas between any ordinate and $R_2$ must be deducted from the area between an ordinate of the curve of loads at $a$ and the point $R_2$, for the shearing stress at the point in question: this deduction is continued until at length the shearing stress becomes zero at $B$.

From the preceding it will be seen that the area of the curve of loads between $A$ and $R_1$ is equal to that between $R_1$ and $a$; also that the area between $R_2$ and $B$ is equal to the area between $R_2$ and $a$.

In the *Victoria and Albert*, *Bellerophon*, and *Audacious* (see figs. 2, 3, and 4, Plate XLVI.), there are four points of maximum shearing stress ($R_1$, $R_2$, $R_3$, and $R_4$), two positive ($R_2$ and $R_4$), and two negative ($R_1$ and $R_3$); hence there are three points of reverse racking, $a$, $b$, and $c$. It is perhaps unnecessary to point out that there must in any case be an odd number of points of reverse racking and an even number of points of maximum shearing stress, half of which will be of opposite sign to the other half.

In finding the areas of these curves the geometrical mode of integration explained at Art. 42 is adopted. If the curve of loads is constructed with ordinates 20 feet apart, the curve of shearing stresses is constructed by means of ordinates placed midway between the others, and therefore also 20 feet apart. The scales adopted are any that will suit the convenience of the calculator; the scale of $AB$ in the figures is 3 inches = 200 feet, and the scale of the curve of loads is 3 square inches = 4000 tons, while the scale of the curve of shearing stresses is 1 inch = 400 tons.

**219. Curve of Bending Moments.**—The bending moment at any point in the length of a beam being the sum of all the shearing stresses between that point and either extremity, it follows that the ordinate of the *curve of bending moments* is determined from the curve of shearing stresses in the same way as the ordinate of the latter curve is obtained from the curve of loads. It is unnecessary to repeat the explanation of the mode of performing the process of geometrical integration; it will, however, be instructive to consider a specific case.

Again, referring to fig. 1, Plate XLVI., where $MM$ represents the curve of bending moments as integrated from the curve of shearing stresses $VVV$, it will be seen that, if we commence at $A$, the ordinates of the curve of bending moments continually get greater as they include more and more of the area of the loop $AR_1a$ of the curve of shearing stresses, until at length a maximum is attained at the ordinate $aa_1$\* through the point $a$. From thence repeated deductions are made, as more and more of the area of the loop $aR_2B$ is taken from the area of the loop $aR_1A_1$, until at length the ordinate at the point $B$ is zero.

In the cases of the vessel shown by fig. 2 of the same Plate, it will be noticed that the *curve of bending moments* crosses the axis, producing three points of maximum bending moment, two being above and the other below the axis, and one of the former in excess of the other. This shows that a portion of the ship near amidships is subjected to a sagging bending moment, and on either side of it the bending moment is a hogging one. Generally there is a hogging moment

---

\* Sections at points such as $a$ divide the ship in such a manner as to render each of the parts before and abaft it separately waterborne. These are termed "*sections of water-borne division;*" $b$ and $c$, figs. 2, 3, and 4, are similar sections.

throughout the vessel's length when she is floating in still water, and in this case it amounts to only 170 foot-tons, while the excess of weight over buoyancy amounts to 210 tons. In almost every case the moment of the downward forces is greater than that of the upward, and thus the tendency is to hog. This is due to the moment of the comparatively heavy extremities, which counteracts the excess of weight over buoyancy at intermediate places. For instance, in the *Audacious* the excess of weight over buoyancy amounts at one place to 265 tons, yet there is no sagging moment, but a hogging moment at that place of 3400 foot-tons.'

The scale of the curves of bending moments, in figs. 1, 2, 3, and 4 of Plate XLVI., is 1 inch = 16,000 foot-tons.

**220. Stresses when among Waves.**—Hitherto we have been considering the stresses upon a ship when she is floating at rest in still water; the results so obtained are useful inasmuch as they afford valuable data for comparing different vessels, especially since the work of obtaining them is of a comparatively simple character. It is, however, obvious that they do not furnish any information regarding the maximum shearing stress and bending moment which a ship may have to resist when performing an ocean voyage. Indeed, it is impossible by any calculation to predict the exact stresses which a ship may undergo during a voyage, inasmuch as the state of the sea is continually varying, so that she may encounter waves of all possible dimensions in a short space of time, and thus her curve of loads may assume a variety of forms. It is evident that there are two conditions in which the maximum stresses possible are exerted, viz., when she is on the crest and in the hollow of a wave of her own length, the stresses in each of these conditions being greater as the height of the wave is increased.

The result of observations made by Mr. Froude shows that the height of sea waves is usually about one-fifteenth to one-twentieth part of their length. A series of calculations have been made at the Admiralty, the results of which will be quoted presently, for the stresses upon ships of different lengths, in which the height of a wave 400 feet long is taken as 25 feet, and that of a wave 300 feet long is taken as 20 feet.

When the vessel is on the crest of a wave (see fig. 1, Plate

CURVES OF BUOYANCY WHEN AMONG WAVES. 313

XLVII.), it is evident that hogging strains are developed, and when in the hollow (see fig. 2, Plate XLVII.) that sagging strains are set up.

In these investigations it is assumed—

1st. That for the moment the ship's vertical motion may be neglected.

2nd. That for the moment the ship is in a position of hydrostatical equilibrium.

3rd. That the methods of calculating bending and shearing stresses, previously used for still water, may be employed here also, in order to approximate to the momentary stresses.

**221. Curves of Buoyancy when among Waves.**—To obtain these curves it is first necessary to draw the water-lines of the vessel in the two conditions, viz., on the crest and in the hollow of a wave of her own length. These water-lines will of course be the curve of the wave (see Art. 164).

We have to draw this curve in such a position on the ship as to cut off a volume of displacement equal to the weight of the vessel, and having its centre of buoyancy in the same longitudinal position as the centre of buoyancy of the displacement in still water. This is a tentative process; a first approximation to its position is made, and then, by a calculation and subsequent corrections, the exact position of the curve is found. An experienced calculator will approximate very closely to the accurate position, leaving but a small correction to be made after calculation.

Having the line drawn, the displacement per foot of length at equidistant sections is calculated, as in the still-water condition, and a curve of buoyancy constructed in the same way as before.

It will be observed that two such calculations must be made, one for the crest and the other for the hollow of the wave. Fig. 3 of Plate XLVII. shows the curves of buoyancy of the *Minotaur* when on the crest and in the hollow of a wave of her own length—400 feet and 25 feet high (see figs. 1 and 2). $FF'$ in fig. 3 is the curve of buoyancy when on the crest of the wave, and $GG$ is the curve when in the hollow. The scale of the curves is 3 square inches = 16,000 tons; also 3 inches along $AB$ is equal to 400 feet. $WW$ is the curve of weights, which is also drawn to the same scale. Fig. 4, Plate XLVII., and fig. 3, Plate XLVIII., show similar curves for the *Bellerophon* and *Victoria and Albert*, drawn upon the same scale as those of the *Minotaur*. These curves were calculated at the Admiralty, and have been published in *Naval Science*.

**222. Curves of Shearing Stresses and Bending Moments among Waves.**—Having the curves of weight and buoyancy, the construction of the curves of shearing stresses and bending moments is very simple, the methods being the same as was explained for still water. Fig. 1 of Plate XLVIII. shows these curves for the crest of the wave, and fig. 2 those for the hollow, in the case of the *Minotaur;* the scale of the diagram being one-half that of Plate XLVI., which shows the still-water curves. In these figures the scale of the curve of loads is 3 square inches = 8000 tons: 3 inches along $AB$ is equal to 400 feet. The scale of the curve of shearing stresses, $VV$, is 1 inch = 800 tons, and that of the curve of bending moments, $MM$, 1 inch = 32,000 foot-tons. It will be observed that when this vessel is on the crest of the wave there is a hogging moment at every point in her length, the maximum moment being at amidships; also, when she is in the hollow of the wave there is a sagging moment throughout the whole of her length, except a small portion right forward, where there is a slight hogging moment. The maximum sagging moment is also at amidships. The sagging moments are, however, much smaller than the hogging moments. The characters of the curves are very much the same in the other two vessels (see figs. 5 and 6, Plate XLVII., and figs. 4 and 5, Plate XLVIII.), but it will be observed that in the *Victoria and Albert* the sagging moments exceed the hogging, and in the *Bellerophon* they are about equal. It should be remarked that all these curves are drawn to the same scale.

The results shown by these diagrams are useful, inasmuch that they point out the relative magnitudes of the maximum hogging and sagging stresses in ships of types so distinct as are those of the vessels considered. The *Minotaur* is an instance of a long vessel heavily armoured throughout her entire length; the *Bellerophon* of a vessel armoured to a slight extent throughout, but especially so at amidships, where there is a heavy armour-plated battery, with guns, etc.; while the *Victoria and Albert* is a vessel of the character of a full-powered merchant steamer, with a light hull and heavy machinery, but not of such extreme proportions as ocean passenger steamers usually are. Thus the two first are useful in judging of the moments of stress to which war ships are subjected, while, as supplementary information to the third case, we give at Art. 229 other particulars regarding vessels of the mercantile marine.

The period of a wave 400 feet long and 25 feet high is rather less than 9 seconds of time; that is to say, such a wave travels a distance equal to its length in that time; hence the changes from the hogging to the sagging stresses occur at intervals of about $4\frac{1}{2}$ seconds. The period of a wave 300 feet long and 20 feet high is rather less than 8 seconds, so that the changes in stress occur at intervals of about 4 seconds.

**223. Table of Maximum Bending Moments and Shearing Stresses.**—The subjoined table of maximum bending moments and shearing stresses, determined from the *Minotaur, Bellerophon,* and *Victoria and Albert,* which are deduced from the curves already explained and other calculations, are published in Vol. II. of *Naval Science.* The moments are given in terms of the displacement of the vessel multiplied by her length, and the shearing stresses are in terms of the displacement. In this form they may be readily applied to determine the approximate values of the same for ships of the same types.

| Conditions. | Minotaur. | | Bellerophon. | | Victoria and Albert. | |
|---|---|---|---|---|---|---|
| | Shearing Stress. | Bending Moment. | Shearing Stress. | Bending Moment. | Shearing Stress. | Bending Moment. |
| | Displacement. | Displacement × length. | Displacement. | Displacement × length. | Displacement. | Displacement × length. |
| In still water, | $\frac{1}{2}$ | $\frac{1}{8}$ | $\frac{1}{3}$ | $\frac{1}{70}$ | $\frac{1}{5}$ | $\frac{1}{80}$ |
| On a wave crest, | $\frac{1}{4}$ | $\frac{1}{6}$ | $\frac{1}{3}$ | $\frac{1}{7}$ | $\frac{1}{5}$ | $\frac{1}{3}$ |
| In a wave hollow, | $\frac{1}{6}$ | $\frac{1}{3}$ | $\frac{1}{4}$ | $\frac{1}{3}$ | $\frac{1}{5}$ | $\frac{1}{3}$ |
| Supported at extremities | $\frac{1}{2}$ | $\frac{1}{7}$ | $\frac{1}{2}$ | $\frac{1}{4}$ | $\frac{1}{2}$ | $\frac{1}{4}$ |
| Supported at middle, | $\frac{1}{2}$ | $\frac{1}{8}$ | $\frac{1}{2}$ | $\frac{1}{8}$ | $\frac{2}{3}$ | $\frac{1}{8}$ |

The displacements of the *Minotaur*, *Bellerophon*, and *Victoria and Albert* are respectively about 9800, 7500, and 2300 tons.

Mr. W. John, of Lloyd's Register of British and Foreign Shipping, in a paper read by him before the Institution of Naval Architects in 1874, gave, as the result of calculations made by him upon the strength of merchant steamers, that the ordinary limit of maximum hogging moments is $D \times \frac{1}{35}$th length, and of maximum sagging moments $D \times \frac{1}{50}$th length. Up to the present time there have been so few calculations of this kind made upon merchant vessels that we are unable to provide further data.

**224. Application of the preceding Results.**—The information furnished by these curves is of no value unless we know the intensities of the stresses which they cause the various portions of the structure to endure; in the same way that it is of no use to know the principal bending moments on a loaded beam unless we know the form and dimensions of its section, as without the latter we are not aware whether the intensity of the principal stress is within the working limit of the material of which the beam is made. Considering the ship then as a beam or girder, the maximum bending moment to which it is subjected being known, we have next to find the tensile stress in tons per square inch on the material farthest from the neutral axis.

**225. Neutral Axis of a Ship.**—By taking moments about the water line or underside of keel, the vertical height of the centre of gravity of the material composing the midship section is soon found. The operation consists simply of multiplying the effective sectional area of each plate, angle-iron, etc. (disposed longitudinally and contributing to the longitudinal strength of the ship), by the distance of its centre of gravity from the axis about which moments are taken; the algebraical sum of these products, divided by the sum of the areas, gives the distance of the centre of gravity from that axis. If moments are taken about the underside of keel, all the products will be arithmetically added; but if about the load water-line, the algebraical sum, or the difference of the sums of the products above and below the axis will be divided by the sum of the areas. The direction in

EQUIVALENT GIRDER. 317

which the centre of gravity is set off from the axis will be determined by the sign of the algebraical sum.

We have stated that the effective sectional area of the plates, angle-irons, etc., is used. By this is meant that the weakest section of the ship is taken, and a deduction is made for the material removed in the rivet holes. As stated in the last chapter, the weakest section of a ship is through a line of frame rivets; and as the rivets in a water-tight or bulkhead frame are spaced closer than elsewhere, the section is taken at such a frame. It is true that the strength is partly made up by means of the wide liners already referred to; nevertheless, in order that the result may not err on the unsafe side, it is usual to choose a water-tight frame, on the supposition that the wide liners do not make it quite so strong as a section of the ship at the other frames. In order to get the effective sectional area, one-sixth of the total sectional area of the iron work is deducted where the work is water-tight, and one-eighth of the sectional area of deck plating and stringers when riveted to beams so as not to be water-tight. The effective strength of wood deck flats is also reckoned, three-eighths of the sectional area being deducted for butts and fastenings (viz., one-fourth for butts and one-eighth for fastenings), and then, to bring the remaining five-eighths to represent an equivalent strength of iron, one-sixth of the five-eighths, or five forty-eighths only, is reckoned of the total sectional area. Plate XLIX. shows a section of an iron ship with the neutral axis drawn through the centre of gravity of its effective sectional area.

226. **Equivalent Girder.**—The neutral axis is sometimes drawn in another way—by constructing a girder which shall represent the sectional area of the material of the ship's section, grouped symmetrically about the middle line of the section as a central axis. Plate L. shows the equivalent girder for an unarmoured ship of war. The materials in the two decks are represented by the two uppermost flanges, which are situated in the same positions as the decks. The upper deck is plated all over, and the lower one has merely a stringer. The web of the girder is made of the materials composing the sides and bottom, concentrated at the middle line, the block at the bottom being due to grouping the effec-

tive sectional areas of the bottom plates, keelson, side keelsons, etc., below the turn of the bilge. By taking moments about any part of this figure its centre of gravity is found to be at $G$; hence the horizontal line drawn through that point is the neutral axis. When the ship is subjected to hogging moments the portion of the section above the neutral axis is under tension, and the portion below under compression; and when it is subjected to sagging stresses the conditions are reversed.

It will be readily seen that, while the presence of rivets weakens a section as regards its resistance to extension, it is not so when the stress is a compressive one, as in that case, if the rivets fill the holes, they resist compression as much as the plate. Hence, supposing this girder to be subjected only to hogging moments, the lower part of it is smaller than the real equivalent, as in constructing it the same deductions were made for rivet holes as elsewhere. Similarly, if the moments are always of a sagging character, the upper part is smaller than the real equivalent. On this account some calculators have constructed two equivalent girders for a ship, one for hogging and the other for sagging moments. In the former case no deductions are made below where it is expected the neutral axis will come (and its position can be very closely approximated to, while, if a slight error be made in the guess, it does not much interfere with the result), and in the latter no deductions are made from the material above the assumed axis. There is, of course, a separate neutral axis for each case.

**227. Moment of Inertia of the Section.**—In order to obtain the intensity of the stress on any part of the section we apply the formula

$$\frac{p}{y} = \frac{M}{I};$$

hence we have to find the value of $I$, or the moment of inertia of the section about the neutral axis. The unit of area employed is a square inch, while distances are measured in feet.

For the moment of inertia of the section we may either calculate direct from the drawing (the usual method, as the girder is rarely constructed), or else calculate from the equivalent girder. If we calculate from the section of the vessel, the moments of inertia of the several parts are found by multiplying the sectional areas of plates, etc., disposed horizontally by the squares of their distances from the neutral axis, while the moment of inertia of a plate disposed vertically is found by multiplying the area of its section by the square of the distance of its centre of gravity from the neutral axis, and adding thereto one-twelfth the area × the square of its breadth. The sum of these results is the total moment of inertia of the section. A similar course is pursued if we calculate the moment of inertia from the equivalent girder, the work being simpler in the latter case when once the girder is constituted. Having the value of $I$ for the section, and the total bending moment known, the intensity of stress at any part of the section is readily found.

**228. Specimen Calculation.**—Suppose a certain vessel, when on the crest of a wave, is subjected to a hogging moment of 50,000 foot-tons, the moment of inertia of her effective section about the neutral axis is 150,000 (units of measurement as in the last Art.), find the tension in tons per square inch on the upper deck plating, which is 18 feet above the neutral axis.

$$\frac{p}{y} = \frac{M}{I},$$
$$p = \frac{My}{I} = \frac{50,000 \times 18}{150,000} = 6 \text{ tons}.$$

**229. Investigations by Mr. John.**—In the paper read by Mr. W. John, of Lloyd's Register, which we have already alluded to in this chapter, a list is given of results of calculations made upon a number of vessels of the mercantile marine, which shows that in such extreme conditions, as on the crest or in the hollow of waves of their own length, the maximum tension per square inch, on the upper works of some of these vessels, is far beyond that which has been hitherto considered desirable. The factor of safety for wrought-iron under tension is considered by many authorities to be 5, so that, allowing 20 tons to the square inch as the ultimate strength of the iron, the maximum tension on a wrought-iron structure should not exceed 4 tons per square inch. As will be seen by reference to the subjoined list of results, this tension is doubled in the cases of some very long ships now in existence, so that it appears either that the conditions which these figures refer to rarely occur, or else that such a high factor of safety as 5 is unnecessary.

| Tonnage of Vessel. | Maximum Tension on the Upper Works in tons per sq. in. | Tonnage of Vessel. | Maximum Tension on the Upper Works in tons per sq. in. |
|---|---|---|---|
| 100 | 1·67 | 800 | 4·59 |
| 200 | 2·36 | 900 | 4·80 |
| 300 | 3·09 | 1000 | 5·19 |
| 400 | 3·55 | 1500 | 5·34 |
| 500 | 3·95 | 2000 | 5·90 |
| 600 | 3·72 | 2500 | 7·08 |
| 700 | 4·57 | 3000 | 8·09 |

# PART IV.

## CALCULATIONS RELATING TO PROPULSION OF SHIPS BY SAILS.

### CHAPTER IX.

Masts—Yards—Sails—Rigs—Sailing—Real and Apparent Motion of the Wind—Effective Impulse of the Wind—Trim of Sails—Effect of the Position of Centre of Gravity (Longitudinally) on a Ship's Sailing Qualities—Centre of Effort—Speed under Sail—Stability under Sail—Steady Impulse and Small Inclination—Steady Impulse and any Inclination—Effect of a Gust of Wind.

**230. General Remarks.**—The only means of propelling a vessel, with which mankind was acquainted until within the last half century, consisted of either rowing by hand or being blown by the action of the wind. Even as recently as the fifteenth century the war vessels of many of the countries of Europe were propelled by rowers, who were seated on board the vessels upon one or more tiers of benches. The labour of continuous rowing was so great that prisoners were forced to perform the work; the name "galley slave," given to these unfortunate creatures, being familiar at the present day. With the rapid development of war ships during the reigns of the Tudors, it became necessary to devise arrangements of masts, rigging, and sails, suitable to propel these vessels; and at that time a style of rig came into use which, with a few modifications, exists at the present day. Indeed, in no other department of naval architecture has so much conservatism been displayed as in the rig of ships; for, if we except certain mechanical contrivances for reducing manual labour, the rigs of ships have remained almost unaltered during the last century.

It would not be consistent with the character of this work to discuss at length the question of the rigs and relative proportions and shapes of sails, as that subject is an extensive one, and belongs rather to the province of the practical rigger. We purpose rather to investigate the relation of sail power to speed and stability; and also to consider the mathematics connected with sail arrangement in regard to the manœuvring qualities of a ship.

It is necessary, however, to explain the meaning of the terms we shall employ, and show by illustrations the nature of the several kinds of sails and rigs.

**231. Masts.**—The sails of a ship are kept at their proper elevation above the deck by means of masts, to which are suspended the yards, booms, etc., and to these latter the sails are immediately attached. Each mast is generally made up of several lengths which lap against and are attached to each other by *caps*. The number of masts in a vessel is governed by the rig: *cutters* have one mast; *schooners*,* *brigs*, and *brigantines* have two; *barques* and *ships* have three; while some exceptionally long vessels have four or more masts. In vessels having two masts, the one nearest the bow is usually named the *foremast* and the other the *mainmast*. When a vessel has three masts, they are styled—commencing at the bow—the *foremast*, *mainmast*, and *mizen mast* respectively. In addition to the mast or masts, there is usually a bowsprit, which is similar in form to a mast, but projects forward, beyond the bow, in a more or less horizontal direction, to support the sails before the foremast, usually styled the *head sails*.

Each mast is made up of several parts, except in some very small vessels, where it is found convenient to make the whole length of one spar. Without going into the technical details of what masts are peculiar to particular rigs, we will merely state that the lowest length and the principal piece of each mast is termed the *lower mast;* thus we have the *fore-lower mast*, *main-lower mast*, etc.; above this there is the *topmast;* thus we have *fore topmast*, etc.; and again,

---

* There is a style of rig upon three masts, which give the vessels carrying it the name of *three-masted schooners* (see fig. 1, Plate 54), while another is termed a *three-masted brigantine*.

above the *topmast*, is the *topgallant mast*, and sometimes the *royal mast*. Generally, however, the topgallant and royal masts are in one piece, the latter portion being termed the *royal pole*. Beyond the bowsprit there is sometimes a *jibboom*, and again beyond that a *flying jibboom*.

The portion of the lower mast between the lower extremity which heels on the step in the ship and the uppermost wedging deck (*i.e.*, the uppermost deck which receives the wedges that tighten the mast in place), is termed the *housing*, and the place where the shrouds are collected on the mast is termed the *hounds*. On the upper extremity of the lower mast is the *lower cap*, through which the topmast passes, the lower extremity of the latter resting on the *trussel trees* near the hounds. The length from the hounds to the cap is termed the *head* of the lower mast. The *head* of the topmast is the length from the crosstrees on the topmast to the topmast cap. Through the latter the topgallant mast passes, resting on the crosstrees. The topgallant and royal masts are usually of one spar, the place where the former ends and the latter commences being termed the *stop*. The portion of the bowsprit inside the ship is termed the *housing of the bowsprit*, and the portion of the jibboom between the bowsprit cap and its after extremity is styled the *housing of the jibboom*.

Except in the cases of some unusual rigs, the masts of a ship incline aft, the inclination being known as the *rake*. The rake is least to the foremast and is greatest to the mizen mast. The deviation of the bowsprit from the horizontal is termed the *steeve*.

**232. Yards.**—The horizontal spars to which square sails are hung are termed *yards*. The lowest yards of the fore and mainmasts are termed the *fore lower yard* and *main lower yard* respectively, while the lowest yard on the mizen mast is styled the *crossjack yard*. Square sails are rarely hung to the last mentioned, it being used only for stretching and working the sail above. The other yards to each mast are known as the fore, etc., *topsail yards*, fore, etc., *topgallant yards*, and fore, etc., *royal yards*.

Each yard is longer than the sails attached to it, the additional length at each extremity being termed the *yard arm*.

To each extremity of the yard arm a ring is attached, through which passes a small spar termed a *studdingsail boom*, which carries a *studdingsail*, and which laps against the yard arm. It should be here remarked that these studding sails are not part of what is termed the *plain* sail of the ship.

Besides the preceding, there is a spar which points upwards, at an angle with the mast, its lower extremity, when in place, being near the hounds. These spars are known as *gaffs;* they support the upper sides of the fore and main *trysails*, and on the mizen mast they support the *driver*. At the lower extremity of the latter is a *boom* which reaches over the stern, and is known as the *driver boom*.

233. Sails.—Sails are divided into two principal classes, viz., *square sails* and *fore-and-aft sails*. The former are most efficient when sailing free, *i.e.*, before the wind, or, in other words, away from the wind. Their mean position is transverse or across the ship, and they can be braced to a considerable angle on either side of that position to suit the direction of the wind, but cannot be braced right fore-and-aft.

*Fore-and-aft sails* are best for sailing close to the wind, or for manœuvring; their mean position is nearly right fore-and-aft, and they can be moved to a considerable angle on either side of that position. Some of these sails are necessary for certain manœuvres, especially going about, or changing the direction of the ship so as to receive the wind from the opposite side. Hence, although some small vessels are wholly without square sails, all vessels have fore-and-aft sails.

The rig of a ship is said to be *square* or *fore-and-aft* according as the principal sails are either square or fore-and-aft.

We have mentioned the principal rigs as being those of the cutter, schooner, brigantine, brig, barque, and ship. In addition to these there are certain combinations or modifications of these rigs, which are adopted in special cases for certain services, some of which are shown by figs. 1 and 2 of Plate LIV. In long steam vessels are found various combinations of the schooner, brigantine, brig, and barque rigs; these being adopted in consequence of sail being but an auxiliary power of propulsion. In such vessels four or more masts are sometimes used in consequence of the great length of the deck, and the desire to have light and easily handled sails and spars. The *Great Eastern* is a remarkable illustration of this, that vessel having no less than six masts, two of which are square rigged and the remainder fore-and-aft rigged.

Square sails are of the form shown by fig. 1, Plate LI. They are four-sided, and generally stand symmetrical with regard to the mast, as shown in the figure, which shows the usual form of these sails.

Fore-and-aft sails are of various shapes. Figs. 2 and 3 of Plate LI. show the general forms, fig. 2 representing such sails as are hung between the foremast and the bowsprit, *i.e.*, *jibs*, *flying jibs*, etc. Fig. 3 is the shape of the principal sails of a cutter and schooner, while in a barque and ship rig they are known as *trysails* when on the fore and main masts, and *drivers* or *spankers* when on the mizen mast. Their general name is *gaff sail*, being hung to a gaff. Figs. 4 and 5 show two kinds of *gaff-topsails*, the former being what is termed a *lug-sail* and the latter a *shoulder-of-mutton sail*. *Staysails* (sometimes hung on the stays of the masts) are of the shape shown by fig. 2.

**234. Rigs.**—We will briefly explain by means of illustrations the nature of the principal kinds of rigs. Fig. 1, Plate LII., shows a *cutter*, all the sails of which are fore-and-aft. *a* is the *mainsail*, *b* the *gaff-topsail*, *c* the *foresail*, and *d* the *jib*. *a*, *c*, and *d* are what is termed the plain sail, and are those generally taken into account in estimating the *trim* of the sails and the proportionate sail power of the vessel. In addition to *a*, *c*, and *d*, a variety of other sails, including some square sails, are occasionally carried in light winds.

Fig. 2, on the same Plate, is a *schooner*, *f* is the *fore staysail*, *a* the *foresail*, *g* the *jib*, *d* the *fore topsail*, *e* the *fore topgallant sail*, *b* the *mainsail*, and *c* the *main gaff-topsail*. A *flying jib* and other sails are sometimes carried in addition to those shown.

Fig. 3 is a *brigantine*, which differs from a schooner, inasmuch as the former carries a *course*, or lower square sail, on the foremast, and has likewise a *top* instead of a *crosstree* at the head of the lower foremast. Brigantines also usually have a fore topgallant mast. In the Plate, *a* is the *foresail*,

$d$ the *fore topsail*, and $e$ the *fore topgallant sau*; $b$ is the *mainsail* or *driver*, and $h$ is the *jib*. These constitute the plain sail of the vessel. Of the others $c$ is the *gaff-topsail*, $k$ the *fore trysail*, $g$ the *fore topmast staysail*, $f$ the *fore staysail*, and and $k$ the *fore royal sail*.

Fig. 4, Plate LII., is a *brig*, $a$ is the *jib*, $b$ the *fore course*, $c$ the *fore topsail*, $d$ the *fore topgallant sail*, $e$ the *main course*, $f$ the *main topsail*, $g$ the *main topgallant sail*, and $h$ the *driver*. These are the plain sail, by which the calculations regarding the sails are made. $k$ and $l$ are the *fore* and *main royal sails* respectively, and $m$ and $n$ are *fore topmast staysail* and *fore staysail* respectively. As will be seen, all these sails, except $a$, $m$, $n$, and $h$, are square.

Fig. 1, Plate LIII., shows a *barque*. In this rig $a$ is the *jib*, $b$ the *fore course*, $c$ the *fore topsail*, $d$ the *fore topgallant sail*, $e$ is the *main course*, $f$ the *main topsail*, $g$ the *main topgallant sail*, $h$ is the *driver*, and $k$ the *main gaff-topsail*. These are all the plain sail of the ship. Of the other sails shown, those marked $l$ and $m$ are the *flying jib* and the *fore topmast staysail* respectively, and $n$ and $o$ are the *fore* and *main royals*. A fore stay sail and a trysail upon the fore and main masts are also carried and used at certain times; these are omitted in the figure, but are similar to the corresponding sails on the fore mast of the brig. It should here be remarked that in the *schooner*, *brigantine*, *brig*, and *barque*, sails are carried upon the stays to the several masts, and are termed *stay sails* (see fig. 2, Plate LIII., and fig. 3, Plate LIV.).

Fig. 2, Plate LIII., shows a *ship rig* of the kind known as a *clipper*. It is very common in fast-sailing ships of the mercantile marine, of which the fig. shows a good specimen. Commencing right forward, $a$, $b$, $c$, $d$, and $e$ are the *flying jib*, *outer and inner jibs*, *fore topmast staysail*, and *fore staysail* respectively. Of the lower sails $f$, $l$, and $q$ are *fore*, *main*, and *mizen courses* respectively. Each of the topsails is in two parts; for instance, $g$ is the upper and $g_1$ the lower fore topsail, and similarly with regard to the square sails on the other topmasts. Also, the top gallant sails are each in two parts, $h$ and $h_1$, being the upper and lower topgallant sails respectively. The yard between the two parts of the sail is made so as to roll up the portion of the sail above it when it is desired to reef, *i.e.*, reduce the area of sail carried; the operation being performed by a reefing apparatus on deck. $k$, $o$, and $t$, are *royals;* and $p$ is what is sometimes termed a *skyscraper*, being carried only in very light winds. In some ships a corresponding sail is also carried on the fore mast. It will be observed that no *royal sail* is carried on the mizen mast in the example shown, but this is not always the case. The sail marked $u$ is the driver, and $v$, $w$, and $x$ show staysails, which are often carried on more stays than in this example. Trysails are also carried when running close to the wind; while in all the rigs studding sails are carried upon booms at the ends of the yards, when running free.

A more usual style of *ship rig*, especially in the royal navy, is shown by fig. 3, Plate LIV. The sails marked $a$ to $h$ inclusive bear the same names as the corresponding sails, similarly lettered, in the *barque rig* shown by fig. 1, Plate LIII.; $k$ is the mizen topsail and $l$ the mizen topgallant sail. These are the plain sail of the ship, and their collective area is given in the table of references above the figure. The following are the names of the other sails shown: $m$ is the *flying jib*, $n$ the *fore topmast staysail*, and $o$ the *fore staysail*, while $p$, $q$, and $r$ are, respectively, the fore, main, and mizen royals. $s_1$ to $s_6$, inclusive, are staysails which, as already mentioned, are carried in the other rigs, but not shown. The *fore* and *main trysails* are shown by $t_1$ and $t_2$.

Figs. 1 and 2 of Plate LIV. are examples of rigs often met with in steam ships. In addition to these there are various modifications and combinations of the schooner, brig, barque, and ship rigs, adopted in such vessels to suit the requirements of particular cases, sail power being merely an auxiliary to the steam power provided.

235. **Sailing.**—The principle of a vessel's motion through the water, in a direction making an angle with that of the wind, has been aptly compared by a writer in *Naval Science* to the motion of a train of carriages on a railway when pushed by a force whose direction is oblique to that of the rails. So long as any portion of the force of the wind can be brought to bear upon the sails, so that there is a resolved component acting in the direction of the keel, the vessel has

a tendency to move in that direction: for the shape of the immersed portion of the vessel's body is such that less resistance is offered to motion in the direction of the keel than in any other direction. Consequently, although the component of the force acting at right angles to the keel may be greater than that in the direction of the keel, yet, owing to the lesser resistance offered to the latter force, it is in general more effective in propelling the ship than the other component. In the case of a carriage on a railway there is no other motion possible but in the direction of the rails, but in the case of a ship, although the resistance to broadside is much greater than to fore and aft motion, yet when the wind is blowing so obliquely with regard to the plane of the sails that only a small portion of its force acts in a longitudinal direction, the vessel makes what is termed *leeway* very rapidly, and that, too, in proportion as the immersion of the vessel is small. Leeway always occurs unless the vessel is running free; but with a strong wind *abeam*, and a good spread of fore-and-aft sail well trimmed, this can be reduced to a small amount. The usual ratio of *leeway* to *headway* varies from about one-fifth to one-tenth, the former fraction being rarely reached. This causes the direction of the ship's course to make an angle with the line of keel, which angle is termed the *angle of leeway*, and varies from about $5\frac{1}{2}°$ to $11°$ (see fig. 1, Plate LV., where the arrows show the direction of the wind and that of the vessel's course is drawn as a ticked line).

236. **Real and Apparent Motion of the Wind.**—By the *real motion* of the wind is meant its motion relatively to the earth; by its apparent motion is meant the motion relatively to the ship when she is sailing. It is, of course, the *apparent motion* with which we are concerned in considering the question of sailing.

In Fig. 2, Plate LV., $AC$ represents in direction and magnitude the real velocity of the wind, and $AD$ represents similarly the velocity of the ship. Through $C$ draw $CB$ equal and parallel to $AD$ and join $AB$, then $AB$ represents in direction and magnitude the *apparent velocity* of the wind.

237. **Effective Impulse of the Wind.**—In fig. 3, Plate LV., $KM$ is the line of a vessel's keel, $AB$ is a sail braced

round so as to make an angle $a$ with $KM$; $PC$ represents the apparent direction and velocity of the wind, $PC$ making an angle $\theta$ with the sail. Resolving the velocity $PC$ into its two components, one perpendicular and the other in the plane of the sail, we have $PC \sin \theta$, the effective velocity of the wind. This is represented by $RC$ in the figure. The pressure of the wind per unit of area of the sail is equal to the change of momentum of the particles of air produced by the action of the sail in each second. Hence this pressure acts in the direction $RC$, and is equal in amount to

$$\frac{PC \sin \theta}{32 \cdot 2}.$$

The weight of air acting upon the sail in a second is the product of the apparent velocity, the density and the sectional area of the wind-current. This sectional area was for some time assumed to vary with $\sin \theta$; with this assumption the impulse varies as $\sin^2 \theta$. Experience has, however, shown that the impulse diminishes much more slowly than the square of the sine of the angle, as is seen by the speed with which vessels can sail close to the wind. Part of this speed is, however, no doubt due to the fact that the apparent velocity of the wind is greater than the real when the wind is before the beam, *i.e.*, blows from an angle on the fore side of a perpendicular to the middle line of the ship. Again, it must be remembered that the surfaces of sails are not flat, but more or less hollow, also the direction of the current of wind on a sail is more or less modified by the influence of other sails in its vicinity.

In fig. 3, Plate LV., if $RC$ represent the impulse perpendicular to the sail, then $RC \sin a = NC$ is the component of the impulse which moves the ship in the direction $KM$, while $RC \cos a = RN$ is the component which produces leeway and tends to heel the ship over.

The result of experience is that, when the sails are braced to the most efficient angle, as deduced from practical trials with the vessel, the forward effect of the wind varies proportionately to the square of the velocity of the apparent wind, and to half the versed sine of the angle between the ship's course and the apparent direction of the wind.

**238. Trim of Sails.**—The principles upon which the area

of the sails for any given vessel is determined will be considered presently; we will, for the present, assume that the area of sails is given, and will now show how to arrange the masts and the sails upon them in such a way that the wind shall cause the vessel to pursue a rectilinear course, when the wind blows across that course, instead of her rotating about an axis.

The motion of a vessel at starting is due to the excess of the impulse of propulsion over the resistance of the fluid in which she moves; the speed of the vessel continues to increase until the two forces are equal, and then she moves with the uniform velocity due to the constant application of the propelling force.

If the propelling force and the resistance act through the same transverse section of the ship, the motion is rectilinear, and if the forces are applied at different vertical heights in that section the ship will heel over, until such an angle is reached that the moment of stability of the ship is equal to the inclining moment of the wind on the sails.

The centre of application of the propelling force is at the centre of gravity of the sails; usually termed the "*centre of effort*," while the centre of application of the resistance of the water when the ship is not running before the wind is a point termed the "*centre of lateral resistance*," which varies in position with the speed of the ship, her form below water, and other conditions of a somewhat complicated character. Hence this point is not determinate. It is usual, however, to consider it to be situated at some fraction of the ship's length before the centre of gravity of her immersed longitudinal vertical middle line plane; the fraction varying according to the ratio of the vessel's length to her breadth and to her form below water. Values of this fraction are given in Table X. The inclining moment of the ship is the moment of stability at the angle of heel; the area of the sails being so fixed that the angle shall not exceed 4 degrees at the ordinary pressure of the wind when plain sail is carried. In all these calculations the plain sails only are taken into account (see Art. 234).

239. **Ardency and Leewardliness.**—If the *centre of effort* of the sails and the *centre of lateral resistance of* the ship are

in the same transverse section, the motion of the ship will be rectilinear. If, however, they are not in the same transverse section a couple is produced which causes the ship to rotate about some axis.

A pair of equal and opposite impulses acting in parallel lines (that is, the impulse of a couple), give no motion to the centre of gravity of the body they act upon; but cause the body as a whole to rotate about its centre of gravity. Hence a ship whose centre of lateral resistance is not in the transverse section which contains the centre of effort of the sails, rotates instantaneously about her centre of gravity.

If the centre of effort is on the fore side of the centre of lateral resistance, the ship rotates in the same direction as the wind blows, or, in other words, she *falls off from the wind* and goes to leeward. Such a ship is said to be *leewardly*, and *to carry lee helm*. In order to sail the required course it is necessary to put the rudder round to windward, and, therefore, the helm to leeward.

If the centre of effort of the sails is abaft the centre of lateral resistance the ship rotates in an opposite direction to the wind, or, in other words, she *flies up to the wind*, and sails to windward of the desired course. Such a ship is said to be *ardent* and to carry *weather helm*, as it is necessary in order to sail the required course that the rudder should be put round to leeward, and therefore the helm should be put to windward.

By the term "centre of lateral resistance," as here employed, must be understood the true centre of lateral resistance, wherever that point may be situated. As already stated, it is usual to draw a vertical line through the centre of gravity of the immersed middle line plane of the ship, and assume that the centre of lateral resistance is at some fraction of the ship's length before that point. In fig. 3, Plate LIV., which shows the sail plan of a ship-rigged vessel, a vertical line is shown through the centre of gravity of the middle line plane, and the centre of effort of the sails is at 15·9 feet abaft that vertical line; so that in the case there shown the true centre of lateral resistance is about 16 feet on the fore side of the centre of gravity of the immersed longitudinal vertical middle line plane of the ship.

Even if it were desirable, it is difficult, if not impossible, to so trim the sails as to ensure that there is never a rotating couple. The plain sails, whose centre of effort is calculated, are not often all set together, and when they are, other sails are often set with them; in short, it cannot be ensured that the computed centre of effort of the sails is the real centre of effort at all times when the ship is sailing. As will be seen presently, when showing how to determine that point, the centre of effort being calculated upon the supposition that the sails are all braced right fore and aft, its position, with the same sail set, does not vary with square sails placed symmetrically in regard to the axis about which they rotate, but it does vary considerably with fore and aft sails, such as the jib, driver, etc., when standing at any other angle. Again, the variations in the position of the centre of lateral resistance at different speeds, already alluded to, prevent us from being able to fix its position under all circumstances. From these considerations it will be seen that the naval architect must have recourse to experience gained by observing other vessels, in order to arrange his sails efficiently. The influence of the position of the ship's centre of gravity on her manœuvring capabilities have also to be taken into account; and data of this character obtained from other ships must also be referred to, as will be seen in the next Article.

The plain sail is so arranged as to ensure that, under ordinary circumstances, the centre of lateral resistance is a little on the fore side of the centre of effort, and thus that the ship shall carry a little weather helm. This is desirable, as the ordinary manœuvres under sails consist of *tacking*, or sailing up in the wind and changing her course in this way, so as to receive the wind from the opposite side of the ship. Hence it is necessary that the ship should carry a little weather helm, as by putting the helm to leeward both rudder and sails act together in changing the course of the ship, and putting her on the other tack.

This *ardent* tendency must not, however, be excessive, as the necessity of counteracting it with the rudder would reduce the speed of the ship.

Should a vessel prove leewardly when plain sail is set, the fault may be rectified in two ways. Either the stern sail may be increased or the head sail diminished, or both; or the trim of the ship may be altered by shifting weights farther forward, and so immersing her more deeply at the bow and diminishing the draught at the stern; in this way the centre of lateral resistance is moved to the fore side of the centre of effort instead of being abaft it as before.

Should a vessel be too ardent the converse of either of these operations will correct the fault. It is worthy of remark that the rake of the masts is sometimes increased to diminish leewardliness, and *vice versa*.

The motion of the centre of lateral resistance with varying speed, already alluded to more than once, is illustrated in sailing a boat close to the wind. When the wind drops, the boat, even if ordinarily ardent, makes leeway very rapidly, and the desired course cannot be kept; but if a sudden breeze springs up, the boat at once, without the rudder being touched, flies up in the wind's eye, and unless checked by the helm, will go about on the other tack. This is due to the pressure of the water against the leeward bow of the boat being increased relatively to that on the after part, and thus the centre of lateral resistance moves forward. It will be readily seen that this excess of pressure forward increases with the bluffness of the fore body; hence the centre of effort must be placed farther forward as the fulness of the fore body below water is increased.

In the old sailing ships of the Royal Navy the centre of effort of the sails was situated at about one-fourteenth of the ship's length before the centre of gravity of the immersed middle line plane; in the fast wooden steam frigates built before the armour-clads it was about one-twentieth to one-twenty-fourth before, and in the iron steam frigate *Inconstant*, whose form below water, especially forward, is much finer than any of the ships already referred to, it is only one-twenty-eighth before.

Table X. contains a list of the positions of the centres of effort of the sails of the typical vessels named therein. The table also contains other particulars of a useful character in relation to the dimensions, positions of masts, and arrangements of sails, in the vessels named. The particulars are copied from Vol. XIII. of the *Transactions of the Institution of Naval Architects*, and were contributed by Mr. J. G. Wildish, of the Admiralty.

**240. Effect of the Position of Centre of Gravity (Longitudinally) on a Ship's Sailing Qualities.**—The influence which the relative positions of the centres of gravity and lateral resistance of a ship have upon her manœuvering qualities, when under sail, has not attracted much attention. Except when a vessel is pitching or scending, or when her trim is altered by the pressure of the wind on her sails, her centre of gravity and buoyancy are in the same transverse section; that being a fundamental condition of her hydrostatical equilibrium. The position of the centre of lateral resistance being governed by the extent and character of the immersed surface of the vessel, and that of the centre of buoyancy by the volume inclosed within that surface, it is evident that two vessels of the same dimensions, draught, trim, and displacement, may have these points at very different distances apart. In the old sailing ships of the Royal Navy the centre of buoyancy—and therefore the centre of gravity—was usually before the middle of the length of the load water-line, the distances varying from one-fiftieth to one-hundredth of the length. The determination of the position was governed by considerations of speed and longitudinal stability, and its effect upon the sailing qualities of the ship do not appear to have been noticed. This was of very little importance at that time, as the ships were short and easily influenced by the rudder. With the introduction of long steam ships, also fully rigged, the question became of more moment, as the power of the rudder in such ships is relatively less. Whether by design or not we are unable to say, but it happens that in the majority of the long steam frigates, which succeeded the sailing ships, the centre of buoyancy was placed much farther aft, and in those which sail best the point is as much abaft the middle of the length as it was formerly before it. An opinion has long been held by many that a short fore body and a long after body is best adapted for speed, but it appears from the results of these ships that no loss of speed resulted when under sail, while the advantages in tacking are very marked in the case of such ships when compared with those ships of the same dimensions in which the centre of buoyancy is before the middle of the length. We will now investigate the cause of these results.

Suppose the force of the wind perpendicular to the sails to be $P$, and the angle which the plane of the sails makes with the keel of the ship to be $a$. So long as the ship pursues a steady rectilinear course the force of propulsion is $P \sin a$ acting on the centre of effort, and this must be balanced by an equivalent force on the ship's bottom, acting through a point in the same transverse section as that which contains the centre of effort, *i.e.*, through the centre of lateral resistance. Now, imagine the action of the wind to suddenly cease, the mechanical work accumulated in the ship will cause her to continue to move in her course, and thus $P \sin a$ will continue to act at the first instant, but instead of doing so through the centre of effort it will now act through the centre of gravity of the ship, where the mechanical work may be supposed to be accumulated. Hence a couple is set up, the resistance against the ship's bottom still acts at the same point as before, while the force moving the ship acts before or abaft that point, according as the centre of gravity (or centre of buoyancy) of the ship is before or abaft the centre of effort. In a brief period the ship loses speed and the centre of lateral resistance moves slightly aft. The effect of this couple is to produce a rotatory motion in the ship about an axis through her centre of gravity. The velocity with which the ship commences to turn is proportional to the moment of $P \sin a$ (acting through the centre of lateral resistance) about the centre of gravity, divided by the moment of inertia of the ship. If, the instant after the wind ceases, the centre of lateral resistance and the centre of gravity are in the same transverse section, the ship does not commence to rotate, and only does so afterward by reason of the centre of lateral resistance moving slightly aft, owing to the reduction in the vessel's speed. Hence, in this case, the course of the ship at first remains unaltered, and afterwards she turns to leeward of her original course. If the centre of gravity is before the centre of lateral resistance, the instant after the wind ceases the ship commences to rotate to leeward; while if the centre of gravity is abaft the centre of lateral resistance she commences to rotate in the opposite direction, or to windward.

In tacking, the helm is placed to leeward, and therefore the rudder to windward, so as to cause the vessel to turn towards the direction from whence the wind blows. Then the head sail is eased off and the driver is hauled amidships so as to increase the efficiency of the sternmost sail, as she turns, and diminish that of the foremost. As the ship continues to turn, all the sails lose their power in maintaining headway, and they do not assist in turning any more until they "draw" on the opposite tack. Hence the only forces then available to turn the ship are the impulse of the water on the rudder and that on the ship's bottom. Now the action of the rudder after the ship has commenced to turn is found, by the strain on the tiller, to be very slight; and if ever the rudder has afterwards to be resorted to, it is in the case of a vessel which "goes about" badly. Thus it is seen that the magnitude and direction of the moment of rotation already alluded to, due to the position of the centre of gravity, and therefore to the centre of buoyancy, is of great importance; for if the centre of gravity is abaft the centre of lateral resistance, and the impulse of the rudder is not sufficient to counteract the opposite tendency to turn, the ship will be very difficult, if not impossible, to tack; whereas, if the centre of gravity is before the centre of lateral resistance, the ship may be tacked by means of the sails alone.

**241. Centre of Effort.**—This term has been already frequently used, and it has been understood to refer to the centre of application of the propelling impulse of the wind on the sails. As the manner in which the wind meets the sails, when the latter are braced so as to be at an acute angle with the wind, is not fully understood, it is impossible to determine the centre of effort exactly. For all practical purposes, however, it is taken at the centre of gravity of the surface of the sails. Only the *plain sail* is taken into account, and in calculating the position of the point the yards, sheets, etc., are supposed to be all braced and hauled into a fore-and-aft line. The sail plans shown by Plates LII. to LIV. represent the sails in this condition.

The first thing to be done is to find the geometrical

centre of gravity of each sail. The methods of finding these points for areas of the kind are given at Arts. 20 to 22. Moments are taken about the load water-line for the vertical position, and about a vertical line through the centre of gravity of the immersed vertical longitudinal middle line plane for the longitudinal position of the centre of effort. The area of each sail is multiplied by the distance of its centre of gravity above the load water-line, and the sum of these products divided by the sum of the areas gives the vertical distance of the centre of effort above the load water-line. A similar course is pursued for its longitudinal position, only that the difference of the products on both sides of the vertical line is divided by the sum of the areas, the distance being set off on that side of the line upon which is the excess of moments. This is invariably found to be on the fore side, but as the centre of lateral resistance is usually at a still greater distance on that side of the vertical line, the tendency is usually in the direction of *ardency* (see fig. 3, Plate LIV.).

242. **Speed under Sail.**—The impossibility of determining the proportion of the force of the wind which acts perpendicular to a sail, especially when the sail is braced to an angle of less than 60 degrees with the apparent direction of the wind, also renders it impossible to determine the total propelling force acting upon a vessel under sail. If it were possible to determine the fluid resistance, direct and frictional, opposed to a vessel when she has attained her maximum speed under a certain area of sail, with the wind blowing at a certain angle to her keel and at a certain pressure per square foot, the proportion which the propelling component of that pressure bears to the whole could be readily determined. But the present state of our knowledge regarding the resistance of fluids and the varying frictional character of the surface of a ship's bottom renders this problem insoluble. Hence, in order to determine the probable speed of a ship under sail, we are compelled to refer to the performance of another ship of similar form, similar surface, and whose area of sail is known.

The chief element in the resistance offered to a ship's motion is the friction of the water on the surface of her bottom.

Hence if there are two vessels of similar form but of different dimensions, then assuming the frictional nature of the surfaces of their bottoms to be the same in both cases, the areas of sail to produce a given driving or propelling force under the same conditions of wind, weather, etc., will be proportionate to the areas of the immersed surfaces of their bottoms. If the vessels are similar the areas of these surfaces will vary as $D^{\frac{2}{3}} : D_1^{\frac{2}{3}}$ where $D$ and $D_1$ are the displacements of the vessels. Let $A$ and $A_1$ be the areas of plain sail so determined for vessels whose displacements are $D$ and $D_1$ respectively. Then, if $S$ and $S_1$ be the speeds of the two vessels having thus proportionate propelling powers,

$$S : S_1 = \left(\frac{A}{D^{\frac{2}{3}}}\right)^{\frac{1}{2}} : \left(\frac{A_1}{D_1^{\frac{2}{3}}}\right)^{\frac{1}{2}}$$

$$= \frac{A^{\frac{1}{2}}}{D^{\frac{1}{3}}} : \frac{A_1^{\frac{1}{2}}}{D_1^{\frac{1}{3}}}.$$

If the speeds are required to be the same

$$\frac{A^{\frac{1}{2}}}{D^{\frac{1}{3}}} = \frac{A_1^{\frac{1}{2}}}{D_1^{\frac{1}{3}}}$$

$$\text{or } A_1^{\frac{1}{2}} = \frac{A^{\frac{1}{2}} D_1^{\frac{1}{3}}}{D^{\frac{1}{3}}}$$

$$A_1 = A \frac{D_1^{\frac{2}{3}}}{D^{\frac{2}{3}}},$$

which gives the area of plain sail required in order that a vessel of given displacement may attain a given speed; the area of plain sail to enable a vessel of similar form, etc., and of given displacement to sail at that speed under similar circumstances being known. It is a necessary condition for the above that the lengths of both the vessels do not fall short of the lowest limits which experience shows to be suited for that speed.

Another kind of resistance is that due to the vessel's bulk being moved through the water at a given speed, and forcing the water away on all sides in the same manner as if she were excavating a canal for herself. This resistance varies as the areas of the immersed midship sections, or as $M$ to $M_1$ say.

With this assumption, the speeds of two vessels of similar form whose areas of plain sail are $A$ and $A_1$ will vary thus:

$$S : S_1 = \frac{A^{\frac{1}{2}}}{M^{\frac{1}{3}}} : \frac{A_1^{\frac{1}{2}}}{M_1^{\frac{1}{3}}},$$

and if $S$ is equal to $S_1$

$$A_1 = A \frac{M_1}{M}.$$

Again, the work performed in moving ships at a given speed, irrespective of friction or form, varies as the weight or as the displacement. By this mode of comparison, in order that the ships may have the same speed,

$$A_1 = A \frac{D_1}{D}.$$

As will be seen by the notes on fig. 3, Plate LIV., it is usual to give each of these three values, viz., area of plain sail per unit of $D^{\frac{2}{3}}$, $M$ and $D$, upon every Admiralty sail drawing, as three valuable criterions whereby the speed of the ship under sail may be determined.

**243. Stability under Sail**—I. *Steady impulse and small inclination of ship.*—In fig. 3, Plate LV., $PC$ represents in direction and magnitude the apparent velocity of the wind, and, as already shown, $RC$ is the component normal to the sail, also $NC$ is the propelling component, while $RN$ is the transverse component that produces heeling and leeway. If $RC = P$, then $NC = P \sin a$, and $RN = P \cos a$. Let $\theta =$ the angle of the ship's heel under the steady pressure of the wind whose intensity is $P \cos a$ acting horizontally. Let $D =$ the displacement, $A$ the area of sail, $GM$ the height of transverse metacentre above centre of gravity, and $CL$ the height of the centre of effort above the centre of lateral resistance. The heeling moment of the wind is $A \times P \cos a \cos \theta \times CL$, and the moment of statical stability of the ship at the angle $\theta$ (supposing $\theta$ so small that the value of $GM$ remains constant) is $D \times GM \sin \theta$. Hence, if the ship is inclined steadily with a uniform pressure of the wind,

$$A \times P \cos a \cos \theta \times CL = D \times GM \sin \theta.$$

It is usual when fixing the area of plain sail which a ship shall carry to assume the heeling component of the pressure of the wind to be 1 lb. per square foot, and the angle $\theta$ is fixed at 4 degrees.

$$A \times CL = D^* \times GM \sin 4°.$$

The figures on the right hand side of this equation being known, those on the other side are easily determined. The value of $CL$ will be governed by the height of the rig generally, it being evident that for the same value of $A$ there may be considerable variations in the length of $CL$. It may here be remarked that the point $L$, or the centre of lateral resistance, is situated at about a half of the mean draught of the ship; but it is usual to measure $CL$ from the centre of effort to the water-line, which gives a length of about an eighth less than the real value.

For purposes of comparison it has been usual in the Royal Navy to obtain the value of $\frac{D \times GM}{A \times CL}$ for each ship, and use it as a measure of her efficiency to stand up under the pressure of wind on her canvas. It, of course, represents the initial power of a ship to resist the inclining force of the wind on her sails, and in most cases has been found to range between 15 and 25 when the ship is at her load draught.

244. II. *Steady impulse and any angle of inclination.*—For comparisons at finite angles of inclination the curve of stability is referred to. As will be remembered, this curve represents by its ordinates the arm of the righting couple at every angle of heel, until the stability vanishes. Thus if it be required to know what angle the ship will be inclined by a steady pressure of the wind at any given intensity; if $P$ be that intensity of pressure in pounds per square foot, $A \times P \times CL$ is the total heeling moment in foot-pounds; and if $D =$ the displacement in pounds, $\frac{A \times P \times CL}{D}$ is the length of $GZ$, or the arm of the righting couple necessary for the ship to remain steady, inclined at the required angle, and by referring to the curve, the angle at which the value of $GZ$ is equal to that required, is the angle at which the ship will be inclined.

In this expression, by using $A \times P \times CL$ we have neglected

---

* D is here expressed in pounds avoirdupois.

the reduction in the effective heeling pressure of the wind
due to the sails being inclined away from the upright position.
At small angles the diminution in the effective pressure
would be very slight indeed, owing to the "bellying of the
sails." We have previously mentioned that the effective
pressure of the wind has been variously taken to vary as the
sine, and the sine squared of the angle of incidence, which
angle is, of course, the compliment of the angle of heel.
Some experiments made by the Royal Academy of Paris
show that neither of these assumed variations is correct,
although that of the sine squared is practically so at angles
of incidence varying from 60° to 90°, or angle of heel varying
from 30° to 0°. As the wind pressure rarely heels a ship
beyond the former angle, it is sufficient for our purpose if we
take the "sine squared" variation as correct. Mr. Wildish,
whose paper has already been quoted in this chapter, has
given therein curves representing the effective pressures of
the wind at every angle of incidence, obtained by the sine
and sine squared assumptions and the curve as found by the
Academy of Paris in their experiments with regard to the
oblique impulses of fluids (see Plate LVI., fig. 2). This last
curve explains what we have stated in Art. 237, with reference to the remarkable effective impulse of the wind when
sailing "close hauled," a phenomenon with which all sailors
and many landsmen are familiar.

In fig. 1 of the same Plate will be found another series of
curves calculated for three typical ships, viz., the *Inconstant*,
a fast corvette, the *Monarch*, a high-sided armoured frigate,
and the *Captain*, a turret ship of low freeboard. The curves
marked $C, C, C$, are the curves of stability of these ships, the
ordinates being the righting levers; those marked $A, A, A$, are
the curves of absolute stability of the same ships, the ordinates in this case representing the actual moments of stability
at the different angles; while the curves marked $B, B, B$,
represent the absolute powers of the ships to carry sail, the
ordinates representing the ratios of the absolute moments of
stability to the moments of the sails at the several angles of
inclination. In these last-mentioned curves the effects of the
oblique impulse of the wind at the several angles of heel has
been taken into account, as given by the Paris experimental

curve. It should be remarked that in these curves it is assumed that the masts have no rake, and that the yards are braced square to the direction of the wind.

**245. III. Effect of a Gust of Wind.**\*—The knowledge of a ship's statical stability at any particular angle, and therefore the area of sail she can carry, so as not to exceed an angle of safety with a steady pressure of the wind of a known intensity, is not sufficient to determine the question of her freedom from or liability to capsizing. In practice the problem must be considered dynamically, as it frequently happens that a vessel is one moment becalmed and the next she is caught by a gust of wind which, if suddenly applied, would have the effect of heeling her over to, approximately, twice the angle which the same force would keep her to if steadily applied. Really sudden gusts of wind are perhaps never met with, nevertheless a ship when passing a headland, behind which she has been shielded from the wind, suddenly becomes exposed to the full intensity of a steady breeze; and even when on the open sea she is frequently assailed by a blast of some minutes duration, exceeding in force the wind under the influence of which she was previously steadily inclined.

Fig. 1, Plate LVII., represents the curve of absolute stability of a ship; the ordinates being proportional to the righting moments at the several angles from zero to 60°, at which angle the stability vanishes. Suppose this ship exposed suddenly to the action of a steady breeze producing a heeling moment of sail pressure equal to 6000 foot-tons. The ship at once begins to heel over, and at 15 degrees† this heeling moment is exactly balanced by the righting moment of the ship. If the pressure had been very gradually applied the ship would remain inclined at this angle, but in the present case the vessel will not stop here, as the mechanical work done while the ship has been inclining to this angle is represented by the area of the rectangle $Oapb$,

---

\* The ideas contained in the following remarks are suggested by a paper contributed to No. 1 of the *Annual* of the Royal School of Naval Architecture, by the Principal, C. W. Merrifield, F.R.S.

† The diminution of the heeling force, due to the oblique impulse of the wind on the sails when the ship is inclined, is neglected in the following considerations.

# EFFECT OF A GUST OF WIND.

whereas the work absorbed by the ship, *i.e.*, the dynamical stability at that angle, is represented by the area of the figure *Ospb*; hence mechanical work has been accumulated equal to the area *Ospa*. The ship will therefore continue to heel over until this work has been expended. This occurs when the ship has gone over to 26 degrees, when the area *ptr* is equal to the area *aOsp*, or, in other words, when the area *Oprc*—the dynamical stability at 26 degrees—is equal to the area of the rectange *Oatc*, for it must be remembered that the wind has been steadily blowing all the time. The ship will then begin a return oscillation under the influence of a righting moment represented by *tr* or *pb*.

Next, suppose that the steady pressure of the wind is equal to a heeling moment of 12,000 foot-tons, and that the wind is again suddenly applied. At 20 degrees the heeling moment is balanced by the righting moment, and if the wind had gradually increased to this force, the ship would remain inclined at that angle. But in this case mechanical work has been performed by the sudden application of the wind, which is represented by the area of the rectangle *Odme*, of which only the portion represented by the area of the figure *Opme* has been consumed, consequently there remains mechanical work represented by the area of the figure *Opmd*, which must also be consumed before the vessel ceases to heel. This occurs at 50 degrees, where the area of the rectangle *Odfh* is equal to the area of the figure *OpMfh*. The rectangle *emfh* represents the work done by the wind while the inclination has been taking place. The work done in heeling her to the statical angle of 20 degrees has now been consumed, and the vessel is inclined at 50 degrees. But her moment of stability at 50 degrees is the same as at 20 degrees; hence, while the wind blows at this pressure the ship cannot right herself, whereas the smallest addition to the heeling moment, or a slight wave disturbance, will cause her to go right over and capsize.

In the preceding observations many things have not been taken into account which would tend to reduce the extent of the heel produced by a suddenly applied breeze of wind. For instance: the reduction in pressure due to oblique impulse of the wind, also the friction of the water on the ship's bottom and the resistance due to bilge or other keels; on the other hand, the effect of waves, which would at one moment tend to right, and at the next to upset the ship, must not be lost sight of. Again, the wind has been supposed to come suddenly upon the ship and last long enough to capsize her. Now this is contrary to general experience, which teaches us that—especially on the ocean—the maximum force of the wind is not at once attained. Consequently, instead of graphically representing the dynamical heeling moment of the wind by a straight line, such as $at$ or $df$ (fig. 1, Plate LVII.), parallel to the base line, it should rather be represented by a curve $Omf$, as in fig. 2 of the same Plate. If this curve could be accurately drawn, so as to represent the worst possible case that could be encountered, then all we have to do is to ensure that the curve of absolute stability is such that the area $mMf$ is greater than the area $Opmd$.

If the effect of waves is taken into account, and their amplitude is known, then since the effect of the wave is to alternately right and incline the ship, we should take the worst view of the case, and consider only the latter effect, which would be to make the curve of absolute stability fall within the other, as showed by the ticked lines $Op_1 m_1 M_1 V_1$. Then the area of $m_1 M f_1$ should be greater than that of $Op_1 m_1 d$. We have, however, no data at present for constructing such a curve as that shown by the ticked line.

# PART V.

## CALCULATIONS RELATING TO PROPULSION OF SHIPS BY STEAM ENGINES.

### CHAPTER X.

Reaction of the Water—Slip, etc.—Experiments on H.M. Ship *Greyhound*—Law of Resistance—Comparative Performances of Steam Ships—Constants of Performance—The Measured Mile—Mean Speed—Trials at varied Speeds—Negative Slip.

**246. Steam Propulsion.**—The application of the steam engine to marine propulsion has not only caused great changes in the forms of ships and their modes of construction, but has also contributed a great element of exactness in regard to calculations of their speeds. The sailing ship is dependent upon the direction and velocity of the winds, which are ever varying, so that it is impossible to predict what speed the vessel will make under any other circumstances than the most favourable. But when steam is the motive power, it is so far under our control that, so long as the engines are in working order and the coals hold out, a definite propelling power can be relied upon.

**247. Reaction of the Water—Slip, etc.**—There are several modes of applying the work developed by a steam engine in propelling a vessel; the principal of which are the *screw* and *paddle-wheel*. All propellors act by driving water in the opposite direction to that of the ship's motion, and it is the reaction of the water so driven back which, being transmitted through the propeller to the bearings of the shaft, and thence to the vessel, drives her ahead. Hence when the vessel is moving with a uniform velocity the reaction of the water is equal to the resistance offered to the ship.

Now if the propeller were acting in an unyielding medium, the speed of the ship would be the same as the fore and aft speed of the propeller. In the case of a paddle-wheel propeller the speed of the ship would be the same as that with which the paddle floats rotate; and in the case of a screw propeller, the speed of the ship per minute would be the product of the number of revolutions per minute, and the pitch of the screw. But water is not an unyielding medium, and hence the propeller really forces back the water it meets, with a certain velocity relatively to still water. This velocity is termed the *slip*. The velocity of the backward current of water relatively to the ship is the sum of the slip and the vessel's speed, and this is termed the *velocity of the propeller*.

*The efficiency of a propeller* is the proportion which the useful work, performed in driving the vessel, bears to the whole energy expended in moving the propeller. If there were no friction in the machinery and shaft bearings, and no action of the propeller on the water, except that of driving it right astern, then the efficiency of the propeller would be simply the ratio of the speed of the vessel to that of the propeller. But unfortunately there is considerable friction among the parts of the engine and at the shaft bearings, there is also the air-pump duty, and in addition there are transverse and vertical motions imparted to the water, and resistances overcome, which reduce the efficiency to a small fraction.

**248. Experiments on H.M.S.** *Greyhound.*—Some experiments recently made on H.M.S. *Greyhound*, by Mr. Froude, have yielded valuable information regarding the efficiency of propellers.* The *Greyhound* is a screw sloop of about 1200 tons displacement, her length between perpendiculars being 172 feet 6 inches, breadth extreme 33 feet 2 inches, and mean draught of water 13 feet 9 inches. These experiments were made by towing the vessel with H.M.S. *Active*, the stress on the tow rope being registered with a dynamometer. At the same time the speed of the ship was accurately observed,

* See Mr. Froude's paper in Vol. XV. of the *Transactions of the Institution of Naval Architects*.

also the power indicated by the engines, and the speed of the screw.

*Law of Resistance.*—It was found in the case of this vessel that up to about 8 knots per hour the resistance is almost exactly proportional to the square of the speed, and that it is expressed by the term $88 V^2$; being about 5600 pounds or $2\frac{1}{2}$ tons at 8 knots. Above 8 knots it increases more rapidly, so that at 12.8 knots—the highest speed attained—instead of being only 14,400 pounds, as it would have been if the law had been unchanged, it has risen to 24,000 lbs., or nearly $10\frac{3}{4}$ tons.

The result of experiments at lighter displacements showed that with $19\frac{1}{4}$ per cent. less displacement, $16\frac{1}{4}$ per cent. less area of immersed midship section, and 8 per cent. less wetted surface, there was a reduction of $10\frac{1}{2}$ per cent. in the resistance, thus showing that near the load draught the resistance does not increase so rapidly as the displacement—a most valuable fact from an economical point of view. Mr. Froude says in his summary of the results: "Lightening, and so diminishing the displacement of the ship, did not seem in the case of the *Greyhound* to be proportionately advantageous. This result, so far as it goes, indicates a superiority as regards resistance in deep rather than broad ships."

The following results are interesting, as exhibiting the small amount of resistance that ships offer. The actual towing strains on the *Greyhound* were as follows, at the several speeds named:—

| | | |
|---|---|---|
| At 4 knots, | ............ | 0.6 ton, |
| ,, 6 ,, | ............ | 1.4 ,, |
| ,, 8 ,, | ............ | 2.5 ,, |
| ,, 10 ,, | ............ | 4.7 ,, |
| ,, 12 ,, | ............ | 9.0 ,, |

Mr. Froude says in his paper:—

"A comparison between the indicated horse-power of the *Greyhound*, when on her steam trials, and the resistance of the ship, as determined by the dynamometer, shows that, making allowance for the slip of the screw, which is a legitimate expenditure of power, only about 45 per cent. of the power exerted by the steam is usefully employed in propelling the ship, and that no less than 58 per cent. is wasted in friction of engines and screw, and in the detrimental reaction of the propeller on the stream-lines of the water closing in around the stern of the vessel."

Mr. Froude further remarks in a foot note—

"This last-mentioned cause of waste in the propulsion of ships is one to which I have for a long time past repeatedly called attention. . . . The subject is of immense importance; for, making every allowance for the power employed in overcoming friction of engines and screw, there remains in the case of the *Greyhound* some 40 per cent. of waste, an amount the true cause of which is certainly worthy of investigation."

In the last sentence Mr. Froude refers to the action of the screw, when close to the stern of a vessel, in diminishing the hydrodynamic pressure of the water against the "run," and thus causing an increase in the head resistance of the vessel. This is especially the case in a ship with a full stern or "run;" and it is seen by the preceding figures to be considerable even in the *Greyhound*, which has a tolerably fine "run."

The following table is very instructive, as it shows a comparison between the apparent thrust of the propeller and the actual resistance of the ship. Mr. Froude has imported into the comparison the results of a trial of the *Mutine*, a sister ship to the *Greyhound*, at precisely the same displacement.

| Ship. | I.H.P. on Measured Mile Trial. | Speed of Screw in feet per minute. | Indicated Thrust in pounds, i.e., $\frac{\text{I.H.P.} \times 33{,}000}{\text{Speed of Screw.}}$ | True Resistance in pounds, deduced from Towing experiments. | $\frac{\text{True Resistance.}}{\text{Indicated Thrust.}}$ |
|---|---|---|---|---|---|
| *Greyhound*, | 786 | 1245 | 20,830 | 10,770 | ·517 |
|  | 453 | 1039 | 14,390 | 6,200 | ·431 |
| *Mutine*, | 770 | 1230 | 20,650 | 9,440 | ·457 |
|  | 328 | 952 | 11,380 | 4,770 | ·419 |

**249. Comparative Performances of Steamships.** — As mentioned in the previous chapter, the surface frictional resistances of ships at a given speed are proportional to the cube roots of the squares of the displacements, provided the lengths of the vessels do not fall short of the lowest limit suited for that speed. It has been usual to assume that under the same limitations the engine power increases as the cube of the speed. By reference to the list of actual towing strains on the *Greyhound*, at different speeds between 4 and

12 knots per hour, which are given in the preceding Article, it will be seen that at the low speeds, from 4 to 8 knots, the resistances varied as the squares of the speeds, but beyond that velocity the resistance increased at a much more rapid rate. For instance, if the ratio between the resistances at 8 and 10 knots were as the cubes of the speeds, then 2·5 tons being the towing strain at the former speed, 4·9 tons would be the strain at the latter speed, whereas the experiment showed that 4·7 tons were required, thus showing that the resistance increased nearly as the cubes. Again, if the ratio were as the cubes, the towing strain at 10 knots being 4·7 tons, therefore 8·1 tons would be the strain at 12 knots, whereas the result showed 9·0 tons. Thus we see that the rate of increase of the resistance from 10 to 12 knots is greater in this ship than from 8 to 10 knots. It will be found that, when a vessel is steaming at a speed for which her length and lines are adapted, the ratio of the increase, or diminution of the resistance at speeds slightly greater or less than that speed, is as the squares of the speeds; and if the vessel is driven at a much higher speed, the rate of increase is given by the cubes, and even higher powers, while if driven at a speed not much in excess of that for which she is adapted, the rates of increase of resistance will be somewhere between that of the cubes and the squares of the speeds. The results given by the experiments on the *Greyhound* show that her lines are best adapted for a speed of from 7 to 8 knots.

It is usual in ordinary calculations to consider that the resistance of a vessel varies as the square of her velocity, and therefore that the power required to produce that velocity varies as the cube, and that the useful effect of the engine, that is, the effect which remains after deducting the power absorbed in overcoming friction, working air-pumps, etc., bears a constant ratio to the power developed in the cylinder, known by the term "indicated horse-power." As ships are usually driven at a higher speed than their lines are intended for, it is probable that the power required usually varies as a higher power than the cube of the speed. In practice, however, it is assumed that if $D^{\frac{2}{3}}$ is multiplied by the cube of the speed and divided by the indicated engine power, a quotient will be obtained whose magnitude is a test of the comparative economy of power in different vessels as the result of the whole combination of ship, propeller, and engine. This quotient is termed the *constant for displacement*. If the displacement is expressed in tons, the speed in knots per hour, and the engine power in indicated horse-power, the value of this constant ranges from about 200 to 260 in good examples. Table XI. gives the values of this constant for displacement of different vessels, as determined by trials on the measured mile at different speeds. The algebraical expression for this constant is—

$$C_d = \frac{S^3 \times D^{\frac{2}{3}}}{I.H.P.}$$

where the denominator represents the indicated horse-power.

In determining the indicated horse-power which will be required to drive at a given speed a vessel whose design is being prepared, supposing that speed to be within the ordinary limit to which such a vessel may be economically driven, it is usual to refer to the constant of performance of a vessel of similar form and similarly propelled when upon trial at the measured mile, at a time when she made about the same speed as it is required the vessel being designed shall make. Then if $S$ is the required speed, $D$ the displacement of the proposed vessel, and $C_d$ the constant chosen—

$$\text{Since } C_d = \frac{S^3 \times D^{\frac{2}{3}}}{I.H.P.}$$

$$\therefore I.H.P. = \frac{S^3 \times D^{\frac{2}{3}}}{C_d}$$

Another constant is used for the same purpose by supposing that the resistance varies as the area of midship section. The basis of this assumption was given in the last chapter; as already stated, it is founded on the supposition that the resistance due to forcing the water out of the vessel's way as she excavates her course, varies in vessels of similar form as the areas of the immersed midship sections. Terming this constant $C_m$, then

$$C_m = \frac{S^3 \times M}{I.H.P.}$$
$$\therefore I.H.P. = \frac{S^3 \times M}{C_m}$$

If the selected case whose constants of performance both of displacement and midship section are used is a good one for comparison, then the values of I.H.P., determined from $D^{\frac{2}{3}}$ and $M$, will be very nearly equal; in which case it is usual to take the mean of the results in deciding upon the indicated horse-power which will be required for the intended speed. Table XI., already referred to, gives the values of $C_m$ and $C_d$ for the several ships therein named.

As will be evident by referring to the expressions for these constants, low speeds with the same values of $D$ and I.H.P. produce low constants, and if the I.H.P. for any speed is excessive, the constant is also low. Thus, considering the speed attained with a certain horse-power as a criterion of a vessel's efficiency, a low constant is an indication of a fault in the ship, propeller, or engines. Of late years it has been found desirable to keep the lengths of armoured ships within the limits which are economically necessary for their speeds, this being done to increase their handiness, reduce their first cost, and the cost of maintenance. These ships show low constants, and although this seems to indicate a fault in the dimensions of the vessels, yet there is no fault in reality, as such results were contemplated and provided for in the engine-power; it being considered more desirable to propel the ships uneconomically than to secure economy of propulsion at the cost of handiness and a large expenditure of money (see constants of *Bellerophon*, as compared with those of *Himalaya*, *Northumberland*, and *Warrior*, in Table XI.)

**250. The Measured Mile.**—When a ship is built and engined, her speed is determined by trial at a measured "knot" or nautical mile. This is done for the twofold purpose of discovering the power indicated by the engines and the speed of the ship. In the event of the former not being so great as was contemplated, or as engines of the particular description should develop, alterations are made, followed by other trials, until the requirements of the engineer are realised. These alterations may affect the nature and pitch of the propeller, as well as the evaporative power of the boilers and the efficiency of the engines. The measured mile trial is necessarily more an engineer's than a shipbuilder's question; nevertheless the latter is deeply interested in the result, in order that he may discover therefrom whether the constants used in the design are suitable, and that he may obtain constants for reference in designing future vessels. Having designed for a certain speed with the development of a given horse-power, it is a matter of importance to him to discover whether with that power the form and dimensions of the vessel are such as to give the desired speed. It is also important to discover the consumption of fuel per indicated horse-power per hour, both with full and half boiler power, in order to know how many days of such full steaming the bunker capacity will permit, and the distance which the coal stowage will drive the ship. At the measured mile trials, too, it is usual to determine the steering qualities of the ship, by measuring the diameter of the circle in which she turns when the helm is hard over. Also, in the case of twin screw vessels, the power of the propellers to turn the ship when acting alone is observed. The slip and general efficiency of the propeller are likewise discovered on these trials.

The limits of the measured mile are known to the pilot by his observing when certain landmarks are in a line with each other, the mile being so set off that at its beginning and termination certain objects on the shore are thus situated with regard to each other. The exact time during which the vessel is running the mile being observed, the rate in knots per hour is readily found. The ship commences to steam at full power some time before reaching the beginning of the course, and the object aimed at is to steam with uniform speed throughout until the vessel is "off the mile." Owing to the currents which continually flow in different directions along our shores, the speed due to the engine power is always either increased or diminished by the movement of the sea due to these currents; consequently runs are made upon the mile in both directions of its length, and the

THE MEASURED MILE.

mean speed of an even number of runs gives the speed due to the engines only. The same precaution eliminates the effect of the force due to the wind on the vessel's hull and rigging.

If the speed of the current and force of the wind were uniform throughout the whole of the trials, the mean of two runs would give the same result—the same boiler-power being supposed to be developed—as the mean of any other even number. But owing to the length of time occupied by these trials such is never the case, for a ship may commence to run aided by a slack current, and make her last run while retarded by a strong current in the same direction. In fact the forces, and even the directions of the currents, within limits, are continually varying; if by some law, that law is unknown, and consequently, in order to eliminate the effect of these currents and that of the wind, the mean of the means of all the speeds of an even number of runs is taken by a method based upon the calculus of finite differences.

For instance, suppose a vessel makes six runs upon a measured mile, three with the current and three against, with the following results as regards speed:—

|     | Knots. |
| --- | --- |
| 1st run, | 16·4 |
| 2nd ,, | 11·1 |
| 3rd ,, | 15·3 |
| 4th ,, | 12·0 |
| 5th ,, | 14·2 |
| 6th ,, | 12·8 |

These figures are arranged as follows, and the means of consecutive speeds continually found until only one mean remains, which is taken as the true speed of the ship in still water.

```
        Knots.
1st, ....16·4 }
              } ..13·75 }
2nd, ...11·1 }          } ...13·475 }
              } ..13·20 }           } ...13·450 }
3rd, ....15·3 }          } ...13·425 }           } ..13·42 }
              } ..13·65 }           } ...13·400 }          } ..13·39
4th, ....12·0 }          } ...13·375 }           } ..13·37 }
              } ..13·10 }           } ...13·337 }
5th, ....14·2 }          } ...13·300 }
              } ..13·50 }
6th, ....12·8 }
      6)81·8
        13·63
```

The *mean* speed is thus found to be 13·39 knots, whereas the *average* speed is 13·63 knots. In the merchant service the latter would frequently be accepted as the speed of the ship, but the Admiralty and some of the principal shipbuilding firms take the former result. The difference, in this case amounting to about a quarter of a knot per hour, is important. Sometimes the method by differences gives a higher result than that of the average, but in any case the Admiralty method is superior in accuracy to the other.

In the example just given, by finding the differences between the real speed of the ship and the observed speed on the mile during the several runs, we shall find that the speeds of the current in the line of the ship's course during the trials were as follow :—

| | | | |
|---|---|---|---|
| 1st run, | 3·01 knots | with | the ship. |
| 2nd ,, | 2·29 ,, | against | ,, |
| 3rd ,, | 1·91 ,, | with | ,, |
| 4th ,, | 1·39 ,, | against | ,, |
| 5th ,, | ·81 ,, | with | ,, |
| 6th ,, | ·59 ,, | against | ,, |

So that the speed of the current in the direction of the course was diminished during the trials from 3·01 to ·59 knots per hour; also that the speeds of the current aiding the ship were 3·01, 1·91, and ·81 knots, or a mean of 1·91 knots; while the speeds retarding the ship were 2·29, 1·39, and ·59 knots, or a mean of 1·42 knots. Thus the ship received more assistance than she suffered retardation from the current, and consequently the average of the speeds gave more than the real speed of the ship in still water. Had the first run been against the tide and the last with it, the variation in the speed of the current being the same as in the example, the average would have given a lower value than the true speed. Hence, if all the trials of a ship are made in the space of about four hours, commencing on the full strength of a tidal current and ending just at high or low water; if the first run is made with the tide, the result by the method of averages will represent the ship's speed to be better than it really is, whereas if the first run is made against the tide, the result is worse than the truth. It is quite within the range of possibility that engineers and shipbuilders have ere now taken advantage of this fact.

**251. Steam Trials at Varied Speeds.**—Mr. Denny, the shipbuilder of Dumbarton, has discarded the conventional system of measured mile trials at full speed and half-boiler power, and now tries each of his ships at four or even five speeds, thereby obtaining data from which a curve of indicated horse-power can be constructed representing its value from the lowest to the highest speeds. By the ordinary measured mile trials only two spots in the curve can be determined, and these at comparatively high speeds, leaving no information regarding the lower speeds. At the annual meetings of the Institution of Naval Architects in April 1876, Mr. W. Froude, F.R.S., read a paper upon the subject, in which he gave the results of some investigations which he had made regarding the ratios of indicated to effective horse-power as elucidated by these trials on certain ships. The results are so important that this chapter would be incomplete without some reference to these ingenious investigations into the several resistances which subtract from the work performed in the cylinders before it is effectively employed in propelling the ship.

Mr. Froude truly says that the "so-called *constants* of performance are invariably *variable* and *inconsistent*," being based, as we have already said, upon the assumption that resistance must vary as the square of the speed, and horse-power as its cube. Mr. Denny's trials furnish important information regarding engine friction, and explain very clearly the sources of that diminution from the indicated power of the engines, which results in only about 37 to 40 per cent. of the whole power delivered being usefully employed.

Mr. Froude says—

"I have always felt that the system of reducing the results of steam trials to indicated horse-power, though no doubt furnishing a true expression in a commercial sense of the relative merits of the ship under trial, tended, nevertheless, to cloud the real significance of the record, viewed as suggestive of those specialities of form or condition which have really governed the ship's performance, not only because indicated horse-power includes in one large term the merits of the ship, the engine, and the propeller, but because the term into which it groups these items is complicated by the introduction of the speed factor, instead of representing them under their more elementary form of force simply. With this view, ever since

I have entered into such investigations, I have invariably converted the horse-power term to a force term by simply dividing it by a speed factor; and, as shaping the reduction into its most natural and opposite form, I have adopted as the divisor the speed of the propeller, expressed, not by its revolutions nakedly, but by its revolutions × its pitch, that is to say, the virtual travel of the force delivered by the propeller. The result thus obtained from the indicated horse-power I have termed 'indicated thrust;' it is, in fact, the thrust which the propeller would be exerting if the force of the steam were employed wholly in creating thrust, instead of partly in overcoming friction, driving the air-pump, and overcoming other collateral resistances. Indicated thrust is simply a constant multiple of the mean steam pressure on the piston; and if this were given in the records of the trials, indicated thrust is

$$\frac{\text{mean piston pressure} \times \text{total piston travel per revolution}}{\text{pitch of propeller}};$$

when, however (as is commonly the case), the I.H.P. alone is given, then the expression for indicated thrust is

$$\frac{33,000 \times \text{I.H.P.}}{\text{pitch} \times \text{revolutions}}.$$

"When decomposed into its constituent parts, indicated thrust is resolved into several elements, which must be enumerated and kept in view.

"These elements are:—1. The useful thrust, or ship's true resistance. 2. The augmentation of resistance, which, as I have pointed out in many previous papers, is due to the diminution which the action of the propeller creates in the pressure of the water against the stern end of the ship. 3. The equivalent of the friction of the screw blades in their edgeway motion through the water. 4. The equivalent of the friction due to the dead weight of the working parts, piston packings, and the like, which constitute the initial or slow speed friction of the engine. 5. The equivalent of friction of the engines due to the working load. 6. The equivalent of air-pump and feed-pump duty.

It is probable that 2, 3, and 4 of the above list are all very nearly proportional to the useful thrust; 6 is probably nearly proportional to the square of the number of revolutions, and thus, at least at the lower speeds, approximately to the useful thrust; 5 probably remains constant at all speeds, and for convenience it may be regarded as constant, though perhaps in strict truth it should be termed 'initial friction.' If, then, we could separate the quasi-constant friction from the indicated thrust throughout, the remainder would be approximately proportional to the ship's true resistance."

He constructs a curve which he terms a *thrust curve* (see fig. 1, Plate LVIII.), representing to scale by its ordinates the indicated thrust at the speeds between the lowest at $a$ and the highest at $e$. The speed represented at $a$ is about 3 to 5 knots. It will be observed that this curve at the lowest end refuses to pass through the thrust zero, but tends towards a point representing a considerable amount of thrust. Mr. Froude justly concludes—

"That this apparent thrust at the zero of speed when there can be no real thrust, is the equivalent of what I have termed initial friction; so that if we could determine correctly the point at which the curve, if prolonged to the speed zero, would intersect the axis $OY$ (fig. 2, Plate LVIII.), and if we were to draw a line through the intersection parallel to the base, the height which would be thus cut off from the thrust ordinates would represent the deduction to be made from them in respect of constant or initial friction, and the remainders of the ordinates between the new base and the curve would, as has been explained, be approximately proportional to the ship's true resistance."

Starting from the experimentally derived fact that with tolerably well-shaped ships of such dimensions as those he is dealing with,* the resistance at such low speeds as from 3 to 5 knots varies as the power 1·87 of the speed. He says:—

"Hence, on this assumption, the lower end of the thrust curve, when divested of the constant friction equivalent, should be a parabola in which the ordinate is as the power 1·87 of the abscissa; and since, as we have seen, the entire thrust, exclusive of the initial friction, is proportionate, at least at the slow speeds, to the true resistance curve, the problem to be solved is the very simple geometrical one of so drawing a parabola of this order, in connection with the axes of co-ordinates of the diagram, that it shall meet or join the existing thrust curve with an identical tangential direction. The construction by which this is effected is extremely simple; at the point $p$, fig. 2, Plate LVIII., near the lower end of the thrust curve, draw the tangent $p'\,p''$; draw the vertical at $h'$ so as to cut the space $oh$ into segments having the ratio indicated by the figured quantities, thus making $oh = 1 \cdot 87\ oh'$; draw a line parallel to $oX$ through the point where this vertical cuts the tangent; the point where this line cuts the thrust axis is the vertex of the required curve.

\* \* \* \* \* \* \*

"Fig. 3, Plate LVIII., shows the process as completed from the records of the trials of Mr. Denny's ship, the *Merkara*. In this diagram the curve of I.H.P., the curve of slip, and the curve of constants, are also shown.

"On comparing five curves thus analysed, it appears that the constant friction is equivalent to from $\frac{1}{8}$ to $\frac{1}{7}$ of the gross load on the

* The *Merkara*: length, 360 feet; breadth, 37 feet; draught, $16\frac{1}{4}$ feet; displacement, 3980 tons.

engine when working at its maximum speed and power. And it is not irrational to accept this relation provisionally as the basis of an empirical formula, since the constant friction depends to a large extent on the diameter and weight of the working parts of the engine, and these must be approximately proportionate to the intended maximum strain, subject, of course, to some allowance for the variation which exists in the types of engine in use. I must admit that the proportion appears to me to be unexpectedly large, but the process by which it is determined is, I think, so certain and definite that I cannot doubt the general soundness of the conclusion deduced by it; and that conclusion seems to me to be one of very high importance and significance, namely, that a screw engine when working, even at its most moderate and economical speed, must be understood to be throwing away in the one element of this friction alone, not indeed $\frac{1}{7}$ of its maximum power, for the engine may be now working at reduced speed, but a power due to $\frac{1}{7}$ of its maximum load. Thus, in the case of the *Merkara*, when the ship is steaming at 5 knots in a smooth sea, one-half of her whole expenditure of power is due to this circumstance. The question of the apportionment of this large amount of inevitable friction between the several working parts of the engine, and of the proportionate degree in which it attaches to different types of engines, as well as the extent to which the evil is remediable, are inquiries of great importance, but they are more or less out of my reach, and are at all events beyond my present purpose, which is satisfied by the proof—an irresistible proof as it appears to me—that the evil does exist to about the degree named."

The power due to the ship's net resistance Mr. Froude designates "effective horse-power," using the symbol E.H.P. The horse-power due to the ship's progress (excluding slip) is styled S.H.P. Experiments made with models by Mr. Froude show that the horse-power due to (1) is 40 to 50 per cent. of the ship's net resistance :—he takes it at 40 per cent.,

Hence H.P. due to $(1) = 0.4$ E.H.P.

The result of his experiments for determining the *water friction of the screw* shows that

H.P. due to $(2) = 0.1$ E.H.P.

As already investigated from the curves found by the steam trials, (3) is equal to $\frac{1}{7}$ of the total load on the engines, when working with the maximum intended speed and pressure—

Hence H.P. due to $(3) = 0.143$ S.H.P.

The *friction due to working load* of engine at maximum speed is, he says, about the same as the dead load friction,

So that H.P. due to $(4) = 0.143$ S.H.P.

## NEGATIVE SLIP. 359

For the *air-pump resistance* he takes the mean of Tredgold's values, viz., 0·075.

Thus H.P. due to (5) = 0·075 S.H.P.

Combining these results he has:

Horse-power due to net resistance ........ = E.H.P.
Augmentation due to net resistance........ = 0·4 E.H.P.
Screw friction due to net resistance........ = 0·1 E.H.P.
Constant friction of engines ................. =    0·143 S.H.P.
Friction due to working load of engines =    0·143 S.H.P.
Air-pump resistance ........................... =    0·075 S.H.P.

or  S.H.P. = 1·5 E.H.P. + ·361 S.H.P.
so that ·639 S.H.P = 1·5 E.H.P.

or S.H.P. = $\frac{1\cdot5}{\cdot 639}$ E.H.P. = 2·347 E.H.P.

To this must be added the slip = ·1 S.H.P.; the whole making the I.H.P.

= 1·1 S.H.P.
= 2·582 E.H.P.
= $\frac{100}{38\cdot 7}$ E.H.P.

or  E.H.P. = ·387 I.H.P.

"This conclusion," says Mr. Froude, "agrees very fairly with what, as I have already pointed out, more general experience has led me to adopt as an average expression of the relation between indicated and effective horse-power, namely, that at high speed the former is about 2·7 times the latter, or the latter 37½ per cent. of the former."

**252. Negative Slip.**—Among other interesting results of the observations on trials of ships upon the measured mile is the remarkable one that sometimes the speed of the ship has been found to exceed that of the screw propeller.* That is to say, the product of the pitch of the screw and the number of revolutions in a given time has been exceeded by the actual distance the ship has moved through during that time. Hence there has not only been an absence of slip, in the ordinary sense of the term, observed upon these occasions, but the ship has actually moved faster than the speed due to the pitch of the propeller. This phenomenon has been termed *negative slip.* Various theories have been offered in explanation of this singular result. Among these it has

* See cases of *Jumna* and *Northumberland* in Table XI.

been conjectured that the screw has been temporarily bent so as to increase its pitch beyond the angle at which it was set, and that when the pressure has been removed the elasticity of the material composing the propeller has enabled it to recover its original form. From want of evidence, and by reason of the improbability of the theory, it has not been accepted by competent authorities. Another theory which received considerable support at one time, and is even mentioned as the real cause of the phenomenon in *Murray's Shipbuilding*, is that there is a body of water following the ship in these cases, and that the screw working in a body of water having a forward velocity communicates a velocity to the ship over and above that due to the pitch and number of revolutions of the screw. That there frequently is a body of water following in the wake of vessels having ill-formed after bodies, is a fact well known to naval architects, and it has already been alluded to in this chapter. Indeed, there is very little doubt that this is a great element in the resistance of most ships, but as the propeller can only act upon a small portion of the following stream, the small additional velocity which can in this way be communicated to the ship is quite inadequate to account for the large percentages of "negative slip" which have been observed in some cases. The explanation offered by Mr. E. J. Reed in a paper read before the Institution of Naval Architects in 1866, and which was first suggested by Mr. J. B. Crossland of the Admiralty, is no doubt the true one. Mr. Reed attributes it to the elasticity of the water. He says, "All former disquisitions upon this subject have proceeded upon the assumption that the water is practically inelastic, and that the motion imparted to the water against which the screw propeller strikes is equal, and only equal in velocity to the velocity of the screw; whereas a little reflection will suffice to show that this can hardly be the case, and that, on the contrary, it is most probable that the water, struck by a high-speed screw, is driven off at a much greater velocity than that of the screw, and that the momentum imparted to it is proportionate to this velocity." It should be added that in cases of negative slip the pitch is usually small, and therefore the velocity of the engine great.

# PART VI.

## CALCULATIONS RELATING TO THE STEERING OF SHIPS.

---

### CHAPTER XI.

Steering—The Rudder—Principle of the Rudder—Angle of Maximum Efficiency—Angle of Maximum Efficiency with regard to Power Applied—Usual Angle of Rudder—Areas of Rudders—Ratio of Pressure and Velocity—The Balanced Rudder.

**253. Steering.**—The operation of guiding and changing the direction of a ship's motion through the water is termed steering. A ship may be to some extent steered by sails, as already explained in Chapter IX., also as mentioned in the preceding chapter, her course may be altered by the proper use of twin screws when she is propelled by steam power.

**254. The Rudder.**—But by far the most efficient, trustworthy, and, indeed, ancient mode of governing the direction of a ship's motion is by the rudder. The rudder is commonly hung to the stern of the vessel, but in some cases when a vessel is double-ended, *i.e.*, intended to move with either extremity foremost, a rudder is hung both at the bow and stern. The immersed part of a rudder has usually the form of a flat plate in a vertical position, capable of turning into different angular positions about a vertical or nearly vertical axis. In the common form of rudder, when it is at the stern, that axis is at the forward edge of the rudder where it is hung to the rudder post by means of hinge connections termed "pintles" and "braces." In what is termed the "balanced rudder," to be described hereafter, the axis is usually at one-third the breadth of the rudder from its forward edge, and the rudder turns on a pivot at its lower end, where it is supported by the projecting after-end of the keel.

**255. Principle of the Rudder.**—In order that the rudder may be employed in turning a ship, it is necessary that the latter shall have motion, and that it may be efficiently employed it is necessary that the speed of the ship shall be sufficient to cause the water to act upon the face of the rudder with enough pressure to turn the vessel. It is also necessary for efficiency that the motion of the water striking the rudder should consist of a steady flow astern relatively to the motion of the ship. Hence it is requisite that the lines of the after body should be fair and fine, so as not to drag a volume of water after the vessel, or set the particles in motion in any other way than directly astern; in proportion as the flow of the stream meeting the rudder deviates from a fore and aft direction, the action of the rudder will fail to be efficient.

When the rudder is right fore and aft, it forms part of the after body of the ship, and being symmetrical, with regard to the middle line longitudinal plane of the vessel, it offers no other than surface resistance to her motion, and this resistance being balanced does not interfere with the rectilineal motion of the ship. But when the rudder is put over to any angle it deflects the particles of water which it meets on that side of the ship. The pressure due to meeting these particles of water with the velocity of the ship's motion may be resolved into two components, one in the direction of the ship's motion and the other perpendicular to it. The first simply diminishes the ship's speed, whereas the other tends to drive her sideways, but acting through a point abaft the centre of the lateral resistance to this sideway motion of the ship, a mechanical couple is set up which causes her to rotate about her centre of gravity. If the rudder is turned to the port side, as shown by $AC$, fig. 1, Plate LIX., then the action of the rotating couple is to turn the bow of the ship likewise to port, as shown by the arrow $B_1$; her instantaneous motion being about her centre of gravity $G$.

Referring to fig. 1, Plate LIX., we will now proceed to examine the action of the rudder more minutely. $AB$ is the middle line of the ship, $AC$ is the breadth of the rudder, which is inclined at an angle $\theta$ to the line of the ship's keel. Let $V$ be the velocity of the ship in knots, and therefore the velocity of the stream which meets the rudder, supposing the direction of that stream to be right astern. The effect of the pressure due to the velocity of this stream upon the rudder may be supposed concentrated at the centre of pressure of the rudder surface. For all useful purposes this centre of pressure may be safely assumed to coincide with the centre of gravity of the surface of the rudder. Suppose then $VP$ to represent the line of action of the resultant pressure in the direction opposite to that of the ship's motion. The component of the velocity $V$ of the stream, normal to the surface of the rudder, is $V \sin \theta$, and if $K$ is the resistance on a unit of surface moving perpendicular to itself with a velocity of one knot, the intensity of the normal pressure produced is $K.V^2 \sin^2 \theta$; supposing that the pressure varies as the square of the velocity. As we shall hereafter see, experiments show that the pressure does not really vary with so great a ratio as the square; the assumption is, however, on the safe side when calculating the stresses on the rudder head.

The normal intensity of pressure may be resolved into two components, viz., a longitudinal component $K.V^2 \sin^3 \theta$, which is the direct head resistance offered by the rudder when at an angle $\theta$ with the middle line, and $K.V^2 \sin^2 \theta \cos \theta$ which gives her sideway motion. This latter pressure acts in the direction $TP$, and after a short time is balanced by an equivalent pressure against the side of the vessel through the centre of lateral resistance $L$. The effect of this couple is to cause the vessel to rotate about an axis through her centre of gravity, while at the same time she moves forward with a velocity somewhat less than $V$, owing to the head resistance of the rudder at that angle. Hence the ship turns in a circle, the smallness of the diameter of which, and the shortness of the time in which the circle is turned, being a criterion of the efficiency of the steering apparatus which, as already stated, it is one of the objects of a steamship's trial on the measured mile to determine.

**256. Angle of Maximum Efficiency.**—To determine the angle at which a rudder exerts its maximum efficiency, we must consider two distinct problems.

I. When the steering force within the vessel, either from manual, steam, hydraulic, or any other motive power, is not limited, to determine at what angle a rudder has the greatest turning power.

II. When a given force is applied, to determine at what angle the rudder is most efficient and what breadth the rudder should have.

We will now consider these problems separately.

**257. Absolute Angle of Maximum Efficiency.**—Firstly, then, we will consider the case when the power applied in turning the rudder is not limited.

Again, suppose the velocity of the stream in knots is $V$, and that it flows directly astern. As already shown (see fig. 1, Plate LIX.), the intensity of the normal pressure is $K.V^2 \sin^2 \theta$. The turning moment of this pressure is $K.V^2 \sin^2 \theta \times RG$, where $RG$ is the perpendicular from the centre of gravity upon $PR$. Hence the turning moment

$$\begin{aligned} M &= K.V^2 \sin^2 \theta \times RG \\ &= K.V^2 \sin^2 \theta \times P_2G \cos \theta \\ &= K.P_2G.V^2 \sin^2 \theta \cos \theta. \end{aligned}$$

Hence, since $P_2G$ is practically of constant length for all angles of the rudder, $M$ varies as $\sin^2 \theta \cos \theta$. Therefore also when $M$ is a maximum,

$$\begin{aligned} \frac{dM}{d\theta} &= \frac{d}{d\theta}\left(\sin^2 \theta \cos \theta\right) \\ &= 2 \sin \theta \cos^2 \theta - \sin^3 \theta = 0; \\ \therefore \quad & 2 \cos^2 \theta = \sin^2 \theta \\ & \tan^2 \theta = 2 \\ & \theta = \tan^{-1} \sqrt{2} \\ & = 54\tfrac{3}{4} \text{ degrees,} \end{aligned}$$

which is the theoretical maximum angle of a rudder's efficiency in turning a ship when the power applied in turning the rudder is not taken into account.

**258. Angle of Maximum Efficiency with regard to the Power applied.**—In fig. 2, Plate LIX., let $AC$ be a rudder of breadth $B$, and $Ac$ another rudder of breadth $b$, each of which is moved by the application of the same power at the rudder head. Suppose the speed of the ship to be the same in both cases, then the ratio between the angles $a$ and $\theta$, to which the rudders $AC$ and $Ac$ will be respectively turned, is determined by the expression

$$\frac{\sin \alpha}{\sin \theta} = \frac{b}{B}.$$

This was proved in the following manner by Mr. F. K. Barnes, in a paper read before the Institution of Naval Architects in 1864.

The normal pressures on the rudders are proportional in the one case to $B \sin^2 \alpha$ and in the other to $b \sin^2 \theta$, therefore the moments of these pressures about the axes of the rudders are proportional to $\frac{B^2}{2} \sin^2\alpha$ and $\frac{b^2}{2} \sin^2\theta$. Hence, since these moments are the same,

$$\frac{B^2 \sin^2 \alpha}{2} = \frac{b^2 \sin^2 \theta}{2}$$
$$B^2 \sin^2 \alpha = b^2 \sin^2 \theta$$
$$B \sin \alpha = b \sin \theta$$
$$\frac{\sin \alpha}{\sin \theta} = \frac{b}{B}.$$

In the same paper Mr. Barnes showed that the effects of the rudders to turn the ship in the two cases will be in the ratio of $\sin 2\alpha$ to $\sin 2\theta$.

For the turning moments of the rudders are, respectively, proportional to $B \sin^2 \alpha \cos \alpha$ and $b \sin^2 \theta \cos \theta$. Calling these $M$ and $m$.

then $M : m = B \sin^2 \alpha \cos \alpha : b \sin^2 \theta \cos \theta$.
But $B \sin \alpha = b \sin \theta$,

as already shown. Therefore,

$M : m = \sin \alpha \cos \alpha : \sin \theta \cos \theta$
$= \sin 2\alpha : \sin 2\theta$.

From this result we gather an important fact. The value of $2\alpha$ or $2\theta$, for which the sine is a maximum, is 90°, and therefore $\alpha$ or $\theta$ is 45°.

Hence the best breadth of rudder for a ship when moving at a given speed is that which allows the rudder to be turned to an angle of 45°, with the steering power available. Since, given a certain power of turning the rudder head, that power is most efficiently applied in turning the vessel when the rudder is at an angle of 45°, hence it is necessary that the rudder should not exceed a certain breadth.

Suppose the values of $a$ and $\theta$ to be 15 and 30 degrees respectively; then

$$\frac{b}{B} = \frac{\sin 15°}{\sin 30°} = \frac{1}{2} \text{ (nearly)}$$
$$\therefore b = \tfrac{1}{2} B \text{ (nearly)}$$

and the effects of the rudders in turning the ship in the two cases will be as sin 30° to sin 60°, or as 1 to 1¾. The ratio between the effects of two rudders in turning a vessel when at angles of 15° and 45° respectively are as ½ : 1 or 1 : 2, supposing their breadths to be in the ratio of sin 45° to sin 15°. Thus narrow rudders at large angles (up to 45°) are equally as efficient as broad rudders at small angles, the speed of the ship being the same.

The speed of the water which meets the rudder of a screw steamship is greater than the speed of the ship, hence such ships require narrower rudders than sailing ships. If it were practicable it would be desirable to have two available breadths of rudder for a ship which steams at one time and sails at another, the narrower one for use when steaming and the broader when sailing.

**259. Usual Angle of Rudder.**—Although 45 degrees is the best angle at which to use a rudder, yet, as will be readily seen, it is but slightly better than at 40 degrees, whereas the power expended in getting the rudder through the additional 5 degrees and the additional head resistance are considerable. Hence it is customary in wood vessels to "beard" the rudder and rudder-post so as to allow of the rudder turning through an angle of about 40 or 42 degrees each way.

The rudder is rarely worked beyond about 15 degrees in large steamships, as the power required to turn it beyond that angle is usually so enormous. There can be little doubt that rudders are frequently made too wide, and that instead of proportioning their width to the area of the immersed middle line longitudinal plane of the ship, only, due regard should be had to the speed of the vessel.

**260. Areas of Rudders.**—The following is a list of the areas of rudder surface and their proportions to the areas of the immersed longitudinal vertical plane in the undermentioned ships of Her Majesty's Navy:—

| Name of Ship. | Area of Rudder in square feet. | Area of Longitudinal Vertical Section. | Area of Section divided by the Area of Rudder. |
|---|---|---|---|
| *Canopus*, | 127 | 4592 | 36·1 |
| *Arethusa*, | 114 | 5359 | 47·0 |
| *Warrior*, | 180 | 9271 | 51·5 |
| *Shah*, | 203 | 7455 | 36·7 |
| *Bellerophon*, | 248 | 7301 | 29·4 |
| *Achilles*, | 166 | 9792 | 59·0 |
| *Himalaya*, | 105 | 6290 | 60·0 |
| *Devastation*, | 165 | 7615 | 46·1 |
| *Cyclops*, | 95 | 3613 | 38·1 |
| *Glatton*, | 163 | 4579 | 28·0 |

The ratios vary from $\frac{1}{28}$ in the *Glatton* to $\frac{1}{60}$ in the *Himalaya*. The former is a full bodied monitor of low speed, and as the motion of the water against the rudder is no doubt deflected from the fore and aft direction owing to the form of the after body, there seems some reason in this case for the apparently excessive ratio. The *Himalaya*, on the other hand, is a fast steam troopship with fine lines, and experience shows that her low ratio of $\frac{1}{60}$ is ample for the vessel. Admiral Halsted stated before the Institution of Naval Architects in 1864 that "reasonable grounds have been shown, from combined sailing experience and successful gunboat experience, that 1 square foot of rudder area to every 38 square feet of immersed longitudinal area of the ship at load draught may be assumed as an effective general standard for rudder surface." We question, however, whether any such standard can be fixed, as the conditions of diverse types of ships are so different.

**261. Ratio of Pressure and Velocity.** — It has been assumed in this chapter that the pressure of the water on a rudder varies as the square of velocity. Experiments made on H.M.S. *Warrior*, by means of a dynamometer, show that when the speeds vary as 1 : 2 : 3 : 4 instead of the pressures varying as $1^2 : 2^2 : 3^2 : 4^2$ or 1 : 4 : 9 : 16, the actual pressures were as $1 : 3 : 6\frac{1}{2} : 8\frac{1}{2}$, which is less than the assumed rate of increase. The error made upon the assumption that the pressure varies as the square of the velocity whenever applied in practice to determine the turning moment or the stress upon the rudder head, will be on the wrong side in the former but on the safe side in the latter case.

**262. The Balanced Rudder.**—The enormous power required in order to get the rudders of high powered armourclads over to an efficient angle, and the consequent stresses on the rudder heads, rudder posts, and stern framing of these ships, has caused our Naval Architects to seek for some form of rudder which, while possessing the same efficiency as the ordinary type, shall yet require the expenditure of less work to get it over to the desired angle, and less power to keep it there while the speed of the ship is maintained. The *balanced rudder* has been found to fulfil these conditions to a useful degree so long as the ship is propelled by steam, but when recourse is had to sail power the rudder has been found objectionable.

The balanced rudder is said to have been invented by Earl Stanhope in 1790, but not in precisely its present form. The credit of having practically tried the balanced rudder is generally assigned to Captain Shuldham, R.N., who experimented with it in the year 1819. It was not, however, until 1863 that anything like a satisfactory test was made of its qualities. Admiral Sir A. C. Key (then captain of the Steam Reserve at Devonport) superintended trials of the balanced rudder on H.M. gunboat *Delight*, which he reported as being "quite successful." Since then it has been fitted in several armour-clad ships of our own and other navies. At first, difficulties were experienced in manœuvering under sail, to meet which, modifications in the rudder were made, as will be explained presently, but more recent experience has shown that there are so many disadvantages attending its use that it is no longer adopted in the Royal Navy.

Referring to Plate LX., $CC_1$ represents a balanced rudder, $A$ being the axis. $P$ is the centre of pressure—still assumed to coincide with the centre of gravity of the area—$PR$ the direction of the resolved normal pressure, and $GR$ is the arm of the turning couple. Let $CC_1 = B$. The turning moment in this case is proportional to

$$B . V^2 \sin^2 \theta \cos \theta \times pG.$$

## THE BALANCED RUDDER.

Let $AC_2$ be an ordinary rudder of the same area as the balanced rudder, and of the same breadth $B$. $P_2$ is its centre of pressure, and $GR_2$ is the arm of the turning couple; hence the turning moment in this case is proportional to

$$B.V^2 \sin^2 \theta \cos \theta \times p_2G.$$

Now $pG$ and $p_2G$ are practically equal, hence the turning moments of the two rudders are practically the same. This is on the supposition that the stream of water inpinging on the rudder meets it under similar circumstances, that is, leaves the surface of the after body with the same direction and velocity. This latter is purely an experimental question, and was answered in the affirmative by Admiral Key in 1863.

Next, we have to consider the relative forces required to turn the rudders to the same angle.

The stress on the rudder head in the case of the balanced rudder depends upon the position of the axis. The best position as determined by Admiral Key's experiment was at one-third the breadth of the rudder from the forward edge. Hence if $AC_1$ is equal to $\frac{CC_1}{3}$, the turning moment at the rudder head to get it over to an angle $\theta$ is proportional to

$$B.V^2 \sin^2 \theta \times \frac{B}{6} = \frac{1}{6} B^2 V^2 \sin^2 \theta.$$

Now, the moment to turn the ordinary rudder is readily seen to be

$$= \tfrac{1}{2} B^2 V^2 \sin^2 \theta.$$

Hence three times the power is required to get the ordinary rudder of breadth $B$ to the angle $\theta$ that is required for the balanced rudder of the same breadth and same efficiency, with its axis at one-third its breadth from the forward edge. It is obvious that the stress at the rudder head diminishes as the axis approaches the middle of the rudder, and supposing the pressure exerted by the particles to be uniform throughout the breadth of the rudder, there would be no more force required in turning than is necessary to overcome the inertia of the rudder. We should here remark that this latter force likewise diminishes rapidly as the axis approaches the middle of the breadth, thus contributing another element of superiority in the balanced over the ordinary rudder.

The advantage of the balanced rudder is apparent only when the speed of the ship is maintained by steam power, or a body of water is driven against the rudder by the screw propeller, even when the vessel's motion ahead is very small. When sailing, the speed of the ship is considerably reduced by putting the helm over, and when the sails are shaking and the head of the vessel points in the direction from whence the wind is blowing, she rapidly loses all "steerage-way," and frequently "misses stays." There is little doubt that owing to the portion $AC_1$ of the rudder being on the opposite side of the axis of rotation, the turning of the ship is impeded when the "steerage-way" is diminished or lost.

An attempt was made to get over this objection by fitting the *Hercules* with a balanced rudder, the fore portion $AC_1$ of which could be locked in a fore and aft direction when desired, leaving the portion $AC$ to rotate with the same effect as an ordinary rudder of that breadth. The fact of this experiment not being repeated in recent vessels is a proof that even this improvement on the usual balanced rudder has not met with sufficient success to warrant its being used in preference to the ordinary rudder rotating about an axis at its forward edge.

# INDEX.

## PART I.—CALCULATIONS RELATING TO THE FORMS AND DIMENSIONS OF SHIPS.

Angular Measurement of Areas, 74.
Application of "Five-eight" Rule, 32.
   ,,      Rule for Displacement, 42, 50.
   ,,      Simpson's 1st Rule, 29.
   ,,      Simpson's 2nd Rule, 31.
   ,,      Trapezoidal Rule, 31.
   ,,      Woolley's Rule, 74.
Areas, Angular Measurement of, 74.
   ,,  of Midship Section, Curve of, 46.
   ,,  of Plane Surfaces, 17.
Axis of Level Motion, 105.

Buoyancy, 13.
   ,,      Centre of, 46.
   ,,      Centre of, by Woolley's Rule, 69.
   ,,      Curve of, 105.
   ,,      Surface of, 106.
Calculation of Displacement, 42, 50, 58, 65.
   ,,      Dynamical Surface Stability, 103.
   ,,      Longitudinal Metacentre, 109.
   ,,      Statical Surface Stability, 97.
   ,,      Transverse Metacentre, 93.
Centre of Buoyancy, 46.
   ,,      Buoyancy by Woolley's Rule, 69.
   ,,      Flotation, 104.
   ,,      Gravity of a Solid, 43.
   ,,      Gravity of Plane Areas, 32, 37.
   ,,      Gravity of Regular Figures, 33.
   ,,      Gravity of Trapezoid, 35.
   ,,      Gravity of Trapezium, 34.
   ,,      Gravity of Triangle, 33.
Coefficient of Fineness of Displacement, 83.
   ,,      Midship Section, 84.
   ,,      Water Lines, 84.
   ,,      (Mean) of Water Lines, 84.
Coefficients of Fineness, Table of, 85.
Comparative Stabilities of different Vessels, 111.

Curve of Areas of Midship Section, 46.
   ,,  Buoyancy, 105.
   ,,  Displacement, 49.
   ,,  Sectional Areas, 47.
   ,,  Tons per Inch, 48.

Displacement, 15, 42.
   ,,      by Geometrical Method, 58.
   ,,      by Woolley's Rule, 65.
   ,,      Calculation of, 42, 50.
   ,,      Curve of, 49.
Dynamical Surface Stability, 102.

"Five-eight" Rule, 29.
   ,,      Application of, 32.
Fixed Metacentre, 89.
Flotation, Plane of, 104.
   ,,  Surface of, 104.
Fractional Intervals, 27.

Geometrical Application of Woolley's Rule, 74.
   ,,  Method, Displacement by, 58.

Hydrostatical Principles, 13.

Intersection of Water Planes, 94.
Investigation of Moments of Inertia, 81.

Level Motion, Axis of, 105.
Longitudinal Metacentre, 108.
   ,,  Metacentre, Calculation of, 109.
   ,,  Metacentric Surface Stability, 110.
Metacentre, 86.
   ,,  Fixed, 89.
   ,,  Longitudinal, 108.
   ,,  Longitudinal, Calculation of, 109.
   ,,  Transverse, 86, 91.
   ,,    ,,  Calculation of, 91.
Metacentric, 106.
   ,,  Surface Stability, 92, 110.
Moments of Inertia, 79.
   ,,  Investigation of, 8

372     THEORETICAL NAVAL ARCHITECTURE.

Moments of Inertia, Table of, 80.
   ,,    Wedge-shaped Solid, 77.
   ,,    Principle of, 35.
More Exact Calculations of Stability, 94.

Plane of Flotation, 104.
Principle of Moments, 35.
Principles, Hydrostatical, 13.

Sectional Areas, Curve of, 47.
Simpson's First Rule, 21.
   ,,    Example of, 22.
   ,,    Proof 1st, 22.
   ,,    Proof 2nd, 26.
Simpson's Second Rule, 28.
   ,,    Example of, 31.
Solids, Centres of Gravity of, 43.
   ,,  Volumes of, 41.
   ,,  Wedge-shaped, 76, 77.
Specific Gravities, Table of, 15.
Stability, 13.
   ,,  Surface, 89.
   ,,    ,,  Calculation of, 97.
   ,,    ,,  Dynamical, 102.
   ,,    ,,  Metacentric, 92, 110.
   ,,    ,,  More Exact Calculations of, 94.
Stabilities of Different Vessels, 111.
Surface of Buoyancy, 106.

Surface of Flotation, 104.
Surface Stability, 89.
   ,,    Calculation of, 97.
   ,,    Dynamical, 102.
   ,,    Metacentric, 92, 110.
   ,,    More Exact Calculations of, 94.

Table of Co-efficient of Fineness, 85.
   ,,  Moments of Inertia, 80.
   ,,  Specific Gravities, 15.
Tons per inch, Curve of, 48.
Transverse Metacentre, 86, 91.
   ,,  Calculation of, 93.
Trapezoid, Centre of Gravity of, 35.
Trapezium, Centre of Gravity of, 34.
Triangle, Centre of Gravity of, 33.
Trapezoidal Rule, 29.
   ,,  Application of, 31.

Volumes of Solids, 41.

Wedge-shaped Solids, Moments of, 77.
   ,,    Volumes of, 76.
Woolley's Rule, Centre of Buoyancy by, 69.
   ,,  Displacement by, 65.
   ,,  Geometrical Application of, 74.
   ,,  Proof of, 67.


## PART II.—CALCULATIONS RELATING TO THE WEIGHTS AND CENTRES OF GRAVITY OF SHIPS.

Adding a Weight, Effect on Stability by 139.
   ,,  Effect on Trim by, 128.
Admitting Water, Effect on Stability by, 144.
   ,,  Effect on Trim by, 134.
Appendages, Corrections for, 193.
Application of Curves, 175, 176.
Approximate Centre of Buoyancy, 156.
   ,,  Gravity, 155.
Approximate Value of G.M., 157.
   ,,  Weight of Hull, 154.
Area of Inclined Water Plane, 192.
Armour Plating, 157.
Assumed Wedges, Moments of, 191.
Axis of Rotation, 209.

Backing, 159.
Beams, 160, 170.
BN and GZ, Values of, 194.
Bottom Plating, 160.
   ,,  C. G. of, 165.
   ,,  Expansion of, 160.
   ,,  Without Expansion, 163.
Bulkheads, 172.

Calculation of Stability Curves, 189.

Centre of Buoyancy, Approximately, 156
Centre of Gravity, 113.
   ,,  Approximately, 155.
   ,,  by Curves, 176.
   ,,  by Experiment 119, 123.
   ,,  Longitudinally, 125.
   ,,  of Armour Plating 157.
   ,,  of Backing, 159.
   ,,  of Beams, 170.
   ,,  of Bottom Plating, 165.
   ,,  of Bulkheads, 172.
   ,,  of Decks, 171.
   ,,  of Framing, 173.
   ,,  of Inclined Water Plane, 192.
   ,,  of Longitudinal Frames, 177.
   ,,  of Protective Deck Plating, 159.
   ,,  of Sheathing, 169.
   ,,  Preliminary Calculations of, 155.
Check Spot at 90 degrees, 195.
Combination Tables, 190.
Correction for Layer, 193.
   ,,  Appendages, 193.

# INDEX. 373

Curves, Application of, 175.
," Metacentric, 180.
," of Dynamical Stability, 186, 197.
," of Statical Stability, 184, 188, 199.

Decks, Weights and C. G. of, 171
Dipping, 217.
Dynamical Stability, 118.
," by Geometrical Method, 198.
," Curves of, 186, 197.

Effective Wave Surface, 223.
Equivalent Pendulum, 210.
Exact Calculations of Stability, 118.
Expansion of Bottom, 160.
Experiment, C. G. as found by, 119.

Fittings, Weight and C. G. of, 177.
Forced Rolling, 231.
Form of Wave Surface, 221.
," and Motion of Sub-surfaces, 222.
Formulæ for Waves, 228.
Frames, Weight and C. G. of, 173, 175.
," Longitudinal, Weight and C. G. of, 177.
Free Oscillations, 209.

GM, Approximately, 157.
Gravity, Centre of, 113.
," Approximately, 155.
," by Experiment, 119, 123.
," Position of, 125.
," Preliminary Calculation of, 152.
Gyration, Radius of, 211.
GZ, Value of, 194.

Heaving, Passive, 230.

Inclined Water plane, Area of, 192.
," C. G. of, 192.
Internal Structure of Wave, 225.
Isochronous Oscillations, 208.

Layer, Correction for, 193.
Light Draught, Stability at, 199.
Longitudinal Frames, Weight and C. G. of, 177.
," Position of C. G., 125.

Metacentric Curves, 180.
," Method, 117.
," Statical Stability, 115.
Moments of Assumed Wedges, 191.
," to Alter Trim, 127.
Motion of Wave Surface, 222.
," and Form of Sub-surface, 222.
," Wave, 220.
Moving Weights, Effect on Stability by, 139.
," Trim by, 125.

Oscillations, Isochronous, 208.

Passive Heaving, 230.
," Rolling, 231.
Pendulum, Equivalent, 210.
," Revolving, 206.
Period of a Wave, 220.
," Dipping, 218.
," Pitching, 215.
Periods of Certain Ships, 237.
Pitching, 214.
Preliminary Calculations, 152.
," Tables, 190.
Pressure, Direction of Resultant, 223.
," Sub-surfaces of Uniform, 222.
Protective Deck Plating, 159.

Radius of Gyration, 211.
Removing a Weight, Effect on Stability by, 139.
Removing a Weight, Effect on Trim by, 129.
Resistance to Rolling in Still Water, 215.
Resultant Pressure, Direction of, 223.
Revolving Pendulum, 206.
Rolling among Waves, 230.
," in a Sea Way, 232.
," in Still Water, 204, 213.
," Passive, 231.
Rotation, Axis of, 209.
Rules and Formulæ for Waves, 228.

Sea-way, Rolling in a, 232.
Stability, Dynamical, 118, 198.
," Effect on, by Adding a Weight, 139.
," Effect on, by Admitting Water, 144.
," Effect on, by Moving a Weight, 139.
," Effect on, by Removing a Weight, 139.
," Exact Calculation of, 118.
Statical Correction for Appendages, 193.
," Layer, 193.
Statical Stability at Light Draught, 199.
," Curves of, 184, 188.
," Metacentric, 115.
Steadiness, 236.
Stiffness, 236.
Still Water Rolling, 204.
," Resistance to rolling, 215.
Structure of Waves, 225.
Sub-surfaces, Form of, 222.
," Motion of, 222.
," of Uniform Pressure, 223.
Surface, Effective Wave, 223.
," Form of Wave, 221.
," Motion of Wave, 222.

Tables, Combination, 190.
," Preliminary, 190.
Trim, Effect on, by Adding a Weight, 128.
," Admitting Water, 134

Trim, Effect on, by Moving a Weight, 125.
Trim, Moment to Alter one Inch, 127.

Uniform Pressure, Sub-surfaces of, 223.
Use of Metacentric Method, 117.

Value of BN and GZ, 194.
,, GM, 157.
Volumes of Wedges, 191.

Water Plane, Area of Inclined, 192.
,, C. G. of, 192.
Waves, 219.
,, Effective Surface of, 223.
,, Form of, 219.
,, Motion of, 220.
,, Period of, 226.
,, Rolling Among, 230.

Waves, Rules and Formulæ for, 228.
,, Sub-surfaces of, 223.
,, Surface of, 221.
Wedges, Moments of, 191.
,, Volumes of, 191.
Weight of Armour, 157.
,, Backing, 159.
,, Beams, 170.
,, Bottom Plating, 160.
,, Bulkheads, 172.
,, Decks, 171.
,, Fittings, 177.
,, Hull, Approximately, 154.
,, Longitudinal Frames, 177.
,, Protective Deck Plating, 159.
,, Sheathing and Planking, 160.
,, Transverse Frames, 173.
Winging out the Weights, 213.

## PART III.—CALCULATIONS RELATING TO THE STRENGTH OF SHIPS.

Axis, Neutral, of a Ship, 316.

Beams, 269.
,, Deflection of, 293.
,, of I-shaped Section, 289.
,, Supported at Ends, 289.
Bending Moments, 271.
,, Curve of, 311.
,, Graphical Representation of, 274.
,, In Terms of Load and Length, 283.
,, Table of Maximum, 315.
,, Various Modes of Loading, 280.
,, Worked Example of, 273.
Bending, Resistance to, 284.
,, Calculation of, 287.
Bent Pillars, 299.
Buoyancy, Curve of, 305.
Butt Straps, 251.
,, Strength of, 253.

Calculation of Bending Moments, 273.
,, Intensity of Stress, 319.
,, Resistance to Bending, 287.
Classes of Stress, 243.
Curve of Bending Moments, 311.
,, Buoyancy, 305.
,, Lading, 307.
,, Shearing Stresses, 309.
,, Stresses among Waves, 314.
,, Weights, 308.
,, Weight of Hull, 306.

Definitions, 239.

Deflection of Beams, 293.
Diameters of Rivets, 245.
,, Table of, 247.
Direct Strain, Measure of, 242.
Distributed Load, 275.
,, and Support, 277.

Edge Connections, 252.
Elastic Strength, 240.
Elasticity, 239.
,, Modulus of, 243.
Equivalent Girder, 317.

Factors of Safety, 241.

Graphical Representation of Bending Moments, 274.
Graphical Representation of Shearing Stresses, 274.

I-Shaped Section, Beam of, 289.
Intensity of Stress, 243.
,, Calculation of, 319.
Investigations by Mr. John, 319.

Lading, Curve of, 307.
Load, Distributed, 275.
,, and Support, Distributed, 277.
Loading, Various Modes of, 280.

Measure of Direct Strain, 242.
Modulus of Elasticity, 243.
Moment, Bending, 271.
,, of Inertia of a Section, 318.
,, of Twisting, 301.
Mr. John's Investigations, 319.

Neutral axis of a ship, 316.

# INDEX 375

Pliability, 240.
Proof Strain, 241.
  ,, Strength, 240.
Properties of Bodies under Stress, 239.

Resilience, 241.
Resistance to Bending, 284.
Rivets, Diameters of, 245.
  ,, Table of, 247.
Rivets, Rows of, 250.
  ,, Spacing of, 247.

Safety, Factors of, 240.
Set, 240.
Shearing Stresses, Curve of, 309.
      Table of Maximum, 315.
Shift of Plates, 262.
Spacing of Rivets, 247.
Spring, 241.
Stiffness, 240.
Still Water Stresses, 304.
Strain, 239.
  ,, Measure of Direct, 242.
Strength, 240.
  ,, of Bent Pillars, 299.

Strength of Butt Straps, 253.
  ,, of Pillars, 297.
Stress, 239.
  ,, Classes of, 243.
  ,, Intensity of, 243, 319.
  ,, Shearing, 270.
Stresses among Waves, 312.
  ,, Curve of, 311.
Stresses, Still Water, 304.
Support, Distributed, 277.

Table of Diameters of Rivets, 247.
  ,, Factors of Safety, 241.
Table of Maximum Bending Moments, 315.
  ,, Maximum Shearing Stresses, 315.
Twisting Moments, 301.

Ultimate Strain, 241.
  ,, Strength, 240.

Various Modes of Loading, 280.

Waves, Stresses among, 312.
Weights, Curve of, 303.
Weight of Hull, Curve of, 300.

---

## PART IV.—CALCULATIONS RELATING TO THE PROPULSION OF SHIPS BY SAILS.

Apparent Direction of the Wind, 328.
Ardency, 330.

Centre of Effort, 330.
Centre of Gravity in regard to Sailing Qualities, 334.

Effective Impulse of the Wind, 328.
Effect of a Gust of Wind, 342.
Effort, Centre of, 330.

Gust of Wind, Effect of a, 342.

Impulse, Effective, of the Wind, 328.

Leewardliness, 330.

Masts, 322.

Real and Apparent Direction of the Wind, 328.
Rigs, 325.

Sail, Speed under, 337.
  ,, Stability under, 339.
Sailing, 327.
Sails, 324.
  ,, Trim of, 329.
Speed under Sail, 337.
Stability under Sail, 339.

Trim of Sails, 329.

Wind, Apparent Direction of, 328.
  ,, Effect of a Gust of, 342.
  ,, Effective Impulse of, 328.
  ,, Real Direction of, 328.

Yards, 323.

---

## PART V.—CALCULATIONS RELATING TO THE PROPULSION OF SHIPS BY STEAM ENGINES.

Comparative Performances of Steam Ships, 348.

Efficiency of a Propeller, 346.
Experiments on the *Greyhound*, 346.

*Greyhound*, Experiments on, 346.

Law of Resistances, 347.

Measured Mile, 351.

Negative Slip, 359.

Performances of Steam Ships, 348.
Propeller, Efficiency of, 340.
„ Velocity of, 340.
Propulsion, Steam, 345.

Reaction of the Water, 345.
Resistances, Law of, 347.

Slip, 345.
Slip, Negative, 359.
Speeds, Trials at Varied, 355.
Steam Propulsion, 345.

Trials at Varied Speeds, 355.

Velocity of Propeller, 340.

---

# PART VI.—CALCULATIONS RELATING TO THE STEERING OF SHIPS.

Absolute Angle of Maximum Efficiency, 364.
Angle of Maximum Efficiency, 363.
Angle of Maximum Efficiency, Absolute, 364.
Angle of Maximum Efficiency, with regard to Power Applied, 364.
Angle of Rudder, Usual, 366.
Areas of Rudders, 366.
„ Table of, 367.

Balanced Rudder, 368.

Efficiency, Angle of Maximum, 363.
„ Absolute Angle of Maximum, 364.

Efficiency, Angle of Maximum, with regard Power Applied, 364.

Pressure and Velocity, Ratio of, 367.
Principle of the Rudder, 362.

Rudder, 361.
„ Principle of the, 362.
„ The Balanced, 368.
„ Usual Angle of, 366.
Rudders, Areas of, 366.
„ Table of Areas of, 367.

Steering, 361.

Usual Angle of Rudder, 366.

---

WILLIAM COLLINS AND COMPANY, PRINTERS, GLASGOW.

Educational Publications of Wm. Collins, Sons, & Co., Limited.

## COLLINS' SERIES OF SCHOOL ATLASES—Continued.

### PHYSICAL GEOGRAPHY—Demy Series.

THE PRIMARY ATLAS OF PHYSICAL GEOGRAPHY, 16 Maps, Demy 4to, 9 by 11 inches, Stiff Cover, ... ... ... 1 0

THE POCKET ATLAS OF PHYSICAL GEOGRAPHY, 16 Maps, on Guards, Demy 8vo, cloth, ... ... ... ... 2 0

1 Hemispheres
2 Physical Map of Europe.
3 Physical Map of Asia.
4 Physical Map of Africa.
5 Physical Map of North America.
6 Physical Map of South America.
7 Physical Map of the British Isles.
8 Maps of the World—shewing Temperature in March, April, May, June, July, and August.
9 Maps of the World—shewing the Mean Temperature in September, October, November, December, January, and February.
10 Map of the World—shewing the Constant, Periodical, and Variable Winds, &c.
11 Map of the World—shewing the Distribution of *Rain*, &c.
12 Map of the World—illustrating Earthquakes, &c.
13 Map of the World—shewing the Ocean Currents, &c.
14 Map of the World—shewing the Distribution of Birds and Fishes.
15 Map of the World—shewing Distribution of Quadrupeds, &c.
16 Map of the World—shewing Distribution of Plants, &c.

### PHYSICAL GEOGRAPHY—Imperial Series.

THE PORTABLE ATLAS OF PHYSICAL GEOGRAPHY, 20 Maps, 11 by 13 inches, mounted on Guards, Imp. 8vo, cloth, ... 3 6

THE STUDENT'S ATLAS OF PHYSICAL GEOGRAPHY, 20 Maps, mounted on Guards. With Letterpress Description and Wood Engravings. By James Bryce, LL.D., F.R.G.S. Imp. 8vo, cl., 5 0

1 Hemispheres—shewing proportions of Land and Water, with Length of Rivers and Heights of Mountains, &c.
2 Physical Map of Europe—shewing Mountains and Rivers, High and Low Lands.
3 Physical Map of Asia—shewing as above.
4 Physical Map of Africa—shewing as above.
5 Physical Map of North America—shewing as above.
6 Physical Map of South America—shewing as above.
7 Physical Map of the British Isles—shewing as above.
8 Various Sections across the Continents.
9 Various Sections in the Oceans, Diagram of Suez Canal, &c.
10 Maps of the World—shewing the Mean Temperature of the Air—March to August.
11 Maps of the World—shewing the Mean Temperature of the Air—September to February.
12 Map of the World—shewing the Distribution of Constant, Periodical, and Variable Winds; Limits of Trade Winds, &c.
13 Map of the World—shewing the proportionate distribution of *Rain*, &c.
14 Map of the World—illustrating Earthquakes and the distribution of Volcanoes.
15 Map of the World—shewing the Ocean Currents and Basins, and principal River Systems.
16 Map of the World—shewing the Geographical Distribution of Birds and Fishes.
17 Map of the World—shewing Geographical Distribution of Quadrupeds and Reptiles.
18 Map of the World—shewing the Geographical Distribution of Plants.
19 Map of the World—shewing the Distribution of Mankind according to Races.
20 Geological Map of the British Isles.

London, Edinburgh, and Herriot Hill Works, Glasgow.

Educational Publications of Wm. Collins, Sons, & Co., Limited.

## COLLINS'

THE POCKET
Maps, 6½ by 11

THE CROWN
Maps, with Le
Imperial 16mo,

THE STUDENT
16 Maps, with
8vo, cloth, ..

1 Roman Empire,
  4th Century.
2 Europe, 6th Cen
  ments of the B
3 Europe, 9th Cent
  of Charlemagne
4 Europe, 10th C
  the German Em
5 Europe, 12th Cen
  the Crusaders.
6 Europe, 16th Ce
  the Reformatio
7 Germany, 16th C
  and Thirty Yea

> This book should be returned to the Library on or before the last date stamped below.
>
> A fine of five cents a day is incurred by retaining it beyond the specified time.
>
> Please return promptly.

THE POCKET
Maps, Imperial

THE CROWN A
with Descriptiv
16mo, cloth let

THE STUDENT
Maps, Imperia
Schmitz, LL.D

1 Orbis Veteribus
2 Ægyptus
3 Regnum Alexand
4 Macedonia, Thra
5 Imperium Roma
6 Græcia
7 Italia, (Septentri
8 Italia, (Meridion

THE STUDENT
CAL GEOGRAPHY, consisting of 30 Maps as above, with Introductions on Historical Geography by W. F. Collier, LL.D., and on Classical Geography by Leonhard Schmitz, LL.D., with a Copious Index, Imperial 8vo, cloth, ... ... ... ... ... 5 0

London, Edinburgh, and Herriot Hill Works, Glasgow